KT-486-666

York St John
Library and Information Services

7 Day Loan

Please return this item on or before the due date stamped below (if using the self issue option users may write in the date themselves)

-5 APR 2012		

Fines are payable for late return

York St John

3 8025 00521993 9

stranger than paradise

stranger
than
paradise

Maverick film-makers
in recent American cinema

YORK ST JOHN
LIBRARY & INFORMATION
SERVICES

GEOFF ANDREW

limelight editions

First Limelight Edition   April 1999

Copyright © Geoff Andrew 1998

Published in the United States by Proscenium Publishers Inc.,
118 East 30th Street, New York, NY 10016,
under license from Prion Books Limited, London

Printed in Great Britain by Creative Print and Design (Wales)

All rights reserved.

No part of this book may be reproduced, stored in a retrieval system,
or transmitted in any form or by any means, electronic, mechanical,
photocopying, recording or otherwise, without the prior written
permission of the publisher.

Library of Congress Cataloging-in-Publication Data

Andrew, Geoff.
        Stranger than paradise : maverick film-makers in recent American
cinema / Geoff Andrew. --1st Limelight ed.
            p.   cm.
        Originally published : London : Prion Books, 1998.
        Includes index.
        ISBN 0-87910-277-2
        1. Independent filmmakers--United States--Biography. 2. Motion
picture producers and directors--United States--Biography. 3. Low
budget motion pictures--United States--History and criticism.
        I. Title.
        PN1998.2.A65   1999
        791.43'0233'092273--dc21
        [b]   98-54603
                                                                  CIP

contents

acknowledgments

While *Stranger Than Paradise* expresses my own opinions, like any book of its kind it is partly the result of countless conversations and shared experiences. Moreover, friends and colleagues offered advice, enthusiasm and help with research materials.

I should, therefore, like to give heartfelt thanks to the following: to my colleagues at *Time Out* – Derek Adams, Brian Case, Wally Hammond, Trevor Johnston and, most especially, Tom Charity – for their overall support and help; to Margaret O'Sullivan and Andrew Rossiter for unearthing clippings of my interviews; to Dominic Wells and the management of *Time Out* for allowing me a sabbatical in which to write the book; to Andrew Goodfellow of Prion for commissioning the book and seeing it through to publication with intelligence, sympathy and patience; and to Ane Roteta, Sarah Carr, Karin Padgham, Mark Sanderson, Gary Oldman and Alejandra de la Paz for making the writing more tolerable than it might otherwise have been. I should also like to thank all those who helped out with providing videocassettes and/or opportunities to see movies unreleased at time of writing: Tony Rayns, Chris Rodley, Maggie Renzi, Jonathan Rutter, Liz Miller, Jim Jarmusch, Stacey Smith, David Cox, Eric Fellner, Nick Fraser, Fiona Morrow, Andrew Weeks, Helene Breyton, Todd Haynes, Scott Meek, Hal Hartley, Matthew Myers, Thierry Cagianut, Steven Bickel, Daniel Battsek, and David Thompson. My parents once again tolerated my reclusiveness with great understanding. I should like to dedicate this book to them, to Tom and Fiona, and to Ane.

foreword by gary oldman

In May of every year, a small, quaint seaside town on the French Riviera is transformed into Times Square on New Year's Eve. I'm referring, of course, to Cannes and its prestigious annual celebration of film. This beautiful resort boasts a renowned shoreline promenade, the Croisette, along which you can find restaurants, casinos, nightclubs, the Palais des Festivals and the infamous Carlton Hotel. It was here, in 1997, amid the splendour of a modest suite, that I first met Geoff Andrew.

He was to interview me for a cover story to run in the London-based magazine *Time Out*. As I've said, we had never met before, but I knew of him through his work as a critic and features writer for the magazine's cinema section. I think it's fair to say that we liked one another almost immediately, so that what was originally planned as a formal one-to-one interview (one of probably fifteen or twenty I had to give that day) soon developed into a conversation that clearly could not be squeezed into the allotted forty-five minutes. We both knew the conversation would not end there.

At that first meeting – and many times since – we talked about our love for film. We discussed those films and film-makers that have been, and continue to be, a source of inspiration to us. We talked about American cinema and, in particular, the world of the independents. The independents have influenced and impacted my own work as a practitioner of film; without a doubt, they have also influenced Geoff, as a spectator, author and critic of film.

There is, of course, no one American director or screenwriter who has brought about the periodic changes in direction in American movie-making single-handedly. But there have been special landmark talents, visionaries, who have emerged in response to the *status quo*, whose work has had a profound and far-reaching effect. Geoff's knowledge of, and passion for, the work of these film-makers is remarkable. So it comes as no surprise to me that he should have turned his critical eye to the most recent American cinema and, more specifically, to the world of the maverick, for the subject of a book. This insightful volume features ten extraordinary talents whose films are a testimony to the best American cinema. Of the many hundreds of films that have been lensed over the last decade, it is their work which has made a significant contribution. Their films have commented on, shaped and redefined the American experience.

Whether concerned with the socio-political and often controversial works of John Sayles, who for me continues to be one of independent cinema's most remarkable phenomena, or the bizarre, mysterious and stylishly comic universe of David Lynch, the pages that follow offer a greater access and understanding to the work of these film-makers. While, arguably, the themes and ideas in these movies have at times been too dark and complex, difficult or disturbing to widen the popular taste for them, in each case the film-maker's passion, energy and vision are unquestionable. It is this vision, its meaning and the core of its creation that Geoff examines here.

With prose that has as much vitality as the movies it discusses, this book is a celebration of cinema, by someone who loves film and understands it. Geoff Andrew has given us the most enjoyable, comprehensive and up-to-date discussion of recent American cinema on our shelves. If you love film, read on...

Gary Oldman 1998

INTRODUCTION

< 1 >

As the movies moved into their second century of existence, the stranglehold exerted by Hollywood over the cinemas of the world was as strong as ever. Budgets for studio movies were continuing to rise at an extraordinary rate (as I completed this book, it was estimated that James Cameron's recently released *Titanic* had cost at least $200 million, little of which appeared to have been spent on trying to furnish a decent script with properly rounded, credible characters); huge amounts were being spent on marketing and promotion, special effects, stars' salaries, screenplays and the optioning of rights to bestsellers; while 'foreign-language' films were finding it harder and harder to reach cinema screens, not only in America but even, very often, in the countries they were made in. At the same time, many felt that the Hollywood movie factory was, aesthetically and spiritually, a spent force. For all the hype and economic clout, it was producing little of genuine artistic interest. It was overly dependent on sequels, prequels and outright rip-offs of previous box-office hits; stories were conceived and written by committee, so that they were formulaic, predictable, banal, and frequently shoddily constructed; characterisation was as two-dimensional as the comic-strip plots – fantasy and action movies predominated, so that films very rarely seemed to be dealing with recognisably 'real' people or situations. Dialogue tended towards the dumb, inarticulate and clichéd. The treatment of social and ethical issues was at best safe, simplistic and sentimental, at worst non-existent. Direction ranged from gratuitously flashy to unimaginatively mundane or even downright incoherent. (Even the action-sequences in, say, *Batman and Robin* came over as just so much meaningless movement and noise, so that there seemed no rationale for the film's existence other than as a cynical merchandising exercise.) The 'boom or bust' philosophy adhered to by the major studios since the 60s had taken its toll: movies were now simply 'product' – bland, gimmicky, mindless 'events' designed, through high-profile marketing, to make a fast buck.

Yet the American cinema was not all bad. In the mid 90s, perhaps the most admired and influential figures working in US film were Martin Scorsese and Quentin Tarantino. And while some felt that Scorsese – who had been widely regarded as the most exciting, rewarding US *auteur* since the 70s, when he made such landmark movies as *Mean Streets, Taxi Driver, New York, New York* and *Raging Bull* – had become a little erratic and lost some of his fire, Tarantino was heralded by many as the new boy wonder. Young cinema-goers, especially, adored his energy, his enthusiasm for movies (however lowly, obscure or disreputable they might be), his sheer bravado both as a film-maker and as a spokesman for a generation accustomed to voraciously devouring pop culture in general and the moving image in particular. Even many older cinephiles, raised on classical Hollywood and the European art-movie, were impressed by his range of reference, by his facility in writing colourful, memorable dialogue, and by his evident readiness to play around with the more conventional methods of cinematic storytelling. He was a maverick, who offered a fresh, iconoclastic alternative to the imaginatively moribund output of Hollywood. In the mid-90s, Quentin appeared to be king, and not surprisingly there were many pretenders to the throne: imitation Tarantino movies proliferated.

< **2** >

Of course, however, he was not a one-off, but only the tip of the iceberg. For one thing, as this book hopes to show, there was already an impressive number of independent-spirited American *auteurs* operating outside or on the margins of the Hollywood system: figures like David Lynch, John Sayles, Spike Lee, Jim Jarmusch, and Joel and Ethan Coen, some of whom had their own imitators – the US indie movement had been gaining momentum for some years before Tarantino appeared on the scene, and by the mid-90s there had been a veritable explosion of new talent. Yet it can be argued that most of the more interesting contemporary film-makers belong to a maverick tradition that stretches back to cinema's early years. How else, if not as mavericks, are we to regard masters of American cinema like Erich Von Stroheim, Josef Von Sternberg, Orson Welles, Nicholas Ray, Douglas Sirk, Sam Fuller or John Cassavetes? Of course, not all the greats were as uncomfortable working in the studio system as the aforementioned; nevertheless, John Ford, Howard Hawks, Alfred Hitchcock and Billy Wilder remained fiercely independent figures who set up their own production companies as soon as they could. The history of the American cinema is littered with free spirits who, rather than merely conform to the escapist ideals fostered by mainstream Hollywood, strove to bring a personal vision to the screen and, in so doing, created lasting works of art that transcend the narrow definition of film as entertainment, pure and simple.

< 3 >

Hence, the *auteurs* of the 80s and 90s whose work will be discussed in the pages that follow are operating in an old and honorable tradition of film-making practice. They are, however, distinguished from the vast majority of their predecessors by the circumstances under which they work. As argued above, Hollywood is now both artistically impoverished, and circumscribed by its devotion to and dependence on enormous financial outlay; and in order to preserve their independence, many contemporary American film-makers actively *choose* to work without the financial support available in Hollywood, preferring to operate within the confines of a relatively small budget rather than have their creative freedom curtailed by conglomerates that will only tolerate so much artistic idiosyncrasy. In terms of 'serious' film-making (as distinct from the Poverty Row B-movies aimed at ethnic minorities and the undemanding audiences who populated drive-ins and porno-houses), working on a low budget was previously seen as an option only for those involved in making experimental, avant-garde and short (as opposed to feature-length) movies; now, however, it's relatively common practice, so that film festivals (notably the influential Sundance event at Park City, Utah, set up by Robert Redford specifically to encourage independent film-making in America) and the more adventurous urban cinemas around the world regularly screen low-budget work to enthusiastic audiences.

< 4 >

As stated above, over the last decade or so there has been a considerable increase in the number of movies made by young, adventurous film-makers willing and able to work on a budget that would barely pay for a major star's make-up bill. Inevitably, the results have been variable (far too many 'wannabes' simply try to rehash the style and subject matter of a current favourite, be it Lynch, Jarmusch, Lee or Tarantino); inevitably, too, many début directors seem to be keen eventually to break into Hollywood. But those who see their film as a calling-card for a successful career in Hollywood should beware: few of the much-vaunted 'movie brats' of the late 60s and 70s – talents like Coppola, Milius, Spielberg, Lucas, De Palma, Scorsese and Carpenter – have made films as original, exciting and uncompromised since they became major players in Tinseltown as those they made before becoming part of the establishment. As can be seen both from the way the studios reacted to the surprise success of *Easy Rider* back in the early 70s and from the way studio buyers and talent-spotters now haunt Sundance in their droves, Hollywood is always keen to cash in on the latest fad, and will put the money upfront to do so – but at what cost to creative freedom and vision? The 1997 Oscars showed that even the establishment is at last beginning openly to acknowledge that its output is less rewarding artistically than that produced by the independent sector – but as long as the blockbusters are more *financially* rewarding, Hollywood will most probably stick to its guns, and shoot down any creativity it considers too risky, idiosyncratic or 'difficult'.

Nevertheless, with more and more of the blockbusters failing to live up to box-office expectations and thus to recuperate or fully justify their vastly inflated budgets, and with more and more quirky, intelligent, comparatively low-budget movies finding an audience, the independent spirit is alive and kicking in the contemporary American cinema. It seems timely, therefore, to take a look at the mavericks who are currently producing the most interesting work in the American cinema; to see where they have come from, and examine their stylistic strategies and thematic preoccupations; to try and discern what they have in common, and how they differ. The assumption underlying this book is that the indie scene now constitutes the healthiest area of American film-making, and that many of the films analysed in the following pages, made by people currently considered mavericks, will come to be regarded, with the passing of time, as landmarks and classics.

< 5 >

But what exactly is a maverick? The dictionary definition tells us that a maverick is 'one who does not conform'. Clearly, with regard to the American cinema, such a definition allows for broad interpretation, and need not be applied only to those who work consistently in the independent sector of the industry, away from the production and distribution facilities provided by the Hollywood majors. Rather, 'maverick' may be seen as a question of attitude and/or achievement; I have taken it to mean those film-makers who, for some or all of their directing careers, have made movies which in one way or another stand outside the commercial mainstream. Clearly, that inevitably includes most of the genuine independents who work without Hollywood financing, but it also embraces figures like Spike Lee, the Coen

Brothers, Whit Stillman or Quentin Tarantino, who work with the majors and 'mini-majors' but whose films, in terms of style or content, betoken a forceful individuality, an artistic sensibility which cannot be contained by the resolutely commercial constraints favoured by Hollywood.

In tracing the developments which led to the current high standing of the US indie scene, I have therefore included many film-makers whose films were not, strictly speaking, independent: people like Altman, Allen, Scorsese, Malick and Mann. Inevitably, whether such borderline figures warrant the term 'maverick' or not comes down to a matter of personal opinion – basically, you just feel it in your bones whether someone is a maverick – and where they are mentioned, I have attempted to offer reasons for their inclusion in the book.

A similar subjectivity of opinion applies especially to those film-makers to whom I have chosen to devote a chapter of their own: the selection was based not only on the number of films they have made, or because they best represent a certain aspect of maverick film-making, but also because I believe their work has an individuality and an artistic worth which makes them important. Hence, though Abel Ferrara is clearly a prolific director with a distinctly maverick sensibility, he does not get a chapter to himself, simply because I find little of genuine artistic merit in his work: to me, his movies seem to be merely incoherent, shoddily made, even exploitative variations on the traditional genres, with a somewhat bogus, unilluminating Catholic subtext thrown in for not-so-good measure. Undoubtedly many will disagree with this assessment of Ferrara's achievements and regret or deplore the fact that I have not dealt with his oeuvre at greater length. I make no apologies for this decision; since I can find little to say that is positive about his work, I would rather deal in detail with, say, Todd Haynes or Steven Soderbergh; while each has made far fewer movies than Ferrara, I believe them to be considerably more interesting, rewarding and important in terms of their respective artistic achievements.

< **6** >

There will, then, be many readers who take issue with some of the choices and statements I have made in this book. So be it: this is not intended as a comprehensive, definitive study, but as an attempt to give some sort of overview of the contemporary US indie scene, and to provide brief but hopefully useful critical analyses of the work of a number of film-makers who, in most cases, have so far received scant coverage in books on the cinema. The aim of this volume, then, is simply to open up a discussion about certain independent-spirited *auteurs* whom this writer believes to be sufficiently important to the future of American film-making to deserve fuller critical consideration than is available in the majority of movie magazines. Their work, which embraces a wide variety of styles and subject matter, is distinguished by its energy, enthusiasm, imagination, and a readiness to experiment and take risks. And as this book intends to show, there is still, thanks to these mavericks, hope for the American cinema.

< 7 >

A brief (pre)history of indie cinema

< **9** >

Although there have always been mavericks making films in Hollywood, it is probably fair to say that the godfather and father of American independent cinema were, respectively, Orson Welles and John Cassavetes. We shall deal with Cassavetes and his films later, but it was Welles who fought hard for and won creative freedom in the making of his 1941 début for RKO, *Citizen Kane*, and Welles who, despite having directed a ground-breaking film widely acclaimed in later years as one of the greatest ever made, soon lost that freedom when his similarly extraordinary second feature, *The Magnificent Ambersons* (1942), was released by RKO in a version cut, re-edited and, in the case of a few scenes, reshot against his wishes. Already the 'boy wonder' of theatre, radio and now cinema seemed to have met, in the words applied to the arrogant, young George Amberson, 'his comeuppance'.

Simultaneously admired and resented, Welles had completed two astonishingly ambitious, intelligent features, and was being punished for it by an industry that didn't want any trouble: be it from enraged media barons like William Randolph Hearst (the alleged inspiration for the eponymous protagonist of *Citizen Kane*); from audiences claiming that they couldn't quite understand or were bored by these unusually dark, complex movies; or from Welles himself, characterised – fairly or otherwise – by his enemies as profligate, arrogant, over-ambitious and difficult. So it was that Welles, now recognised as one of the finest film-makers of all time, was reined in by Hollywood, and forced to work under tighter constraints, either by 'behaving himself' and turning out supposedly more conventional thrillers – *The Stranger* (1946), *The Lady from Shanghai* (1948), *Touch of Evil* (1958) – for the major studios, or by making films funded by minor companies like Republic (*Macbeth*, 1948) or by European investors. But *Othello* (1952), *The Trial* (1962), *Chimes at Midnight* (1966), *The Immortal Story* (1968) and *F for Fake* (1975) were not only made without the help of Hollywood finance; they were also made very cheaply, often over lengthy periods as Welles struggled to get the money together, partly paying for them out of his own pocket with earnings from the acting chores he was meanwhile performing for other, lesser film-makers. Amazingly, he managed to complete the majority of these mostly very fine films (though there were other unfinished films such as *Don Quixote*, *The Deep* and *The Other Side of the Wind*). Amazingly, too, he never seemed to give up trying – film-making was his life, and in his determination to remain true to his artistic vision (even at the cost of appearing on TV in chat-shows and ludicrous commercials), he embodied a spirit of independence that remains an inspiration to maverick film-makers to this day.

Not that Welles was alone in his creative battles with the studios in the 40s and 50s. In the years after the Second World War, America was very different from what it had been beforehand, and those changes were both felt and reflected by Hollywood. The film industry was undergoing a crisis as it struggled to fend off the twin threats of television and (supposedly) the Red Menace. America had become more conservative, more devoted to conformist values; paranoia about Communists and other 'un-American' groups (basically ethnic minorities) was widespread, and the great ideal for many WASP Americans, after the upheaval of the war years, was to own a nice, clean, quiet home

< **10** >

in the suburbs, complete with TV, washing machine, car and a couple of well-scrubbed kids. Accordingly, Hollywood was finding it increasingly difficult to tempt audiences away from the family hearth and the small screen; responding with movies in colour, 3-D and new widescreen formats like Cinerama or CinemaScope did little to stop the decline in audiences.

Overall, films generally became a little blander, more concerned with extravagant spectacle and fantasy or with the depiction of happy families in safe suburban settings; and those screenwriters and directors who dealt with more serious social issues were closely watched, or sacked and blacklisted, by studio moguls eager to avoid problems with Senator Joe McCarthy's House Un-American Activities Committee. Hollywood was worried: it was beleaguered by loss of talent and by an atmosphere of uncertainty and betrayal as film folk 'named names' of colleagues and friends in their rush to clear themselves of any suspicion of Communist behaviour, and it had little time for potential trouble-makers in the shape of 'difficult' or flamboyantly idiosyncratic artists.

< 11 >

But artists there were. Some, hounded or simply disenchanted by the McCarthy 'witchhunts', left for Europe: Joseph Losey, John Berry and Stanley Kubrick were among their number. Others (mainly writers) were forced to work anonymously under pseudonyms. And others, like Nicholas Ray, Douglas Sirk and Sam Fuller, worked on within the industry: Ray and Sirk, often finding themselves in conflict with studio executives, tended to 'smuggle' their more subversive critiques of American life into seemingly conventional genre films, while Fuller managed to preserve his independence as an *auteur* who wrote, directed and produced his own films by working for the most part in lower-budget studio output. At the same time, two other groups were beginning to make their presence felt in the world of film production: on the one hand, stars – like Burt Lancaster, Randolph Scott, Ida Lupino, Charles Laughton and Jerry Lewis – who formed their own production companies or turned to

directing; and at the other extreme, avant-garde figures like Maya
Deren, Kenneth Anger, Stan Brakhage, Bruce Conner, Robert
Frank and Shirley Clarke, whose films, while ignored for obvious
reasons by Hollywood, began to find audiences in specialist ven-
ues in cities like New York and San Francisco.

Though 'underground' cinema, as such experimental work
later came to be called, is by definition maverick and independent, it is sufficiently different from the films discussed in the
following pages to stand beyond the scope of this book. I have
mentioned it, however, since its flowering (not unconnected with

< 12 >

the rise of the 'Beat' movement) coincided with the directorial
début of John Cassavetes, who since the mid-50s had established
himself as an accomplished, charismatic and unusually intense
actor in movies like *Crime in the Streets* (Don Siegel, 1957) and
Edge of the City (Martin Ritt, 1958). Based on improvisational
exercises at his actors' workshop, *Shadows* (1959) was not only
his first outing as writer-director, but a landmark in American
independent cinema. The fact that it was made for $40,000 and
yet won awards and found an audience was a rare achievement in
itself, but the film's subject matter and style proved equally influential. About the relationships and everyday lives of three young
New Yorkers, the film impresses with a subtle, frank exploration
of attitudes to race and sex within a narrative so elliptical, rambling and seemingly spontaneous it can barely be called a 'story'.
Even more distinctive, however, is the technically raw feel of the
film: shot in grainy black and white, with an evident disregard
for (or dislike of) consistently crisp focus, and featuring nervy,
jagged editing, it simultaneously looks so improvised as to be virtually documentary, and focuses squarely on the performances.
As in *cinema vérité* (a documentary style which arose at around
the same time in the work of film-makers like Richard Leacock,
Albert and David Maysles, Robert Drew and DA Pennebaker),
and as in most of Cassavetes' later films, the emphasis was firmly
on character-study through gesture, which was closely observed
by a free-focus, sometimes hand-held camera, while narrative

Shadows (1959), Cassavetes' first feature, made the same year as Godard's **Breathless**, shares many of the same impulses towards a new form of film-making. Cassavetes' style pioneered the quintessential mix of American and European filmic sensibilities, that has subsequently been emulated by so many indie film-makers.

pacing and structure were partly defined by the performances. Cassavetes' aesthetic differentiated itself from the classical Hollywood tradition in two crucial respects. On the one hand, its rough-hewn, intensely 'naturalistic', spontaneous tone was an explicit rejection of the polished escapism of most Hollywood storytelling; on the other, the very fact that the method is so observational results in the viewer often being unusually aware of the camera (particularly as it slides in and out of focus) and, therefore, of the film-maker. Ironically, in making the visual style more 'relaxed' yet less 'invisible' than in most Hollywood films, Cassavetes draws our attention to the fact that what we are actually watching is filmic artifice – something being acted out – and not reality.

Hence, there is a very modern element of self-consciousness, of self-reflexivity at work in Cassavetes' films: to some extent, they are not only about the characters they portray but about the very act of performance, of depicting those characters' emotions. As I hope to show later, that sense of cinematic artifice, that awareness of the relationship between the fiction we are watching and the 'reality' it is describing, and the relationship between the film-maker, the film and the viewer is frequently inscribed, in one way or another, in the work of many contemporary American independent film-makers. Also very influential, however, were Cassavetes' interest in the kind of characters – not heroes or villains, but 'ordinary' people – seldom seen in Hollywood films; his repeated use of a small, 'repertory' group of actors (usually friends like Peter Falk, Ben Gazzara and Seymour Cassell and his wife Gena Rowlands); and his antipathetic attitude to the Hollywood majors, for whom he would regularly work as an actor in order to fund his own films.

< 14 >

The two studio movies he made after *Shadows* – *Too Late Blues* (1961) and *A Child is Waiting* (1963) – were both unhappy experiences for Cassavetes, and they remain fascinating but profoundly flawed. Far more rewarding were films like *Faces* (1968), *Husbands* (1970), *A Woman Under the Influence* (1974) and *Love Streams* (1984) – bleak, rambling but enormously insightful dissections of dysfunctional relationships – and his surprisingly fruitful attempts to inflect lighter, more generic material with his naturalistic aesthetic in the romantic comedy *Minnie and Moskowitz* (1971), the noir thriller *The Killing of a Chinese Bookie* (1976), the backstage drama *Opening Night* (1977) and the gangster drama *Gloria* (1980). Indeed, it is arguably these later movies, in which traditional genre elements are, as it were, interrogated and transformed by Cassavetes' distrust of movie clichés, that have exerted the most influence on modern film-making.

During the 60s, however, Cassavetes the director was such a marginal figure that his influence on American film-making was quite minimal. The crisis afflicting the studios in the previous decade had, if anything, worsened, and the pictures produced by Hollywood during the 60s fell largely into two distinct groups. On the one hand, the studios continued to churn out expensive, outdated spectaculars which failed dismally to take account of the changing times. Though this was the age of the Beatles, Bob Dylan and 'flower power', of John F Kennedy and Martin Luther King, of the Cuban missile crisis, student unrest and Vietnam, Hollywood remained largely unresponsive to the contemporary zeitgeist and tried mostly to emulate its biggest box-office hits: the enormous success of *The Sound of Music* (Robert Wise, 1965), for example, sparked off a series of elephantine musicals like *Star!* (Robert Wise, 1968), *Funny Girl* (William Wyler, 1968), and *Hello, Dolly!* (Gene Kelly, 1969). On the other hand, there were also more serious, politically and ethically probing films, mostly by directors who had already distinguished themselves in TV drama. For all their intelligence and craftsmanship, however, many of these movies – *Fail-Safe* (Sidney Lumet, 1963), *To Kill a Mockingbird* (Robert Mulligan, 1963), *Hud* (Martin Ritt, 1963) and *Seven Days in May* (John Frankenheimer, 1964) are among the best-known examples – remained cinematically conservative, and were marked by a certain portentousness in style and tone.

< 15 >

There were, however, causes for hope. The 60s also saw the rise of the film schools at universities like UCLA and NYU; there was increased access to and interest in world cinema, notably in the 'new wave' *auteurs* of France, Italy, Eastern Europe and Latin America; and there was Roger Corman, who had begun directing in the mid-50s, specialising in lowly but imaginative B-movies, often made for AIP (American International Pictures) and aimed at the drive-in youth market. In terms of form and content, most of Corman's own films – the finest included *Sorority Girl* (1957), *Machine Gun Kelly* (1958), *A Bucket of Blood* (1959), *The Pit and the Pendulum* (1961) and *The St Valentine's Day Massacre* (1967) – were more remarkable for their inventive responses to budgetary limitations and for their speedy exploitation of any current fad – be it sex, drugs, rock 'n' roll or the popularity of sci-fi, horror and gangster movies – than for any intrinsic artistic worth. His importance, however, lies not only in his having been a genuinely successful independent director, but in his having given work, in one capacity or another, to an astonishing array of cheap, youthful, enthusiastic talent through his production company New World: among those who worked for him over the years can be counted Francis Ford Coppola, Jack Nicholson, Dennis Hopper, Peter Bogdanovich, Peter Fonda, Monte Hellman, Martin Scorsese, Joe Dante, Jonathan Demme, Robert De Niro, Jonathan Kaplan, Paul Bartel, Penelope Spheeris and John Sayles – in short, many of the prime movers of the independent scene of the 60s, 70s and early 80s. The Corman 'graduates' were united in their desire to make films, however disreputable (sex, nudity, violence and a rock soundtrack were virtually a *sine qua non* as elements in Corman productions), with sufficient cinematic flair and invention to off-set the paltry budgets and often formulaic subject matter: lessons taken fruitfully to heart when they moved on to making bigger movies.

< 16 >

The Corman 'school' was not, however, the sole haven for the maverick spirit in the 60s. Even the studios – often against their better judgement – sometimes found themselves working with adventurous, free-spirited directors, most notably Sam Peckinpah, Arthur Penn and Robert Altman, who all graduated from television, and Dennis Hopper. Though he worked mainly in the Western – the most hallowed and traditional of American genres – Peckinpah subverted the form by painting a bleaker, more brutally violent portrait of the West than had been seen in classic movies by the likes of Ford, Hawks, Anthony Mann and Budd Boetticher; his most influential (and controversial) film was *The Wild Bunch* (1969), a dark, brooding epic in which the fatally flawed heroes finally meet their destiny in an extraordinary bloodbath, a massacre shot largely in slow motion to lend a partly mythic, partly orgasmic resonance to their dying paroxysms. Besides being much imitated itself, the scene echoed the final sequence of Penn's *Bonnie and Clyde* (1967), in which the gangster couple appear to writhe in a black parody of sexual ecstasy as they are riddled with bullets. If anything, Penn's film – initially written by Robert Benton and David Newman in the hope that it would be directed by Godard or Truffaut – was even more influential than Peckinpah's: in turning his Depression-era outlaws into cool, young, attractive and sympathetic outsiders oppressed and destroyed by an uncaring, hypocritical, vengeful society, Penn caught the mood of an age when youth was openly rebelling against an unjust, imperialist, capitalist America. In this respect, the film anticipated Dennis Hopper's surprise success in 1969 with *Easy Rider*, in which two drug-dealing bikers travel across a mythic contemporary America, only to die at the hands of reactionary Southern rednecks. Such cult hits were the film

Dennis Hopper starred in, with Peter Fonda, and directed the seminal 60s counter-culture road movie **Easy Rider**. The disasterous critical and commercial reception of Hopper's next film **The Last Movie** (1971), served to steel Hollywood against the funding of more independently-minded movie projects.

and its accompanying soundtrack album of rock favourites that Hollywood decided not only to jump belatedly on the youth-market bandwagon (with dire results, financially and artistically), but to give Hopper – subsequently something of a hero as an actor on the indie scene – *carte blanche* for his next outing as director. Sadly, *The Last Movie* (1971), a bizarre and ambitiously allegorical film about an American stunt-man trying to shoot a Western in the Peruvian Andes, was so chaotic, self-indulgent and obscure that its critical and commercial failure ensured Hopper would not direct again until 1980, when he made the raw, edgy domestic drama *Out of the Blue*.

< 18 >

But it was perhaps Robert Altman who best exemplified the maverick spirit in American film-making after the success of his 1969 film *M*A*S*H*. A black comedy depicting the crazy antics of the various staff of a Mobile Army Surgical Hospital during the Korean (for which read Vietnam) War, the film – his fourth feature, but first hit – established the hallmarks of Altman's style and deeply ironic, sometimes even cynical attitude towards power, heroism and authority. The narrative is a sprawling series of illuminating vignettes rather than a tight story; the quirkily but carefully selected cast offers a large number of deftly drawn characters whose often semi-audible lines of dialogue constantly overlap; the shallow focus of the telephoto lens helps us to pick out telling moments from the hubbub of multi-tracked conversation and hectic activity; and the film's status as cinematic artifice and genre pastiche is repeatedly invoked by self-reflexive comparisons between the characters' actions and media versions of the same announced over the camp's PA system.

In the years that followed, Altman turned his caustic gaze on to a vast range of subjects, prolifically working his subversive way through genres – crime movies in *Thieves Like Us*, *The Long Goodbye* (both 1973) and *Kansas City* (1996); Westerns in *McCabe and Mrs Miller* (1971) and *Buffalo Bill and the Indians* (1976); psychological dramas in *Images* (1972) and *3 Women* (1977); the buddy-movie in *California Split* (1974); backstage

Tim Robbins in Robert Altman's **The Player** (1992), a dazzling satire on Tinseltown's methods and mores. With his subversive genre-bending in films throughout the 70s like **McCabe and Mrs Miller** and **The Long Goodbye**, Altman was a major influence on and inspiration to the next generation of independent directors.

drama in *Nashville* (1975); the romantic comedy in *A Perfect Couple* (1979); soap-style suburban drama in *Short Cuts* (1993) – and, at times when he found it difficult to obtain Hollywood financing, mounting cinematically imaginative adaptations of plays like *Come Back to the 5 & Dime Jimmy Dean, Jimmy Dean* (1982), *Streamers* (1983) and *Secret Honor* (1984). If Altman's free-wheeling, garrulous style was occasionally copied in other Hollywood films, the imitation was rarely successful, for his laid-back but intellectually sharp sensibility and his strangely bemused romantic pessimism were at odds with the more simplistic feelgood attitudes favoured by Tinseltown. Indeed, though he accepted financing whenever it was made available, and seldom complained about his experiences with the studios, he made no secret of his disdain for the absurdities of the film factory's methods and mores, and expressed it dramatically with dazzling wit and stylistic sophistication in *The Player* (1992), a shrewd satirical account of greed, hypocrisy, deceit and dog-eat-dog instincts in contemporary Hollywood.

< **20** >

It is perhaps unsurprising that Altman was at his peak in the 70s, when America was undergoing a period of disenchantment: the Woodstock generation's summer of love had ended at Altamont, the Vietnam War has ended in costly defeat, and the Watergate scandal had further undermined faith in political leaders. It was during this period that Hollywood produced some of its darkest, most ambitious films in years, made for the most part by 'movie brats' like Coppola, Scorsese, Brian De Palma and John Milius; even Lucas and Spielberg began their Hollywood careers with (for them) atypically adult films like *THX 1138* (1970) and *Sugarland Express* (1974). For a decade, Coppola led the way with *The Godfather* (1971), *The Conversation* (1974), *The Godfather Part II* (1974) and *Apocalypse Now* (1979) – brooding, haunted stories of corruption by power. Milius offered elegiac explorations of the mythology of American heroism in films like *The Wind and the Lion* (1975) and *Big Wednesday* (1978). De Palma gave us dark studies in psychic torment in

Robert De Niro and Harvey Keitel come to blows in Martin Scorsese's **Mean Streets** (1973). Scorsese's continued pursuit of personal obsessions, avoidance of hackneyed Hollywood plot structures and energetic visual style has made him a model for many of the new auteurs.

such movies as *Obsession, Carrie* (both 1976) and *Blow Out* (1981). Yet, eventually, they came to be overshadowed by the considerably more complex, consistent achievements of Scorsese. Indeed, if Welles and Cassavetes can be said to be the godfather and father of the contemporary US indie scene, then Scorsese is surely the brilliant elder brother. Although his films were for the most part financed by the Hollywood studios, with movies like *Mean Streets* (1973), *Taxi Driver* (1976), *New York, New York* (1977), *Raging Bull* (1979), *King of Comedy* (1982) and *GoodFellas* (1990) he understandably came to be regarded as the quintessential maverick *auteur*.

His films were visually stylish but extremely visceral in their treatment of violence, obsession and paranoia; they were partly confessional, grounded in Scorsese's personal experiences of having

< **22** >

grown up as a Catholic on the fringes of the underworld in New York's Little Italy, and partly a manic cinephile's hommage to his many favourite movies; they avoided the hackneyed storytelling methods and happy endings beloved by Hollywood; his pop-culture credentials were proclaimed by his exhilarating and imaginative use of rock music on the soundtrack; and his upfront treatment of intense human emotions – especially in the nervy, troubled waters of male-female relationships – was often reminiscent of Cassavetes, who had himself once encouraged the fledgling director to make more personal movies. Not only was Scorsese clearly a major film-making talent, but unlike the other 'movie brats', for many years he proved resistant to the notion of 'going Hollywood'; after Lucas and Spielberg broke box-office records with films like *Jaws* (1975), *Star Wars* (1977) and *ET The Extra-Terrestrial* (1982), many of the young Turks once apparently destined to transform American film-making seemed to decide that if they couldn't beat Hollywood at its own game, with its safe, commercial ambitions, they might as well join it. Scorsese, on the other hand, remained true to his obsessions.

Nevertheless, even though Scorsese, by the end of the 70s, was almost unique among the 'movie-brats' in this respect, their example had encouraged many other film-makers to try and forge a career with movies that didn't fit easily into the Hollywood mould. After the staid, dispiriting achievements of the 60s, there suddenly seemed to be an exciting effusion of mature, thought-provoking movies. Bob Rafelson looked at dysfunctional families, alienation and thwarted ambitions in *Five Easy Pieces* (1970), *The King of Marvin Gardens* (1972) and *Stay Hungry* (1977). Peter Bogdanovich paid fond, imaginative hommage to the likes of Ford and Hawks with *The Last Picture Show* (1971), *What's Up, Doc?* (1972) and *Paper Moon* (1973). Monte Hellman followed up his two stark, low-budget Jack Nicholson Westerns – *The Shooting* and *Ride the Whirlwind* (both 1966) – with likewise laconic contemporary existentialist fables like *Two Lane Blacktop* (1970) and *Cockfighter* (1978), both starring

Warren Oates, a Peckinpah favourite and one of the key actors of 70s maverick cinema.

Genre specialists emerged. Despite having his greatest successes with the Hawksian siege-thriller *Assault on Precinct 13* (1976) and the 'slasher-movie' *Halloween* (1978), John Carpenter's interest in sci-fi produced inventive hommages like *Dark Star* (1974), *The Fog* (1980) and *The Thing* (1982). George Romero, who had made what was arguably the most influential contribution to the modern horror genre with his low-budget *Night of the Living Dead* (1969), continued to work inventive variations on the genre with darkly allegorical tales of social collapse like *The Crazies* (1973), *Martin* (1976) and *Zombies – Dawn of the Dead* (1977). Larry Cohen moved from superior 'blaxploitation' thrillers like *Bone* (1972) and *The Godfather of Harlem* (1973) to outrageously subversive, often semi-parodic horror and sci-fi fare like *It's Alive* (1973), *Demon (aka God Told Me To)* (1976), and *Q – The Winged Serpent* (1982), while taking time out to tackle political chicanery in the film noir-inspired *The Private Files of J Edgar Hoover* (1977). High-level corruption filtered through a noir sensibility also fuelled the 70s films – *Klute* (1971), *The Parallax View* (1974) and *All the President's Men* (1976) – of Alan J Pakula, while Walter Hill inflected the macho conventions of various action genres with an ultra-laconic existentialism (recalling Peckinpah and the Americanophile French noir master Jean-Pierre Melville) in films like *Hard Times* (1975), *The Driver* (1978), *The Long Riders* (1980) and *Southern Comfort* (1981).

< **23** >

Comedy, meanwhile, was supplied by several very different talents. From exploitation thrillers for Corman like *Caged Heat* (1974) and *Crazy Mama* (1975), Jonathan Demme progressed to a series of gently satirical populist comedies about ordinary people caught up in extraordinary situations: *Handle With Care (aka Citizen's Band)* (1977), *Melvin and Howard* (1980), the TV featurette *Who Am I This Time?* (1982), *Swingshift* (1984) and *Something Wild* (1986). Another Corman associate, Paul Bartel specialised in intentionally tacky 'bad-taste' humour with films like *Private Parts* (1972), *Death Race 2000* (1975), *Cannonball* (1976), *Eating Raoul* (1982) and *Lust in the Dust* (1984), while yet another, Joe Dante, applied an equally wicked and engagingly anarchic sensibility to parodies like *Hollywood Boulevard* (1976), *Piranha* (1978), *The Howling* (1980), *Gremlins* (1984) and *Explorers* (1985). Meanwhile, the determinedly autonomous Woody Allen had shifted from ragbag parodies like *Bananas* (1971), *Sleeper* (1973) and *Love and Death* (1975) to more substantial comic explorations of middle-class neuroses and male-female relationships in ever more ambitious and stylistically confident films like *Annie Hall* (1977), *Manhattan* (1979), *A Midsummer Night's Sex Comedy* (1982), *Zelig* (1983), *Broadway Danny Rose* (1984), and *Hannah and Her Sisters* (1985). With limited success, Allen interspersed these comic gems with more insistently 'serious' films like *Interiors* (1978), *Stardust Memories* (1980) and *September* (1987), which often provoked charges of self-indulgence – a criticism also frequently (and more justifiably) directed against the likewise 'semi-autobiographical' films of Henry Jaglom. Certainly, Jaglom may be viewed as a genuine independent (unlike many of the other Hollywood-employed mavericks mentioned above), but while he often attempted, in work like *Sitting Ducks* (1979), *Can She Bake a Cherry Pie?* 1983), *Always* (1985) and *Someone to Love* (1987), to emulate the inventive editing style of his friend Orson Welles' last films (notably *F for Fake* and the 1977 documentary *Filming Othello*), he rarely managed to transcend a sloppy, self-indulgent formlessness or to avoid an overwhelming ambience of narcissistic navel-gazing.

Similarly scrappy in terms of structure and direction (but deliberately so) were the films of John Waters, whose deliriously tacky 'underground' comedies like *Mondo Trasho* (1969), *Pink Flamingos* (1972) and *Desperate Living* (1977) – mostly centred around the appallingly slobby antics of characters played by the portly transvestite Divine – became cult favourites. At first,

< 24 >

Waters' grasp of film language was rudimentary (he seemed more interested in provoking a sensation of disgust in his youthful audiences than in hazarding a coherent attempt at filmic 'style', minimalist or otherwise), but as his infamy spread beyond the late-night circuit and he became more successful, his films – including *Polyester* (1981), *Hairspray* (1988) and *Cry-Baby* (1990) became more polished, less likely to offend and more concerned with revelling in lurid kitsch and dubious taste.

At the other end of the aesthetic spectrum were a number of idiosyncratic craftsmen who with each new film they made became – successfully or otherwise – more ambitious, applying their distinctly personal vision to a range of genres and topics. In Alan Rudolph, who after directing an undistinguished low-budget horror movie (*Premonition*, 1972) became an assistant to Altman, Hollywood found one of its most eccentric, mercurial and, it must be said, erratic talents. His first feature of note, *Welcome to LA* (1977), a kaleidoscopic, stylish and somewhat stilted satire on the life-style of various well-heeled Angelenos, was all too obviously indebted to Altman, who produced both that film and its successor, an imaginative, updated gloss on the Joan Crawford-style melodrama entitled *Remember My Name* (1978). Neither movie performed well commercially, however, and for some years Rudolph found himself directing impersonal chores like *Roadie* (1980) and *Endangered Species* (1982). Only with *Choose Me* (1984), *Trouble in Mind* (1985) and *The Moderns* (1988), about a group of expatriate American artists, art-collectors and dealers in 20s Paris, did his true sensibility manifest itself: 'realistic' characters, places and situations were subtly transformed, by small, odd but telling details, into the stuff of stylised fairy-tale, while the tone trod a tightrope between fragile romanticism, cool irony and a somewhat arch, hip self-consciousness. Indeed, it was sometimes difficult to pinpoint exactly what interested Rudolph as he moved magpie-fashion between a variety of subjects and genres: *Love at Large* (1990) and *Mortal Thoughts* (1991) were brittle, intricate, but strangely

< **25** >

dissatisfying reworkings of the noir thriller, while *Equinox* (1992) was a bizarre, mystifying psychodrama about twin brothers separated at birth whose very different characters and lives become interlinked by contrived circumstance. More rewarding was *Mrs Parker and the Vicious Circle* (1994), in which Rudolph's penchant for whimsy was firmly reined in to provide an affectionate but unsentimental portrait of the Algonquin set.

< **26** >

Restless, audacious, full of ideas, adept with actors, and clearly at odds with Hollywood's mainstream, Rudolph nevertheless has yet to produce a fully satisfying movie; his films seem never quite to deliver what they promise. Certainly, that could not be said of Terrence Malick, the most enigmatic and intriguing of this particular generation of mavericks. A former Rhodes scholar and philosophy lecturer, he made his début as writer-director with *Badlands* (1973), widely regarded as one the finest films of the 70s. The subject matter was not itself especially original: based on the killing spree undertaken by a real-life couple in the 50s, the story fits snugly within the lovers-on-the-run sub-genre previously dignified by such movies as *You Only Live Once* (Fritz Lang, 1937), *They Live By Night* (Nicholas Ray, 1948), *Gun Crazy* (Joseph H Lewis, 1949) and *Bonnie and Clyde*. In its treatment of this material, however, Malick's film differed significantly from these and, indeed, most other movies. Instead of casting the young garbage collector and his teenage girlfriend in the usual heroes-or-villains mould as misunderstood outcasts or thrill-crazy delinquents, Malick provides them with no simple, easily digestible motivations for their murderous deeds: the boy, polite and pleasant enough in most of his actions, is merely keen on seeing himself as a kind of James Dean figure, while the girl views everything that happens around her (we hear excerpts from her diary in voiceover) as if it were part of a story in the low-brow teen-magazines she obsessively reads. Coupled with Malick's use of Carl Orff's music and the lyrical, painterly images (the opposite of those usually found in violent crime movies), the dialogue and characterisations serve to reinforce the mysterious nature of the couple's actions while exploring the nooks and crannies of the yawning gulf between the banality of real life and its more romantic counterpart as purveyed by the media.

Malick's cool, oblique, subtly ironic narrative style – which anticipated in some respects the work of later indies like Jim Jarmusch, the Coen Brothers, Hal Hartley and Todd Haynes – was taken even further in his second film, *Days of Heaven* (1979), a strange, finally tragic tale of a love triangle set in the Texan farmlands in 1916. Again Malick used a young girl's inarticulate but strangely expressive thoughts as voice-over to comment on the story; again, too, as the film touches on matters of love, class, economics and social injustice, the astoundingly beautiful images of the elements and nature draw our attention away from the human drama to something more awesomely mysterious, even metaphysical; it is as if individual motivation counts for little in the larger scheme of things.

< 27 >

Sadly, for reasons best known to himself, the perfectionist, reclusive Malick didn't make another film for two decades, and only returned to directing in 1997 with an adaptation of James Jones' war novel *The Thin Red Line*. At one point, after the resounding box-office failure of the costly *Heaven's Gate* (1980), it looked as if the same fate might befall Michael Cimino. Having started his directing career modestly enough with *Thunderbolt and Lightfoot* (1974), an imaginative variation on the heist- and buddy-movie genres made for Clint Eastwood, Cimino went on to make *The Deer Hunter* (1978), an impressively mounted, epic exploration of the effects of the Vietnam War on ordinary Americans. Though flawed by its racist depiction of sadistic Vietcong forcing American POWS to play Russian roulette, the film's stately pace and eye for detail lent it an almost mythic dimension, a quality that would also be found in the similarly lengthy *Heaven's Gate*, in which Cimino recreated the 1892 Johnson County Wars between immigrant farmers and Wyoming cattle barons as a vast, sweeping, vividly detailed historical pageant. Given virtual *carte blanche* by United

Artists, Cimino appeared to represent the triumph of the young Turks over the old Hollywood until, with a budget run extravagantly out of control and a narrative (running almost four hours) which many at the time found dull and confusing, the film achieved notoriety as a commercial and critical disaster. With hindsight, much of the outrage seems unfair – the movie is intelligent, elegant and eloquent on the muddled mores underlying the mythology of the pioneer spirit – but the damage was done, and Cimino's career went into seemingly irreversible decline with the sporadic appearance of overblown follies like *Year of the Dragon* (1985), *The Sicilian* (1987), *Desperate Hours* (1990) and *Sunchaser* (1996). More importantly, perhaps, given that the *Heaven's Gate* catastrophe virtually brought down a studio singlehandedly, the film's failure probably did irreparable damage to the maverick strain's standing in the eyes of Hollywood, which proved quite happy to furnish increasingly large budgets, but only, for the most part, for spectacular escapist fare.

< 28 >

Two other idiosyncratic talents who slowly graduated from comparatively low-budget output to more prestigious work were Phil Kaufman and Michael Mann, who both originated from Chicago. After a false start with two low-budget satires – *Goldstein* (1964) and *Fearless Frank* (1965) – Kaufman began to attract attention as the writer-director of intelligently off-beat features: *The Great Northfield Minnesota Raid* (1972) undermined Western heroics to witty and inventive effect, *White Dawn* (1974) charted a fateful encounter between American whalers and Eskimos at the turn of the century, *Invasion of The Body Snatchers* (1978) updated Siegel's 1956 classic to paint a scary, partly satirical portrait of contemporary Californian life, while *The Wanderers* (1979) was a lively, stylish slice of nostalgia about life in the Bronx gangs in 1963. Kaufman's prime sensibility, however, was literary, and his greatest triumph came with his adaptation of Tom Wolfe's *The Right Stuff* (1982), a truly epic study of modern American heroism in which the largely unsung exploits of test-pilot Chuck Yeager are weighed against the far more heavily publicised achievements of the seven astronauts who pioneered NASA's Mercury programme. Remarkably, Kaufman's tone is at once celebratory and ironic: he applauds the men's courage ('the right stuff') while casting a beady eye over the media hype, political opportunism and souped-up jingoism that accompanied the moon-shot. The film has all the majesty and grace of a great Western, but there is also an almost European sense of critical distance applied to the events shown, a strategy later applied to Kaufman's sensitive, resourceful but emotionally cool version of Milan Kundera's Prague Spring novel *The Unbearable Lightness of Being* (1987). Thereafter, sadly, he seems to have lost his touch, with *Henry & June* (1990) and *Rising Sun* (1993) both disappointing his admirers.

< 29 >

Though a similarly cool, quasi-European sensibility may also be discerned in the films of Michael Mann – his taut, taciturn scripts and his fascination with loyalty, betrayal, professional codes of honour and self-definition recall the crime thrillers of Jean-Pierre Melville – Mann's work is considerably less literary and ironic in tone than Kaufman's. After *The Jericho Mile* (1979), a superior TV movie about a prisoner who overcomes boredom and asserts his individual worth by training to become an Olympic-standard runner, Mann revealed his true colours with *Thief (aka Violent Streets)* (1981), a gripping psychological study of a master safecracker whose sense of self-respect and professional freedom are threatened by mobsters determined to keep him under their control. The film was distinctive both stylistically and in its unsentimental existentialism: emphatically modern in its use of sleek, Expressionist iconography (semi-abstract shots of high-tech machinery and architecture have become a trademark of Mann's style), electronic rock music and long, wordless, virtuoso action set-pieces, *Thief* set the tone for most of his subsequent studies of wary, world-weary obsessives trying honourably to make their way in a dangerous, hostile world. For some years, Mann found it hard to build a career in features – his next movie, *The Keep* (1980), an ambitious, bizarre but uneven study of evil with Nazis beseiged by a mysterious ancient power in the Romanian mountains, failed to find an audience – and he devoted himself to his TV series *Miami Vice* and *Crime Story*. But after *Manhunter* (1986), one of the first, and best, of modern serial-killer thrillers, he scored a hit with a visually ravishing, impressively complex adaptation of James Fennimore Cooper's *The Last of the Mohicans* (1992), and came up with one of the very finest crime movies in decades: *Heat* (1995), an enormously detailed, magisterially directed epic charting the cat-and-mouse contest between a brilliant, workaholic cop and his similarly single-minded counterpart, a reclusive master-thief.

< **30** >

The tendency towards the epic mode increasingly displayed by Mann, Kaufman, Malick and Cimino may also be found in the career of Oliver Stone, the screenwriter-turned-director who in the 80s and 90s countered Hollywood's preference for mind-less escapist blockbusters with a series of ever more bombastic movies about serious political subjects. After scripting several high-profile, somewhat controversial films like *Midnight Express* (Alan Parker, 1978), *Scarface* (De Palma, 1983) and Cimino's *Year of the Dragon*, and having directed two eminently forget-table horror-shockers – *Seizure* (1973) and *The Hand* (1981) – Stone hit his stride with *Salvador* (1986) and *Platoon* (1987), dealing, respectively, with the USA's pernicious involvement with right-wing governments in Central American politics and with the experiences of the lowly 'grunts' fighting with no clear sense of purpose in Vietnam. If neither film was particularly subtle, sophisticated or original in terms of its cinematic style or political analysis, each had sufficient visceral force and sense of injustice to suggest that Stone might eventually have something interesting to say about modern America. Certainly Stone him-self appears to have believed as much, for he embarked upon a prolific series of movies that dealt in turn with unbridled capi-talism (*Wall Street*, 1987); the media's relationship with violence (*Talk Radio*, 1988); America's treatment of its wounded Vietnam veterans (*Born on the Fourth of July*, 1989); the counterculture of the 60s (*The Doors*, 1991); the conspiracy behind the assassination of John F Kennedy (*JFK*, 1991); the Vietnam War and its aftermath as experienced by the Vietnamese (*Heaven and Earth*, 1993); the media's relationship with violence, again (*Natural Born Killers*, 1994); and the rise and fall of a corruptible president (*Nixon*, 1995). Big subjects, all, and just as Stone became more ambitious in terms of his material, so he resorted to an increasingly flamboyant array of cinematic trickery (fragmented narratives, different film stocks and speeds, distorted angles and strange superimpositions) and lengthier running times to convey the complexity of his vision. Unfortunately, very often his analysis of the chain of events he was exploring was needlessly complicated rather than complex, so that one emerged bemused, bludgeoned and not a little bored by the sledgehammer tactics of his storytelling style. While there is no question that Stone is – and probably sees himself as – a maverick, he is in danger of taking his work too seriously as a socio-political force, although *U-Turn* (1997), an expensive, semi-comic variation on the B-movie crime-thriller, seemed a self-conscious attempt to forego serious comment in favour of the post-modernist pyrotechnics pioneered in *Natural Born Killers*.

< **31** >

Other film-makers were content to express their personal vision of American society in subtler, more intimate ways. Paul Schrader, for example, moved from *Blue Collar* (1978), a modest heist-thriller that managed to offer insights into working-class aspirations, union politics and organised crime, and *Hardcore* (1979), an overheated but harrowing morality play about religious faith in conflict with the contemporary profanities of the sex industry, with a series of obsessive films concerned with the problems and possibilities of finding grace through spiritual and moral redemption. Intriguingly, Schrader's intelligent cinephile sensibility led him through a variety of filmic forms: *American Gigolo* (1979), for example, was a glossy, sensualist's update of Bresson's *Pickpocket* (1959); *Cat People* (1981) a study in sexual obsession inspired by Val Lewton's 40s horror film of the same name; *Mishima* (1985) an ambitious attempt to fashion a new kind of biopic that might throw fresh light on the relationship between life, art and politics; *Light of Day* (1987) a poignant study in familial conflict brought about by differences in age, lifestyles and religious belief; *Light Sleeper* (1991) a modern urban fable about a disenchanted drug-dealer jolted out of his self-destructive habit by a murder; and *Affliction* (1997) a cool mix of crime mystery and psychological drama as it examines the emotional shortcomings of a smalltown cop haunted by his experiences at the hands of a tyrannical, abusive father. If Schrader's work can seem occasionally portentous, his clear-eyed intelligence and overall reluctance to compromise his fascination with contemporary ethics make for compelling, provocative and frequently unsettling drama.

< **32** >

Similarly concerned with the dilemmas faced by protagonists torn between sensual abandon and intellectual self-control are the autobiographically-inspired films of James Toback who, apart from having written memorably personal scripts for *The Gambler* (Karel Reisz, 1974) and *Bugsy* (Barry Levinson, 1991), has also directed a handful of his own movies. Most impressive was *Fingers* (1977) in which a classical concert pianist is enthralled and tormented by the violence he encounters while debt-collecting for his mobster father; the film is raw, at times even crude, but such is the courage of its convictions in documenting its flawed hero's psychic anguish that it achieves a strangely rigorous power. Toback's following films – *Love and Money* (1980), *Exposed* (1983) and *The Pick-Up Artist* (1987) – were basically sillier, more baroque variations on the same theme, but with *The Big Bang* (1989), a simple, admirably direct documentary in which he talks to various colourful characters about their lives, loves, hopes, fears and beliefs, he was quietly and wittily back on form.

Not entirely dissimilar to Toback in terms of his professed interest in the conflicts between spirituality and carnality, God and Mammon, crime and punishment is Abel Ferrara, who has emerged from the lower echelons of the exploitation industry to become something of a cult favourite among certain film-goers. Making his name with the infamous *The Driller Killer* (1979), in which he took the lead role as a New York painter so deranged by his punk band neighbours that he embarks on an odyssey of killing down-and-outs (but, interestingly, no women) with a power drill, Ferrara moved steadily into slightly more upmarket productions, mostly in the crime genre. *Ms .45 (aka Angel of Vengeance)* depicted the deadly revenge taken against a variety of male chauvinists by a mute garment worker after she has been raped twice in one day; *China Girl* (1987) relocated the Romeo and Juliet story to Little Italy and Chinatown as its young lovers try to ignore the bloody battles between rival ethnic gangs; *Cat Chaser* (1989), *King of New York* (1989) and *The Funeral* (1996) were more conventionally polished but uninspired crime sagas; *Bad Lieutenant* (1992) was one of Ferrara's more extreme efforts, a rambling, raw psychodrama about a New York cop hooked on drugs, booze and sex but redeemed by his interest in the case of a gang-raped nun; the paranoia about authoritarianism in *Body Snatchers* (1994) gained little resonance from relocating the classic story to a military base; and the attempt to explore the philosophical dimensions of vampire mythology in *The Addiction* (1995) was not helped by the self-indulgence of Ferrara's direction. All too often, the more ambitious, thoughtful elements in the scripts by the director's frequent collaborator Nicholas St John – the Catholic concern with crisis of conscience and faith, the attempts to define good and evil in a chaotic world beset by compromise, corruption and social injustice – are rendered murkily incoherent by Ferrara's insistent, gloating fascination with low-life sleaze and by the apparent difficulties he has in organising a focused, structured narrative; it is as if he hopes to transform a genre film into something more artily significant but hasn't the self-discipline to do so, with the result that his films look at best efficient, at worst hollow and pretentious.

Even when he has moved away from genre, the consequences

< 33 >

have been disappointing. About a film-maker who exploits the tensions between his two lead actors to enhance his movie about marital breakdown, *Snake Eyes (aka Dangerous Game)* (1993) explores the fraught relationship between life and art to somewhat obvious effect, while *Blackout* (1997), about a movie-star so into intoxicants that he can't remember whether or not he has murdered his lover, is so sloppy, inarticulate and salaciously entranced by the stoned depravity on view that it looks depressingly like self-parody.

< 34 >

If the film-makers whose work I have described above may be included among the most important American mavericks of the late 70s, 80s and early 90s, few of them may be seen as genuine independents. The majority of their films were made for the Hollywood majors. Indeed, for years, the anti-Hollywood ethos and production/distribution methods initiated by Cassavetes seemed to have led nowhere: there were a few independent films being made, but they were so infrequent, and usually achieved such a low audience profile, that there was little sense of continuity, let alone of any kind of 'movement'. Occasionally, following in the tradition of Paul Morrissey, whose association with pop artist and minimalist film-maker Andy Warhol had taken him from such spaced-out sex sagas as *Bike Boy* (1967), *Lonesome Cowboys* (1968) and *Flesh* (1968) to modishly camp drive-in fare like *Flesh for Frankenstein* (1973), figures would emerge from the 'underground' to reach, briefly, a wider audience: Mark Rappaport with *Casual Relations* (1973) and *The Scenic Route* (1978), Curt McDowell with *Thundercrack* (1975), Eric Mitchell with *Underground USA* (1980), Amos Poe with *Subway Riders* (1981), Kathryn Bigelow and Monty Montgomery (later an associate of David Lynch) with *The Loveless* (1981), Slava Tsukerman with *Liquid Sky* (1982), and Jon Jost, who exhibited the heavy influence of Godard in quizzical films about the American Dream like *Angel City* (1977), *Last Chants for a Slow Dance* (1977) and *Slow Moves* (1983). Women directors, too, tended to work in low-budget and independent films: Claudia

Weill (*Girlfriends*, 1978), Amy Jones (*The Slumber Party Massacre*, 1982; *Love Letters*, 1983), Susan Seidelman (*Smithereens*, 1982; *Desperately Seeking Susan*, 1985), Penelope Spheeris (*The Wild Side, aka Suburbia*, 1983; *The Boys Next Door*, 1985), and Lizzie Borden (*Born in Flames*, 1983). So, too, did African-American directors like Charles Burnett (*Killer of Sheep*, 1977; *My Brother's Wedding*, 1983), Charlie Ahearn (*Wild Style*, 1982), and Bill Duke (*The Killing Floor*, 1985), whose main inspiration – this was before the success of Spike Lee's *She's Gotta Have It* (1986) – was perhaps the provocatively satirical, dramatically ramshackle anti-racist allegories of Melvin Van Peebles (*Watermelon Man*, 1970; *Sweet Sweetback's Baadasssss Song*, 1971).

< 35 >

The view that Hollywood's marginalisation of women and black directors was at least partly motivated by ideological factors, as opposed to talent, finds further support in the fact that films dealing seriously with sensitive political issues were also frequently independent, rather than mainstream, productions, such as Robert Young's *Alambrista!* (1977) and Gregory Nava's *El Norte* (1983), about the harsh prospects facing Latin American immigrants, and Rob Nilsson and John Hanson's *Northern Lights* (1978), about Dakota farmers organising themselves politically.

As a result, independent film-making during the 70s and 80s was not the healthy, high-profile phenomenon it is today. Even when David Lynch made a splash with his remarkable *Eraserhead* (1976), a surreal, nightmarish, profoundly personal cinepoem financed by the American Film Institute, the film was so idiosyncratic – it was impossible to categorise it as belonging to any one genre – that it spawned no real imitators. Even so, however weird Lynch's vision of the world, the mainstream – in the form of Mel Brooks' production company and Dino De Laurentiis – tried to harness his peculiar talents to a more conventional form of filmic narrative with, respectively, *The Elephant Man* (1980) and *Dune* (1984), and while the former is certainly an extremely impressive film, it was not until *Blue Velvet* was released in 1986

that we were again able to see Lynch's unique sensibility untaint-
ed by commercial considerations. This time around, however, his
decision to work without making artistic compromises found
him in good company, for in the intervening years two other
determinedly independent talents had arrived on the scene: John
Sayles, whose 1979 film *Return of the Secaucus Seven* had been
welcomed as a landmark in low-budget film-making; and Jim
Jarmusch, whose successful second feature *Stranger Than Paradise*
(1984) was also seen as something of a watershed movie. Both,
of course, were courted by Hollywood; both, however, were
keenly aware of just how far the mainstream might accommodate
the kind of movies they wanted to make (in the case of Sayles, a
little; not at all, in the case of Jarmusch). And make movies they
most certainly would. American independent cinema was back,
and this time it had made up its mind: it was here to stay.

< **36** >

But what, precisely, differentiated the new mavericks and
indies from the film-makers featured in the preceding pages, and
what encouraged or allowed them to make the offbeat, original
movies they did? In order to answer the former question, it is
perhaps best first to consider the second. America in the 80s was
marked by a return to outright conservativism and conformism
under the presidencies of Reagan and Bush, a conservatism and
conformism reminiscent of the 50s and mirrored in Hollywood
itself, which produced ever more anodyne, formulaic, expensive
spectaculars dominated by special effects and the star system.
Idiosyncratic or 'personal' films were increasingly difficult to
make unless you were an established favourite like Woody Allen,
while the studios shied away from treating issues like poverty,
racial and sexual inequality, AIDS, or the rise in crime – all problems afflicting 80s America – other than in the blandest, most
reassuring terms. As a result, any young film-maker who felt the
need to avoid or transcend the escapism favoured by the studios
had to find finance outside of the mainstream, foregoing big
budgets, stars and state-of-the-art special effects. Happily, such
film-makers could look not only to the example of Cassavetes

and other mavericks, but to original work in other fields, most notably in music (where the garage sensibility of punk and avant-garde bands and indie record labels had successfully provided an alternative to the more technically polished dinosaurs supported by the major record labels) and in the rise of the pop video-promo and MTV, forms which not only were frequently made with comparatively minimal resources but which experimented in playful post-modern fashion with styles of narrative, assuming a high level of cineliteracy and tolerance among the audience for the weird, eccentric and innovative. (Not surprisingly, a number of indie film-makers of the 80s and 90s including Jarmusch, Lee and Hartley supplemented their income by making occasional pop-promos.) As a result, not only has there been a degree of cross-fertilisation between cinema, music and video, but aficionados of rock, MTV and other related forms of art and entertainment are perhaps more open-minded with regard to the experimental stylistic strategies, narrative modes and low-budget resources of indie film-making.

< **37** >

Not, of course, that the film-makers whose work is analysed in the following chapters all share the same concerns or styles. Indeed, their respective movies are distinguished by a highly individual artistic personality which is very much at odds with the comparatively anonymous creative signatures of directors who work within the Hollywood mainstream. The work of Sayles, Wang, Lee and Haynes is marked by their notably different approaches to social and political issues; that of Lynch, the Coen Brothers and Tarantino by subversive, playfully anarchic but similarly diverse reworkings of traditional genres; that of Jarmusch and Hartley by apparently more personal, less clearly generic considerations of narrative methodology and emotional substance; while Soderbergh appears to be a restless, unsettled talent, exploring radically different themes and different narrative styles as he moves from film to film. Each, therefore, with the arguable exception of Soderbergh, may be regarded as an *auteur*, with his own thematic and stylistic trademarks. At the same time, however, in one way or another they all share a basic disinclination towards toeing the mainstream line. Whether working for a Hollywood major, for a partly independent outfit like Castle Rock, Fine Line, Miramax or October (now aligned, respectively, to parent companies Buena Vista and Paramount), for their own independent companies (sometimes, as in the case of Jarmusch, Haynes or Hartley, in collaboration with foreign companies like Japan's JVC or Britain's Zenith), or even putting together a budget through family, friends, private investors and personal outlay, each of these film-makers tends either to avoid genre conventions or to interrogate them by means of subtle transformations, so that their work is fresh, eccentric, and – explicitly or implicitly – critical of the Hollywood norm.

Moreover, in terms of working methods, while some of these *auteurs* are happy enough to make use of Hollywood financing when the opportunity arises, they are all for the most part prepared to work on comparatively low budgets, foregoing major stars, extravagant sets and visual effects (though these last are increasingly available now that computer technology has become widespread and relatively cost-effective), and favouring both a repertory group of actors and technicians and invention fostered by financial necessity. And it is finally that invention – the imaginative fecundity, the desire, willingness and ability to go out on a limb and offer a more rewarding, challenging alternative to the safe, stale homilies and clichés that now figure so strongly in the American mainstream cinema – that marks out the film-makers investigated in the following chapters as fertile creative talents deserving of serious consideration and acclaim. If the American cinema is to offer us anything other than bland, formulaic entertainment, contrived by committee and aimed at the widest, least demanding audiences – in short, if it is to give us something artistically worthwhile – then it is the mavericks and indies who will surely lead the vanguard.

< 38 >

David Lynch

< **39** >

While, at time of writing, it remains impossible to foretell the progress and more particularly the box-office success of Quentin Tarantino's film-making career, it is ironic that David Lynch has come closer to reaching, and satisfying, a wide audience than any of the other indie *auteurs*. While the Coen Brothers and Spike Lee have worked on relatively big-budget movies, not one of the mavericks and indies of the 80s and 90s has been entrusted with directing a film on the scale of Lynch's *Dune* (1984), and none of them has reached an audience as large as that which regularly tuned in to Lynch's much-imitated TV series, *Twin Peaks* (1989-91). Yet Lynch was always an unlikely contender for mainstream success; while his film work is arguably no more 'experimental' than that of, say, Jim Jarmusch, Hal Hartley or Todd Haynes, his apparent disregard for the conventions of plot, characterisation, theme and even meaning makes it difficult to fathom how he could have achieved the popularity he has.

For Lynch – who trained as, and remains to this day, a painter firmly in the modernist tradition – is emphatically not a natural storyteller. From *Eraserhead* to *Lost Highway*, his films have been more concerned with creating strange worlds, unsettling moods and bizarre images than with forging a tidy, linear, easily com-prehensible narrative peopled by rounded, recognisably 'real'

< **40** >

characters. Indeed, his films, which frequently dispense with the traditional plot-logic of cause and effect, seem more closely aligned to the workings of dream; it is no accident that he has frequently been described as a Surrealist (although he lacks the strict Surrealist's anti-bourgeois thrust), and Lynch himself has spoken of his interest in the films of Cocteau, Fellini and Man Ray, as well as in the writings of Kafka and the paintings of Bacon. Like that of the Surrealists, Lynch's work exhibits an abiding fascination with the unconscious, with the inexplicable, and with uninhibited emotional responses to sex and death, and may fruitfully be interpreted in Freudian terms. For Lynch, creativity is a matter not of carefully reasoned intellectual activity, but of allowing intuition and imagination free rein; unsurprisingly, then, he is famously reluctant to discuss his films in terms of any exact meaning, preferring instead to safeguard the mystery that is both their prime characteristic and their subject matter.

Perhaps inevitably, that extreme dependence on intuition and the reluctance to interrogate the precise meaning of his work are probably responsible for both its strengths and its weaknesses. At times, Lynch's tendency simply to 'go with the flow' of his unfettered imagination results in cinema that is stylistically and thematically bold, original and imbued with a hallucinatory, visionary power; at others, it can seem mannerist, self-indulgent and undisciplined almost to the point of incoherence. There is no doubt that Lynch can create enormously effective images, moments, scenes; yet only in a few movies has he managed to make them make proper sense or harnessed them to an entirely gripping narrative.

His films are probably best understood as attempts to imagine worlds that are subtly but significantly different from the one we live in: expressionist worlds of the mind, where what we see and hear tells us about the dark, hidden desires, anxieties and fears that make up the inner lives of his characters. In order to communicate those emotions clearly, however, the worlds created must function according to their own, persuasive inner logic, and when Lynch's disregard for the conventional demands of narrative results in a lack of cohesion, his exploration of that emotional/ mental landscape can seem unrewardingly vague, unilluminating and even, in films such as *Wild at Heart* (1990) and *Twin Peaks: Fire Walk with Me* (1992) – profoundly flawed works which nevertheless have much to recommend them – tainted by a hint of insincerity or cynicism.

At the same time, however, it would be unfair to make too much of this last charge when Lynch is so clearly keen to plough his own idiosyncratic artistic furrow, and has done so with such fruitful results. Despite remaining true, as we shall see, to his own very personal preoccupations, and despite his evident lack of interest in simply conforming to mainstream storytelling methods, he has tended to work for the most part in recognisable genres – horror, sci-fi, film noir and domestic melodrama – and, in so doing, has managed to revitalise them by means of wit, stylistic invention, and sheer audacity in confronting the darker excesses of human behaviour. If Lynch's fascination with both the squeaky-clean banal facade and the sinister underbelly of modern America occasionally leads him to indulge in, respectively, kitsch and sensationalism, his imaginative fecundity is such that even his least satisfying films proffer a refreshing alternative to the bland, hackneyed clichés favoured by the Hollywood mainstream. No Lynch film, not even *Dune,* is wholly without worth or interest; and to see his finest work – *Eraserhead, The Elephant Man, Blue Velvet* and the pilot episode of *Twin Peaks* – is to submit to an experience as unsettling, provocative and viscerally affecting as any provided by the modern American cinema.

Even in the two shorts he made before *Eraserhead* – both of which blend drawn animation with the use of live actors (treated, by means of stop-motion camerawork and grotesque make-up, as if they were animated cartoon characters) – certain preoccupations later recognisable as typically Lynchian can be discerned. In the four-minutes-long *The Alphabet* (1968), a small, pale girl lies in bed listening to children chanting their ABCs; as adult voices

< 41 >

take over to sing about the value of learning the alphabet, the letters take shape in the darkened room, but when plant-like tentacles constrain the girl, she writhes in agony and vomits blood over her pristine white sheets. And in the half-hour-long *The Grandmother* (1970), a young boy, ignored and beaten by his parents for wetting his bed, sows a seed in a pile of earth on the bed, from which grows a plant that gives birth to an elderly woman who comforts him with kindness; when, however, she becomes ill, his parents merely laugh at his unhappiness, and she dies, leaving the boy to return to his lonely room, and sleep.

< 42 >

Already, we can see Lynch's concern with dysfunctional families, children abused and made unhappy by adults, emetic bodily functions, and the traumatising rites of passage from innocence to experience; already, too, a distinctive visual style is evident, intriguingly situated between stark, gritty, pared-down 'realism' and the more fantastic strategies of Surrealism and Expressionism; and already we see a tendency towards partly symbolic narratives that cannot be explained away in terms of conventional 'realist' logic. These shorts, then, seem in retrospect to be like Lynch's features in embryonic form; impressive as they are, however, as animation (which has always proved fertile territory for film-makers keen to articulate the 'impossible'), it was only with the shift to live-action in *Eraserhead* that Lynch's peculiar talent for the vivid creation of imaginary worlds came properly to the fore.

Though, at the time of its release, Lynch's début feature first found an audience with the late-night crowd – many of whom seem to have regarded it in much the same cultish light as, say, the 'sick' bad-taste comedies of John Waters, disreputable, over-the-top horror-shockers like *The Texas Chainsaw Massacre* (Tobe Hopper, 1974), or even camp horror-parodies like *The Rocky Horror Picture Show* (Jim Sharman, 1975) – *Eraserhead* was an altogether more serious, experimental and discomforting undertaking than those more easily categorised movies.

Made on a low budget over a period of five years, the film inhabits a strange grey area lying between genre pastiche and personal confession, nightmare fantasy and social satire. Superbly shot in (for the most part unusually dark) black and white, and set in an only remotely familiar urban hell of empty, underlit streets, ravaged wastelands, and grimy, semi-derelict industrial architecture, it charts the humiliating, anguished experiences of the hapless Henry Spencer (Jack Nance), a perpetually worried, baby-faced innocent with a fearsome shock of hair, who lives in a dark, dank, squalid one-room apartment. Upon returning home, Henry learns from his strangely seductive neighbour that he is invited to dinner to meet his girlfriend Mary's parents; the awkward silences of the encounter turn to outright aggression when Mary's mother reveals that her daughter is pregnant and that he must marry her. The 'baby', however, is born prematurely, and its monstrously embryonic appearance and incessant crying soon drive Mary back to her parents, leaving Henry to deal with his sickly, precociously malicious offspring alone. He copes with the ordeal by fantasising about a smiling, hamster-cheeked young woman who performs a bizarre song-and-dance act – which involves crushing spermatazoa-like creatures beneath her feet – in a little theatre behind his radiator; but after nervously yielding to the advances of his neighbour, who is so disturbed by the presence of the grotesque baby that she later transfers her attentions to another man, Henry suffers a weird nightmare in which, during a visit to the Lady in the Radiator's stage, his head is replaced – decapitated, in fact – by the baby's, and taken to a workshop where his brains and skull are turned into erasers to be put on the end of pencils. Awakening from the dream to further cries from the infant, he cuts open the bandages swaddling its body, sending it into horrifying, deadly paroxysms of agony; all hell breaks loose in the room – or even, perhaps, in the universe – until after a white flash accompanied by 'heavenly' choral music, Henry is reunited with the Lady in the Radiator, who embraces him.

< 43 >

Jack Nance plays Henry, the hapless victim of Lynch's surreal imagination in the director's first feature **Eraserhead** (1976). Already in place are Lynch's signature mix of dark psychology and unsettling humour and his expressionist use of sound and lighting.

While it's certainly possible to hazard an interpretation of the film which grounds its inspiration in Lynch's personal life – at the time of filming, he was working under severe budgetary contraints, at the same time as trying to support a wife and daughter – it resonates far beyond purely autobiographical concerns. Clearly, the movie is a phantasmagoric meditation, loosely disguised as a kind of horror movie, on problems associated with marriage, parenting, and the whole cycle of sex and birth, love and death: besides the anxieties and catastrophes Henry suffers with regard to his evidently non-committal 'shotgun' marriage to Mary and to his troublesome experiences with an unwanted, mutant 'child', there are numerous scenes featuring images disturbingly evocative of intercourse and castration. The Lady in the Radiator destroys the sperm-like creatures that drop on to her stage by stamping them underfoot (smiling as she does so – after all, Henry is unhappy about fatherhood); when Mary unexpectedly and briefly returns from her parents, Henry awakes to discover her beside him in bed, scratching and writhing in her sleep, only to find, beneath the clammy, tangled sheets, bizarre umbilical cord-like creatures emanating from her body, which he strenuously pulls out and hurls against the wall; and when, half-terrified, half-aroused, he submits to his neighbour's slightly sinister sexual advances, the bed on which they make love is transformed into a milky pool into which the couple sink, as if drowning.

< 45 >

Still more perversely suggestive of sex, conception and birth, however, is the film's 'poetic' opening sequence. Henry's head floats as if disembodied against a black background and a dark, organic-looking 'planet'; the camera then floats over a strange, murky landscape before plunging through a gaping orifice. We then see a mute, putrescent, twitching and tortured figure (credited as 'the man in the planet') who looks out a window and then, after the mouth of Henry's floating head yawns open to allow a worm-like creature to emerge, jerks a series of levers: the worm flies off-screen to fall, in the next shot, into a shining white pool, before the image fades to be replaced by our first proper view of Henry, looking worried and miserable in the street.

This opening sequence is crucial to any interpretation of *Eraserhead* since it can be read in several ways. On one level, it may symbolise the act between Henry and Mary which brings about the birth of the 'baby', and which reflects Henry's very apparent unease about physicality, sex and women. (With the sole exception of the girlish, consolatory Lady in the Radiator who, cherub-like and emphatically asexual, sings a song promising that 'in Heaven everything is fine', the women in the film – including Mary's mother, who forces him against a wall and kisses his neck – are generally seen as unpredictable, demanding and predatory.) On another, it may also depict an act of creation by which the 'man in the planet', a Godlike figure who controls human activity with his levers, creates Henry himself. Moreover, since the first image of the film is Henry's horizontal head, it may even be that Henry is actually dreaming this act of creation, in which case the entire movie might be seen as Henry's reverie, born of his anxieties not only about sexuality, physicality and parenthood but about his fragile hold on existence itself. Certainly, this last interpretation helps to make sense both of the dream sequence that gives the film its title, in which Henry's head – his most conspicuous defining characteristic, as it were – is removed by the 'baby' rising out of the collar of his jacket, and of the scene in which Henry watches his neighbour arriving home with another man and, as she returns his gaze, sees himself as he believes she now sees him: as the grotesquely monstrous 'baby'.

< 46 >

Eraserhead, then, while impossible to pin down to any one meaning, concerns anxieties about identity and existence, and its eloquence and power in speaking about those fears lie less in the film's story than in its execution, in its *mise-en-scène*. We have already noted Lynch's use of ill-lit streets and seedy industrial architecture – traditionally associated with film noir, a genre much given to moods of menace and paranoia, in which danger may lie in wait in the black shadows and the hero may be consigned to the darkness of oblivion – but Lynch takes his designs further still, so that exteriors impinge upon interiors, just as the world impinges on and reflects (or may be the product of) his protagonist's state of mind: in Henry's likewise underlit room, there are piles of dirt on tables, sprouting spindly, sickly-looking plants, while in a drawer, for no evident reason, there is a bowl of water – 'civilisation' is too thin a veneer to hold back the elemental chaos and decay of the natural world over which it has been built. Aurally, too, Henry cannot escape the hostile outside world: whether walking the streets or sitting in his room, he is surrounded by a persistent rumbling, roaring and hissing, as if the pipes, radiators and walls, even the elements, are threatening an apocalyptic explosion. (Lynch's expressionist 'sound design', usually executed with the help of his long-term collaborator, the late Alan Splet, has continued to be a hallmark of his style to the present day.)

But it is perhaps Lynch's morbid fascination with the sheer physicality of the flesh that best expresses Henry's anguish about sex and death. Besides the various worm-like creatures that emanate from Henry's mouth or Mary's womb, or fall on to the Lady in the Radiator's stage, another repulsive feature is the tiny 'man-made' chickens served up for dinner by Mary's parents; when carved by Henry, one begins to move as if in pain and spews forth pints of bubbling blood. More disturbing still, of course, is the 'baby', a fleshy, skinless, emphatically inhuman head attached to a legless, armless torso swaithed in bandages; monstrous from the start, the creature becomes even more repellent when it develops spots and sores, or when finally, after Henry has cut open its bandages, its innards begin to swell and bubble and its neck extends wildly, until its enlarging head seems to take over the room and, hence, to complete its malign conquest of Henry's life.

< 47 >

In terms both of the fertility of Lynch's imagination and of the cinematic expertise that enabled him to express his ideas on screen, *Eraserhead* introduced a distinctive, original talent to the film world, though at the time it appeared unlikely that his darkly eccentric vision could ever be fruitfully accommodated by the commercial mainstream. Remarkably, however, the film's cult success and reputation were such that for his next movie he was taken on by no less an establishment figure than the comedian Mel Brooks, who invited Lynch to direct, for his production company Brooksfilms, *The Elephant Man*.

Set in 1880s London, the film told the real-life story of John Merrick, an appallingly deformed man exhibited in circus freak-shows until he was 'saved' by Frederick Treves, a surgeon who, in electing to take Merrick under his wing for personally ambitious purposes of scientific study, discovered that his charge, far from being a brute, insensitive imbecile, was in fact a charming, intelligent and enormously 'civilised' individual deserving of friendship and respect. Had the film been made purely according to Hollywood conventions, it would surely have emerged as a cynical exercise in maudlin sentimentality; but while it was in many respects more 'mainstream' than *Eraserhead* and most of Lynch's subsequent work, it benefitted hugely from the fact that there were aspects of Merrick's story which closely coincided with many of Lynch's own obsessions. (Indeed, one might even argue that the film had some autobiographical resonance for Lynch, whose progress as a reputedly 'freakish' experimental film-maker moving into the 'respectable' arena of the mainstream, courtesy of Brooks' patronage, paralleled that of Merrick from circus freak-show into well-to-do Victorian society through the kindly understanding of Dr Treves.)

< 48 >

In terms of narrative, for the most part Lynch maintained a straightforward linear trajectory. Only a few impressionist shots – most notably an opening montage (of a woman's eye, a photo of the woman, elephants, the woman knocked over and writhing, white smoke and the sound of a baby crying) which refers to the freak-show myth that Merrick's condition was attributable to his mother having been trampled by an elephant – evoke the realms of dream and fantasy; it is almost as if Lynch is showing he can 'behave himself' and make a movie that is accessible to a wider audience than the one which enjoyed *Eraserhead*.

At the same time, however, the film's *mise-en-scène* and thematic development are wholly in keeping with Lynch's other work. Victorian London, as depicted by Freddie Francis' high-contrast black and white camerawork, Lynch and Splet's sonic design and Stuart Craig's production design, is a dark, cruel, hostile place, much of it ravaged by poverty and the pollution of the Industrial Revolution in full swing: behind the 'civilised' veneer of the hospital, the homes of the wealthy, and the West End theatre (where Merrick is taken on his one happy public excursion), lies a festering world of steaming factories, sinister alleys and the circus, where more disturbing spectacles are enjoyed than those played out on the legitimate stage. And Merrick himself, played with enormously expressive dignity by John Hurt under mounds of make-up, is both a physically grotesque incarnation of sickly, rotting flesh and a childlike innocent whose experiences of the adult world – whether at the hands of his exploitative 'owner', the habitually violent freak-show proprietor Bytes, or at those of the initially disgusted hospital staff – are regularly a source of pain, fear and confusion. Even the kindness and sympathy he eventually inspires in the likes of Treves and the actress Mrs Kendal gives cause for sadness, in that his 'education', his introduction to a society more refined and humane than that of the circus, makes him all too aware of the severe limitations his illness, and his resulting appearance, have placed upon his life.

< **49** >

In this regard, Lynch's film, with its antithetical story of a 'good', innocent outsider being civilised by a partly 'bad', i.e. unfeeling 'normal' society, belongs to a tradition of films about 'noble savages' that includes such titles as *The Miracle Worker* (Arthur Penn, 1962), *L'Enfant Sauvage* (François Truffaut, 1969) and *The Enigma of Kaspar Hauser* (aka *Every Man for Himself and God Against All*) (Werner Herzog, 1974). In other ways, however, Lynch's film may be seen as more closely aligned with *Freaks* (Tod Browning, 1932), in its insistence that physical beauty – or its absence – is no index of spiritual, moral or intellectual worth; in its recognition of the sense of community that leads society's outcasts to support each other in their sufferings (when Bytes abducts Merrick to take him with the circus to Europe, the other 'freaks' liberate him); and in its refusal to sensationalise its subject by pandering to our basest voyeuristic impulses. Just as Browning introduced his cast of (real-life) 'freaks' by showing them first in a lyrical long-shot of a picnic, then acclimatised viewers to their physical abnormality with mundane shots of them performing 'normal' everyday tasks, so Lynch reveals the precise nature of Merrick's deformity only bit by bit, showing him first in silhouette or under his cape and hood before allowing us to see his body clearly and in full.

As we shall see later with *Blue Velvet* and, to a lesser extent, *Lost Highway*, Lynch is clearly fascinated by the phenomenon of voyeurism, and in *The Elephant Man* he is not only aware of the need to engage our sympathies with Merrick while minimalising any opportunities for us simply to indulge our morbid curiosity (which might easily provoke feelings of revulsion), but he inscribes the very theme of voyeurism into the text of the movie. Not only are we made to feel uneasy by the sight of visitors to the circus staring (like us) at Merrick's affliction; when he is taken to the theatre – a magical, joyous evening for a man recently kept hidden in his room, away from the prying gaze of the public – the sense of triumph engendered by Mrs Kendal's well-meaning tribute (she introduces him, in his box, to the rest of the audience, who applaud enthusiastically) is counterbalanced by our nagging awareness that once again he is being held up as a spectacle to gratify the self-congratulatory humanism of enlightened society and, by implication, of ourselves. It is that awareness which allows us to understand the true complexity of Merrick's plight, and of the film, rather than just wallowing in sentimental drama.

< **50** >

Sadly, Lynch's next encounter with mainstream production was less happy. Encouraged by the critical and commercial success of *The Elephant Man*, Lynch accepted an invitation from the producer Dino De Laurentiis to film Frank Herbert's sprawling sci-fi novel *Dune*. With the benefit of hindsight, it is perhaps hard to see what attracted the director to an epic project dealing with the deadly rivalry between two warring dynasties to wrest control of a consciousness-expanding, life-prolonging spice and thus of the universe itself. Admittedly, there is, in the ambivalently heroic character of Paul Atreides, a protagonist who is 'awakened from his sleep' by a sentimental and intellectual education that will allow him to control both his own destiny and that of the cosmos, but the plot is so intricate and all-consuming that Lynch found little opportunity to develop the theme of innocence transformed by knowledge and experience. Indeed, as it stands – whether in the frequently incomprehensible two-hour theatrical release, or in a clearer, four-hour TV assembly (which is probably closer to Lynch's original intentions, though it has a ludicrous, tacked-on explanatory prologue which persuaded him to take his name off the credits) – the film features few Lynchian elements other than a physically repulsive Baron Harkonnen (all sweating obesity and bursting boils), and two mythical species: an enormous, pink, phallic-looking Supreme Being, and the gigantic sandworms who erupt from the desert, again phallic in shape but endowed with huge, gaping jaws clearly evocative of a vagina dentata. While, at least in its four-hour version, *Dune* is not nearly as bad as its reputation as a box-office catastrophe would suggest – the action sequences are efficient, the sense of scale impressive, and the set designs and camerawork imaginative – it remains, for all its extravagance, a minor contribution to the Lynch canon.

< 51 >

Working with De Laurentiis did, however, have compensations, for the producer next allowed Lynch considerable creative freedom in making a project dear to the writer-director's heart: *Blue Velvet*. As with *Eraserhead* and *The Elephant Man*, the basic thrust of the film was to expose the dark, disturbing core beneath the surface of civilisation, but here the effect was more subversive and unsettling, simply because the society explored by the film was far more familiar: that of modern smalltown America (a world, incidentally, that Lynch knew well and remembered affectionately from his childhood). The story also took the familiar form of a detective mystery. In Lumberton, clean-cut student Jeffrey (Kyle MacLachlan, who had played Paul in *Dune* and would come to be seen by many as Lynch's alter ego) visits his father in hospital, and in a patch of wasteland on his way home finds a severed ear. Handing in the ear at the police station, he later learns from a detective's daughter, Sandy (Laura Dern), that investigations have somehow linked it to a local cabaret singer, Dorothy Vallens (Isabella Rossellini). Jeffrey determines to find out more for himself, and with Sandy's help breaks into

Dorothy's apartment, in a reputedly dangerous part of town. Eager for new experiences, Jeffrey is nevertheless unprepared for the dangers he encounters – not merely the almost schizophrenic volatility of Dorothy herself, who on finding him spying on her from her closet, makes him undress at knifepoint and starts making sexual advances to him, but the psychopathic aggression of Frank Booth (Dennis Hopper), who arrives at Dorothy's and, with Jeffrey once again watching from the closet, begins to subject her to violent sexual abuse and humiliation. Shocked and disturbed, Jeffrey tells Sandy he believes Frank has abducted Dorothy's son and husband (whose ear it was) in order to avail himself of her favours. When he visits Dorothy again, she asks him to make love to her and hit her – reluctantly he complies – until Frank arrives and forces them to accompany him and his henchmen to Ben's, where Dorothy's child is being held, and where Jeffrey is repeatedly threatened and humiliated. Shaken by his experiences, he confesses his love to Sandy, but their blossoming romance is interrupted first by her jealous boyfriend and then by Dorothy, whom they find naked and beaten outside Jeffrey's home, and who later informs Sandy and her family that she and Jeffrey have had sex. Though Dorothy is taken to hospital and Sandy is upset, Jeffrey returns to the singer's apartment and finds the murdered bodies of her husband and a corrupt policeman involved in Frank's drugs-ring. Calling Sandy's father for help, he makes to leave but is chased back into the apartment by Frank, whom, by hiding in the closet, he manages to shoot and kill. Order has been restored – Jeffrey wakes in his garden to find himself surrounded by his and Sandy's families and by Dorothy, released from hospital, with her son.

In *Blue Velvet*, Lynch was able, for the first time, to frame his customary preoccupations and stylistic preferences within a genre film made on an adequate budget. If the story has a certain naïve unreality about it (Jeffrey's boyishly enthusiastic methods of detection are somewhat reminiscent of, say, the Hardy Boys adventures popular in the 50s), Lynch simply takes as much as he

< **52** >

needs from the mystery-thriller format in order to concentrate on more serious, disturbing elements. From the opening shots, which introduce Lumberton in a series of emphatically idealised images of cosy suburban life – red roses and yellow tulips sway against an impossibly blue sky and white picket fence, a fireman waves at the camera from a passing fire-engine, Jeffrey's mother sits watching an old crime movie on TV, while his father waters the garden – it is clear that Lynch is going to show us a world familiar from 50s movies and TV but entrancingly off-kilter. The pastiche of smalltown life is quickly shattered: even before a word has been spoken, Jeffrey's father keels over (whether as a result of a heart attack or an insect bite – he slaps the back of his neck – is unclear), his dog snaps at the hose-water spraying from his loins, and the camera plunges into the grass of the neatly-mown lawn to uncover a sinister, hitherto invisible world of black, chaotic, battling insects. Evidently, this is to be no ordinary tale of the solid, traditional, homely virtues of smalltown America.

< **53** >

Nor, however, will it be an ordinary crime movie. Not only are Jeffrey's investigations, as stated above, risibly naive and frequently irrational (precisely why, for instance, does he – or for that matter Frank – return to Dorothy's apartment at the end of the film, when she is no longer there?); there's also the fact that the exact nature of Frank's criminality, his links with Ben and the corrupt cop, and the true motivation for his having taken Dorothy's husband and son, are given little dramatic or thematic weight by Lynch, whose real interest lies in the psychopathology of the violent sexual behaviour witnessed, and later participated in, by Jeffrey during his descent into a hellish underworld that fascinates, frightens and repels him. Intriguingly, his first sexual act is not an innocent kiss with Sandy, an archetypical girl-next-door familiar from countless movies, but an act of voyeurism, watching the more mature Dorothy – a cabaret singer and therefore, by generic convention, a *femme fatale* – undress through the slats of her closet. But Dorothy's sexual status – especially in her dealings with Frank – is also predicated in part on the fact that she is a mother, and her relationships with Frank and Jeffrey are perhaps best understood in Freudian terms as Oedipal: Jeffrey desires the mother Dorothy, and so needs to replace the 'father', Frank – who has sex with Dorothy and has control of her real son – by killing him. Even this explanation of the dangerously fraught relationships between the three is insufficiently complex, however, since Frank himself may be seen in the role of both father and son: when, like Jeffrey, we first see him violently abuse Dorothy, after initially insisting that she address him as 'Daddy', he calls her 'Mommy, Mommy', and tells her that 'Baby wants to fuck.' Moreover, while his actions at first give the impression of turning into a conventional (if psychopathically aggressive) rape, what he actually does is far more perverse: after ordering her to open her legs so that he can stare at her crotch (all the while inhaling some kind of gas and yelling at her not to look at him), he whines, 'Baby wants blue velvet,' and Dorothy places a piece of her robe into his mouth. He then climbs astride her as if to rape her, but actually stuffs the fabric between her legs, growing increasingly excited by the mock intercourse until he finally shouts, 'Daddy's coming home'. It is as if Frank is undecided whether he wants to play the son, husband or father, and can only begin to express his desire with help from the hallucinatory gas and from the violence he uses to take control; there is a strong suggestion that he would like to return to the womb, and that he is impotent (which might explain his constant rage and, perhaps, his inability to speak more than a few words without recourse to the word 'fuck').

But just as Frank and Dorothy, who in her dealings with Jeffrey alternates between tender vulnerability and a domineering aggression which imitates the way Frank torments her, are 'split' characters, so Jeffrey is revealed to be more complex than his square-jawed, squeaky-clean appearance and demeanour initially suggest. His investigations, we come to see, are motivated not only by a desire to solve a crime but by his becoming sexually aroused by Dorothy (it is no accident that Sandy tells him

< **54** >

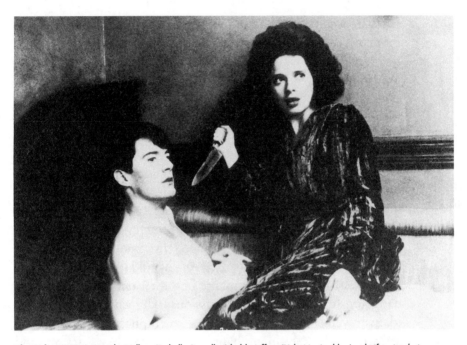

Blue Velvet (1986): Dorothy Vallens (Isabella Rossellini) holds Jeffrey (Kyle MacLachlan) at knifepoint during one of their schizophrenic sexual encounters – a path that leads the naive 'hero' into a dark underworld of the psyche.

she is unsure whether he's 'a detective or a pervert'); not only does he take evident pleasure in watching her (either from the closet or at the club where she performs), but he readily agrees to have sex with her even when, traumatised by Frank's recent abuse, she imagines that he is her husband. And although he first refuses to hit her as she asks (her masochistic tendencies are clearly the psychological result of her being tormented by Frank), he does comply: in exploring the dark underbelly of Lumberton life, he also discovers a dark side of himself, so that Frank's claims that Jeffrey is just like him, and his repetition of the lyrics from the Roy Orbison song mimed to by the charming but profoundly sinister Ben (Dean Stockwell) – 'In dreams I walk with you/ In dreams I talk with you/ In dreams you're mine, all of the time/ Forever, in dreams' – make perfect sense of their relationship.(Indeed, it could be argued that much of the perversity he sees and participates in is something he himself imagines or dreams: soon after the scene in which he finds the ear, the camera zooms right into the dark orifice, while the final sequence of domestic bliss, coming immediately after Jeffrey's killing of Frank, begins with the camera pulling back from a close-up of Jeffrey's own ear, so that most of the film could be seen as having taken place within the confines of his mind.)

Nevertheless, even if we accept what we have seen as 'real' rather than imagined, the film's 'happy ending' is partly ironic: as we see Jeffrey's family and friends reunited in sunny suburban idyll, a line is reprised from Dorothy's cabaret rendition of the song 'Blue Velvet' ('And I still can see blue velvet through my tears') which reminds us that she, Jeffrey and quite probably everyone else present (particularly, one would imagine, Dorothy's infant son) will be forever marked by their encounters with the dangerously unbridled primal passions indulged in by Frank (the id, as it were, to Jeffrey's ego). As if to emphasise the frailty and artifice of their restored happiness, Lynch shows Jeffrey and Sandy finding solace in the sight of a beetle-munching robin on their kitchen window-sill (reminding us not only of the beetles in the lawn at the film's opening, but a dream recounted by Sandy in which robins, representing love, bring light back into a dark, troubled world) – only the bird is clearly a clockwork creature.

Stylistically the film is imbued with artifice: Jeffrey and Sandy's conversations are full of lines that are deliberately naive or corny ('It's a strange world'; 'Why are there people like Frank?'), while Frank's profanities are excessive even for a psychopath ('Fuck… let's drink to fucking!'; 'Let's fuck – I'll fuck anything that moves!'); the colours are often super-saturated, and the compositions – most memorably when Ben mimes to 'In Dreams' using a torch as a microphone, and when Jeffrey finds the two corpses in Dorothy's apartment – like strangely formal, nightmarish *tableaux vivants*, while the overall design, in terms of architecture, decor, cars, etc., suggests a world as evocative of the

< **56** >

50s (a famously conservative era often regarded as somehow more pure and/or innocent, morally and sociologically, than the decades that followed) as it is of the mid-80s, when the film was made. This level of artifice not only lends the film considerable irony and wit, and allows Lynch to stage scenes so horrifying in their evocation of evil menace that they need not be constrained by considerations of 'realism', but gives the film the feel of a fairy-tale, in which knight-in-slightly-tarnished-armour Jeffrey rescues damsel-in-distress Dorothy from the child-eating ogre Frank, and wins the pure princess Sandy as his prize.

Blue Velvet's critical and commercial success was doubly welcome after Lynch's unhappy experience with *Dune*; his star was once more in the ascendant and he embarked upon a period of, for him, frantic activity. His next film was a 22-minute contribution to a compendium movie entitled *Les Français Vu Par...* (the other episodes were by Jean-Luc Godard, Werner Herzog, Andrzej Wajda and Luigi Comencini); entitled *The Cowboy and the Frenchman* (1988), it is a playful, characteristically off-the-wall little comedy about three none-too-bright cowboys (led by the extremely deaf Slim, played by Harry Dean Stanton) who are bewildered by the sudden arrival of a Frenchman on their ranch. Basically, the film is a gentle, rather silly satire on national stereotypes – the cowboys are xenophobic, rodeo-riding gamblers prone to shout 'What the hell!' and 'Yippee-kay-yeah!', while the Frenchman is a beret-sporting romantic with a pencil moustache, a poetic turn of phrase (he's forever babbling on about how the Indians sold Manhattan Island for a bunch of palm-leaves), *escargots* in his pockets, and wine, baguettes, cheese and miniature Eiffel Towers in his suitcase. Patchy amusement can be had from the various linguistic and cultural misunderstandings that occur, while the final rapprochement, which involves much singing of corny Country ballads and the cowboys (now also joined by an assortment of bar-room whores and Parisian gamines) learning phrases like '*Voulez-vous coucher avec moi ce soir?*' and '*Vive la France!*', should clearly not be taken too seri-

< 57 >

ously as a model of international tolerance and understanding.

Far more ambitious and rewarding was Lynch's first foray into television with the 'soap' series *Twin Peaks*, written and co-produced with Mark Frost, with several episodes directed by Lynch himself (including the opening pilot which, with the addition of a number of scenes from later instalments, was given a theatrical release in some territories as a feature).

Given the experimental style and controversial content of *Eraserhead* and *Blue Velvet*, one might have assumed that Lynch's idiosyncratic sensibility would have felt even more frustrated by the conventions of television soaps than it was by mainstream film-making, especially as the 'plot' of *Twin Peaks* is ostensibly driven by an investigation into the torture and murder of a young woman which eventually leads to revelations that involve incest, violent sexual abuse, prostitution, diabolical possession and drug-taking. Nevertheless, while Lynch never shied away from the serious implications of the sexual, violent and psychologically warped subject matter of his story, very little explicit sexual or violent activity was shown on-screen; rather, his interests seemed to lie, again, in revelling in the sheer strangeness and perversity of the relationships that define the seemingly strait-laced, tranquil community of the rural north-western logging town (again evocative of Lynch's early years, not to mention the hammy TV and cinematic stereotypes he grew up with) of the series' title.

Hence, while FBI special agent Dale Cooper (Kyle MacLachlan, once again so cheerily clean-cut and open in his manner that he can bear little resemblance to the Bureau's real-life agents) and local sheriff Harry S Truman make their investigations into the demise of Laura Palmer (whose corpse is discovered at the start of the first episode, and whose name echoes that of the heroine of Otto Preminger's 1944 classic *Laura*, another alleged murder victim whose 'ghost' continues to tantalise and haunt the minds of both those who knew her and the detective investigating her death), the story quickly opens out to examine the secret lives of a large gallery of often eccentric characters.

< 58 >

Not only do Cooper and Truman find that the reputedly unblemished homecoming queen Laura was regularly taking cocaine and probably involved in prostitution at an establishment frequented by her father (who, we eventually learn, committed the murder while possessed by a mysterious, demonic figure named Bob), but we discover that the entire town seems to be caught up in clandestine and adulterous affairs, business intrigue, and various other unsavoury, illicit activities. Despite the fact that this concern with moral and spiritual degradation ties in once more with Lynch's interest in the corruption of innocence, it is also, certainly, standard fare for TV soaps. Where Lynch's series differs from the standard soaps like *Peyton Place*, *Dallas* or *Dynasty* is in its blatant refusal to adhere to a conventionally 'logical' plot structure or a 'realist' aesthetic: plot strands are needlessly complicated or simply left hanging untied, the otherwise recognisably smalltown lifestyle of Twin Peaks is regularly invaded by fantasy figures and elements more familiar from sci-fi or horror, and a number of characters – such as 'the Log Lady' – are included more for their bizarre eccentricity than for any precise function in the development of plot. The overall effect, at least in the pilot and the first series, is strangely hypnotic as the mood shifts suddenly but smoothly from the darkly mysterious to comically whimsical, from 'natural' to supernatural, from tearful melodrama to noir parody, playing with and warping our generic expectations.

< 59 >

If, finally, the series has little that is particularly significant or insightful to say about such troubling issues as incest, domestic violence, teenage prostitution or drug abuse, there is no denying the fact that Lynch's imagination and sure grasp of style make for many memorable moments. The tense, edgy mood in the morgue where Laura's body is kept is accentuated by malfunctioning fluorescent lights flashing off and on; Laura's grieving mother has a terrifying vision in which she finally recalls glimpsing the scowling figure of Bob hiding at the foot of her daughter's bed; another girl, who has survived a torture session similar

< **60** >

to that inflicted on Laura, walks scarred, semi-naked and traumatised by shock over a railway bridge leading from the forested wilderness surrounding the formerly safe haven of Twin Peaks; and yet another displays her talent for working in a brothel by tying a knot in a cherry stalk with her tongue. (Less successful are those scenes simply too abstract or fantastically bizarre to fit into the generic scheme of things, such as those set in a displaced, curtained 'Red Room' where Cooper encounters, among others, both Laura Palmer herself and a dwarf – listed in the credits as the Man from Another Place – who makes his arcane utterances in a barely recognisable English and for no evident reason performs a weird little dance.) Most affecting, however, is the brooding intensity of the treatment of emotional pain: when Laura's father and mother first learn, during a telephone conversation, of their daughter's death, or when the headmaster, himself on the brink of tears, announces her death over the PA system to classrooms of stunned pupils, Lynch lingers on their grief at such length that we are almost embarrassed to be witness to their naked anguish.

So popular was the first series of *Twin Peaks*, with viewers revelling in the colourful characters, in repeated motifs like Cooper's antiquated, oft-stated love of cherry pie or another character's absurd obsession with her curtains, and in the plangent strains of the much-used music of Angelo Badalamenti (who first collaborated with Lynch on *Blue Velvet*, to similarly memorable effect), that a second series was embarked upon. With its meandering narrative, even more insistently emphatic oddness, and greater dependence on off-the-wall whimsy, the series soon became quite tiresome; in determinedly subverting the conventions of TV soap, it had replaced outmoded formulas with tired clichés of its own. The decline may perhaps be attributable to the fact that Lynch himself was less closely involved in the second series than the first, since he was at work on his next feature film, *Wild at Heart*, which won the prestigious accolade of the Palme d'Or when it premièred at the 1990 Cannes Film Festival. As ever, the new movie was a stylish, visceral piece of film-making, but in loosely adapting Barry Gifford's story about two young lovers on the run from the girl's jealous mother and the criminals she enlists to end their relationship, Lynch seemed to lose the sharp focus that had distinguished his most interesting explorations of a single, precisely imagined community.

The story itself is simple and straightforward: Sailor (Nicolas Cage) and Lula (Laura Dern) are passionately in love with one another, united in their addiction to hot, wild sex and rock 'n' roll. But when Lula's mother Marietta (Dern's real-life mother Diane Ladd) tries to prevent Sailor – just out of prison after serving almost two years for killing a man she had hired to attack him – from seeing her daughter, the couple leave Cape Fear for New Orleans. Marietta persuades a lovestruck admirer, private detective Johnnie Farragut (Harry Dean Stanton in nicely morose form), to follow them, but, doubtful of his determination, she

< **61** >

The road to nowhere for Sailor and Lula (Nicholas Cage and Laura Dern) in **Wild at Heart** (1990) – where Lynch's visual flair and kitsch eccentricities lack the defining motivation they had in **Blue Velvet**.

then panics and enlists the help of the drug-dealer Marcello Santos, who threatens to kill his rival Farragut. As the runaways drive on west to Texas, swapping thoughts on the terrible ways of the world and exchanging memories about the precise circumstances of Lula's father's death in a fire (as Santos' driver, Sailor saw the conflagration which, he suspects, was an act of murder on the part of Marietta and Santos, who therefore want to silence him), a remorseful Marietta joins Farragut in New Orleans, too late to prevent his death at the hands of Santos' associates.

< **62** >

Meanwhile, Sailor and Lula reach the small town of Big Tuna where, at their motel, they are befriended by the sinister Bobby Peru, who makes lascivious advances to the now pregnant Lula before persuading the impoverished Sailor to join him in a robbery. The crime is a set-up – Peru is actually working for Santos – but it is he who gets killed; Sailor merely ends up in jail again. When the still devoted Lula and their son meet him upon his release six years later, Sailor bids his farewell, believing they'll be better off without him. Beaten unconscious, however, by a gang of youths, he has a vision of the Good Witch from *The Wizard of Oz* (Lula has frequently imagined her mother as that film's Wicked Witch of the West); told that Lula still loves him, and that he should fight for his dreams and run away from life no more, he returns to Lula and, by way of proposing marriage, sings a version of his hero Elvis Presley's 'Love Me Tender'.

As this brief synopsis may suggest, *Wild at Heart* takes a situation familiar from countless films about misunderstood young lovers on the run from oppressive adults, and decks it out with idiosyncratic details. Indeed, for all its visual audacity (Lynch uses the wide Scope screen with considerable flair) and despite some chillingly atmospheric set-pieces (most notably a scene, itself virtually irrelevant to the plot, in which Sailor and Lula come across and are horrified by a gruesome car crash at the side of the road), many of the film's details suggest that Lynch, left without a precise milieu to delve into, is often merely indulging in kitschy eccentricity for kitschy eccentricity's sake. Much is made of Sailor's snakeskin jacket being a representation of his 'belief in individuality and personal freedom'; of the couple's favourite slogans ('Rockin' good news!') and colourful dialogue (Lula is 'hotter than Georgia asphalt'); of their obsessions with Elvis and The Wizard of Oz; and of the other characters' various grotesque characteristics (Bobby Peru's swollen gums and stunted, rotting teeth; a gangster called Mr Reindeer, constantly attended by semi-naked women; a one-legged female killer, or another woman – played by the famously dark and elegant Isabella Rossellini – wearing a hideously obvious blonde wig). All of this makes for reasonably entertaining viewing; none of it, however, appears to have any particular significance or purpose, except, maybe, to alert us to the feverish, overheated imaginings of the romantic couple on the run and, perhaps, of their creator.

< 63 >

Where the irony and deliberate artifice in *Blue Velvet* lent a genuine complexity to its commentary, in *Wild at Heart* the most obvious departures from generic 'realism' seem like aesthetic posturing, a crowd-pleasing provision of self-conscious 'Lynchian' weirdness that adds little or nothing to whatever the film has to say. Nor is Lynch's use of repeated visual and aural motifs especially interesting: the most obvious – the striking of a match in enormous close-up, usually followed by shots of roaring flames – which forges links between the fiery passion Sailor and Lula feel for one another (signified by their sharing cigarettes) and the deaths of Sailor's parents from smoke-related illnesses and of Lula's father by arson, is hardly original in its conjunction of love and death, while the visual and verbal allusions to *The Wizard of Oz* serve merely to remind us that Lynch's film is also a fairy-tale and a road-movie about youngsters endangered by the world around them. Small wonder, then, that the 'happy ending' reuniting Sailor and Lula, based as it is on the intentionally risible *deus ex machina* apparition of a fairy queen and on a knowingly camp rendition of a schmaltzy pop ballad, seems so hollow, cynical and dissatisfying.

The impression that Lynch had perhaps run out of imaginative steam and was coasting on the back of his 'weirdo' reputation was not diminished by the work he produced over the next two years. The mercifully short-lived TV sitcom series *On the Air* (1991-92), about the ludicrously inefficient antics of the eccentric staff of a New York television station in the late 50s, suffered from cartoon-thin characterisation and a poorly-paced, all too broad comic style. Still more dispiritingly, for his next feature Lynch returned to the world of his TV success with the prequel *Twin Peaks: Fire Walk With Me* (1992) which, after a barely coherent, insistently bizarre 20-minute prologue outlining an earlier FBI investigation into the murder, in the small north-western town of Deer Meadow, of waitress Teresa Banks, moved on to chart the final seven days in the life of Laura Palmer. True, the main body of the film, which jettisoned the detective format, the catch-phrases and comic turns, and many of the characters of the TV series to focus more closely on the drug addiction, pros-titution and incestuous violence that marked Laura's last, miser-able days on earth, was as dark and cruel as anything Lynch had ever shown. True, too, that its relationship to the TV series threw up some intriguing temporal and spatial conundrums: when Laura awakens in her bed to find the dead body of Annie Blackburn (a future murder victim) beside her, she is told that 'the good Dale is in the Lodge', referring back to the TV series' final scenes of the FBI agent's possession by Bob, which of course take place some time after Laura's own death; and some interest-ing play is made with a picture, given by an old woman to Laura to hang on her wall, of an open door in a darkened room, through which Laura (in dreams?) walks, eventually to find her way to the 'Red Room' of the Lodge.

That said, however, the overall impression is of Lynch raking over old ashes, without quite being sure why he is doing so. The prologue is mostly silly, devoted to indulgent scenes such as one where a female FBI agent performs a grotesque, incomprehensible mime to a male colleague who later deciphers its arcane symbols in order to receive his instructions.

< 64 >

Meanwhile, the main story seems often to wallow in sequences depicting Laura's degradation, so that whatever few serious insights it offers into the theme of sexual abuse (and it is psychologically astute to suggest that Laura tries to cope with her fearful, guilty feelings about being repeatedly raped by her father by imagining him as the diabolical Bob) are counterbalanced by a mood of lurid sensationalism, most notably in a disco scene in which Laura and her friend Audrey, both semi-naked, indulge in delirious, drug- and booze-induced depravity. Too often, also, Lynch resorts to clichés associated with the horror genre, as when Laura is transformed before our very eyes into an obscene vampire-like figure; such moments may enhance the film's capacity to shock or create suspense, but they serve no purpose in terms of a coherent narrative or a serious study of psychological torment.

< **65** >

While Lynch's inventive use of sound, colour, composition and decor made for several unsettling scenes, the organisation of the movie as a whole seemed confused, caught between a genuine desire to delve deeper into Laura's wretched experiences and a complacent readiness to settle for the suspenseful conventions of a teenage horror shocker. Perhaps unsurprisingly, then, it fared badly both with the critics and at the box-office; many of the former saw it as a cynical attempt to cash in on the success of the TV series, while fans of the series, deprived of its lighter moments, found the movie intolerably dark and disturbing. Lynch himself, apparently distressed by its critical and commercial failure, didn't return to feature film-making for five years. In the meantime, he contented himself with a number of relatively low-profile projects. He directed two Barry Gifford-scripted dramas for his 1992 TV trilogy *Hotel Room* – *Tricks* and *Blackout*, both stylistically restrained but gripping, subtly unnerving studies of characters confused and haunted by death, desire and despair – and a 55-second, silent, black and white film made for the cinema-centenary compilation *Lumière and Company* (1995), which in five brief shots tells the eery, impressionistic tale of a couple being informed of the murder of their son by what seems to be a

Satanic sect, who may already have their next victim – a naked woman kept submerged in a water tank – in their grasp. At the same time, he continued with his painting, wrote and produced (with Angelo Badalamenti) 'The Voice of Love', an album of songs performed by Julee Cruise (the roadhouse singer in *Twin Peaks*), and produced Michael Almereyda's experimental vampire fantasy *Nadja* (1994) and Terry Zwigoff's *Crumb* (1995), a documentary about the acclaimed, controversial and sexually obsessive comic-strip artist Robert Crumb. Only in 1997 did Lynch himself finally make a proper big-screen comeback with *Lost Highway*.

< **66** >

If the film constitutes something of a departure from much of Lynch's earlier work – it is recognisably set in the ultra-modern, comparatively sophisticated world of Los Angeles, rather than one of the writer-director's beloved small towns, and it is only partly or tangentially concerned with an innocent's rites of passage to experience – it remains unmistakably Lynchian in terms of its style

On the road again. Fred and Renee Madison (Bill Pullman and Patricia Arquette) in **Lost Highway** (1997) – a disturbing piece of psychological noir every bit as experimental, in its own way, as **Eraserhead**.

and its disregard for conventional narrative. It begins, slowly but surely, as a kind of twisted psychological film noir: after the opening credits, which show us a two-lane highway illuminated by the headlights of a speeding car, we see a haggard-looking Fred Madison (Bill Pullman) listen to an anonymous, unseen caller announce over his apartment's intercom that 'Dick Laurent is dead'. Evidently, Fred is mystified by the call, but he has other concerns on his mind: very soon we gather, as he asks why his wife Renee (Patricia Arquette) will not come to listen to him at the club where he plays jazz saxophone, that he is unsure of her fidelity, a suspicion fuelled by her lack of enthusiasm for their love-making and, later, by the attentions paid to her by a man named Andy at a party the couple attends. Moreover, the Madisons are both anxious about two videocassettes mysteriously left on their doorstep, the first simply showing the exterior of their house, the second, far more disturbingly, shot inside the house at night and ending with footage of the couple asleep in their bedroom. Fred has an inkling of who might have sent the tapes when, at the party, he is approached by a strange, gnome-like Mystery Man who insists they've already met at Fred's house, and who demonstrates that he is actually there now, by asking Fred to call home: the man's voice answers the phone. When Fred and Renee return home (she remaining enigmatic about how she knows Andy), Fred suspects someone is in their apartment; though he finds no one there, he cannot sleep, and wanders through the dark corridors until he decides to watch the second tape again: it now ends in carnage, with a blood-spattered Fred beside his wife's mutilated corpse. He's horrified by what he sees, but the next thing he knows he is being interrogated, tried and sentenced to death for a murder he can't remember having committed.

< 67 >

At which point, Lynch and Barry Gifford's narrative takes a completely unexpected twist: though Fred starts suffering awful headaches and hallucinatory visions of a flaming cabin, we are unprepared for the discovery one morning of an entirely different prisoner in the cell. Not only are the guards amazed to find Fred replaced by Pete Dayton (Balthazar Getty), a young man with a cut on his head, but Pete hasn't a clue how he got there. Released to go home with his parents, he presently returns to his garage mechanic job and his girlfriend Sheila, but soon begins to find himself in trouble again when he allows himself to be seduced by Alice (Patricia Arquette, now blonde instead of brunette as for Renee), the girlfriend of Mr Eddy, a dangerous and jealously possessive hoodlum who has hitherto admired Pete's car-fixing talents. When, in time-honoured fashion, Alice suggests she and Pete (who is now having some trouble focusing his eyes) escape the increasingly suspicious Eddy by robbing a rich acquaintance who works in porn-movies and who first introduced her to Eddy, he nervously agrees, but when he arrives at the man's mansion, a fight develops which ends with Andy (for it is he) dead. Alice, unrepentant, refuses to give a clear reply to Pete's questions about a photo he finds showing Alice and Renee with Andy and Eddy, and instead insists they drive to meet a fence who has a cabin in the desert. Upon arrival, they first make love in the sand in the light of the car's headlights; after Alice walks off to the cabin, telling her lover, 'You'll never have me', Pete becomes Fred once more. The fence – the Mystery Man from the party – emerges from the cabin to say that the woman Fred is asking for is not Alice but Renee. Fred drives off to the Lost Highway Hotel where (in a room already envisaged by Pete at Andy's place) Renee is having sex with Mr Eddy; after she leaves, Fred emerges from the room opposite, beats up Eddy at gunpoint, packs him in the trunk of his car, and drives back into the desert. There, in the fight that ensues between the two men, Fred is saved by the Mystery Man who makes the wounded Eddy watch, on a tiny portable TV, footage of himself and Renee watching porno-movies at Andy's. The Mystery Man then shoots Eddy and vanishes, leaving Fred holding the gun; he drives home, rings the doorbell and announces into the intercom that Dick Laurent (whom we have known as Eddy) is dead. Spotted

< **68** >

by the cops who are now working on Andy's murder, he then speeds into the desert; as the sirens and flashing lights follow in hot pursuit, Fred screams, and we see the white lines of the highway rushing towards us in the headlights.

If I have dwelt on the plot of Lost Highway at some length, it is not merely to suggest the complexity of the storyline, but because whatever originality or significance the film may have exists at the level of narrative structure rather than in the *mise-en-scène*. For once, in terms of tone Lynch plays both story and characters fairly straight: besides a scene exhibiting Eddy's psychopathic obsession with road courtesy (he nearly kills a rude tail-gater), there is very little comedy, and with the exception of the Mystery Man – an odd, ghostly figure perhaps best viewed as Fred Madison's unconscious or id – the characters are mostly presented as fairly ordinary human beings. Indeed, what is most immediately distinctive about the film are two unusual, perhaps inexplicable narrative tropes: firstly, that the story ends at the point at which it began (in which respect it may be seen either as circular or, perhaps, as a spiral or figure 8), and secondly, that one character (played by one actor) for a while 'becomes' another character (played by another actor who in no way resembles the first), while remaining involved either with two women very similar in appearance or, perhaps, with one woman who changes her name and, subtly, her appearance.

Of course, in 'realistic' terms, it is impossible to make sense of these extraordinary narrative choices, and on a first viewing *Lost Highway* can give the impression of being muddled, pretentious nonsense. Repeated viewings, however, suggest that it may be open to interpretation on a more metaphorical level. One reading might infer that Fred is so confused and alienated from reality by his paranoia about his wife's fidelity that he simply cracks up. Whether or not he kills her (the film never lets us know for certain) is relevant only insofar as his guilt over such an act might prove intolerable; he simply imagines himself as a younger, less world-weary man who, at least initially, proves to be more attrac-

< 69 >

tive to women than Fred, but when things start going wrong again, his memory and true identity are restored, so that he takes vengeance on a man he suspects has ruined his life. Another reading might argue that, chronologically speaking, the story actually begins when Pete Dayton spends the night in jail. He becomes involved with a deceitful temptress who leads him into robbery and murder, they start afresh in a more comfortable life with new identities, but his guilt leads him to suspect that she is deceiving him once more, and so he kills her. Still another, perhaps more fanciful interpretation has been mooted, suggesting that the film's concept of human identity/personality is not unlike that believed in by certain 'primitive' spirit religions, where the self wanders or flows, as it were, from body to body, a fluid entity entirely at odds with our notions of a fixed, unique soul that serves as the defining characteristic of individuality.

Unfortunately, none of the above interpretations can wholly defend *Lost Highway* against charges of incoherence, since Lynch frequently over-eggs the pudding. The Mystery Man, for example, may serve for much of the story as some kind of alter ego or id to Fred Madison, but then why does Fred imagine Renee, looking at him in bed, with the mystery man's face? Likewise, Pete's parents and Sheila, his girlfriend, keep hinting ominously that something strange happened to Pete the night before he landed in jail, but Lynch never offers any further information as to what that event may have been; it is as if he wants to imply that there is some rational explanation for what happened, but is reluctant to give us one because he's not quite sure what it might be. As in *Twin Peaks: Fire Walk with Me*, where he vacillated between generic suspense and a more serious consideration of domestic abuse, he appears in *Lost Highway* to want to have his cake and eat it: it's possible, the narrative implies, to make sense of the mystifying circumstances in which Fred and Pete find themselves trapped, but Lynch loves the mystery far more than any possible explanation, and is not about to help with any clarification.

That said, the film is certainly an improvement on its imme-

< **70** >

diate predecessor and, save for Patricia Arquette's insipid, stilted, low-charisma performance as both Renee and Alice, it is executed with considerable confidence and flair by all involved, particularly in the creepy early scenes set in the bewildering landscape of Fred and Renee's cold, sparsely decorated, seemingly haunted apartment whose shadowy corridors, typically for Lynch, seem constantly to echo with a sinister, apocalyptic rumbling. Once again, he has fashioned an unnerving, often compelling drama from his anxieties about loss of identity, sexual paranoia and man's capacity for violence. (Indeed, just as the film's story turns full circle, one might argue that, in returning to a style of film-making as experimental in its own way as that in *Eraserhead*, Lynch's career had done the same.) It is only a pity, then, that he still seems unable or unprepared to frame his preoccupations within a persuasively coherent narrative.

< 71 >

Lynch's career is at once one of the most fascinating and one of the most frustrating in modern American cinema. Stylistically, there is no question that he is both innovative and influential, adept at fashioning convincing imaginary worlds from the filmic raw materials of inventive production design, strikingly vivid imagery and intensely expressive use of sound. Thematically, too, his abiding and deeply ambivalent interest in sexual desire, in voyeurism and violence, innocence and experience, civilisation and chaos has produced works that combine the magical, fabulous simplicity of fairy-tale with a sophistication born of an ironic yet affectionate approach to cinematic genre.

At the same time, however, there is an unexpectedly conservative side to his work: the evident (and oft-proclaimed) nostalgia for the simplicities and moral certainties of rural smalltown life, the anxieties about sexual desire and women, and the sense that the world is on the brink of slipping into a diabolical maelstrom of violence, drug-abuse and sexual licentiousness sit strangely at odds with the progressive aesthetic strategies of his films, however much one might prefer to dismiss these elements as the stuff of affectionate parody, allegorical psychodrama or pure fantasy. Moreover, his reluctance to fully confront the meaning of his work, and disregard for narrative coherence is, perhaps, intellectually cautious. Certainly, he is one of the great intuitive film-makers of recent years; but were he to proceed, occasionally, beyond the limits of his intuition, he might find himself making more genuinely audacious and fully realised films like *Blue Velvet*, and fewer flawed movies such as *Wild at Heart* or *Twin Peaks: Fire Walk with Me*.

< **72** >

john sayles

< **73** >

Ever since he made his directing début with *Return of the Secaucus Seven* in 1979, John Sayles' reputation has rested largely on both the sociopolitical acuity of his work and on his deft skills as a storyteller, a writer of impressively naturalistic dialogue, and creator of psychologically rounded characters (indeed, the Los Angeles Film Critics awarded him the the Best Screenplay award for *Secaucus Seven*). At the same time, however, there has been a widespread assumption that Sayles is more interested in (or at least more adept with) the written word and the performances he elicits from his actors than in *mise-en-scène* – a view with which this writer, for one, disagrees.

Moreover, Sayles' critics have tended to argue that his more openly political works are too preachy or didactic. While they are certainly serious and sincere in their commitment, his films are mercifully free of the bombastic polemical excesses that can be found in the work of, say, Oliver Stone. Sayles is left-wing in the old tradition of a fundamentally decent, humanist belief in the right of any individual or group to be accorded equality, freedom and justice; unlike Stone, he is not prone to fashionable conspiracy theories, being more interested in the way particular societies work in the social, political and ethical arena. Furthermore, he does not make films that proclaim their political import as the primary subject in hand (as, for example, Stone has done with *Born on the Fourth of July, JFK* or *Nixon*) but allows the politics to emerge naturally from his study of a particular milieu or situation. Use of genre, accordingly, is one of his prime narrative strategies; and rather than going out of his way to subvert the conventions of, for example, the Western, the soap opera, the teen romance or the sports movie, he hitches a ride on those conventions, subtly playing with them to lend the issues he is dealing with both greater clarity and, at times, a mythical dimension, much in the way, say, that Douglas Sirk used melodrama to mount his critiques of American society in the 50s. And it is in his use of genre, with its attendant iconography, that Sayles may be regarded as an imaginative director as well as a talented, perceptive writer.

< 74 >

It is perhaps only natural, however, that the view of Sayles as being primarily a writer should have arisen, given his credits prior to making his début as a full-blown *auteur* (he regularly writes, directs, edits and acts in his films). After studies in psychology and a variety of jobs (at one time or another he worked as a nursing-home orderly, construction worker and meat-packer), in 1975 he won an O Henry award for his first published short story, and wrote his first novel, *Pride of the Bimbos*, about the members of a drag softball team. A second novel, *Union Dues*, about the labour movement, was published (and nominated for a National Book Award) two years later, and while he was working as an actor in summer stock, he adapted Eliot Asinof's *Eight Men Out*, a book about the notorious 'Black Sox' baseball scandal of 1919, into a movie screenplay. Though a decade would pass before Sayles himself was finally able to direct *Eight Men Out* (1988), the script did attract the attention of Roger Corman, and over the next few years Sayles established a name for himself as the writer of a number of superior exploitation movies made by Corman's New World Pictures: *Piranha* (Joe Dante, 1978), *The Lady in Red* (Lewis Teague, 1979), *Battle Beyond the Stars* (Jimmy Teru Murakami, 1980), *The Howling*

(Dante, 1980) and *Alligator* (Teague, 1980). Though all were basically cheap and cheerful genre movies, transparently made to cash in on the success of films like *Jaws* and *Star Wars*, Sayles' scripts were engagingly up-front about their derivativeness, packed with wittily absurd dialogue, over-the-top set-pieces and allusions to movie lore: *Battle Beyond the Stars* was a sci-fi rehash of the Japanese classic *Seven Samurai* (Akira Kurosawa, 1954), while *The Howling*, a werewolf thriller, featured characters named after horror-movie directors like Freddie Francis, Terence Fisher and Erle Kenton, and made sly references to such diverse cultural phenomena as the Little Red Riding Hood story, Allen Ginsberg's poetry volume *Howl*, and the legendary disc-jockey Wolfman Jack. Even more idiosyncratically, the films were often structured around a generically unusual or even gently subversive premise: *The Lady in Red* was a Depression-era gangster saga seen from the perspective of a woman, while *Alligator* had a neat ecological thrust to its tale of a reptile flushed down the toilet as a baby and become monstrously outsized from feeding on the corpses of animals used in scientific experiments.

< 75 >

It was with the proceeds from writing such films that Sayles was able to finance his directing début; the ultra-low budget – usually estimated at somewhere between $40,000 and $60,000 – was amply rewarded when the film grossed over $2 million in the USA alone. Typically of his early films as director, *Secaucus Seven* was necessarily modest in scale but wide-ranging in the scope of its subject matter. About a bunch of mostly unmarried, childless middle-class WASPS in their late twenties and early thirties, who get together for their annual long-weekend reunion in a small New Hampshire summer-resort town, the film is a witty, light-hearted, deceptively slight study of a particular segment of American society at the end of the 70s. Though the individual characters in the group are clearly delineated – they include teachers, a medical student, a failed actress, a singer-songwriter hopeful of finally finding fame and fortune in LA, a social work-er who helps heroin addicts kick their habit, and a Senator's speech-writer (whose new, seemingly strait-laced lover Chip – also a political aide – is a stranger to the group, and thus serves as an audience surrogate in his desire to learn about the tangled history of the friends' various relationships) – the film never attempts to paint a cross-section of America at large. Instead, it is more concerned with how the characters' moral and political values have changed (or endured) since they first met in the late 60s.

Not that the film is at all portentous or didactic; indeed, it is only very late in the film, when several of the group have come across a dead deer in the road on their drunken drive home from an evening in a local bar, and are asked by the police to state if they have any record of criminal activity, that we and Chip finally find out about the event that gives the film its title. Back in the late 60s, seven of the group were on their way to a demonstration in Washington, DC, and were forced to spend the night in a cell after police on the look-out for 'pinkos' found a rifle and some marijuana in the car they were driving. Until this confession, neither we nor Chip have had any idea of the group's radical past. At the same time, Sayles makes no big deal of it politically – as it transpires, the car they were driving was borrowed, the group was released the next day without being charged, and the 'Secaucus Seven' tag was simply an in-joke; even the social worker, who confesses to a cop a lengthy list of conspiracy-related charges from the years 1969-73, admits somewhat ruefully that in every case the charges were dropped.

Characteristically for his utterly plausible, naturalistic film, Sayles avoids a contrived, melodramatic revelation in favour of something more subtle: we realise (though they never say as much) that it was the shared experience of that night that brought these people close together, giving them a sufficiently tolerant sense of common humanity and purpose for their friendship to be able to endure both the passing of time and the many complicated shifts and changes in their various relationships. Even over the weekend that constitutes the film's time-span, couples break up, romantic hopes are disappointed, and

< 76 >

unwise one-night stands are indulged in; but, for all the tensions, gossip and argument that intrude on the general air of nostalgic camaraderie, the bonds between the various members of the group manage to hold fast, such is their intimate knowledge and understanding of each other.

If all this sounds a little smug, sentimental and hermetic, Sayles effortlessly sidesteps such pitfalls both by means of his sharp, ironic dialogue and by showing us that there is indeed a world beyond that of his central characters. When Katie (played by Maggie Renzi, Sayles' long-term partner and oft-times actor and producer) tells her husband Mike that she's worried their marriage will eventually fall prey to the same forces that have destroyed most of their peers' relationships, his reassurance that their neighbours are still happily married prompts her, with a rather bitchy sense of superiority, to reply, 'The Whites are Born Again – they don't count'; in fact, while all the group are affectionately observed, no one is romanticised. Their liberalism frequently comes unstuck, particularly in the somewhat snobbish attitude expressed by some of their number towards Ron (David Strathairn, who would become another stalwart Sayles regular), an amiable, intelligent, local garage mechanic whom Mike has known since school, and whose job and decision to stay in town rather than move to the city become the object of some cautiously-voiced contempt. Indeed, Ron and a penurious married couple with three kids (the husband, incidentally, is beautifully played by Sayles himself) serve to throw a sharper, more objective light on to the endless emotional problems discussed by the middle-class, once radical weekenders.

Sayles' acute understanding of the relationships on view is not only evident in his deft delineation of character and his confident way with dialogue (which covers a multitude of topics, from sex, birth control and Washington's involvement in Latin American politics to 'progressive' rock, changes in the education system, and the relationship of food to flatulence), but in his direction. Since the film was made on such a low budget, costly, complex

< 77 >

camera movements were avoided, but Sayles shows subtlety in charting the shifting allegiances between characters by the way he groups or separates them, either within the frame or by cross-cutting, and displays great flair in shooting a basketball game, cutting with increasing speed between overhead, eye-height and low angles to suggest the exhilaration (and, to some extent, the aggression) the men feel as they work off steam away from the women. True, compared to many modern film-makers, Sayles is not a 'flashy' visual stylist, but his innate sense of camera placement and timing, and his ear for music that is wholly appropriate to a scene's mood, rhythm and meaning (he has worked closely with the very versatile composer Mason Daring ever since his début) were already apparent in this his first film.

< **78** >

While the sociopolitical concerns of *Secaucus Seven* emerged, as it were, organically from its loosely structured narrative, Sayles' tendency to focus his films on a particular issue was far more evident in his next movie as writer-director, *Lianna* (1982). About an intelligent, attractive, hitherto heterosexual woman in her thirties (warmly devoted to her children but increasingly disenchanted by her arrogant, philandering film-lecturer husband) who falls in love with a rather older lesbian who teaches at the night-classes she attends, the film provides a sensitive if slightly predictable account of the difficulties faced both by anyone who 'comes out' in a predominantly straight, conformist society, and by those who dare to undergo a dramatic change in their lifestyle at an age when most people are settled in their ways. Not only does Lianna face fearful prejudice (even from her close friend Sandy, who wonders if Lianna was sexually aroused by their past moments of emotional intimacy together), and witness the homophobic hatred that underlies the hitherto liberal veneer of her husband's attitudes towards sexual dalliance (he has sex with his students, but objects to her fucking her teacher), but as soon as she moves out to live alone, she realises the solitude and sense of strangeness that can afflict an individual's efforts to remain true to his or her feelings: she spends evenings alone in her newly

Ruth (Jane Hallaren) and Lianna (Linda Griffiths) in Sayles' take on lesbianism **Lianna** (1982) – distinguished by its refusal to adhere to the usual movie stereotypes.

rented flat, and is forced to support herself by working as a supermarket cashier. Nor does Ruth, her lover, offer much help: though comfortable with her sexuality and lifestyle, she is both anxious about being too open about being a lesbian in what she considers a small-minded community, and torn between her desire for Lianna and her troubled relationship with a woman she has known and loved for years.

While American film-making outside of the underground had seldom dealt with lesbian experience (and, when it had, had done so without the frankness or sensitivity of Sayles' film), it's to some extent true that Lianna inhabits much the same territory as the 'social-conscience' drama beloved by television movies or by mainstream 'liberal' film-makers like Robert Mulligan, Norman Jewison and Martin Ritt (the directors, respectively, of such anti-racist or 'feminist' films as *To Kill a Mockingbird*, 1962; *In the*

Heat of the Night, 1967; and *Norma Rae*, 1979); the film is coloured, here and there, by a rather staidly humanist worthiness and by an overall predictability in the plotting. Nevertheless, *Lianna* is distinguished by Sayles' refusal to adhere to the usual movie stereotypes and by his psychological insights. Crucially, Ruth, who has her own emotional problems, is neither demonised as a predatory lesbian nor romanticised as an entirely sympathetic, free-spirited mentor. Moreover, Lianna does not face prejudice from everyone outside the lesbian community. While her husband is disgusted (or, rather, his masculine pride is wounded) by Lianna engaging in what he describes as 'unnatural acts', and while Sandy is frightened and uncomfortable about Lianna's new-found attraction to women, others react more positively. Her teenage son has no problems with the fact that his 'old lady is a dyke', while her young daughter's silent sulking is clearly attributable to the fact that she feels abandoned by her mother and, being too young to understand about sex, has no idea of what is going on.

< **80** >

Lianna's neighbour Sheila (Maggie Renzi again) doesn't care about her sexual preferences, nor does her husband's colleague Jerry (Sayles himself) who, after coming on bluntly but unsuccessfully to what he sees as the newly unattached Lianna, proclaims himself tolerant of lesbians simply because (in a nicely absurd touch) he's from California. Most interesting of all, however, is the reaction of Sandy's football-coach husband, who finds his wife's fears faintly embarrassing: in pointing out that he once had a great black player in his team who happened to be gay, and that he never worried about his activities in the showers because the player 'had more important things on his mind' than seduction, he inadvertently hits the nail on the head – we are not defined by our sexuality alone.

Typically, Sayles leavens his story with numerous witty lines which, along with the scenes depicting the sheer sensual joy of Lianna's initial infatuation with Ruth, prevent the film from turning into just another earnest problem drama. None the less, he doesn't downplay the difficult situation Lianna has put herself in. In a final scene that eschews the uplifting, feelgood mood favoured by most such movies (and in one of the film's few outdoor sequences – it is, after all, about different kinds of emotional entrapment), Lianna returns to the kids' playground shown at the film's opening, where once again she finds Sandy, who admits that she has missed her friend and that, while she is not sexually interested in women, she does still love her. At the same time, however, as Lianna takes comfort in Sandy's embrace, she, like us, is all too aware that Ruth has returned to her former lover, and that she must continue alone in her search for commitment and happiness.

< 81 >

Sayles' next film, which, with its $3 million budget, cost almost four times as much as *Lianna*, nevertheless took a likewise downbeat approach to that standby of Hollywood film-making, the teen romance. Kicking off in 1966 in Hoboken, New Jersey, *Baby It's You* (1983) tells the story, familiar from 'Romeo and Juliet' and countless imitations, of two High School students whose love for one another is constantly undermined by their very different backgrounds and aspirations: Jill, the Jewish daughter of a well-to-do doctor, is planning to go on to college, while Albert (who prefers to call himself 'the Sheik') is a smart-suited, smooth-talking womaniser from a blue-collar Italian-American family who, between occasional forays into petty crime, dreams of making it big like his hero Frank Sinatra. While, true to tradition, it is partly the disapproval voiced by the couple's parents, teachers and friends that continually threatens their efforts to be together, Sayles effects a sharper, more comprehensive and honest analysis of their situation, not only by showing how the pair's characters, needs and ambitions are shaped by their particular experiences of the world (the liberal Jill is initially both repelled and attracted by the Sheik's rather macho, domineering attempts to date her), but by showing, finally, that first love, however romantic it may seem, is not necessarily built to last.

Hence, the Sheik, who has never had it easy financially or at home (his father constantly criticises him), is determined to have things his own way, whatever the cost, be it expulsion from school for getting into a fight with a teacher, sleeping with one of Jill's friends when he can't get close to her at a backstage party after her success in a school play, or leaving Hoboken for Miami Beach after participating in a none-too-successful armed robbery. Jill, on the other hand, is strong enough secretly to resist her elders' suggestions that she shouldn't see the Sheik, but is middle-class enough to realise that his hopes of becoming a singing star are just pie-in-the-sky, and that his chauvinism and his lowly prospects would hold her back in any career she chooses to follow. Indeed, where Sayles' film differs most from other examples of the teen-romance genre is in following the two lovers into their post-high-school years, when the difference in their aspirations and abilities becomes even plainer to see: at college the hitherto comparatively strait-laced Jill gets caught up in the hippy world of drugs and free love (often with students imported from Yale and Harvard whom she doesn't even like much), while the once seemingly non-conformist Sheik ends up rather pathetically miming to easy-listening standards at a Miami bar frequented by tourists and the elderly. Ironically, too, it is the Sheik – formerly so sure of his strength, individuality and appeal to women - who cannot accept the demise of their romance; only when he realises he is losing Jill does he let down his proud facade (it is surely no accident that he is content to mime to Sinatra and others, while Jill puts in hours of practice in her efforts to become an actress). But it is too late: for all the violent anger and aggression he displays when he unexpectedly turns up to visit her on campus, she cannot, and will not, hide the fact that she no longer loves him – not, at least, in the way that he wants her to, with a view to marriage and parenthood. Before he leaves, however, she asks him to accompany her one last time to a college dance; someone has stood her up. Hesitantly, he agrees and, at the ballroom, makes a 'weird' request of the rock band, who

< **82** >

begin to play 'their song', 'Strangers in the Night'; as the former lovers dance, with the other students gradually joining in, Sinatra's voice replaces the half-hearted band on the soundtrack, a poignant reminder not only of their past romance, but of the fact that, in growing up, Jill and the Sheik have become 'two lonely people'.

Despite, therefore, the film's initially more upbeat mood (Sayles respectfully shows, with wit and brio, such hallowed teen rituals as the introductory chat-up session, the fast car-ride, the first lingering kiss, the teasing of schoolfriends, etc., all accompanied by a selection of vintage pop songs, including some by a later New Jersey alumnus, Bruce Springsteen), *Baby It's You* echoes its immediate predecessor in its study of how individuals are affected by society even in their intimate emotional lives, and in its ambivalent, bitter-sweet conclusion. (The wrangles between Sayles and the film's distributor, Paramount, over the emphasis given to its darker second half, persuaded him that he should thereafter insist on the right to final cut.) Perhaps unsurprisingly, then, as if to compensate for, or move away from, the somewhat over-familiar dramatic strategies of these two films, he returned with his next movie to a very low budget, and to a deliciously offbeat exercise in shaggy-dog storytelling. Although *The Brother from Another Planet* (1984) dealt with the predicament of the African-American community living in Harlem, it did so as a wittily imaginative, small-scale variation on the sci-fi genre so popular at the time in Hollywood (indeed, it has been described as a low-budget riposte to Spielberg's *ET*). Of course, Sayles had already proved himself adept at playing with cinematic convention in his work for Corman, but with *Brother* his use of genre was taken much further in terms of it being a tool with which to explore and reflect on the serious issues at hand.

As if to show that sci-fi films need not rely on expensive special effects, Sayles' alien falls to earth in the simplest of scenes: all we see are a few flashing lights inside his capsule, until the sign for the Ellis Island Immigration Center is lit up from the reflec-

< 83 >

tion of his crash (heard on the soundtrack), and we see (in a shot clearly meant to evoke Jack Arnold's classic 1954 B-movie, *The Creature from the Black Lagoon*) a black hand rising from the water to grasp the dock, with the Statue of Liberty in the background. Indeed, as the Brother – a fugitive slave from another planet – attempts to find sanctuary in New York, learning about human hardship and injustice as he tries to acclimatise to his new home, the question of freedom will remain an important issue in the lives of those he meets, even though it is rarely discussed upfront. After making his way through the Immigration Center – now a national monument, but still echoing (as the Brother discovers by touching its walls) with the pain and confusion of all those who once passed through it in their quest for freedom and a better life – he finds his way to Harlem and a bar where the proprietor and the regular clientele (a young guy addicted to sci-fi video games and a pair of elderly barflies continually

< **84** >

In **The Brother from Another Planet** (1984) Sayles puts his apprenticeship under Roger Corman to good use, exploiting the sci-fi genre to explore the black urban experience in a light-hearted low-budget entertainment.

engaged in absurd philosophical discussions about the strange ways of the world) try to fathom whether the mute visitor is deaf, crazy or wino. Happily, after he proves himself adept at repairing a faulty video-game simply by touching it faith-healer-style, they decide to help by enlisting one of their number – a civil servant who works in Welfare – to find him a job (mending video-game machines) and lodgings (with a white woman whose black lover has left her to look after their infant son alone). True to tradition, however, the Brother's well-being is threatened, not only by the hazards of life in an impoverished city neighbourhood (he is soon mugged by junkies), but by two sinisterly robot-like white aliens (Sayles and David Strathairn), bounty-hunters bent on taking him back to his life of slavery.

< 85 >

In terms of conventional plotting, not a lot happens in the film: the Brother tracks down the rich, white businessman who is supplying Harlem's drug-dealers and gives him a taste of his own medicine, before finally managing to escape the bounty-hunters once and for all when, faced with a whole group of black aliens (whose supportive presence in Harlem the Brother has divined by means of scrawled messages disguised as graffiti), they self-destruct. Nevertheless, by having the Brother silently observe those around him, Sayles touches on a variety of contemporary issues: the erosion of black youth through exploitative drug-dealing (appropriately, the Rastafarian who leads the Brother one night through the hellish world of the junkies and dispossessed is named Virgil, after the guide in Dante's 'Inferno'); the importance of historical awareness (one of the ageing barflies rightly insists that the young should remember Harlem's past glories, while the Brother accompanies his landlady's son to an exhibition about slavery); the inefficiency of a Welfare system embroiled in bureaucratic red-tape; and the racism encountered in even the friendliest individuals (such as two white Mid-Western businessmen who hilariously assume the worst when they discover they are lost in Harlem). Excepting only the Brother's hunting down of the drugs-lord (which nevertheless inventively involves the Brother taking out his eye and leaving it to record, camera-fashion, the activities of various addicts and pushers), the film's many serious points are handled with a warm, good-natured humour, most notably in the bleary barflies' endless banter (one, absurdly and morbidly obsessed by diseases, opines that the first victim of leprosy is the penis: 'Go to those Polynesian islands, you see some long faces, man!'). Minor, meandering and light-hearted it may have been, but in its successful attempt to mix populist entertainment with intelligent social comment, *Brother* was not only a delight in itself, but looked forward to the considerably more ambitious achievements of his next three films.

< **86** >

With *Matewan* (1987), *Eight Men Out* and *City of Hope* (1991), Sayles can be said to have attained a new confidence and maturity as a writer-director. In each film, he deployed an extremely large cast and the trappings of genre (respectively, the Western, the sports film and the urban crime movie) to trace the various intricate, interwoven threads that make up the fabric of American life on both a personal and a political level. Story, character, conflict and relationships are presented and understood not only in terms of the psychology of the individual – the norm for most Hollywood films – but in a wider context which embraces ethnic, sexual, economic, cultural, historical and ideological factors; there is, accordingly, a constant tension between the needs of the individual and the demands of society, between aspiration and achievement, idealism and pragmatism, the private and the public. At the same time, moreover, because these analytical studies of American society were partly structured in accordance with the formal conventions of genre cinema, there is in addition an intriguing, revealing relationship between fact and fiction, popular myth – or heroic legend – and social 'reality'.

In *Matewan*, perhaps the most fruitfully generic of Sayles' films, he drew upon a traditional narrative form – of the lone outsider coming into a divided community in an attempt to restore justice and peace – to resonant effect. Matewan is a small West Virginian mining township wholly owned, in 1920, by a greedy coal company which is forever increasing the cost of living for its employees and their families, while simultaneously cutting the rates of pay. The locals are understandably incensed, especially as the company has begun importing cheap labour in the form of Italian immmigrants and blacks from Alabama; inevitably, both groups fall prey to the Virginians' xenophobic racism and desire for a scapegoat. It is an explosive situation, and when union organiser Joe Kenehan (Chris Cooper) comes to town, hoping to lead the workers into non-violent industrial action against their bosses (instead of turning their anger against each other), he finds himself not only greeted with suspicion by the locals, many of whom would rather take the law into their own hands, but openly threatened by the professional strike-breakers hired by the company. For a while, he manages to instill a sense of unity among the townsfolk and their black and Italian colleagues, who live in a camp on the edge of town; but when a local businessman who acts as a quisling for the company succeeds in bringing the union man into disrepute and instigates a crisis in which a young miner is murdered by the strike-breakers, Joe is powerless to prevent a full-scale gunfight between workers and company agents.

< 87 >

Sayles' decision to film his account of the beginning of the real-life Coal Wars of the 1920s as a Western succeeds in several respects. For one thing, it allows him to impose a tight, ordered narrative structure on the messier chaos of historical events; we are rarely in doubt, despite the various groups and allegiances involved, as to who are the good guys and who are the villains, besides which we feel, from the familiar sweep of the narrative, that there's almost a tragic inexorability to the events on view. For another, the Western format lifts the story into the realm of American myth; in being reminded of the oft-depicted range-wars between pioneer farmsteaders and robber land-barons, we are made aware of the heroic courage of those poor 'ordinary' workers who, in West Virginia as late as the 1920s, fought and in many cases gave their lives in the war between Capital and

Labour. Thus, the union movement – generally neglected, or even demonised, by the movies – is here associated with the pioneer spirit that brought civilisation to the wilderness; that it fails, in this case, to restrain the workers from taking up arms against the company's thugs is not merely a matter of historical accuracy but, in the film, a regrettable, partly self-destructive course of action on the part of the workers which may nevertheless be attributed, to some degree, to the devious, violent ways of the company itself.

< **88** >

But the use of Western iconography (the town constable, for example, as played by an uncompromisingly fair, gun-toting David Strathairn, is clearly evocative of the Old West's sheriff) and Western story elements not only lends the film a mythic clarity and resonance; it also allows us to understand the relevance of more poetic, lyrical scenes which in themselves may have little to do with developing the immediate conflict between heroes and villains. For example, the many camp-fire scenes, which underline the increasing tolerance between the locals and the blacks and Italians by depicting their common love of music and need for food, evoke the social gatherings and rituals lovingly shot by John Ford; in a similar way, the strike-breakers' brute, boorish behaviour, whether at the meal-table of the boarding house run by the intimidated but brave widow Elma Radnor (Mary McDonnell), or in the church where her lay-preacher son (the story's narrator) delivers a Biblical parable which informs the congregation that Joe is no traitor to their cause, comes across as an effrontery against the traditional virtues of community which has as much to do with the bullying of the meek and innocent by powerful 'outlaws' as it has to do with the politics of labour. The strength of Sayles' script and *mise-en-scène* (which merges gritty, low-key realism with more stylised elements such as the magnificently staged final shoot-out) lies in the way they ring new changes on filmic conventions: a preacher's hellfire sermon (spoken by a memorably rabid Sayles) equates 'the Prince of Darkness' with communists, socialists and unionists; a potentially deadly stand-off between the unarmed Joe and the strike-breakers is suddenly and unexpectedly averted by the intervention of some hitherto unseen mountain-trappers, who will leave the workers' camp in peace just as long as they don't kill any hogs (they too have have been deprived of their land by the mining company); and the climactic shoot-out comes to an end not, as might be expected, with Joe taking up arms (in fact, for all his pacifist ideals, he ends up dead), but with the main thug gunned down by the hitherto trouble-avoiding Elma Radnor, as he tries to make his escape through her washing-lines. Nor is the workers' victory final; as the now aged Danny's voiceover informs us, this was merely the start of the Coalfield War, and as Joe predicted, the miners took the worst of it – and just as we saw Danny as a boy down the mine at the film's start (appropriately, the opening sequence ended in an explosion), so we see him as a man at its end, still toiling in the cramped, stifling darkness.

< 89 >

Without in any way romanticising the workers or the outcome of their struggle, Sayles nevertheless pays tribute to the sense of community fostered in them by the union, and evokes a critical moment of change for that community. A similar strategy was to be found in *Eight Men Out*, in which he proposed that the Black Sox scandal, which rocked the 1919 baseball World Series, was a defining moment for American sport and, by implication, for the nation's faith in itself. As in *Matewan*, the underpaid workers – here, the players of the enormously successful Chicago White Sox – fall prey to the greed, hypocrisy and divide-and-rule tactics of a variety of self-serving money-grabbers: the team's miserly owner Charlie Comiskey; rival groups of gamblers who go about persuading team-members to throw the series; the gangster Arnold Rothstein, who profited most from the fixing of the games; and the sundry lawyers and legal figures who found fame and fortune through their involvement in the trials that ensued when the fix was uncovered in newspaper reports.

Since the sports movie is a less 'mythical' genre than the Western, it must be said that the overall structure of the film, which loosely divides the characters into two distinct groups – on the one hand, the players, their wives, their innocent young fans and the truth-hungry sports-writers, and on the other, the exploitative hangers-on who stand to make money from the team's efforts – makes it seem rather more schematic than *Matewan*. Nevertheless, in tracing the complex web of connections between the various 'bad guys' that lead to the team's downfall, and in charting the domino effect that sees one underpaid player after another fall victim to the gamblers' plans, Sayles shows great narrative expertise in organising a wealth of information into a taut, coherent drama. Crucially, the players yield to temptation for a variety of reasons: some feel resentful at being so poorly treated by their boss, others fall in line simply because a respected colleague has already done so, others are happy just to make a fast buck with little risk of discovery – while others, like Buck Weaver and 'Shoeless' Joe Jackson, barely take part in the fix at all, so devoted are they to the feelings of pride and exhilaration their playing gives them. Indeed, only a handful of the players are easily corrupted, and the gamblers' schemes begin properly to bear fruit only after a petty piece of penny-pinching on the part of Comiskey: by giving the team a meagre celebration with flat champagne instead of the financial bonus he'd promised, he inadvertently pushes the pitcher Eddie Cicotte (Strathairn) – an honest, much-admired man nearing retirement – into joining the few young players who have already agreed to the fix, with the result that others follow his example. There is little profit to be had from the deal, however; the gamblers pay them only a fraction of the sum agreed, and when one player refuses to throw any more games, gangsters threaten to kill his wife.

Sayles is not primarily bemoaning, however, the sad fates of the individual players; indeed, when four of the team are found not guilty in a grand jury hearing (prior, it turns out, to their being banned from ever playing professional baseball again by a commission instigated, ironically, by Comiskey, who wants only

< **90** >

to clear his own name of any suggestion of corruption), the reporter who exposed the fix, Ring Lardner (played by Sayles himself), declares the verdict as 'a bigger fix than the series'. Rather, Sayles pinpoints a moment when sport first became tainted by the malign influence of big money: baseball, and America's attitudes towards the 'heroes' that played it, had lost their innocence – a notion eloquently expressed by a young fan who, as Jackson emerges from the hearing where he has been accused of corruption, utters the famous plea, 'Say it ain't so, Joe, say it ain't so.' That nostalgia, for a time when sport was simply participated in for the sake of pure enjoyment, rather than for financial gain, is invoked still more poignantly in an epilogue, in which, half a decade later, Buck Weaver goes to see his old team-mate Jackson playing, under the name of Brown, in an amateur game. As Weaver, listening to other spectators, now realises, if he's remembered at all, like his former friends it will only be as a member of the discredited 'Black Sox'; nevertheless, as we see Jackson turn in slow motion to smile towards the camera and applause rises on the soundtrack, it's clear that he for one still loves the game and plays as if his life depended on it.

< 91 >

Though Sayles' analysis of the effect of money on sport may, as we said, seem a little over-schematic at times, his organising of a narrative that includes numerous baseball games and a large cast is exemplary in its clarity; indeed, much of his success in defining and differentiating such a large number of characters may be attributed to the fact that, even though he was now able to work on a bigger budget than previously, he continued to work regularly with a 'repertory' group of actors often (though not always) apparently chosen in terms of 'type'; Strathairn, for example, brought the same air of unpretentious honour to the role of Eddie as he had to *Secaucus Seven* and *Matewan*, while Kevin Tighe was as morally repellent as one of the gamblers as he had been as a strike-breaker in *Matewan* (and would be again as an opportunist detective in *City of Hope*). Time and again, Sayles has cast relatively unknown but very capable, facially memorable actors to populate his complex, multiple-character narratives, a strategy used to great effect in his next film, which had around forty significant speaking parts.

City of Hope was arguably his most ambitious movie to date, a sharp, lucid dissection of the many forces that have brought a New Jersey city to the brink of social and economic collapse. There is no single predominant story; the narrative instead consists of a number of intersecting stories which serve to illustrate and interrelate the various allegiances and animosities – to do with race, class, family, the legal and political systems – which divide Hudson City as a community. A young Italian-American, Nick (Vincent Spano), turns to petty crime out of disgust for his wealthy building-contractor father Joe (Tony Lo Bianco), whom he considers to be both excessively devoted to the memory of his dead Vietvet-hero son and tainted by his dealings with corrupt, self-serving local politicians and businessmen; a black councillor, Wynn (Joe Morton), in danger of losing the support of his black constituents due to his moderate political stance, faces a moral and professional dilemma when he is pressurised to defend two black kids (whom he believes guilty) accused of mugging a white teacher they claim molested them; Joe reluctantly hires Carl (Sayles), a crooked garage-owner crippled in the car accident that killed Joe's son, to torch one of his tenement slums which the Mayor wants demolished in order to secure his re-election; and Nick finds himself hounded by a hot-headed cop, not, as it transpires, for his suspected role in a robbery, but because the psychotically jealous cop objects to Nick, an enemy since school, dating his ex-wife Angela.

Such a brief synopsis barely scratches the surface of *City of Hope*'s densely woven narrative texture – there are countless other sub-plots and revealing vignettes involving a host of other significant characters – but it does begin to suggest the way the various individuals and groups that make up the population of Hudson City are embroiled in constant conflict and compromise; for most of these people, politics and ethics are less a mat-

< **92** >

ter of ideological choice than of personal expediency, of looking after one's own best interests in terms of deciding who one joins forces with. Nepotism, back-handers and clandestine deals are the norm among businessmen and politicians; almost everyone, rich or poor, powerful or weak, is so determined to lose neither face nor foothold on the social ladder that deceit, aggression and crime have become constant options. Members of ethnic groups, families, the police and local politicians tend to believe they should look after each other, whatever the cost. Favours are given, recalled, repaid, resented. Activism is reduced to partisan sloganeering. Truth and the common weal are widely deemed secondary to personal ambition. The American dream has become a nightmare.

< **93** >

Not that Sayles is overly insistent on humanity's capacity for corruption. There are numerous 'good', generous, tolerant characters in the film – it's just that they tend to wield less power. Moreover, no one here, to paraphrase Renoir's 1939 classic *La Règle du Jeu* (a film whose criss-crossing characters and loose narrative structure must surely have influenced *City of Hope*) is without their reasons. Even someone as immediately unappealing as the sleazy, vengeful Carl (it's interesting how Sayles will often take one of the least sympathetic parts for himself) finally wins our understanding, if not our admiration, when we learn that his resentment of Nick stems from his having been crippled by Nick's brother, who caused the car accident – which resulted also in the death of a woman – with his drunken driving, and from Joe's having covered up the incident. Nor are the enmities, prejudices and conflicts impossible to resolve; with honesty, understanding and a little effort, a sense of common purpose can be regained, as when one of the young muggers finally starts up a conversation with the teacher whose career he has almost ruined by dishonestly accusing him of paedophilia, or when Nick, wounded by a gunshot fired by Angela's manically possessive ex-husband, is reconciled at last to his father's love by the latter's explanation that he allowed the torching of the tenement simply because he thought it would help Nick, who was wanted by the police for the robbery. At which point Joe calls into the night for medical aid for his son, only to hear his plea – 'Help, we need help!' – echoed over and over again by Asteroid (Strathairn), a deranged derelict to whom nobody ever listens, since all he ever does is repeat the slogans of the TV advertisers and political campaigners he hears around him. As the high overhead shot of Asteroid fades, with him still clutching at a fence and screaming, unheeded, for help, the film ends, leaving us in no doubt as to the uncertainties faced by a contemporary urban America devoted to financial, political and moral expediency, and guided by no real sense of common purpose.

< **94** >

Hope, for Hudson City, is certainly in short supply, so it is only appropriate that Sayles should to some extent adopt the noir-ish visual style of such despairing urban-corruption dramas as *Force of Evil* (Abraham Polonsky, 1948), *On Dangerous Ground* (Nicholas Ray, 1951) and *On the Waterfront* (Elia Kazan, 1954); many of Sayles' scenes take place in the streets at night, with red (the colour of danger and overheated passions) and black predominating on the palette. At the same time, however, by using long takes shot by a fluidly mobile camera, and by shifting the centre of attention of a shot from one character (or group of characters) to another, and maybe to yet another, as their paths cross and diverge, Sayles' elegant, imaginative *mise-en-scène* underlines not only how any one person's actions will almost certainly affect someone else, but how various elements in the film (property, money, class, sex, race, family, friendship, politics, the law, etc.) are inextricably built into the way a society functions and defines itself as a community.

Characteristically, Sayles' versatility and anthropologist-like curiosity about people and places then led him into a very different (and noticeably smaller-scale) genre: the 'sickness' movie. Typically *Passion Fish* (1993) bore scant resemblance to the 'disease-of-the-week' dramas and soaps beloved by television (and, indeed, subtly parodied in Sayles' movie). We don't even see the accident that cripples and paralyses soap-star May-Alice (Mary McDonnell) from the waist down: our first view of her are close-ups of her hand twitching and her eyes flickering open as she regains consciousness in a hospital bed. (In a neat, ironic twist, her first words – 'It's all so strange; all I remember is that I wasn't happy, was I?' – are actually from the soundtrack of the soap playing on the TV; as she looks up at her healthier, happier self on the small screen, she and we are soon made aware of the discrepancy between the ludicrously sanitised representations of ill-health marketed for home consumption, and the more challenging realities to be faced by May-Alice.) Though Sayles is certainly not one to sidestep the physical side of her condition (we presently see her struggling in vain to regain use of her legs, angry and embarrassed at having become incontinent, and bitter and frustrated about having 'a freezer compartment for a pussy'), he is more interested in how the constraints suddenly imposed on her life affect her psychologically and socially. Self-pity is her immediate response, and the moment she can get out of hospital, she leaves New York and retreats to her remote, now deserted childhood home in Louisiana, where she takes solace in alcohol and endless re-runs of her soap series, and makes life hell for a succession of nurses she reluctantly hires and fires to attend to her daily needs.

< **95** >

Only with the arrival of the proud, taciturn and similarly stubborn young black woman Chantelle (Alfre Woodard) does 'the bitch on wheels' finally meet her match. May-Alice's domi-neering sarcasm, aggression and tantrums are, we come to realise, a self-defence strategy with which she tries to conceal, from her-self and the nurse, her vulnerability and her fear of being alone. But Chantelle has her own reasons for putting up with her employer's irascibility (though she firmly draws the line between what she's paid to do and anything else May-Alice expects of her): after a while, May-Alice discovers that Chantelle is a recov-ering crack-addict, and that this is the only job she could get, a job she needs in order eventually to win back custody of her daughter, currently living with Chantelle's strait-laced doctor father.

It is the nurse's determination to overcome her own problems and her own addiction that finally gives May-Alice the will-power and strength to stop wallowing in drunken self-pity and start to live again. Looking for a bottle one night, in an old dark-room formerly used by her gay uncle (her only living relative), she begins to print the photographs she has taken with a camera he left behind during a visit; entranced by the pastime, she takes up photography and begins, as it were, to look at life anew, to appreciate once more the natural beauty of the world around her. Encouraged by Chantelle, she also manages to give up drinking, and begins occasionally to enjoy the company of others, notably the Cajun odd-job man and swamp-guide Rennie (Strathairn), whom she had a crush on as a schoolgirl but who is unfortu-nately now married (to a puritanically religious woman) with five kids. Like Chantelle, who has embarked on a tentative affair with a zydeco-musician and blacksmith named Sugar (who has a long list of wives and offspring to his name), May-Alice begins hesitantly to feel that there may be hope after all, and invites Chantelle to stay on a while, both as her nurse and as her friend.

Though the story of *Passion Fish* is inevitably far simpler than those of his three previous movies, Sayles' unerring sense of detail makes for a film of considerable insight and subtlety. May-Alice's problem is that she is so caught up in self-pity and fear that she cannot come to terms with her new predicament: at the film's beginning in the hospital, her self-absorption is mirrored in the way the camera never shows the faces of the medical staff who dance in attendance on her. Only much later, after Chantelle takes her outside to do back-strengthening exercises by the lake (and replies to her complaint that she can't wheel herself back to the house because 'It's uphill' with the terse 'So's life!'), does May-Alice begin properly to look beyond herself and see how she might fit into the world. Without her acting ('the only thing I

< **96** >

was ever good at'), she feels lost, unable to find a place for herself in society, as her various visitors illustrate: while she gets on well enough with her gay uncle Reece, he, as the 'black sheep' of the family, serves only to reinforce her impression of herself as a freakish outcast; she has outgrown two local gossips who inadvertently remind her that she was bullied at school (she was a misfit even as a child); while three actresses who visit from New York (giving rise to a hilarious scene in which one, recalling a one-line part she had in a dim sci-fi saga, delivers a ludicrous series of variously emphasised renditions of the deathless phrase, 'I never asked for the anal probe') serve only to remind May-Alice that she's no longer part of their glamorous theatrical world. She needs to rediscover, even reinvent herself, which is only possible by accepting the world immediately around her for what it is – which is why a magically atmospheric boat trip to an island in the bayoux with Rennie and Chantelle, and a visit to a Cajun dance in the company of Rennie, Sugar, Chantelle and her father and daughter, prove to be so revitalising and therapeutic. Crucially, it is at these two moments, away from the confines of her house, that she not only begins to regain a sense of her roots and her place in the community, but at last openly confronts what is perhaps the most difficult problem for her to overcome: her continuing need for physical love. Heartened, on the island, by Rennie smearing mud over her legs – useless but, to him, still beautiful – to protect them from mosquito bites, she later tells him at the clambake that he doesn't need the excuse of a job to do at her house in order to visit; indeed, she adds when he smiles, he should visit soon. (Incidentally, this brief exchange, while marking an important stage in May-Alice's regeneration, is quite extraordinary, in that it seems to condone adultery, which of course is generally presented in American film as a sin or, at the very least, as an aberration best avoided.)

< 97 >

Chantelle's recovery is charted with similar subtlety as she moves from simply regarding the time she spends with May-Alice as a necessary job to seeing it as a chance to get back out into the normal world, meet people, and prove her responsibility by caring for another person. Interestingly, Sayles makes little of how the women's relationship is affected by their racial backgrounds – that is not the issue between them (they are too caught up in the physical trials and tribulations of everyday existence to worry about the colour of each other's skin). Nevertheless, attitudes towards race are noted in the old-fashioned assumption, made by May-Alice's visitors, that Chantelle is some kind of servant, and the pair do discuss the status of Cajuns and Creoles in Louisiana society.

< **98** >

Once again, besides offering a totally credible account of the steady blossoming of mutual respect and friendship between the two women, Sayles also manages, in the film's second half, to paint a persuasive, lyrical picture of Louisiana life. If it is a more positive portrait than in his other films, that is because it is seen through the eyes of his two protagonists, both of whom seek a reason to live; accordingly, as they emerge from their respective shells, the world around them seems to come alive with a magical, life-sustaining sensuality (most notable in the trip to the island, shot by Roger Deakins in warm, shimmering tones that match the intimacy of the moment) and a genuine sense of community, expressed, as in *Secaucus Seven*'s bar-scenes, *Baby It's You*'s college dance finale and *Matewan*'s campfire sequences, through a shared enjoyment of traditional music. It is that sense of tradition, community and the magical vibrancy of the natural world that links Sayles' next, in some ways least typical film to the rest of his oeuvre.

The Secret of Roan Inish (1993) was unusual for the writer-director not only in that it was adapted from a novel (Rosalie K Fry's *Secret of the Ron Mor Skerry*) rather than an original screenplay; it was also a 'family-movie', shot not in America but in and around a remote fishing village on the west coast of Ireland. Set in the late 40s, it tells of a ten-year-old girl who goes to stay with her grandparents (her widowed father, working in the city, can no longer look after her properly) and finds out about her family history: hearing strange tales about, and subsequently searching for, her young brother Jamie, rumoured to be living with the seals and seagulls ever since his cradle was washed out to sea when he was a baby, the inquisitive, very determined Fiona first discovers that there is allegedly a strain in her ancestry that derives from a woman who was a selkie (half-human, half-seal) and then, with her cousin's help, convinces her grandparents that the only way to persuade the seals to return her brother is by moving back into their old cottage on Roan Inish, a nearby island which the family and their friends evacuated when it became too hard to sustain a living. The plan works, and Jamie is finally reunited with his family.

< **99** >

Despite the Celtic myths that make up much of the narrative (and, with Fiona learning about her ancestral past from the tales related by her grandparents and cousins, this is very much a film about the traditional art of storytelling as oral history), Sayles roots the almost 'magical' events on view within a vividly delineated social, economic and historical context. The 'legends' related, which centre on seals, birds, storms and shipwrecks, reflect the community's dependence on the sea for work and food; the selkie myth mirrors not only the family's mixed blood, but their fragile, double-edged relationship with a place which, on the one hand, they love, and which, on the other, is responsible for many of the hardships and deaths they have suffered. Poverty, unemployment and the migration of the younger generation to the industrialised cities is eroding a traditional way of life, and even though the old folks are as happy as Fiona to return to Roan Inish, their future there remains uncertain.

While the sheer joy Sayles takes in the recounting of legends is evident throughout, he is fully aware that modern audiences may be sceptical as to their veracity: even Fiona's old grandmother, hearing her husband tell the girl yet another story of a man being saved from drowning by a seal, mutters that it is just superstitious nonsense. Crucially, the film never lapses into cute prettiness or whimsy. For all the hints at supernatural goings-on, in visual terms, the activities of the seals and gulls are largely and wisely restricted to simply swimming, flying, and warily watching humans; on the rare occasions when they are shown to be involved in what might be seen as anthropomorphic activity (as when a seal sits in an empty cottage with the infant Jamie, as if at a tea-party), the point of view is usually that of Fiona, a child who, after all, is deprived of her brother and parents, and therefore eager to believe that the legends are true. Likewise, with his characteristically sharp ear for demotic idioms and his customary concern for how people actually make a living – much of the activity depicted in the film revolves around catching, gutting and cooking fish – Sayles effortlessly avoids 'Oirish' stereotypes, even as he acknowledges the harsh, earthy natural beauty of the Donegal coastline by means of Haskell Wexler's shimmering camerawork and the poignant folk-melodies of Mason Daring's score.

< **100** >

Whereas movies like *Matewan* and *Eight Men Out* had already offered evidence of Sayles' interest in American history, it was only in *Roan Inish* that he really confronted the question of how our lives may be influenced, one way or another, by the actions of our forefathers. In his next film, *Lone Star* (1995), the theme of how the present is coloured by the past moved centre-stage to accompany Sayles' equally keen interest in the social, political and psychological dimensions of place. In the town of Frontera, on the Texan side of the border between the USA and Mexico, sheriff Sam Deeds (Chris Cooper) investigates the discovery of a human skeleton in the desert; when the dead man is identified as Charlie Wade (Kris Kristofferson), a 'bribes-or-bullets' sheriff who used to terrorise the Mexican and black inhabitants of the town back in the 50s, Sam begins to suspect that he was murdered by his own father Buddy, a deputy who after Wade's mysterious and sudden disappearance became the sheriff, and who is still viewed by the community as a paragon of fair, honest law-enforcement. As Sam questions those who knew Buddy – whom Sam appears to want to discredit, partly because he is forever being told by the older citizens that he is a pale shadow of his father, partly because, 20 years earlier, Buddy broke up his romance with a Mexican named Pilar (Elizabeth Peña), now a widowed history teacher with kids of her own – he unearths a crime far more wide-ranging in its effects and implications, both for the community and for himself, than he ever imagined.

As with *Matewan* and *City of Hope*, Sayles adapts genre in *Lone Star* – here, the Western and the detective mystery – to clarify the conflicts and explore the various divisions and allegiances that make up the community of Frontera. Inevitably, many of the tensions afflicting the town are racial: the Mexican population, albeit in the majority, is still mostly subordinate, economically and politically, to the WASPs (some of whom remain quite openly racist), while the small population of blacks is largely confined to the army base on the edge of town. But just as these ethnic groups are not homogeneous and wholly isolated from each other, but made up of diverse individuals, some of whom regularly mix with members of the other groups, so individuals are complex characters, full of seemingly contradictory impulses. Pilar's mother Mercedes, who considers herself American, looks down on her compatriots who still speak Spanish; a white army officer plans marriage with a black colleague; a black teenager feels closer to his estranged grandfather (who teaches him about their partly Seminole ancestry) than to his disciplinarian father, who wants him to follow in his footsteps by going to West Point; and Sam and Pilar, much to Mercedes' disapproval, revive their love affair. Symptomatically, Pilar tells a school parents' committee that history is never a simple, straightforward one-sided affair, a lesson Sam too needs to learn. Ironically, his investigations lead to the discovery not that Buddy robbed and murdered Wade (as many townsfolk privately believe), but that Wade's other deputy, now Mayor Pogue, shot him in order to prevent him killing a young black, now a bar-owner known as 'the Mayor of Darktown'; Buddy merely helped Pogue and the intended victim cover up the crime, handing over the dead sheriff's ill-gotten

< **101** >

Chris Cooper plays Sam Deeds and Elizabeth Peña plays Pilar Cruz in **Lone Star** (1995) – perhaps the finest example of Sayles working the conventions of a genre (in this case the Western) to excavate the more complex and difficult reality that lies buried underneath traditional mythologies.

money to Mercedes, whose husband Wade had recently killed in an incident involving the illegal smuggling of Mexicans across the Rio Grande. Not that Buddy was the saint of legend: Sam also finds that his father, besides occasionally using his job for personal gain, later had an adulterous affair with Mercedes and, more disturbingly, was actually Pilar's father (his determination to keep the young Sam and Pilar apart was thus motivated not by racism but by his fear of incest). Nevertheless, at the film's end, when Sam tells Pilar of this last discovery, they decide to 'forget the Alamo' and put love and personal happiness above the constraints of social taboo by continuing their relationship. (This conclusion is even more unusual and radical – if reasonable, since Pilar can no longer bear children – than the condoning of adultery in *Passion Fish*.)

Lone Star, as Sayles has noted, is about borders, whether geo-graphical, political, cultural, psychological, social, legal or moral; and borders, like legends (the title refers both to the 'Lone Star State' and to the reverence accorded Buddy Deeds), are artificial, man-made constructs, the result of historical choice and social conditioning. While, therefore, their presence should be acknowledged and understood, they may also be crossed when the need arises; it is important, in order to achieve a proper sense of self-knowledge, to make one's own choices, rather than simply conform to the expectations of society. The past may – indeed, does – hang heavily over a group or individual, but progress can be made only when aspects of history are examined with an open mind, and then accepted or rejected according to their worth: our predecessors may have been racists, illegal immigrant 'wet-backs', or even the leaders of a community, but we have to make our own way through life, and take proper responsibility for our actions.

< **103** >

In adding the extra dimensions of time and place to his analy-sis of the mechanisms that affect the workings of a society, Sayles achieved even greater sophistication in his insights than in his earlier work. Furthermore, not only was his writing at its sharpest (a marvellous example comes when one character explains that his black fiancée's family are tolerant of her marrying a white man because at least it means she's not lesbian, to which his friend replies, 'It's always heartening to see a prejudice defeated by a deeper prejudice'), but his direction was perfectly in tune with the theme of the film. Most notably, in staging the crucial scenes from the past, as remembered either by Sam or by those he questions, Sayles avoids the dissolves and cuts usually used to introduce and exit from flashbacks, and instead simply pans the camera to left or right, or up or down, to show an event from the past in exactly the same spatial setting. The result – which, as it were, involves the camera crossing temporal borders – not only suggests that the past is always with us, exerting an influence on the here and now, but even allows Sayles to show, by beginning

a 'flashback' with one character in the present and then ending
on another character in the present, that what we are seeing is a
shared memory. The strategy, in fact, is if anything even more
subtle than that used in *Citizen Kane*, whose 'multiple-memory'
narrative also served to explore the contradictory facets of a personality perceived as legendary. Where, however, Welles' film
explores the legend only to end in defeat – an individual's private,
inner self is ultimately unknowable – Sayles comes to a more tentatively optimistic (if ironic) conclusion: Sam discovers the truth
about Buddy, but decides to bury it once more and allow the
people of Frontera to abide in their belief in the legend; after all,
Buddy is fondly remembered as a figure who managed to bring
justice and a modicum of racial harmony to the bordertown, and
to undermine that myth would rob the melting-pot community
of a (supposedly) shining example it badly needs to follow.

That same blend of irony and muted optimism was also to be
found in *Men with Guns* (*Hombres Armados*) (1997), shot in
Spanish and Mayan in Mexico, with a mostly Latin-American
cast and crew. Like *Roan Inish*, the film is given a mythic dimension by being structured as a series of stories within stories: an
Indian woman tells her small daughter of a doctor from the city,
whose journey into the mountains is itself interrupted by
flashbacks of his own memories and of the experiences of the
people he meets. And like *Lone Star*, the central story is of an
investigation made by an idealistic but naive, at first seemingly
innocent protagonist who gradually comes to realise that his
beliefs, rooted in 'official versions' of history and politics, are a
travesty of the truth.

When the elderly, successful city doctor Humberto Fuentes
(Federico Luppi), mourning the recent death of his wife, decides
to use his vacation to visit some of his former students, now
working as doctors in remote Indian communities, he is advised
to abandon his plans both by his son (who considers Indians lazy
and undeserving of help) and by one of his patients, an army
general who warns him of dangerous guerrillas. Nevertheless,

< 104 >

after bumping into one of the students, who has given up professional medicine to run a black-market pharmacy in the city's slum areas, Fuentes decides to proceed with his journey. His search first takes him to a small village where, after being pointedly avoided by the locals, he is told by an old blind woman that the young doctor was burned to death by 'men with guns'; unlike her friends, she is willing to tell the truth because she is no longer afraid of strangers, since all her family has been killed. Mystified, the doctor moves on to look for other students, against the advice of a police officer who claims that the dead man was kidnapped by guerrillas; but as Fuentes continues his search, and is joined by the orphaned young Conejo, the army deserter Domingo, and Padre Portillo, a priest whose cowardice in the face of army atrocities against the Indians has resulted in a loss of faith, he comes to realise that the Indians, underpaid and oppressed by the rich and powerful, are being tortured, raped and murdered by the army, and even sometimes killed by guerrillas should they give in to threats and help the soldiers. The ill-assorted group travels deeper into the mountains and finally, after an encounter with the army which results in the priest's 'disappearance', makes its way, together with Graciela, a young woman traumatised into silence ever since she was raped by soldiers, to a mountain community so remote that its very existence is a matter of dispute: neither the army, the guerrillas nor the whites who run the country have ever been able to find it. When they reach Cerca di Cielo ('Close to Heaven'), where the small population appears to live without food or proper accommodation, there is again no sign of a doctor, and Fuentes dies from the exhaustion of climbing the mountain. Reluctantly, the hitherto cynical Domingo, who studied medicine before being forced to join the army, agrees to treat a woman injured by a landmine; it is she whom we have seen telling the story of Fuentes' journey to her daughter. Heartened by the soldier's restored humanity, Graciela looks down from the mountain-top and smiles to herself.

< 105 >

If the revelations of Sayles' story (whose central character was inspired by the figure of Dr Arrau in Francisco Goldman's novel *The Long Night of White Chickens*) are hardly original – it is now widely accepted that authoritarian regimes often cover up their deliberate oppression of poor indigenous populations by blaming their own atrocities on guerrillas – there is no denying the insights he brings to bear on Fuentes' oydssey, which is not only geographical but psychological and moral. As a good liberal intent on improving the Indians' lot by passing on his medical expertise, Fuentes acknowledges that the battle is against both bacteria and ignorance. Nevertheless, his own ignorance about the political realities of his country is explicable in terms both of governmental deceit and of a certain reluctance to face up to the truth about his comfortable lifestyle; when he tells a couple of American tourists (Mandy Patinkin and Kathryn Grody) who ask him, in comically inept Spanish, about atrocities against the Indians, that the media and 'common people' love drama and that such evils exist only in other countries, his blinkered attitude may derive from an unwillingness to accept that his own position (he is rich and has army bigwigs among his patients) is predicated partly on the exploitation of the under-paid, underfed, undereducated and systematically dispossesed Indians. Only in moving away from the city and encountering a variety of impoverished communities (who survive by gathering salt, sugar, coffee, bananas, gum and corn) does he begin to have any real understanding of the inequalities of the society in which he lives; even then, as his assumptions are completely overturned – he learns that medical instruments are used for torture, schools for interrogation, the 'protective' army for unprovoked genocide – he is educated in the ways of the world by a blind woman, a child, an army deserter who repeatedly threatens him at gun-point, a faithless priest (who calls himself 'The Ghost' ever since the shame of letting his parishioners die while he himself escaped the army executioners) and a mute Indian girl: all, at least theo-retically, less intelligent, worldly and liberal than himself. Even

< 106 >

the American tourists – whose comical aspects may, one suspects, be Sayles' typically self-deprecating way of owning up to his own politically right-on outsider's view of oppressive authoritarian societies – know more about what is going on in the further reaches of Fuentes' country than he, and point out that it was the colonising Europeans, coming from a history of feuding warlords, who introduced genocide to Latin America. Not that Fuentes is 'bad': as the priest explains to him, the sin of 'omission' (not doing the right thing) is not as serious as the sin of 'commission' (doing the wrong thing), so that 'idiots' who fail to understand or act properly may still go to heaven.

< 107 >

Hence, even though *Men With Guns* concerns a society in which poor, 'innocent', rural Indians are oppressed and persecuted by a rich, powerful, urban, originally European oligarchy, it at the same time insists that ethics, which involve different levels of awareness and responsibility, are relative. The blind woman says that when Indians put on army uniforms they become white (and so, by implication, bad), yet we see that some soldiers do have a conscience: not only was Domingo forced by his colleagues into committing murder and rape but, ashamed of what he has become, he deserts and, for all his gun-brandishing, finally helps Fuentes in his quest. Most of the Indians encountered by the doctor are unfriendly, refusing to speak to him about his missing students, and even steal his camera and car hub-caps, but they do so out of suspicion, fear and poverty. The priest betrays his parishioners, but his all-too-human cowardice does not prevent him being a deeply moral man: he punishes himself by cutting himself off from society and eventually gives his life to save Fuentes, Conejo and Domingo. In a world where the oppressed are given no real choice (the army insists that five of the priest's fold sacrifice their lives to save the village, only to massacre the entire population after he makes his escape), absolute morality is an unaffordable luxury; the only means of survival are pragmatism and faith.

It is faith, finally, which allows Sayles' characters to overcome the tragic injustices of the society they inhabit: the doctor's faith in medical progress, Portillo's in the possibility of redemption through self-sacrifice, Conejo's in his own ability to survive as a scavenger, Domingo's in the chance to atone for his sins by taking up as a doctor where Fuentes and his murdered students left off, and Graciela in the hope that her own wounds will be healed in the remote, peaceful, white-free community of Cerca di Cielo. There is, however, an ironic poignancy to Sayles' ending, in that this community seems to be Utopian in the sense not only that the oppressors are absent but that it is unclear whether it is anything more than a world imagined by the Indian mother as she relates Fuentes' story to her child. She knows that he will never leave Cerca di Cielo, and he dies (fittingly, since he has overcome his ignorance) 'close to heaven'; the whole film, then, may be seen as a parable ending in a dreamlike haven where, in the words of one character, the Sky People 'eat air and shit clouds': where wounds are healed, human sympathy is rediscovered and hope regained. Like *Roan Inish*, *Men with Guns* not only reflects and celebrates the oral storytelling tradition, but proposes that tradition as a way of making sense of tragedy, which not only constitutes a denial of the 'official version' of conflicts disseminated by self-serving governments, but provides a means of hanging on to one's faith in the face of apparently insurmountable hardship and injustice. Moreover, as the film's simple title suggests, by structuring his story along the lines of a mythic parable, Sayles is in effect implying that it should not be read as a specific indictment of any particular country but as a more abstract, universal analysis of the forces – economic, racial, social and political – that operate in any authoritarian society where oppression, injustice, violence and the manipulation of information are rife.

In certain respects, *Men with Guns* may be placed generically alongside investigative, anti-authoritarian movies by directors like Costa-Gavras, Gillo Pontecorvo and Francesco Rosi, as well as *The Official Version* (Luis Puenzo, 1985) and a number of other Argentinian films about 'the disappeared'. At the same

< 108 >

time, however, Sayles' decision to merge gritty visual realism with a format more akin to that of myth or fable once again speaks of his originality and ambitions as a storyteller, just as his use of various kinds of Latin American music (echoing the evocative soundtracks compiled for his earlier work) testifies to his wide-ranging interest in traditional popular culture. If the film sometimes lacks the visual flair and acting finesse of his best work (though the lead performers are all very impressive), that is probably evidence of the difficult circumstances under which it was made. Nevertheless, its blending of the personal and the political, its analytical sharpness and emotional sincerity, and the unpatronising integrity of its portrait of Latin-American and Indian culture again place its maker head and shoulders above most 'serious' or 'political' directors of the mainstream.

< 109 >

In working within, and sometimes against, the conventions of traditional genres to explore the sociopolitical and moral fabric of twentieth-century America, Sayles has proved himself a worthy successor to a cinematic tradition that includes such diverse figures as Ford, Welles, Ray, Sirk and Altman, albeit working, of course, from a more politically radical, leftist perspective. But it is not merely for the content and insights of his films that he should be seen as one of the most important American mavericks of the last two decades; his integrity in remaining true to his singular vision, and his ability to work wonders on comparatively low budgets also deserve praise. Even as he has continued both to work as a script-doctor on many big-budget Hollywood movies and to persevere with his writing in other fields (in 1989 he scripted several episodes of *Shannon's Deal*, a superior TV series about a hard-working, unconventional lawyer, while 1991 saw the publication of *Los Gusanos*, an epic, multi-layered novel about the relationship between Cuba and the United States), his films as writer-director have gone from strength to strength. Credit in this respect must also go to the colleagues who have repeatedly worked with him, either behind or in front of the camera. Many have collaborated with him twice or more: not only Mason Daring, David Strathairn and Maggie Renzi (who, besides taking small but memorable acting roles in many of his movies, instigated a number of them), but actors like Chris Cooper, Stephen Mendillo, Kevin Tighe, Gordon Clapp, Nancy Mette, Jace Alexander, Joe Grifasi, Bill Raymond, Leo Burmester, Randle Mell, Tom Wright, Joe Morton, Josh Mostel, Jo Henderson, Michael Mantell, Vincent Spano, Mary McDonnell, Clifton James and Angela Bassett, cameraman Haskell Wexler, production designer Dan Bishop and producers Sarah Green, Peggy Rajski and Paul Miller. At least in terms of actors, he may

< 110 >

be seen as having been instrumental in helping to advance the careers of such performers as Rosanna Arquette, Matthew Modine, Robert Downey Jr, John Cusack, Michael Rooker, and DB Sweeney (not to mention Alfre Woodard, Strathairn, McDonnell, Bassett and Morton), while Ernest Dickerson (later a cameraman for Spike Lee and the director of *Juice*, 1992), Skip Lievsay (regularly a sound editor for a number of the major film-makers in this book) and Nancy Savoca (director of *True Love*, 1989) are among those who also worked for Sayles in one capacity or another in the early stages of their film careers.

It is perhaps appropriate that so many people later involved in some of the most rewarding American films of recent times have crossed paths with a film-maker devoted to celebrating community and disentangling the many threads that make up modern American society; but it is also indicative of the impression he has made on modern American film-making. (Indeed, many felt that Lawrence Kasdan's *The Big Chill*, 1983, was directly influenced by *Secaucus Seven*, although the strong resemblance of Kasdan's *Grand Canyon*, 1991, to *City of Hope* can only have been accidental, given that it was released only a few months after Sayles' film). Influence apart, however, he remains one of the most distinctive, ambitious and insightful *auteurs* working today, and the originality, power and complexity of his work amply reward repeated viewings – the mark, surely, of any great film-maker.

wayne wang

< **111** >

Though Wayne Wang has alternated, with variable critical and commercial success, between low-budget, personal movies and more mainstream, comparatively big-budget productions, seen as a whole his output is distinctive and for the most part very impressive. Indeed, while it has often been said that he virtually invented the Chinese-American movie single-handedly, it should perhaps also be remembered that his films were exploring issues of ethnic and cultural identity several years before Spike Lee came to the fore with his own very different take on questions related to the experiences of African-Americans. If Wang has yet to match Lee's high profile, that's partly because the more con-frontational (and so more controversial) tone of much of Lee's work has made him a 'spokesman' (willing or otherwise) for the African-American community, partly because Wang's films – not all of which treat Chinese-American subjects – are clearly the work of a mercurial artistic personality who prefers to change stylistic methods from film to film.

Perhaps too, Wang's more quizzically philosophical interest in cultural identity is less immediately grasped and less easily marketable than Lee's upfront concern with the social and political problems faced by America's black population. What political content there is in Wang's work is not only less obviously polemical than the work of Lee and Stone, but a number of his finest films are formally experimental, less straightforwardly aligned to the conventions of genre and linear narrative than, say, the work of Sayles (Wang's more popular, accessibly mainstream movies also tend to be his most anonymous). Rather like Soderbergh, he seems to have a magpie sensibility, drawing on whatever influences he deems appropriate for any given project; hence, one film may be playfully Godardian, another in the style of Ozu, another self-consciously neo-noir, yet another in the vein of the traditional Hollywood melodrama, so that, his evident interest in Chinese-American subjects aside, it is often hard to predict what he will do next.

< 112 >

Wang – whose father named him Wayne after John Wayne, anticipating his son's interest in the collision between Eastern and Western cultures – was born in Hong Kong after his parents fled there from mainland China. Educated at an English-language Jesuit school, he remained in the British colony until his late teens, when he went to the Bay Area to study at the California College of Arts and Crafts, where he developed his interests in painting, photography and film. In 1975, with two friends, he made a low-budget American feature entitled *A Man, a Woman and a Killer* – it made little impression, and apparently Wang has no interest in resurrecting it – which he followed with a number of shorts and, after returning to his birthplace, regular work in TV drama. It was only upon his subsequent return to San Francisco that he first produced cinematic work of any real note, when in 1981, for approximately $20,000, he co-wrote and directed the art-house hit *Chan is Missing*.

Loosely structured along the lines of a detective mystery (it might easily have been called *Chinatown*, though it differs from Roman Polanski's film of 1974 by investigating the Chinese-American community from the inside), the film follows the search of two taxi-drivers, Jo (Wood Moy) and his nephew Steve (Marc Hayashi), for a Taiwanese acquaintance named Chan Hung, who has suddenly and mysteriously disappeared with

$4,000 they gave him to buy a licence that would set them up in their own cab business. As the pair make their enquiries, various theories are offered as to the reason for Chan's disappearance – that he was involved in a car accident and chose not to appear in court; that he was implicated in, and maybe even committed, the murder of an elderly supporter of the People's Republic after a dispute about which flag should be raised to mark a Chinese New Year parade; or that he had never really adjusted to America, and felt it was time to return home to the old country. The deeper Jo and Steve investigate, the more contradictory the 'clues' become; but just as Jo has given up on ever finding out what actually happened, or even who Chan really was, Chan's daughter returns the money (though she, too, has no idea of her father's whereabouts). Chan himself, however, never turns up, and Jo concludes that the only way to solve the mystery is to 'think Chinese', to realise that what isn't there is just as important as what is there: in short, to acknowledge that some things happen without reason.

< 113 >

While the unorthodox conclusion to Wang's investigative mystery both points to a fundamental difference between Western and Chinese thinking and suggests the crucial importance of what is absent (i.e. China itself, as the shots of water at the film's end imply), the prime point of interest of *Chan is Missing* is not the conclusion to the search but the multifarious clues unearthed during the search itself. Despite Jo's noir-style voice-over, the movie is no ordinary detective mystery: there's little real sense of danger, much of the film is intentionally funny, and the whole thing – shot on location in raw, grainy black and white, with its rambling structure often giving rise to digressions that are only indirectly relevant to Chan's disappearance – is in many ways as reminiscent of a documentary as it is of a conventional genre movie. Accordingly, Wang allows himself sufficient leeway to explore the many contradictory aspects of the Chinese-American experience, which embraces a wide range of social, political and cultural attitudes, not to mention the various geographical homes of the Chinese diaspora.

The Chinese encountered in the film hail from the People's Republic of China, Taiwan, Hong Kong and, of course, in the case of the younger generation, America itself. Furthermore, much is made of the differences between FOBs (Chinese who have arrived in America fresh off the boat) and ABCs (American-born Chinese), between those who embrace the culture of their new country and those who are so determined to remain true to their Chinese roots that they don't even want American citizenship, and between the older and younger generations. Jo, for example, while in many ways Americanised, is sympathetic to those FOBs who feel confused by their new home, and understands the seemingly paradoxical way of Chinese thinking, while Steve thinks that all that 'identity shit' is old news (i.e. irrelevant to his experiences) and often falls into a slangy mode of speech which Chan's daughter rightly likens to the rhythms and idioms of Richard Pryor (to which Steve responds that Jo reminds him of Charle Chan, himself a detective and an old-fashioned stereotype of the CHinese-AmericAN favoured by the movies).

< 114 >

Indeed, the main thrust of the film appears to be that Chinese-American or even Chinese identity, like the missing Chan, is impossible to define, not only because of its inherent contradictions but because of its enormous adaptability. While one may recognise the difference between, say, Cantonese and Mandarin cuisine, or between faithful PRC communists and those loyal to the breakaway nation of Taiwan, there is no escaping the fact that 'Chinese' is at once a unifying and a divisive factor, just as 'Chinese-American' works both ways: Steve may have been assimilated, at least in his own eyes, into American culture, but China too has a tendency to appropriate facets of American life, as is made clear by the film's opening song, a version of 'Rock Around the Clock' by Hong Kong pop star Sam Hui with lyrics about the inflationary costs of rice. It is as if Wang is saying there is no simple, single definition of what it means to be Chinese or Chinese-American, just as Jo and Steve look bemused and sceptical when a young lawyer, who is something of an academic expert on the linguistic problems of cross-cultural communication, expounds her hilariously arcane theory as to why Chan, interrogated about his role in the car accident, confessed his guilt when he really intended to proclaim his innocence.

With *Chan is Missing*, Wang had introduced himself as a wry, quirky, magpie talent, drawing in a way sometimes reminiscent of early Godard upon a diversity of moods, styles and allusions to create a bizarre but coherent comedy-thriller, a vehicle for incisive insights into cultural questions, inhabited by colourful characters and propelled by an energetic sense of pace. At least in terms of its style, his next film, *Dim Sum - A Little Piece of Heart* (1985), suggested that the writer-director should certainly not be pigeon-holed too soon, since its miniaturist study of an almost completely westernised Chinese-American family was notable chiefly for its gently affectionate humour, the delicate nuances of its insights into family relationships, and a leisurely pace and a restrained, carefully composed visual style reminiscent of the films of Yasujiro Ozu.

< 115 >

As in several of the Japanese master's films (most notably, perhaps, *Late Spring*, 1949, and *An Autumn Afternoon*, 1962), the story centres on an elderly widowed parent keen to see a grown-up daughter get married and leave the family home. In *Dim Sum*, the parent is Mrs Tam (Kim Chew), a 61-year-old seamstress who, despite a certain trepidation about living alone, repeatedly tries to persuade her daughter Geraldine (Kim's real-life daughter, Laureen) that she should finally tie the knot with her long-term boyfriend Richard, particularly as she was once told by a fortune-teller back in the old country that she would die at the age of 62. Geraldine, however, is far from sure that her apparently healthy mother is about to die, and resists the many suggestions, from her mother, her uncle (Victor Wong) and her mother's friends, that she should leave home and settle down. Eventually, she does move into a friend's apartment, but returns after her mother is suddenly taken into hospital. Happily, Mrs

< 116 >

Tam makes a speedy recovery, and makes a long-planned last visit to China; in her absence, Uncle Tam tells Geraldine that his sister-in-law really is upset that she has not yet married. Upon her mother's return, Geraldine is about to tell her about a momentous decision she has come to with Richard, but Mrs Tam interrupts her, saying that the fortune-teller told her that she had now entered upon the second 61-year-long cycle of her life, and that there is therefore no longer any need for Geraldine to rush into marriage. Geraldine smiles and cries to herself, although a closing shot of shoes left, according to the Chinese tradition, by the hearth suggests that Richard is now at least finally allowed to stay overnight without incurring Mrs Tam's disapproval.

While Wang is in *Dim Sum* again dealing with San Francisco's Chinese-American community, the movie's quiet tone, dedramatised, elliptical narrative and its focus on the experiences of a small family group arguably make it a less ambitious but more perfectly achieved film than its predecessor. Its success lies not only in the discreet, understated way it touches on a variety of aspects of Chinese-American life – for example, the desire of Mrs Tam, who seldom speaks in English, to return to China only after she has become a US citizen is evoked in two brief scenes, one of her being questioned, none too successfully, by Geraldine about the American presidents, the other of her smiling gleefully at being presented with a celebratory cake decorated with the Stars and Stripes – but in the rich tapestry of emotions it untangles as it explores the mother and daughter's attitudes to the question of whether Geraldine should marry. On the one hand, Mrs Tam genuinely wants to see her daughter settled down, partly for traditional Chinese reasons, partly because she believes her daughter wants to marry and because she wants to know that her own responsibility for her daughter is over; on the other hand, she is afraid that she will be lonely, and quite selfish enough to ignore Geraldine's feelings in the matter. Meanwhile, for her part, Geraldine is torn between traditonal filial duty (as her uncle observes, 'You can take a girl out of Chinatown, but

you can't take Chinatown out of a girl'), and the sense of individual independence and freedom her generation has grown
accustomed to; she is concerned about her mother's ability to look
after herself (somewhat unnecessarily – Mrs Tam is sufficiently
shrewd to cast a beady eye over the accounts for her brother-in-
law's bar), and at the same time, however much she loves Richard,
she is far from sure that she actually wants to marry him.

The strength of Wang's film lies in the way he reveals these
various factors only bit by bit, a strategy that both makes his dramatically slight narrative consistently engrossing throughout
and, like the casting of Kim and Laureen Chew, lends it an
authentic feeling of everyday life. Indeed, that authenticity also
derives from the fact that the question of Geraldine's future is
finally left as unresolved as the questions of Chinese cultural
identity were at the end of *Chan is Missing*. Just as, in that film,
the search for Chan was at least as revealing as its conclusion, so

< 117 >

Geraldine (Laureen Chew) and her uncle (Victor Wong) in **Dim Sum** (1985), Wang's restrained, Ozu-esque meditation on Chinese-American family relationships.

here it is Wang's sense of detail, as he explores the texture of the Tams' lives, that provides the film's most memorable moments. The settled ways of Mrs Tam's life are beautifully evoked in the film's opening Ozu-like montage: static shots of curtains billowing in a gentle breeze, Mrs Tam entering the room to sit at her sewing machine, a bird in a cage, a longer shot of the room, an exterior shot of a San Francisco street, and of a ship passing under the Golden Gate Bridge, then of Geraldine sitting alone looking at the water, not only locate the setting for the film and introduce the themes of absence and solitude, but also evoke the comforting daily routine currently enjoyed by Mrs Tam but threatened by the possibility of Geraldine's departure. Another result of this attention to detail is our sense of the generosity extended towards the characters; even though Wang's gentle humour frequently casts an ironic light over their stated motives (as when uncle Tam's encouragement of Geraldine to get married is shown to be at least partly motivated by his own desire to marry Mrs Tam), we are never in any doubt that, in the words of Renoir, 'everyone has his reasons'.

< 118 >

As if yet again to confound expectations, *Slam Dance* (1987) saw Wang take off in still another direction. A comparatively big-budget contemporary film noir, which shows no interest in the Chinese-American community whatsoever, it centres on the talented but complacent cartoonist CC Drood (Tom Hulce) who suddenly finds himself not only suspected by the police of murdering a girl with whom he had a brief affair, but menaced by the perpetrators of the crime, who wrongly believe that the dead girl told or gave him something which could ruin them. True to this Hitchcockian premise, Drood sets about clearing his name and safeguarding his life by solving the labyrinthine mystery; in so doing, he comes to see the error of his selfish ways, to accept responsibility both for the unwitting part he played in the girl's demise, and for the consequences of his actions towards his estranged wife (Mary Elizabeth Mastrantonio) and daughter, with whom he is reunited at the film's end.

The victimised Drood (Tom Hulce) is reluctantly involved in an argument between two criminals in **Slam Dance** (1987) – one of Wang's less personal films.

While it is hard to make a strong case for *Slam Dance* being in any way a personal film for Wang, it remains an extremely well-crafted conspiracy thriller, with more than enough suspense, offbeat comedy and emotional substance to hold the attention. If it can be said to share any common ground with its predecessors, it is surely in the interest accorded the notion of family (not only has Drood's idle daydreaming and casual attitude to the responsibilities of adult life alienated him from his wife and child, but also his landlady, who inadvertently sets off the crisis that will threaten his very existence by holding on to a parcel intended for his eyes only, raids the mail because it allows her to fantasise that her own family still cares about her), and in the conceit that a simple, straightforward definition of people is impossible. Buddy (Don Opper, the script's author), the thug who repeatedly beats up and threatens Drood unless he hands over the incriminating parcel, actually loved the girl he accidentally killed (while putting pressure on her for his lesbian boss, who was jealous at her dating Drood), and eventually shoots himself in remorse at her death. Smiley (Harry Dean Stanton), the cop Drood most wants to avoid, is ironically so convinced of his innocence that he lays down his life for the cartoonist, while Drood's friend Jim (Adam Ant) is not only involved in covering for the real culprits but also has designs on Drood's wife. While these revelations are par for the course in noir thrillers, it is also true that Wang makes the most of such ironies in both plot and characterisation: it is appropriate, for example, that Drood eventually disguises himself as Buddy in order to ensure his own safety, for like his late tormentor he too has learned to accept responsibility and love again.

< 120 >

Visually, too, Wang excels, his painter's eye coming into its own to create sharply defined images that speak of Drood's isolation, his tendency to see his life as a dream, and the chaos into which it is thrown. Perhaps most impressive, however, is the slyly ironic black humour brought to an otherwise conventional, if slick and suspenseful, narrative: particularly memorable is a scene which nicely exaggerates Drood's perilous predicament when, taken for questioning at the police precinct, he's forced to wait handcuffed to a chair between two seemingly homicidal psychopaths whose argument with one another inevitably and hilariously comes to include the reluctant and terrified Drood.

While *Eat a Bowl of Tea* (1989) found Wang returning to his fascination with Chinese-American subjects, in its own way it was as polished and conventional as *Slam Dance*, although it must be said it was some kind of breakthrough in itself to centre a classic American melodrama entirely on the experiences of Chinese-American characters played by an authentically Chinese-American cast.

Set in New York in 1949, it concerns the trials and tribulations experienced by a newly-wed couple, the thoroughly Americanised ex-serviceman Ben Loy (Russell Wong) and the bride he brings back from China, Mei Oi (Cora Miao), the daughter of a close friend of his father Wah Gay (Victor Wong). At first the marriage is blissfully happy, but soon pressures of work (he is made the manager of a restaurant) and the persistent attentions of his extended family render Ben Noy impotent, with the result that Mei Oi, lonely and desperate for affection, succumbs to the advances of a local womaniser. Soon after she announces she is pregnant (the baby was conceived during a restful trip with Ben Noy to Washington, away from the prying eyes of the Chinese community), the affair is discovered: her husband, feeling betrayed, announces his plans to divorce her, while Wah Gay takes his revenge on the seducer by slicing off his ear, before taking off for Cuba in the mistaken belief that he is now wanted for murder. Weeks pass, and Ben Noy, still in love with Mei Oi, admits his responsibility for the collapse of their marriage; reconciled, they decide to start a new life in San Francisco where, after the birth of their child and with another on the way, they are visited by their fathers.

< 121 >

In many respects, *Eat a Bowl of Tea* is a throughly engaging, intelligent, skilfully mounted mainstream period drama, notable primarily for allowing us an insight into the everyday lives of New York's Chinese-American community in the late 40s; there's pleasure enough to be had from seeing the various social rituals and gatherings, which Wang recreates with impressive accuracy and dramatic flair. Nevertheless, the crux of the film is the crisis which threatens Ben Noy and Mei Oi's marriage, the reasons for which allow Wang to explore not only the pressures placed upon the couple by their families and friends, but also the pressures placed upon the Chinese-American community as a whole by the American government. Wah Gay's narration at the film's beginning explains that until the end of World War Two, during which China had become an ally and young Chinese-Americans had distinguished themselves as servicemen, America's Exclusion Laws had meant that Chinese men were not allowed to bring their wives and families with them to America; the result was not only a society made up wholly of men but, when the Exclusion

Laws were finally repealed, an overwhelming eagerness to make up for lost time: sons were sent to China to find a bride as quickly as possible, and couples encouraged to have children without delay. Ben Noy's impotence, then, is not merely the result of his overworking, but of the fact that the importance traditionally given to raising a family by the Chinese has been distorted and exaggerated by a community of old men artificially brought together by American immigration policies which were themselves destructive to the bonds of the Chinese family. Ironically, it is the old men's ever-watchful and oft-voiced desire that Ben Noy father a child that renders him initially unable to do so, and which drives the neglected Mei Oi into the arms of another man; only when the couple are allowed to be themselves, rather than representatives of Chinese-American society, are they given the chance to find happiness together, based on mutual love rather than a sense of social duty. First, however, they must rid themselves of the doubts and suspicions fostered by the unusual social and political circumstances of their marriage: Mei Oi fears Ben Noy only married her to please his father, while he worries that she only accepted his proposal because it enabled her to leave China and come to America.

< 122 >

If this aspect of the film sees Wang exploring connections between the personal and the political, in most other respects it conforms to the conventional melodrama's focus on the psychology and experiences of individuals, even as it forges tentative links between the vicissitudes of the couple's romance with historical events in the outside world (at one point, Wang cuts wittily from a gossip warning friends not to breathe a word to anyone about Mei Oi's adultery, to a close-up of a newsboy yelling 'Extra! Extra! Read all about it!' – the news, in fact, concerns China's entry into Korea and America's decision henceforth to treat the People's Republic as an enemy). True, it pinpoints a moment of change in the development of a more 'complete' Chinese society, when they were finally allowed to live like other Americans, and thus to beget proper first-generation Chinese-Americans, but the real focus of the story is the relationship between Ben Loy and Mei Oi. And while Wang lucidly shows the various social forces that influence their marriage, the film never quite avoids the sentimental pitfalls of conventional Hollywood romance: everyone in the film, with the arguable exception of the local gossip and the womanising seducer, is just a little too nice and wholesome properly to convince. That said, Wang's *mise-en-scène* shows him to be keenly aware of the disadvantages of such a closely-knit, inward-looking society: the predominance of murky interiors and the Ozu-like shots of Mei Oi isolated in darkened rooms point to the way a warmly supportive but conformist community can have an oppressively claustrophobic, constraining effect on its members.

< **123** >

The more ambitiously experimental side of Wang's artistry came to the fore in his next film, the delightfully titled *Life is Cheap...But Toilet Paper is Expensive* (1990), in which, as in *Chan is Missing*, he employed a combination of genre pastiche and semi-documentary observation to explore aspects of life in modern Hong Kong. Again, the story is (very loosely) structured as an investigative crime thriller, though there are also echoes of the Western as a cowboy-hatted Chinese-American, The-Man with-No-Name (Spencer Nakasako), arrives from San Francisco to deliver a mysterious briefcase to a Hong Kong Triad boss. As he attempts to carry out the task, encountering a bewildering gallery of locals en route, who warn him about being ripped off, steal the case, threaten his life, and literally make him eat shit, the man becomes increasingly mystified by this 'final frontier at the edge of China', and leaves for San Francisco, concluding that everybody in Hong Kong is looking for the same thing (though what, he doesn't say), and wondering what will happen to the city when it is finally taken over again by China.

Wang's ragged narrative – which takes in straight-to-camera 'interviews', brief inserts from nightmare fantasies (notably of a hand being severed with a cleaver), a love-song performed by a prostitute, and a great deal of hand-held camerawork (including a seven-minute sequence of the hero pursuing the briefcase-robbers through crowded streets, department stores, dark alleys and run-down tenement corridors, all shot with a 'subjective' camera that eventually shakes so much that the images resemble a kinetic action-painting) – is less concerned with coherent characters and plot than with evoking the wildly chaotic contradictions of contemporary Hong Kong life. The film opens with a man eating in a bloody abbatoir (where we later see ducks hung upside down and cruelly left to die after having their throats slit according to Chinese tradition); he waxes lyrical about five thousand years of Chinese culture, hacks, spits, and then, laughing madly, utters the line that gives the movie its title. Thereafter, the hero's uncle, after delivering a none too enlightening lecture on how to dance, warns him to keep out of trouble and always be humble, a lesson the hero learns to his cost when, wrongly suspected of having an affair with the gang boss's mistress Money (Cora Miao), he is forced to eat shit (beautifully served on a silver

< 124 >

Spencer Nakasako plays The-Man-with-No-Name in **Life is Cheap...But Toilet Paper is Expensive** (1990) – a return to freewheeling experimentalism for Wang, using genre pastiche and vérité trickery.

platter, of course). Ironically, it transpires that Money is in fact in love with the boss's daughter, an affair over which the boss, who has himself never fucked Money, might 'lose face'. Nothing in Hong Kong, the hero discovers, is quite what it seems; since everyone is so concerned with keeping up an appearance, Money explains, it is hard to live according to one's true feelings. (It is that emotional freedom, presumably, which the hero believes everyone in Hong Kong is looking for.)

< 125 >

By way of reinforcing this argument, Wang stages a number of vérité-style 'interviews' with Hong Kong characters all intent on proudly preserving a façade of aggressive independence: a cabbie (played by director Allen Fong) rants in incredibly foulmouthed fashion at other 'bad' drivers, while boozing, looking behind him at the camera, and driving dreadfully himself; a wealthy couple bemoan the fact that so few Chinese have been featured on the TV series *Lives of the Rich and Famous*; a prostitute, protesting somewhat implausibly that there are certain things she won't do, then confesses that what really upsets her is when people won't pay for the services she has rendered. Most of these 'insights' into the Hong Kong character are surreally comic and absurd. At the film's end, however, an ex-concert pianist from the People's Republic reveals that, during the Cultural Revolution, rather than play the Communists' propaganda music (or, indeed, pretend he was free by playing Chopin for visting US diplomats), he cut off his own arm in order to safeguard his integrity: the desire to remain true to one's feelings in any society where keeping up appearances counts for so much can be costly indeed.

Mostly, however, Wang's exploration of his birthplace is a hilariously offbeat, gleefully provocative and exhilaratingly fragmented, free-wheeling account of a wild Eastern city on the brink – of an ocean, of political change, of social and moral collapse. With its relentlessly profane dialogue, its scenes of carnage and gore, and its strong scatological content (besides the shiteating sequence, one scene has the hero addressed by a Triad man visibly in the process of evacuating his bowels), the film is clearly intended both to shock, disturb and amuse, just as its jagged editing, its mix of carefully composed and grainy hand-held images, and its elliptical, often barely comprehensible storyline are designed to keep us alert to the small but telling details of Wang's diffuse, digressive thesis. Nothing could have been more different from his subsequent film, *The Joy Luck Club* (1993), a big-budget adaptation (by Hollywood screenwriter Ronald Bass and the author) of Amy Tan's novel, made under the aegis – and, unfortunately, the influence – of executive producer Oliver Stone, to whose overblown, tub-thumping melodramas it bears more than a passing resemblance.

< 126 >

Basically, the film uses a series of flashbacks to depict key moments in the lives of four Chinese-American women and their mothers, moments which counterpoint the comparative ease of life in America in the 90s with the extreme hardships – concubinage, arranged marriages, poverty, war, infanticide, suicide, etc – suffered by earlier generations in China. While Wang directs the movie with characteristic efficiency, with his by now regular cameraman Amir Mokri's lush, widescreen images of the Chinese landscape reminiscent of the visual splendour of the films of Chen Kaige and Zhang Yimou, and while it certainly provided more substantial roles for Asian actresses than had been the Hollywood norm, the film is marred by maudlin sentimentality. As in much of Stone's work, it exhibits a disturbing tendency to stage glossily picturesque tableaux of human misery, while moving towards a facile resolution of the stereotypical tensions which initially define the relationships between the various mothers and daughters. There is no detailed analysis of the way lives are shaped by social and historical forces, merely a flaccid humanism and sense of its own worthiness that tips the film fatally in the direction of lachrymose soap opera. Indeed, were it not for the Chinese subject matter, it would be near-impossible to recognise such a mainstream tear-jerker as a Wayne Wang film; and as if to make amends for such an error of judgement, the writer-director next turned to a far more offbeat, personal project: the diptych of *Smoke* and *Blue in the Face*, shot back to back in 1995.

While the two films are in no way concerned with Chinese-American experience, and are clearly inspired by the writings of Paul Auster (indeed, each film is credited to both Wang and the novelist), they figure among the director's most personal projects for several reasons. Firstly, it was Wang who approached Auster, after reading his *Auggie Wren's Christmas Story* in the Christmas 1990 edition of the *New York Times*, and suggested they collaborate on building a film around the story: Wang wrote the first treatment for *Smoke* himself, after which they worked on the script together. Secondly, like many of his films, the diptych is about a specific community – this time, the New York borough of Brooklyn – noted for its cultural diversity. And thirdly, the diptych form allowed Wang simultaneously to indulge his interest both in well-wrought linear storytelling and in more spontaneous, fragmented, improvisatory and semi-documentary collages.

< 127 >

Though the original intention was simply to make *Smoke*, the production progressed so well that Wang and Auster were able to persuade Miramax, the film's producers, to allow them to make, immediately after the completion of shooting on the first film, a second, less rigidly structured, low-budget movie which would serve as a complement to the first. Only one of the lead actors was able to work on beyond the original deadline – Harvey Keitel, who plays Auggie Wren, the manager of the Brooklyn Cigar Co. corner-store, which functions as the geographical focus of each film – but various bit-players from *Smoke* and a host of star cameos filled out the cast of *Blue in the Face* to gloriously off-beat effect.

The two films are intended to complement each other and are best seen together in sequence. Yet for the sake of clarity we shall deal with them separately. In *Smoke*, Paul Benjamin (William Hurt), a novelist who frequents Auggie's cigar shop and is finding it hard to write since the death of his pregnant wife in a shooting incident, offers a homeless young student, Rashid

(Harold Perrineau), a floor to sleep on for a few nights as a thank-you for the boy's having prevented him walking under a bus. After the boy leaves, Paul discovers not only that his real name is Thomas, but that he has left in his flat a package of cash he picked up following a robbery committed by a local gangster. He persuades Auggie to give Thomas a job; when the boy inadvertently ruins a case of expensive Cuban cigars, he reimburses Auggie with the stolen money, which the shop-owner then hands on to his old flame Ruby (Stockard Channing), who has been pestering him to help her drug-addict daughter, whom she claims (not altogether convincingly) Auggie fathered. Paul, meanwhile, discovers that Thomas has been working, under another false name, at an out-of-town gas station run by his father Cyrus (Forest Whitaker), who abandoned his son after his wife died in a car crash caused by his own drunken driving; Paul and Auggie go to the garage and force Thomas to reveal his true identity. Inspired, perhaps, by these events, Paul overcomes his writer's block but, over lunch with Auggie, confesses he has no ideas for a Christmas story he's been commissioned to write. Auggie helps out by relating what he claims is a true story: after finding a wallet dropped by a boy who had been stealing magazines from his store, he returned it to the boy's address, where he was welcomed by, and shared Christmas dinner with, a lonely, blind old woman who mistook him for her grandson. While there, he found a pile of stolen cameras and took one for himself; thinking better of it months later, he returned to the tenements only to find the old lady gone. Hence, he kept the camera, and embarked on his life's work, taking one photo from the same position outside his shop, at the very same moment every single day.

Despite the very conspicuous differences, in terms of race, age, class and history, between the various characters who weave their way through the seamless, carefully designed tapestry of *Smoke*'s narrative, it is by subtly pointing to the experiences and emotions they share in common that Wang and Auster not only

< **128** >

bring out the novelist's abiding interest in the strange workings of chance, but highlight the film's thematic substance. For one thing, all the main characters are to some degree haunted by the death or absence of a loved one: Thomas by his parents, Cyrus (a manual worker who has a false, mechanical arm to remind him daily of the fateful car crash) by his wife and son, Paul by his wife, and Auggie not only by a sense that Ruby betrayed him (or vice versa, perhaps) but by a feeling that if he had kept Paul's wife talking in his shop a little longer one morning, she would not have been shot and killed. Each, too, through the course of the story, manages to assuage his pain and loneliness by finding, through friendship with the other characters, a surrogate family. Rhymes abound: Ruby's daughter is four-months pregnant, as was Paul's wife when she was killed; when Thomas first meets Cyrus, he introduces himself using Paul's name; Cyrus' false arm has a counterpart in Ruby's eye patch; Auggie's daughter denies he is her father, just as Thomas initially says his father is dead; to reassure a shop assistant he invites out for a drink with them, Thomas claims he is Paul's father (even more unlikely given that Paul is white), which recalls a story Paul told him earlier about a man looking on the face of a long-lost father younger than himself, buried in ice for 25 years.

< 129 >

Further echoes, moreover, are to be found in Auggie's final story: the boy, who comes from the same Projects as Thomas, is a thief like the gangster whose money Thomas has 'stolen', while his lonely old grandmother finds a surrogate relative in Auggie. The point is essentially humanist – our lives are simultaneously the same and different – and is illustrated further, albeit in reverse, when Paul asks Auggie the purpose of his photographic mission. As Auggie explains, while showing him just some of the four thousand pictures he's taken (one of which includes Paul's wife, not long before she was shot), all human life is there on the corner outside his shop – you only have to open your eyes to see it: the location, time of day and framing may be identical from photo to photo, but the content is infinitely varied.

A similar irony attaches to the money that passes from hand to hand throughout the story. It was first stolen from a shop by a hoodlum, before falling into the hands of Thomas, who hides it away until giving it, at Paul's suggestion, to Auggie, to appease his anger over the ruined cigars; he in turn gives it to Ruby to pay for the rehabiliation of a junkie who may not be his child. While the money is a source of temptation and causes considerable upheaval (at one point the gangster beats up Paul, believing he knows of its whereabouts), it finally becomes a selfless gift to be used for beneficial purposes; similarly, Auggie's deceit in pretending to be the old lady's grandson was in fact, as Paul says, 'a good deed', since with his company he brightened up what may very well have been her last Christmas.

< 130 >

Indeed, deceit is a leitmotif in the film; and, like money, it is not presented as necessarily 'bad'. As Paul says, smiling sceptically at the end of Auggie's story, bullshit can be 'a real talent': it is not what one says or does that counts, or even why one says or does something, but the effect of one's actions or words. Thomas' lies reunite him with his father; Ruby's possibly false claim that Auggie is her daughter's father produces a cure for the girl's drug-addiction; Auggie's pretending to be the old lady's grandson makes her happy; and even if his Christmas tale is a fabrication, it serves a purpose in giving Paul an idea for his magazine story (the film ends with him beginning to type it up, before the closing credit sequence shows, in black and white, a wordless re-enactment of the story, which looks noticeably less plausible than it sounded when Auggie was telling it.) Indeed, it may be said that the main theme of *Smoke* (which consists of five chapters entitled 'Paul', 'Rashid', 'Ruby', 'Cyrus' and 'Auggie') is storytelling itself – everyone has his or her own story – and it makes the point that it is the sharing of stories, true or false, that brings people together and forges friendships; and as Paul says, smiling and smoking with Auggie as the film draws to a close, without friendship life wouldn't be worth living.

Reinforcing the theme of friendship, of shared stories and

Harvey Keitel and William Hurt in the cigar shop which provides the focus of both **Smoke** and **Blue in the Face** (1995), Wayne Wang's diptych of Brooklyn-based collaborations with writer Paul Auster

experiences, Wang's *mise-en-scène* is for the most part limited to medium shots which show two or more characters sharing the frame; only when Auggie tells his lengthy tale does the camera slowly zoom into an extreme close-up on his smiling mouth. In *Blue in the Face*, Wang adopted a far more flexible and varied approach to narrative, as befits a largely improvised film which is basically a discursive, celebratory essay on the cultural diversity of life in Brooklyn. Even more than in *Smoke*, Auggie's cigar shop serves as the dramatic and geographical focus of the film, which offers very little in the way of a conventional plot, most of it being an intentionally ragbag assembly of brief comic sketches, direct-to-camera anecdotes, video-shot documentary footage of Brooklyn streets, local inhabitants reeling off statistics and explaining what's special about Brooklyn, archive newsreel footage about the Brooklyn Dodgers, and even songs. Such plotline as there is tells of Auggie's relationship with his girlfriend Violet, whose anger over his forgetting his promise to accompany her to a gig by her brother's band is assuaged when he commits to her and they have a baby, and of his boss Vinnie's plans to sell off the shop, with which Auggie, who sees the place as an essential meeting-place for the neighbourhood's inhabitants, strongly disagrees. Happily, Vinnie (Victor Argo) changes his mind after being visited by the ghost of baseball star Jackie Robinson who, in bemoaning the fact that the Dodgers moved to LA, points to the need for a sense of pride in one's local community.

< **132** >

While the central theme of *Blue in the Face* is certainly the value of such a pride – a 'small is beautiful' attitude to urban life that celebrates the ability of Brooklyn's many ethnic groups to hang out and have fun together (after a singing telegram girl, played by Madonna, announces that Vinnie has decided not to sell the store after all, crowds immediately join Auggie and Violet to dance in the street) – the film covers a multitude of topics as it light-heartedly proceeds from one short sketch to another. A young woman (Mira Sorvino) berates Auggie for threatening to have arrested a kid who has stolen her handbag, so that he eventually hands the bag back to the kid who runs off with it. Jim Jarmusch, who drops into the shop to smoke what he vows will be his final cigarette (some hope!), offers hilarious observations on smoking in the movies. Lou Reed comments, equally absurdly, on his new-fangled (i.e. lensless) spectacles. A derelict (an unrecognisable Lily Tomlin) seeking the Belgian Waffle Shop prompts a discussion of the difference between Belgian and Brooklyn waffles. A local explains his obsession for removing plastic bags from trees (they symbolise 'chaos'). And a rap-singing watch-salesman argues with Tommy (Giancarlo Esposito) over racial identity – though the man offers discounts to African-Americans, Tommy insists he's Italian – and with Vinnie (who, given the chance, performs cowboy songs) over his musical taste, before returning a year later disguised, very unconvincingly, as a white-suited, straw-hatted Cuban cigar-salesman.

While *Blue in the Face* may be slight, its shaggy-dog charm and absurdist wit perfectly embody Wang and Auster's affectionate celebration of a diverse but unified community; just as the film pays tribute to Brooklynites' ability to get on well together, so there is a sense that the movie itself is the product of friendly collaborative efforts (amazingly, it was shot in only six days). At the same time, of course, it reflects back on *Smoke*; the spirit of generosity extended by Wang and Auster to the central characters in that film is now extended to a whole neighbourhood. Moreover, *Blue in the Face* – less Godardian in style than *Chan is Missing* or *Life is Cheap...*, though no less playful or offbeat – is arguably Wang's most fruitful and entertaining blend of fiction and documentary to date. Warm and witty, experimental and accessible, energetic and insightful, it highlights the advantage of working cheaply but imaginatively outside the constraints of traditional genres – a working method which Wang, judging from his promising but erratic career to date, would do well to resort to whenever the opportunity arises.

< **133** >

6

jim jarmusch

< **135** >

Jim Jarmusch is remarkable for having achieved both critical and a degree of commercial success with work that in many respects bears a far stronger resemblance to experimental, 'underground' film-making than to either the Hollywood mainstream or the European art-movie. In their own way, his films differ from the tidy, conventional narratives of most commercial film-making as much as those of David Lynch. Yet whereas Lynch opts for a surreal, nightmarish weirdness, Jarmusch's work is distinguished by its adherence to slight, elliptical, seemingly inconsequential 'stories' drained of the usual dramatic climaxes – they are only very tangentially linked to traditional American genres – and by a subtle, experimental, modernist play with the formal aspects of cinematic language. Crucially, in terms of the films' influence on other directors and their accessibility to audiences, this latter characteristic never seems arch or academic, since even his more aesthetically austere work is firmly rooted in a warm, amused interest in people; indeed, in terms of their narrative scope, focus and tone, his movies – with the exception of *Dead Man* (1996) – are perhaps best understood as the filmic equivalent of a miniaturist's short story rather than of the novel.

In fact, the Ohio-born Jarmusch first had ideas of becoming a poet, but after a spell in Paris, during which time he immersed himself in the wide array of films shown at the Cinémathèque, his ambition turned towards film-making. During his time as a student at Columbia University and as an assistant to Nick Ray at NYU, he became closely involved with New York's underground music and film-making scenes, playing in a band called the Del Byzanteens, working on Eric Mitchell's *Underground USA* and Wim Wenders' film about Nick Ray, *Lightning Over Water* (1980), and hanging out with the likes of John Lurie, saxophonist and composer for the Lounge Lizards. (Even now the structure and editing of his films suggest an abiding interest in musical form and rhythm.) In 1980, he made his first feature, *Permanent Vacation,* in which disaffected young drifter Aloysious Parker (played by 16-year-old Chris Parker) wanders aimlessly around New York until deciding to take a boat to Paris.

< **136** >

Seen today, despite the prizes it won at festivals in Mannheim and Figueira da Foz, the film looks strangely stilted in comparison with Jarmusch's later work, and very much a product of its times: though Parker's insistent assertions, that his fickle rootlessness derives from a tendency to get quickly bored with people and places, are treated with a degree of scepticism, there remains a whiff of modishness about the film, both in its rather po-faced portrayal of adolescent ennui and in the hints of allegory that colour the boy's random encounters with various losers, derelicts and poseurs. Leaving his likewise laconic girlfriend with little explanation for his sudden departure, he embarks upon an odyssey through a blighted urban wasteland, where he meets a deranged war veteran (to the sound of unseen artillery attacks and air-raids); visits his crazed, institutionalised mother; enters a cinema foyer (cue for an allusion to Ray's *Savage Innocents,* 1960), where an eccentric black relates an ingenious joke involving a jazz saxophonist, the song 'Somewhere Over the Rainbow' and the Doppler effect (whereby sounds change pitch according to their distance from a listener); bumps into a saxophonist (Lurie) playing an almost unrecognisable free-form improvisation around the same song; steals a car only to get ripped off by a fence (Mitchell); and, using the cash to buy his ticket to Paris, meets a young Parisian drifter on his first trip to New York on the quay. Evidently, the movie is about alienation in a world beset by insanity, poverty, industrial decay, and no real sense of community; unfortunately, however, the meandering, picaresque narrative and Parker's flat, unappealing performance provide no proper focus of interest and result in sequences where Jarmusch's exact intentions remain frustratingly obscure; most damagingly, it is hard to care about the protagonist or his fate.

That said, *Permanent Vacation* is not wholly without virtues. The location camerawork by Tom DiCillo (later the writer-director of films like *Johnny Suede*, 1991, and *Living in Oblivion*, 1995) is impressively crisp and atmospheric, while Lurie contributes an unusual soundtrack (co-written with Jarmusch himself) for chimes, sax and percussion that is eerily evocative of a ghost-city; most memorably, the final long shot of Manhattan Island, seen from the departing boat, features Lurie's haunting sax spiralling through different keys as its tentative, oblique allusions to 'Somewhere Over the Rainbow' recall the Doppler effect gag. It is also, however, possible to discern, in embryonic form, certain themes and motifs that would recur in the writer-director's later, more mature work: the notion of an outsider passing through a strange land; masculine ennui and the desire for escape; random meetings charged by a sense of strange coincidence; and a view of America markedly less glamorous than that usually seen in the movies, ravaged by poverty and urban dereliction. Finally, then, though the film is marred by the kind of pretensions often to be found in student work, its ambitions and achievements belie the fact that it was made for a mere $12,000.

< **137** >

Nevertheless, Jarmusch's following feature, *Stranger Than Paradise* constituted a giant step forward, even though it was made under straitened circumstances. Originally, Jarmusch was able to shoot, over one weekend, only the first third of the film – with leftover black-and-white stock given him by Wim Wenders after the completion of *The State of Things* (1982) –

which was screened as a short at festivals in Rotterdam and Hof, where it received both a warm reception and, in Holland, a critics prize. At this point, further finance was made available by Paul Bartel and the German producer Otto Grokenberger, and Jarmusch was able to complete the rest of the movie, which went on not only to win the prestigious Camera d'Or in Cannes, but to attract audiences around the world significantly larger than those usually prepared to watch such experimental, low-budget work (the film eventually came in at around $110,000). As in his debut, the 'story' was so simple and slight as to be almost non-existent: Willie (Lurie), a young, profoundly Americanised Hungarian expatriate living in New York, reluctantly agrees to let Eva (Eszter Balint), his 16-year-old Hungarian cousin, stay in his cramped apartment for 10 days until she moves on to live with their Aunt Lottie in Ohio. They don't get on very well, but by the time she leaves they have come to some sort of mutual under-standing, and a year later Willie and his friend and gambling partner Eddie (Richard Edson) borrow a car and visit Eva and Lottie in snowy Cleveland. Bored, Willie (whose real name turns out to be Béla) and Eddie decide to take Eva with them on a quick trip to Florida, but she soon becomes irritated by them leaving her alone to bet their remaining money at the racetrack, so that when a drugs-dealer mistakes her for one of his contacts and hands her a package stuffed with cash, she makes for the air-port, intending to return to Europe. When the men return flush with winnings from the horses, they hurry to the airport in the hope of stopping her, but Willie is forced to buy a ticket for the Budapest flight simply to catch up with her on the plane. Eddie then sees the plane take off, presumably with both Eva and his friend on board – but the girl returns alone to the now aban-doned motel room, having decided to stay in America.

What is most immediately notable about Jarmusch's film is its narrative style. Structured in three parts (entitled 'The New World', 'One Year Later' and 'Paradise'), it is wholly made up of single-shot scenes (separated by black film) in which the fixed

Studied ennui – Eddie (Richard Edson), Eva (Eszter Balint) and Willie (John Lurie) are unmoved by the delights of Florida in the (now distinctive) dedramatised cool of Jarmusch's **Stranger Than Paradise** (1984).

camera either remains absolutely still, or simply pans around a room to follow the characters; there are no dissolves, wipes or cuts within scenes, merely 67 discrete shots (roughly 20 to each 'chapter'), a strategy which makes both for a paring-down of film language and for an elliptical narrative style wholly in keeping with Jarmusch's tendency to 'dedramatise' his films, to focus our attention on those seemingly 'dead' moments usually deemed too unimportant, in terms of plot development, by other film-makers. The effect at first seems quite austere, an odd combina-tion of mimimalist/Warholian 'real time' aesthetics and a more tersely economic approach reminiscent of Robert Bresson and Yasujiro Ozu (both of whom Jarmusch greatly admires), but as the film proceeds it becomes easier to see what Jarmusch's aims are: to concentrate on those unspoken minutiae of human gesture and movement which say at least as much about the characters' emotions and states of mind as would any dialogue or dramatic plot-twist, and to explore new methods of cinematic storytelling. Moreover, in 'flattening' the narrative, he is able to create and sustain, throughout the film, a mood and tone tantalisingly pitched somewhere between poetic melancholy and deadpan, ironic, faintly absurdist humour.

In this respect, the performances – particularly that of Lurie – are crucial. When the film first appeared, some viewers greeted Willie and Eddie's cool, laconic demeanour as evidence of Jarmusch's ultra-hip boho pretensions, an interpretation which fails to take account of the ironic distance he maintains between the attitudes of the characters and the droll perspective of the film itself. Willie's bored, often arrogant, selfish posturing is seen not as a virtue but a weakness, a self-defeating delusion: as his refusal to admit to his Hungarian roots (and name) shows, he is more preoccupied with maintaining a facade of fashionable self-sufficiency than with acknowledging his feelings for others. (The more garrulous, easy-going and boyishly innocent Eddie is ironically rather more mature in this respect, and is visibly delighted that Eva remembers him when he turns up with Willie in Cleveland.) Nevertheless, Eva's invasion of Willie's complacent, self-consciously 'cool' and affected lifestyle serves not only to provoke him into a tentative recognition of the importance of friendship but to remind him of his roots: presumably, he could have got off the plane when he found that Eva wasn't on it, but decided to make a return visit to the old country instead. Not that the trip will necessarily change Willie very much; as Eddie says, seeing the plane take off: 'Oh Willie, I had a bad feeling – what the hell you gonna do in Budapest?' Still, he has at least dragged himself out of the rut of his idle, empty existence.

That, perhaps, is not exactly a hugely dramatic conclusion for a film, but Jarmusch leads us to it with considerable warmth, wit and a subtle poetry. Aunt Lottie and Eddie, in particular, are enormously engaging, amusing characters: the former babbles on in Hungarian, barely bothering to notice whether anyone is in

< 140 >

fact listening to her, and repeatedly beats her two guests, who both take a ridiculous pride in their gambling skills, at a card game; Eddie, meanwhile, is so eager to impress Eva that when she announces she is going to Cleveland, he tells her the city is so beautiful she is sure to love it – before admitting that he has never been there. (Of course, when he and Willie finally go there themselves, all they see are characterless suburbs and enormous, ugly industrial sites, just as their later experience of Florida – 'Paradise' – is, as far as we actually see, largely confined to a motel room.) At the same time, however, Jarmusch makes use of Tom DiCillo's bleached monochrome camerawork to often stunning effect, so that a snow-covered Lake Erie and a Florida beach look as bleakly beautiful as each other. Music, too, is used to lend an air of strangeness to an otherwise mundane landscape, with Lurie's string quartet (appropriately echoing the style of the Hungarian composer Bartók) providing a melancholy backdrop to the sometimes dreamlike images on view.

< 141 >

Both stylistically and thematically, *Down By Law* (1986) was in many regards a reworking of *Stranger Than Paradise*, since its tripartite structure – basically depicting self-willed inertia, enforced inertia and a journey towards freedom (or even, perhaps, Hell, Purgatory and Paradise) – again featured feckless, self-regarding, determinedly cool no-hopers vaguely revitalised by the unexpected arrival in their lives of a foreigner.

Jack (Lurie) is a New Orleans pimp whose dreams of hitting the big time, as his girlfriend says, are destined to amount to nothing, while radio DJ Zack (Tom Waits) is thrown out of their apartment by his lover who complains that he's so proud and obstinate in his attitude to life, love and work that he's digging his own grave. Both men, it seems, have their enemies: Jack, sent by a rival pimp to meet a new hooker, is arrested when he is found in the girl's room (she turns out to be under-age), while Zack, drowning his sorrows in booze, is also set up when he agrees to drive across town a car which he believes merely to be stolen but which actually has a corpse in the trunk. The pair end

< 142 >

up sharing the same cell in the New Orleans Parish Prison, but are so concerned with maintaining a tough, hip facade that they barely communicate (unless it is to argue or fight) until a third cellmate arrrives in the shape of Roberto (Roberto Benigni), an irrepressibly cheery Italian with a poor grasp of English and a passion for old movies and the poems of Walt Whitman and Robert Frost. (By chance, Zack had already briefly met 'Bob' during his drunken reverie on the streets, when the Italian had made the observation that 'Is a sad an' beautiful world'.) Ever optimistic, Bob tells the cynical Jack and Zack of his plans for escape; unexpectedly, they succeed, and head for the bayoux, where they soon get lost. At last, after going around in circles with Jack and Zack bickering endlessly, they come upon an isolated diner deep in the forest. Immediately, Bob falls in love with Nicoletta, its Italian owner, agreeing to stay on with her forever ('like in a book for children'), while Jack and Zack decide to move on, going their separate ways – it doesn't matter in which direction, just as long as they break up – at a suitably Frostian fork in the road.

As before, Jarmusch's film proceeds by taking two habitual loners, unable or reluctant to commit to others, to a point where they grudgingly and hesitantly acknowledge the existence and the benefits of friendship: Bob's good humour and innocence, his readiness to throw himself whole-heartedly into new relationships and even a new romance, and his determination to move on until he finds something worth stopping for, serve as a catalyst for Zack and Jack's partial regeneration. The pair's feigned, world-weary 'experience' is in fact illusory: both end up in jail after being duped by people who appeal to their vanity and worldliness; both act as hard men in prison while protesting their legal innocence, and are thus wholly taken aback when they learn that Bob, whom they condescendingly regard as something of a buffoon, confesses that he really did kill a man (in self-defence, as it transpires, by throwing a billiard ball at a man pursuing him for cheating at cards). And both pour contempt on Bob's revela-

Jailbirds Zack (Tom Waits), Jack (John Lurie) and Bob (Roberto Benigni) make their escape (to nowhere in particular) through the stagnant wastes of the Louisiana bayoux in **Down By Law** (1986).

tion that he has found a means of escape, but are all too happy to take advantage of his undying faith in his own adaptability when he leads them, as if by magic, to freedom (Jarmusch's elliptical narrative style allows him to omit showing how they actually manage to get from the exercise yard to the sewer-tunnel leading to the bayoux, confirming the impression that his film is partly a metaphorical fairy-tale). Even when they have regained their liberty, Zack and Jack are so preoccupied with asserting their superiority over Bob and each other that they end up literally going round in circles; it is Bob's desire that they should stick together and head for the Texas he has seen in old movies that finally takes them away from the stagnant, threatening swamp towards the safe haven that is Nicoletta's cabin. Indeed, Bob's childlike faith in his hopes and dreams is their salvation (at one point, he even draws a window on the cell wall so that they can at least imagine a way out of their confinement), whereas Jack and Zack's ludicrous mutual animosity is initially expressed by them each saying, by way of insult, that the other doesn't even exist. In short, Bob's belief in a 'sad an' beautiful world' is positive, pragmatic and inspirational, whereas their pathetic delusions of cool grandeur are largely negative and self-defeating.

If this metaphorical aspect to the film (which also connects Bob's references to Robert Frost with the fork in the road where his fellow travellers are finally forced to make a decision about their futures) had been allowed to dominate the narrative, *Down By Law* might well have declined into pretentious whimsy and half-baked allegory. Happily, as in his second film, Jarmusch leavens the brew with a great deal of humour: Bob's wide-eyed innocence (beautifully evoked in his pidgin-English repetition of recently assimilated phrases like 'If looks could-a kill, I ham a dead man now' and 'I ham no criminal, I ham a good hegg', and his absurd boyhood reminiscences about his 'very strange' mother's methods of killing and cooking his pet rabbit) is crucial in this regard. Jarmusch's colourful way with idiosyncratic dialogue also extends to the other characters, notably in a scene where Zack, persuaded by Jack to convince him that he is really a DJ, riffs on, radio-style, about the weather, and when the pimp Fatso (Rockets Redglare), reassuring Jack that his offer of a new hooker is an honest one, claims that he's 'serious as cancer'.

Furthermore, the film is shot through with a number of formal devices that reflect its thematic content. It begins by alternating the first introductory shots of Jack and Zack with three montage sequences showing travelling shots of New Orleans' seedier, less glamorous architecture (fittingly, given the theme of regeneration, the opening shot is of a hearse in a cemetery); the first montage features shots moving from right to left, the second from left to right, the third from right to left again, as if foreshadowing the pair's antagonism and their indecision. At the same time, the fact that they are far more like one another than they would like to admit is shown by the fact that their respec-

< 144 >

tive introductory scenes end with each climbing into bed next to a woman who, though her eyes are open, keeps her back to the man in order to pretend, in her anger, that she is asleep. Besides such structural devices, Robby Muller's fine black-and-white camerawork also has a precise thematic thrust, moving from the vaguely sinister, noir-ish night-time cityscapes of the first part, through the stark, static scenes in the confined space of the prison cell in the second, to the lustrous, silvery, wide-open vistas of the bayoux in the third: the journey for Jack and Zack is spatial and emotional, exterior and interior, as they are progressively forced to open their eyes to life's new horizons.

< 145 >

In 1986, Jarmusch began work on a project which took him in a rather different direction: a series of shorts, going by the title of *Coffee and Cigarettes*. At the time of writing, five of these conversation pieces have been shot, but only the first and third episodes, of what Jarmusch intended as an on-going series that might one day be assembled as a feature, have been completed and released. (The second, shot in 1989 in Memphis, stars Joie and Cinque Lee – sister and brother of director Spike – and Steve Buscemi; the fourth, shot in 1992, features the French-African actors Isaach de Bankolé and Alex Descas; while the fifth, also shot in 1992, features Renee French and EJ Rodriguez, formerly of The Lounge Lizards.) It is a shame these still await completion, because *Coffee and Cigarettes* (1986) and *Coffee and Cigarettes (somewhere in California)* (1993) are delightfully funny, shot with minimum fuss in black and white, and written with an acute ear for the absurd banalities of everyday small talk. In the first, Roberto Benigni, so 'wound up' that he shakes violently whenever he takes a sip of coffee or a drag on his cigarette, is joined in a run-down café by a similarly tremulous Steven Wright. Little happens: the pair discuss their common love of coffee and cigarettes, swap seats because of the noise and then immediately swap back again, and when Wright confesses that he is reluctant to keep a dental appointment, Benigni offers, for no good reason, to stand in for him, and leaves. Much of the humour, as in *Down By Law*, derives from Benigni's eccentricity and poor understanding of English, and it has to be said that the later short is more consistently amusing. As before, Iggy Pop waits in a rather more upmarket café (complete with juke box and swirling dots of light reflected from a revolving globe) until he's joined by Tom Waits, who explains his late arrival by saying that he has delivered a baby and used his medical expertise on the victims of a four-car pile-up (even performing a tracheotomy with a ballpoint pen). The pair speak of their love of coffee and, while proudly proclaiming that they have given up smoking, both take cigarettes from a pack left on the table. At first they get on well, agreeing that they are members of the 'coffee and cigarettes' generation as opposed to the 'pie and coffee' generation of the 40s (invoking Abbott and Costello as proof of this theory), but after Iggy notes that there are no Waits songs on the juke box, his tetchy friend says he might feel more at home at a Taco Bell or International House of Pancakes. Iggy's enthusiasm for a new drummer he's played with is taken by Waits as an insult about the percussion in his own music, and an awkward silence ensues until Iggy decides to leave. They wish each other well, but after Iggy departs, Waits notes triumphantly that none of his work is on the juke box either, and furtively lights another cigarette.

< **146** >

The virtue of these shorts, besides their comic observation, is the fact that Jarmusch manages to make so much from so little; using only close-ups, two-shots and the occasional overhead shot of the coffee-and-cigarette-strewn table, he focuses attention squarely on the characters and their troubled attempts to get on with each other. In the first, the lack of communication is largely linguistic; in the other, more interestingly, it is down to pop-star pride and paranoia, with each musician making great self-congratulatory claims for himself while falling victim to a suspicion that the other is subtly putting him down. Indeed, the pair – Waits especially – would seem to be closely related to the characters played by Lurie and Waits in *Down By Law*.

With his next feature, many felt that Jarmusch was returning

Iggy Pop and Tom Waits exchange absurd banalities in one of Jarmusch's on-going series of comic shorts **Coffee and Cigarettes (somewhere in California)** (1993)

to the style, structure and concerns of *Stranger Than Paradise* and *Down By Law*, albeit in vividly saturated colours and with a far larger cast than previously used. Nevertheless, despite the fact that it consisted of three stories ('Far From Yokohama', 'A Ghost' and 'Lost in Space'), and was ostensibly concerned with the experiences of strangers or, rather, foreigners in a strange land, *Mystery Train* (1989) was altogether more ambitious, complex and original than his earlier work. Each of the 'stories' centres on a guest or guests spending a night in a seedy Memphis hotel, hilariously overseen by an eccentrically morose night clerk (Screamin' Jay Hawkins, whose classic rendition of the song 'I Put a Spell on You' had been used to superb effect in *Stranger Than Paradise*) and his ludicrously pillbox-hatted, down-trodden bellboy (Cinque Lee). In the first, a young Japanese couple, Jun (Masatoshi Nagase) and Mitzuko (Youki Kudoh), arrive by train on a pilgrimage to the home of Sun Studios and rock 'n' roll heroes like Carl Perkins, Howling Wolf, Jerry Lee Lewis, Roy Orbison and the King himself, Elvis Presley: after a tour of the studio, they forego a visit to Graceland and check into the hotel, where they inspect the girl's scrapbook of photos which remind her of Elvis, discuss whether Memphis is like Yokohama, make love, listen to Elvis sing 'Blue Moon' on the radio (the DJ's voice is that of Tom Waits – did Zack move on to Memphis after the end of *Down By Law*?) and, next morning, as they prepare to leave the hotel, hear a gunshot in a neighbouring room. In the second tale, the Italian Luisa (Nicoletta Braschi, from *Down By Law*), waiting for a flight that will allow her to take her husband's coffin back to Rome, wanders the city streets and, after being followed by a faintly menacing man who approaches her in a diner insisting she buy what he claims was Elvis' comb for $10, takes refuge in the hotel and agrees to share a room with Dee Dee (Elizabeth Bracco), a nervy, talkative woman who has just left her English boyfriend, 'Elvis'. Talking a while, they fall asleep listening to 'Blue Moon' on the radio, until Luisa is woken by a vision of Presley's ghost (he apologises for coming to the wrong address and vanishes when she tries to wake her room-mate). The next morning, as the women are about to leave, they hear a radio news item about local police looking for dangerous armed criminals, and then hear a gunshot in a neighbouring room. ('Maybe a .38,' says a seemingly unperturbed Luisa; was her late hubby by any chance a mafioso?)

It is only about halfway through this second story, when Luisa and Dee Dee hear love-making in the room next door, that we realise it is taking place not only in the same hotel but at the same time as its predecessor. Accordingly, when the third story opens with Johnny (Joe Strummer), a young Englishman nicknamed 'Elvis', sitting drunk in a bar, embittered about losing his job and his girlfriend Dee Dee, and waving a loaded gun around, our interests immediately become aroused as to what will be the cause and outcome of the gunshot heard in the previous two

< 148 >

episodes. As the final story proceeds, further links are established. To help look after Johnny, his friend Will (Rick Aviles), whom we have already briefly seen mending his car during Luisa's walk around Memphis, calls Charlie (Steve Buscemi), also glimpsed briefly outside his barbershop by Jun and Mitzuko and mentioned in passing by his sister Dee Dee. After Will and Charlie collect Johnny, taking him on a drive around town, they decide to drown their sorrows at his sad predicament and call at a liquor store, whose owner is shot by Johnny during an argument provoked by the man's racist remarks to the black Will. The trio drive on, listening to 'Blue Moon' on the car radio, until they decide to hole up for the night in a hotel where Will's brother-in-law is night clerk (i.e. Hawkins); when they awake next morning, Charlie, seeing the depressed Johnny put the gun to his head, struggles to take it away from him. At which point, Jarmusch mischievously cuts downstairs to the night clerk, who on hearing the gunshot immediately knows which room it came from, and sends the bellboy to investigate.

< 149 >

Only when the boy reaches the room does Jarmusch reveal the answer to the mystery that has been haunting us since the end of the first story: typically, it is not as dramatic as most movies have led us to expect. No one is dead: the shot was an accident, and we see that it has merely wounded Charlie in the leg. The image fades, before a brief epilogue depicting Luisa rushing to catch her plane at the airport, Will and Johnny driving their truck with Charlie in the back, passing on their way to a doctor in Alabama a train leaving Memphis, which is carrying Mitzuko, Jun and Dee Dee (whom the Japanese have still never seen or met) away from town. A montage of shots of the train gathering speed – in a direct reversal of the opening sequence which showed the Japanese arriving in Memphis – plays out to the strains of Elvis singing 'Mystery Train'.

If I have described the narrative of Jarmusch's film in some detail, that is because its originality lies less in its often very witty portrait of Memphis as seen by strangers than in the way

Jarmusch uses his three subtly interlinked stories as a means of exploring the nature of cinematic storytelling. As a matter of fact, there are many other connections between the stories which I haven't yet mentioned: in each of the three hotel rooms there is a painting of Elvis but no TV (both are commented on in each episode); Jun and Dee Dee look out of their respective windows to see a train pass over a bridge, under which we later see Johnny and his friends driving; Luisa and Dee Dee are embarrassed by the sound of a couple (Mitzuko and Jun) making love next door; the couple's walk around Memphis takes them past the bar in which we later see Johnny getting drunk; and Luisa at one point exactly (but, of course, unknowingly) retraces the steps taken earlier by the Japanese. The result of Jarmusch revealing the connections between all these disparate elements only gradually is not only that we are forced into the position of having to investigate the 'mystery' of the narrative – to piece together

< **150** >

The young pilgrims to Elvis' Memphis, Mitzuko (Youki Kudoh) and Jun (Masatoshi Nagase), make up just one of the interlinking tales in **Mystery Train** (1989) which together subtly explore the nature of cinematic storytelling.

the jigsaw, as it were – for ourselves; it also means we are continually required to reassess the meaning of what we have already seen and heard, as people, places, events, sounds, objects and sounds recur in different contexts or are shown from different perspectives. The film, then, explores, and makes explicit, both the fundamental methods of cinematic storytelling and the experience of watching and understanding a film: in each activity, meaning is derived by positing some sort of relationship between characters, actions, objects, sounds, time and place, and alters precisely according to the changes that occur within those very relationships.

< **151** >

That the art of storytelling is at least partly the self-reflexive theme of *Mystery Train*'s three stories is born out by Jarmusch's description of the film as 'a modern minimalist's version of "The Canterbury Tales"'. (Indeed, early in the film, Jun and Mitzuko are seen walking past a signpost announcing that they are in Chaucer Street.) The reference alludes not only to the fact that the film, despite being set entirely in Memphis, is to some degree a road-movie – almost every character is either passing through or thinking of leaving the city, while the young Japanese rock 'n' roll fans are certainly modern-day pilgrims – but also to the fact that it consists of tales within tales, just as a train consists of separate but connected carriages: there are the endless stories about Elvis, different accounts of the break-up between Johnny and Dee Dee, the absurdly funny banter between the night clerk and the bellboy on topics such as how much Presley would have weighed had he died on Jupiter (648 lbs, apparently), and Will and Johnny's drunken discussion about why a hotel run by blacks in a black part of town should feature as its décor pictures of Elvis rather than, say, Otis Redding or Martin Luther King. Moreover, as a subtle echo of the film's fascination with making links between diverse narrative elements, Mitzuko and Jun argue over the facial resemblance to Elvis of such unlikely figures in her scrapbook as the Buddha, a Sumerian King, the Statue of Liberty, and Madonna (this last accepted as conclusive evidence of just how influential Presley has been!).

At the same time, of course, *Mystery Train* succeeds and enter-tains on levels other than as a study in storytelling. Like Jarmusch's earlier work, it is about relationships, and chance encounters (though in this case the various groups inhabiting the three rooms don't actually meet – even though some of them are acquainted with one another – but pass on, blissfully unaware of the others' proximity). Like his previous two features, it shows a fascination with changing light as an index of time and place (Robby Muller's moody camerawork is as elegant and precise as the Edward Hopper paintings it sometimes echoes). It also serves, to some extent, as a playful exercise in genre: its three parts may be viewed as offbeat variations on the romantic comedy, the ghost story, and the crime thriller. Indeed, the film is so rich in its ambi-tions and achievements that it may be seen as something of a landmark in American independent film-making. Its complex three-part structure, with the stories interrelating either in terms of narrative content or overlapping chronology, anticipated Hal Hartley's *Flirt* (1995) (which also included accidental gunshots, a variety of nationalities – including Japanese characters, one played by Masatoshi Nagase – repeated dialogue and situations, and deadpan humour); Steven Soderbergh's *Schizopolis* (1996) (another jigsaw puzzle about film language, which also includes Japanese and Italian characters); and Tarantino's *Pulp Fiction*, which has arguments about pop culture (Johnny, Will and Charlie's discussion about the TV series *Lost in Space* could easily be transplanted to a Tarantino film), an accidental shooting, and a narrative whose precise time-span becomes clear only late in the movie). Of course, Jarmusch's film also included a larger role than usual for Steve Buscemi, who not only had a cameo in *Pulp Fiction* but also appeared in *Reservoir Dogs* (1991) (which again featured accidental shootings and a complex time-structure, not to mention regular interruptions from a radio DJ, voiced by *Coffee and Cigarettes'* Stephen Wright); indeed, Buscemi himself, who has arguably become the 90s indie actor *sans pareil*, went on

< 152 >

to cast Elizabeth Bracco and Rockets Redglare (who, after cameos in *Stranger Than Paradise* and *Down By Law*, played the liquor-store owner in *Mystery Train*) in his feature début as writer-director, *Trees Lounge* (1996).

Although Jarmusch's next film, *Night on Earth* (1991), shared with its predecessor the anthology structure of separate stories (here five, rather than three) related sequentially but actually depicting events that take place contemporaneously, its concerns, ambitions, scope and effect are somewhat different from those of *Mystery Train*; crucially, the five stories are connected only in that they begin and end at precisely the same moment in time (but in five different cities around the world, and therefore in different time zones), and in that they depict an (in most cases fairly inconsequential) encounter between a taxi driver and his or her fare. In Los Angeles, at 7.07 p.m., the young Corky (Winona Ryder) takes Hollywood casting agent Victoria (Gena Rowlands) to Beverly Hills; when the older woman tells her that she is exactly right for a movie she is working on, Corky turns down the chance to become a star, since she intends to become a mechanic. In New York at 10.07 p.m., Yoyo (Giancarlo Esposito) has trouble finding a cab that will take him from Broadway to Brooklyn; eventually he is picked up by Helmut (Armin Mueller-Stahl), an ex-circus clown from East Germany whose driving and knowledge of New York are so poor that Yoyo takes over the wheel. While comparing their lives on the way home, they pick up Yoyo's foul-mouthed sister-in-law Angela (Rosie Perez) who argues constantly with Yoyo but wins the admiration of Helmut. On arriving in Brooklyn, Yoyo gives Helmut directions on how to return to Manhattan, but he soon gets lost. In Paris, at 4.07 a.m., an African driver (Isaach de Bankolé) throws out two African passengers who keep insulting him, and picks up a young blind woman (Béatrice Dalle) whom he thinks will give him less trouble; she, however, responds to his solicitous curiosity about her affliction by contemptuously insisting that she is far more able to live life to the full than he. When he drops her off by the

< **153** >

< 154 >

Seine, she smiles to herself when she hears him drive off and crash his cab into another car. In Rome, also at 4.07 a.m., Gino (Roberto Benigni), an eccentric whose driving is as manic as the non-stop conversations he conducts with himself, picks up a priest (Paolo Bonacelli) whom he insists on addressing as a bishop; when he takes the opportunity to confess his sins, with graphic descriptions of his sexual encounters with pumpkins, a sheep and his sister-in-law, the priest dies of a heart attack, and Gino leaves his body propped up on a roadside bench. Finally, in Helsinki at 5.07a.m., Mika (Matti Pellonpää) picks up three paralytically drunken men, one of whom, Aki, has the previous day been sacked, seen his new car wrecked, learned that his teenage daughter was pregnant, and been thrown out by his wife. Mika has his own, even more depressing story: he and his wife finally saw their prematurely-born baby daughter die after trying for years to conceive. Chastened and in tears, two of his fares walk off home, leaving Aki slumped on the sidewalk to regain consciousness as day breaks.

While the only explicit link between the five stories, apart from the driver-passenger encounters and their temporal setting, is the way Jarmusch introduces each with shots tracking into a ticking clock and into the dot marking the relevant city on an old-fashioned globe, followed by a brief montage of static shots of mechanical and architectural features – cars, clocks, public phones, diners, bridges, squares, docks, etc – introducing the city in question, two themes recur throughout the film: blindness (literal in the Paris story, metaphorical in the others, although Gino mostly drives around the dark Roman streets wearing shades) and confession. Each episode depicts, in one way or another, how driver and passenger don't really understand each other's needs or feelings; each, too (except for the black comedy of the Roman tale), ends with a hint that, through their brief encounter, the strangers may have arrived at some kind of temporary, improved awareness of how the lives and attitudes of others may differ from their own. (Indeed, as in *Stranger Than Paradise* and *Down By Law*,

the encounters may even be viewed as a meeting of innocence –
Victoria, Helmut, the African, the priest, the drunks – with experience – Corky, Yoyo, the blind girl, Gino, Mika – though these
qualities might also, of course, be attributed the other way
round; no one involved can be described as wholly innocent or
experienced.) That said, Jarmusch's customary determination to
play down any potential climaxes or conclusions lends the film a
very engaging air of inconsequentiality (a rare quality in the cinema, in which inconsequentiality is usually seen as, and often is,
a failing; another example of this kind of low-key narrative subtlety is the Taviani Brothers' *Kaos*, 1984, itself a compendium of
five stories by Pirandello). Whatever emotional punch or sense of
dramatic completeness, coherence and closure the film provides
is the result of an accumulation of detail, of Jarmusch's assured
handling of mood, of his generosity towards the characters, and
of the neat structural conceit of compiling a sequence of five contemporaneous tales which begins at sunset and ends at sunrise,
thus provoking a sense of regeneration through life's endless
cycle. Misunderstandings may occur, hopes may be dashed,
tragedy and death may befall both individuals and families, but
the world continues to turn.

< 155 >

As ever, although the film ends on a note of melancholy, as a
whole the mood is leavened not only by an impression of people
somehow coping with the various misfortunes life has to offer,
but by Jarmusch's affectionate sense of humour. The New York
and Roman stories are especially funny, and much of the comedy
in the former is designed to show just how much the very different Yoyo and Helmut have in common: both wear aviator hats
with the ear flaps turned down (though Yoyo insists, with absurd
'attitude', that his is far more fashionable), both, in their own
way, are clowns, and both have a rather eccentric grasp of English
(while Yoyo guffaws at Helmut's name, which he likens to a hat,
he can't see the absurd echoes of his own). Indeed, Jarmusch
makes a point throughout of subtly suggesting the shared
humanity of his often diametrically opposed characters: Corky

may be young, scruffy and unambitious, and Victoria a middle-aged, well-to-do career-woman, but they share similar attitudes towards men, a tendency to curse at frustrating phone-calls (both say 'shit!' at exactly the same moment as they finish calls at the airport), and a determination to live their lives as they please.

If the film's five stories lack the intertextual complexity of the narrative of *Mystery Train*, *Night on Earth* is nevertheless an impressive achievement. For one thing, despite the technical and visual constraints Jarmusch imposes on himself by centring each episode on a cab journey, his adept assembly of establishing shots of the cities, exterior shots of the taxis, interior shots of the drivers and their fares, and shots of the streets as seen through the window from the passengers' point of view, means that the film never seems claustrophobic or dramatically and visually tedious. For another, he creates a subtly different mood for each episode by playing off the distinctive characteristics of each location. This is not merely a question of depicting a city's topography and architecture, or even of highlighting a particular aspect of its social life (the racial melting pot and aggressive conversational manners of New York, for instance, or the presence of African immigrants in Paris, or the influence of the Catholic Church in Rome), but of playing variations on the way the cities have been represented in the movies. The first episode shows how the film industry dominates certain areas of life in Los Angeles, and cannily counterpoints a newly bankable star (Ryder) with an older woman widely regarded as one of the great screen actresses (Rowlands, who also, of course, was the wife of John Cassavetes, an indie very much after Jarmusch's own heart); the second drafts in two New York actors (Esposito and Perez) known for their work in Spike Lee's *Do the Right Thing* (1989), arguably a seminal film in terms of its study of the city's racial tensions; the third – besides using Dalle, whose feistiness recalls her role in Jean-Jacques Beineix's *Betty Blue* (1986), and de Bankolé, best known for his work in *Chocolat* (1988) and *S'en Fout la Mort* (1990), both made by Claire Denis, assistant director to Jarmusch on

< 156 >

Down By Law – also pays tribute to Jacques Rivette's *Le Pont du Nord* (1981) by including a scene on the Quai de l'Oise; the fourth, with Benigni providing typically broad Italian comedy, pays a brief hommage to Pasolini's *Accattone* (1961) with a shot of the Cafe Tevere and a scene featuring roadside prostitutes; while the last borrows both its actors and its morose, booze-sodden mood from the movies of Aki Kaurismäki, whose film-maker brother Mika also gets a name check. (Crucially, many of the performers, not to mention some of those paid hommage, are personal friends of Jarmusch, who prefers to write roles specifically for people he knows personally, and still describes his film-making methods as essentially 'amateur'.)

< **157** >

Not that these allusions and echoes are part of some movie-buff's showing off; indeed, just as Tom Waits' score goes through a series of imaginative variations – bluesy jazz for New York, lilting accordeon for Paris, Nino Rota-style circus music for Rome – on the waltz (a poignant song appropriately titled 'Back in the Good Old World') that accompanies the opening and closing credits, so these references are subtly and seamlessly interwoven into the fabric of the film's evocation, through the characters, the mood, architecture and changes in the light, of each city's lifestyle and atmosphere. In short, as in *Mystery Train*, every detail, however seemingly insignificant, has its precise function or purpose.

While *Dead Man* (1995) would first appear to be significantly different from Jarmusch's earlier work – it is set in the past (the late nineteenth century), is more closely aligned with a recognisable genre (the Western), has a single linear storyline, an altogether looser, more extenuated narrative, and a number of lyrical scenes notable for their hallucinatory, non-naturalistic tone – it remains a natural progression from its predecessors. Again, it charts a stranger's journey in a strange land, which might be interpreted as a spiritual odyssey from hell, through purgatory, to heaven; again, it shows a fateful chance encounter between two culturally very different individuals, and the slow but steady blossoming of friendship and mutual respect; again, too, it can be seen as a meeting of innocence and experience and, like *Night on Earth*, suggests that life may be seen as a cycle. Indeed, its opening pre-credits sequence is as tautly economic, impressionistic and formally stylised as anything Jarmusch had done to date. As young Cleveland accountant William Blake (Johnny Depp) travels to take up a job in an industrialised outpost in the wilderness of the far western frontier, the social, cultural and geographical changes this initial journey takes him through are beautifully signified in a terse montage which plays telling variations on a repeated motif. In each brief segment (separated by fades to black which denote Blake's falling asleep), shots of the train – its wheels, axles or billowing steam – are followed by shots of the accountant reading or waking up, of the landscape seen from his window and, again reflecting his point of view, of the other passengers looking at him; as the exteriors change from farmlands and forests to mountains, deserts and desolate Indian reservations, so the suited businessmen and neatly bonneted women surrounding Blake in the early stages of his journey are steadily replaced by scruffier, tougher trappers and downright aggressive ruffians armed with guns with which, at the first opportunity, they blast at the buffalo herds grazing nearby. The only dialogue that interrupts this highly formalised yet informative montage is when the engine fireman (Crispin Glover), his face blackened by coal dust, comes to sit opposite Blake, and after asking why he has chosen to come out to hell (the accountant has recently lost both his parents and his fiancée, and is looking to start a new life), mutters some enigmatic words about being in a moving boat, and darkly warns that instead of a job, he's just as likely to find his own grave.

That much is clear as soon as the story proper begins to run its looser, less tautly edited course after the credits, with Blake heading through the streets of Machine (where he witnesses a range of foreboding sights, including piles of buffalo skulls, a busy undertaker's, and a woman performing fellatio on a gun-

< **158** >

man in broad daylight) to the industrial hell-hole of the Dickinson Metalworks. As predicted, Blake doesn't get his job: his letter of application arrived months late, and the factory's irascible owner, John Dickinson (Robert Mitchum), sends him packing at gunpoint. Drowning his sorrows outside a saloon, he befriends a downtrodden paper-flower seller, Thel; but when they are caught in bed by her former lover Charlie, a gunfight develops which leaves Thel and Charlie dead and Blake, wounded in the chest, fleeing on the dead man's horse. Charlie, it transpires, was the son of the tyrannical Dickinson, who hires three ruthless gunmen to find the man who killed his heir (and, equally importantly, stole his favourite horse); meanwhile, Blake is being tended to by Nobody (Gary Farmer), a native American who, having had the dubious benefit of a European education and seen the genocidal treatment of Indians back east, is now viewed as an outcast and a liar by his tribe (they call him 'He who talks loud but says nothing'), and who believes Blake is the reincarnated spirit of the English visionary poet whose name he shares.

< 159 >

Described superficially, much of the rest of the story would seem to be rather conventional Western fare: the three gunmen and a pair of US marshalls pursue Blake, who with the help of his new Indian ally manages to evade them. Since Jarmusch, however, never adopts a conventional approach to narrative, characterisation or thematic content, *Dead Man* is nothing if not audacious and highly original. For one thing, there never seems to be any real hope of Blake recovering from his wound (though Nobody rubs a traditional mud remedy into his chest, he cannot remove the bullet), so that we are all too aware that to some degree he is already, as Nobody says, a dead man; the narrative 'question' is not whether he will survive, but what will befall him and what he will learn on his voyage towards death. For another, as Nobody escorts him to the point of departure for his final journey (lying alone in a boat sent out, like a Viking's burial, into the ocean, recalling the fireman's earlier conversation), Blake's experiences of the world around him become increasingly hallucinatory, his perceptions transformed by physical weakness, peyote, and the revelations he is told by Nobody about the world of the spirit: at one point he sees Nobody's face as a skull, at another (just before he shoots the two marshalls) he appears to believe he really is the poet William Blake, and at another he lies down to sleep embracing a dead fawn, as if he too now senses that he is part of the natural world. And finally, Jarmusch feels no need to romanticise Blake's friendship with Nobody according to the 'noble savage' tradition: not only is the youth understandably sceptical about the meaning and import of much that Nobody tells him (which he describes as 'Indian malarkey'), but Nobody's own motives for helping Blake are grounded at least as much in a desire to befriend a visionary poet (who has also, impressively, killed white men), as they are in any sense of humane altruism. Nevertheless, while Jarmusch is no apologist for Indian mystical beliefs, we, like Blake, begin to recognise that the native American feels more at one with the land and the natural world, and that he sees life and death as a continuum or cycle, in contrast to the white man, who sees death as the end of life, and as a punishment for the transgressions committed within that life.

Death for the white settlers, then, is essentially negative, which chimes with Jarmusch's depiction of the 'civilisation' they have brought to the huge, beautiful wilderness of north-western America. The adage 'Go west, young man', with its evocation of the land of golden opportunity, is viewed with profound irony by Jarmusch's film. Machine, especially as represented by the 'dark Satanic mills' of the Dickinson Metalworks, is a living hell of industrial 'progress'. Morality is concerned with possession and power (whether it be Charlie's jealousy over Thel, Dickinson's anger over the theft of his horse, or the open racism directed at Nobody by a Christian missionary who runs a remote trading post). Life is cheap, as is evidenced by the three trigger-happy gunmen, two of whom are murdered by the other, Cole (Lance Henricksen), long before he even catches up with Blake and Nobody (who shoots and is shot by Cole) as the former's funereal

< **160** >

William Blake (Johnny Depp), a stranger in a strange land, embraces a dead fawn in one of the more hallucinatory sequences from **Dead Man** (1995) – Jarmusch's predictably idiosyncratic take on America's most hallowed genre.

canoe drifts out to sea. (Crucially, Jarmusch's handling of violence, while showing it to be horrific – Cole crushes the head of a dead marshall he finds with his shoe, and is later seen eating the cooked arm of one of his colleagues – is marked by its restraint: there is no suspenseful build-up, slow-motion or lingering visual emphasis on gore to romanticise or sensationalise its perpetration.)

As ever, Jarmusch peppers what is fundamentally an elegiac poem for lost innocence and a meditation on different attitudes to death with moments of drole, deadpan humour and colourfully eccentric, yet credible, characters. One bounty hunter (Michael Wincott) is killed by his partner Cole simply because he cannot stop discussing whatever trivial topic enters his mind; Nobody and Blake come across a bizarre trio of settlers (including the grotesque transvestite Sally Jenko) arguing over Nero's killing of Christians, the possum and beans they're eating, and the meaning of the word Philistine ('a real dirty person,' opines Sally); the first question almost everyone asks of anyone they encounter is whether he has any tobacco on him. At the same time, however, poetry is again present, both in Nobody's quotations from Blake (appropriately, 'Every night and every morn,/ Some to misery are born'), and in Robby Muller's extraordinarily lustrous photography (in monochrome and 'Scope) of the silvery glades, snowy mountainsides and dense forests of the vast northwestern landscape. Indeed, with its mix of pastoral beauty and industrial blight replacing the more familiar depictions of the west as a place of dusty townships, towering mesas and rocky canyons; its offbeat cameos played by a cast that includes such unlikely faces as John Hurt, Gabriel Byrne, Alfred Molina and, as Sally Jenko, Iggy Pop; its throbbing, hypnotically repetitive electric guitar score by Neil Young; and the leisurely, dreamlike rhythms of its episodic narrative, *Dead Man* constitutes a determinedly different take on the traditional iconography, atmosphere and action-led drama of America's most hallowed and sharply delineated genre.

< **162** >

Year of the Horse (1997) took Jarmusch in still another direction, that of the rock documentary. In making a film about Neil Young and the band Crazy Horse, the director typically made imaginative use of his medium, not only intercutting his own footage of concert performance and interviews (shot on tour in 1996) with similar footage from 1976 (shot by a British crew) and 1986 (shot by Young himself under the name of Bernard Shakey), but revelling in low-budget stylistic strategies: the film, 'made loud to be played loud', features an excellent Dolby soundtrack but was mostly 'proudly filmed in 8mm' – with additional footage shot in 16mm and on Hi-8 video – which lends the images of the band in concert (mostly in long- and medium shot, evoking the sensation of actually being there at the concerts) a raw, grainy immediacy entirely in keeping with the heads-down, no-frills, raunchy style of the rock 'n' roll they are playing. Indeed, the movie is basically a straightforward tribute to the band and their music: their numbers are reproduced in their entirety in no-nonsense fashion, with Jarmusch simply overlaying a few appropriately evocative, poetic shots of the American landscape and highways to provide visual variety, while the interviews and off-stage footage never pretend to offer a definitive history of the band's career but merely depict them warts and all, paying fond tribute to their longevity (a tribute enhanced by the use of the earlier footage). The overall modesty and quiet integrity of the project (the band are shown having fiery rows) extends to the director himself who – besides eschewing visual pyrotechnics (though he does make use of some fast- and slow-motion, and even a little animation) – includes scenes in which guitarist Frank 'Poncho' Sempedro jokingly takes him to task for being a 'hip, trendy, New York artsy-artsy film producer'. At the same time, however, Jarmusch does provide the film's funniest moment when he explains, by way of reply to a question about the difference between the Old and New Testaments, that basically the former is 'when God is really pissed all the time' because men are fuck-ups, before going on to read aloud passages outlining the effects of the Creator's wrath, savouring the gruesome, blood-curdling details with his deep, deadpan drawl.

< 163 >

Though *Year of the Horse* might seem something of an oddity in Jarmusch's oeuvre, with its unassertive, low-budget technique, its droll wit, and its respect for Crazy Horse's music, it is wholly in keeping with his overall outlook. (The role of music in his work should not be underestimated, and he has often likened his methods to those of the 'garage bands' of the 70s). He remains a true original, difficult to define on any terms other than his own. His films are at once accessible yet experimental, affectionate yet ironic, elegiac yet comic, simple and austere yet packed with subtle detail; they reveal an interest in formal innovation, yet they are to some extent about that most humane of emotions, friendship. They are profoundly American in both their concerns and sense of place, and yet almost European or Asian in mood and style. (His films' characters and settings reflect his love of 50s B-movies, especially film noir, but his narrative and visual style – particularly in his use of landscape – and his preference for understated performances are symptomatic of his admiration for Bresson, Ozu, Antonioni, Godard, Rivette, Wenders and early Fassbinder.) His gently ironic, dedramatised, barely generic narratives, his refusal to sell out to Hollywood, and his sense of his work as essentially 'amateur' and personal have made his influence on the independent film-making scene, both in America and abroad, considerable: it is hard to imagine the likes of such admittedly diverse directors as Hal Hartley, Tom DiCillo, Richard Linklater, Kevin Smith or Aki Kaurismaki reaching the enthusiastic audiences they have without the example set by Jarmusch. Indeed, it might be argued that his occasional cameo appearances in films by other indie directors – including *Blue in the Face* (Wayne Wang, 1995), *Sling Blade* (Billy Bob Thornton, 1996; the director had taken a small role in *Dead Man*), *Leningrad Cowboys Go America* (Aki Kaurismäki, 1989) and *Tigrero* (Mika Kaurismäki, 1994) – are acknowledgements of the affection and respect in which he is held. If he continues to experience some difficulty in finding finance for his projects, that is only further evidence of his having remained true to his artistic ideas and principles, while others are trying to make their name as the new Scorsese, Tarantino or whoever; as such, he deserves recognition as a valuable, talented, highly influential elder statesman of the American indie scene.

< 164 >

тhe coen вrothers

< **165** >

Since they first burst on to the movie scene, in 1984, with *Blood Simple*, the Coen Brothers have gone from strength to strength, and may now be counted among the most exciting, adventurous and original film-makers working in the American cinema. If at first they seemed to be merely virtuoso stylists, given to expert genre pastiche that was most notable for the precision of its plotting and dialogue, as time has passed the Coens' peculiar talents and obsessions have come into sharper focus, so that we may divine not only a consistent philosophy of human experience (which may be summed up, perhaps, in a line from *Miller's Crossing*, 1990: 'Nobody knows anybody… not that well'), but a fascination with the formal aspects of cinematic storytelling. The more closely one examines their complex, tortuous narratives, the more likely one is to discover, beneath the labryrinthine plotting, the wise-cracking dialogue and the overall bravura of their visual style, a tendency to structure the films around repetitions, paradoxes, symmetries and doubles, so that each movie may be seen as a series of imaginatively executed variations upon the same theme.

Almost every one of their films is to some degree aligned to a specific genre – the film noir, the gangster thriller, the horror film or the screwball comedy. Yet their films always bear some resemblance to art-movies, in which story and characters serve partly as a means of exploring/deconstructing a philosophical or formal/aesthetic idea. In this respect, and in their constant refusal to pretend that they are 'realist' narratives – the frequent use of voice-overs by (perhaps unreliable) narrators and of emphatic stylistic tropes draws attention to the films as fictional constructs – the Coens' films remain undeniably modernist in approach.

Not that the brothers – who, despite crediting themselves as co-writers, with Joel directing and Ethan producing, actually collaborate closely on all aspects of the film-making process, from initial conception of the story to the editing – would be likely ever to subscribe to such a 'serious' interpretation of their films. In interview they have repeatedly proved reluctant to discuss the 'meaning' of their work, preferring to limit their statements to jokey anecdotes (indeed, humour plays a strong role in all their movies). Perhaps, too, Joel's pre-directorial career – after film studies at NYU, he worked on the editing of such low-brow horror films as *Fear No Evil* (Frank Laloggia, 1981) and *The Evil Dead* (directed by their friend Sam Raimi in 1982), while his younger brother studied philosophy – failed to suggest the rather more cerebral attitude to genre their films would adopt.

Nevertheless, right from the narration that opened *Blood Simple*, it was already clear that the Coens were not content to stick to tried and tested formulae. As a montage shows us bleak, lifeless vistas of the Texan landscape, we hear a voice – later revealed to be that of the seedy, duplicitous private detective Visser (M Emmet Walsh) – introduce the film's setting, and indeed its moral universe, with the following words: 'The world is full of complainers. The fact is, nothing comes with a guarantee. I don't care if you're the Pope of Rome, President of the United States or Man of the Year – something can always go wrong. Go ahead, complain, tell your problems to your neighbour, ask for help – watch him fly... Now in Russia, they got it mapped out so that everyone pulls for everyone else; that's the theory, anyway. But what I know about is Texas, and down here, you're on your own.'

< **166** >

It might be possible to argue that this brief but memorably cynical monologue was just a clever, colourful pastiche of the 'hard-boiled' style of classic crime writers like James M Cain (an influence, certainly, on the film) and Dashiel Hammett, were it not for the fact that *Blood Simple* then proceeds to illustrate the thesis that 'you're on your own' with all the rigorous logic of a philosophical syllogism. While the plot revolves around such stock pulp-fiction elements as adultery, jealousy, greed, deceit and murder, what is immediately noticeable about the film is that each and every character is so caught up in their own obsessions that they are fatally oblivious to what is going on around them; only we, the audience, has any idea of the deadly chain of events that leads to the deaths of three of the four main characters, since they all act out of ignorance, repeatedly deceiving each other or misinterpreting each other's words, actions and motives.

< 167 >

To simplify an enormously tortuous, impressively detailed story: Abby (Frances McDormand) leaves her manically possessive husband Julian Marty (Dan Hedaya), and spends the night with Ray (John Getz), Marty's friend and employee at the Neon Boot saloon. Suspicious that Abby is having an affair, Marty has hired Visser, who photographs the couple in bed; Marty's response to the photos is to hire the private detective to kill Abby and Ray for $10,000 dollars. Visser supplies evidence that he has shot the lovers in bed, by means of a doctored photo, and taking the money, shoots Marty with Abby's gun (which he stole to leave as incriminating evidence). Visiting the bar, Ray finds the seemingly dead Marty and, assuming that Abby shot him, drives him into the countryside where, after a long struggle, he manages to bury his dying boss. He then tells Abby he has 'taken care' of things and, distrustful of her air of innocence, starts acting distantly towards her, so that she in turn suspects he may have murdered her husband. Reassured by another saloon employee, who tells her that Marty only recently left him a phone message accusing Ray of having stolen $10,000 from the safe, she is ready to make up with Ray when he visits her apartment to tell her that he has now found the doctored photo and suspects someone else of having shot Marty; Visser, however, who wrongly believes they are on to him, is waiting outside Abby's apartment, and shoots Ray dead through the window before he can say more about his suspicions. Terrified that Marty is out for revenge, Abby finally manages to shoot and kill Visser, whom she believes to be her husband when he breaks into her unlit apartment.

Blood Simple is an elaborately plotted, tautly directed thriller, full of grotesque set-pieces (notably Ray's gruelling, lengthy endeavours to finish Marty off in a roadside field, and Visser's invasion of Abby's apartment, when he is forced to punch his way through a wall in order to extract, with his left hand, a knife with which she has pinned his right hand to a window-sill) and atmospheric details suggesting the sordid, overheated passions that drive the plot (Visser sweating endlessly, dead fish left to rot on Marty's desk after he is shot); especially impressive is how the story shows small, simple misunderstandings leading to murderous actions.

Yet the narrative structure (whose repeated scenes and lines of dialogue emphasise the way the characters, despite being fatally connected through their actions, inhabit separate mental and emotional worlds) is far more formal than that of the average thriller. Marty warns Ray that Abby is more duplicitous than he realises and will one day tell him, feigning innocence, that she has no idea what he's talking about – the exact words she uses when Ray later tells her he's 'taken care of things' (of course, being unaware that Marty is dead, she really doesn't know what he's talking about, and his vagueness, born of his distrust of her, only makes her suspect in turn that he has killed Marty). Such ironies are scattered throughout the film: Marty wrongly believes Visser has killed Ray and Abby; they each believe that the other may have killed Marty (though for the most part Abby wrongly believes her husband is alive, and even trying to kill her); Visser, who knows more than the others, thinks that she knows he has killed Marty and is therefore a threat to him, whereas in fact she

< **168** >

remains unaware of his very existence until after she has shot him. Locations (the saloon and Marty's office, Abby's apartment, Ray's house) and objects (Abby's gun, Visser's cigarette lighter and Volkswagen, ceiling fans, the photos and rotting fish) recur in scene after scene, often taking on a new, different significance: Visser's lighter, first implied to be an incriminating clue, is merely a red-herring, while Abby's gun is not only believed by each character to have a different relevance to Marty's death, but used by each character to shoot at another. If the material elements of the characters' relationship with the world around them keep changing in this way, how can they even begin to arrive at some sort of understanding of 'the truth' of what is happening to them? Most of the time, they don't even know if someone is dead or alive, let alone who killed that person.

< 169 >

In this last respect, a scene towards the end of the film is indicative of the way the Coens simultaneously play games with

Sleazy private detective Visser, played by M. Emmet Walsh, tries to free his hand which has been pinned to the window-sill with a knife in **Blood Simple** (1984) – the Coen's stylistical fluid and formally complex début.

audience expectations and make their narrative function on an altogether deeper level. Having visited the office where Marty, unbeknownst to her, was earlier shot, and found it in a state of disarray that suggests Ray may have killed him (in fact, Visser returned there to try and find the lighter and photos that might incriminate him), Abby returns home only to be woken by the sound of smashing glass; she first assumes it is Ray, but finds Marty in her room, coughing blood. It is, of course, a nightmare, which plays mischievously on our own confusion as to whether Marty may still be alive (we have already seen him, as it were, 'return from the dead' when Ray was trying to dispose of his body); but the dream is also an expression of Abby's growing anxiety that Ray may have killed her husband and that she, partly responsible, will be haunted by guilt. The scene, then, is symptomatic of how everything in the film has more than a single, simple meaning.

< 170 >

Even the music accompanying the closing credits – 'It's The Same Old Song', by the Four Tops – resonates in a variety of ways: we have already heard the song earlier in the film, so the title may be taken quite literally; the words 'It's the same old song,/ But with a different meaning since you've been gone' point both to Marty's reactions to his wife's adulterous departure and to the way objects and actions take on 'a different meaning' as the film proceeds; and the fact that the number starts the moment Visser dies reminds us that death itself is the 'same old song', since all the main characters except Abby have by now succumbed to its dominion. In effect, the film is saying, the wages of deceit, distrust and ignorance – of treating the world as a place where 'you're on your own', of acting without examining the potential consequences of that action – is death.

While critics and audiences alike were impressed by *Blood Simple*'s fluid camera style, razor-sharp editing and excellent performances by a comparatively obscure cast (the Coens have always been adept at discovering relatively unknown actors or foregrounding previously unexplored qualities in well-known actors), few appear to have noted the formal and thematic aspects of the film. The same might be said of *Raising Arizona* (1987) which, rather like *Crimewave* (1985), an excessively broad, loud comedy the brothers wrote with and for Sam Raimi, adopted a jokey, larger-than-life, comic-strip approach to narrative and characterisation. Again, much of the praise heaped on the film centred on the snappy, witty dialogue. But as the film relates the bizarre tale of HI 'Hi' McDonagh, habitual convenience-store robber (Nicolas Cage) and his wooing of police booking officer Edwina (Holly Hunter) and their misbegotten attempts to abduct and raise a baby, it is as intriguing for its formal and thematic elements as for the offbeat originality and humour of the Coens' writing.

< 171 >

Like the characters in *Blood Simple*, Hi and 'Ed' embark on what at first to them appears a comparatively 'innocent' crime (abducting one of the quintuplets born to the wealthy, unpainted-furniture tycoon Nathan Arizona – Ed's infertility and Hi's criminal record mean they are unable to conceive or adopt), without due regard for the complications that are bound to ensue. Similarly, from the very start, when Hi claims that, 'I was writing hot checks which, when businessmen do it, is called an overdraft; now I'm not complaining, mind you, just saying there ain't no pancake so thin it ain't got two sides,' it seems the Coens' attitude towards the various crimes and misdemeanours on view is one of moral relativism. Hi and Ed, for sure, are wrong to assume that their needs outweigh those of the Arizonas, but are they worse than the Arizonas (Nathan, after all, uses the TV newscasts about the abduction to promote his chain of stores), or than Hi's foreman Glen and his wife Dot who, besides raising their own kids to be unruly monsters, and suggesting to Hi that he and Ed join them in a wife-swapping session, demand the couple hand over 'Junior' to them as soon as they realise the baby's true identity? Or than Hi's erstwhile cellmates Gale and Evelle, who, hiding out with the couple after their prison escape, not only try to tempt Hi back into a life of crime, but abduct

Convenience-store bandit 'Hi' and his ex-cop wife Ed (Nicolas Cage and Holly Hunter) contemplate the patter of tiny feet in **Raising Arizona** (1987).

Junior to get the ransom for themselves? At least Hi and Ed's crime is motivated by their love for one another; even so, Hi experiences guilt about it, as he confesses when he dreams into existence ('I feared that I myself had unleashed him') the Fury-like Leonard Smalls, a 'Lone Biker of the Apocalypse' who rides through the Arizona desert scorching the earth as he hunts down the kidnappers. (That Hi envisions him being 'especially hard on the little things, the helpless and the gentle creatures' – rabbits, lizards and plants are killed as he passes – is surely an allusion to the evil preacher in Charles Laughton's 1955 film *The Night of the Hunter*, another deceptively naive tale of a battle for the possession of innocent children.)

In a sense, not only is the Lone Biker Hi's nemesis, but Gale and Evelle may be seen as his id: they are first introduced, immediately after Hi, having his photo taken with Ed and Junior, insists that everything will be 'decent and normal' from now on, as they erupt, miraculously, from the earth itself, crawling out of the mud and howling during a violent thunderstorm. This scene, like the shots of Smalls' fiery, supernatural journey through the desert, is not just flashy showing-off on the Coens' part (though the film is notable for the technical virtuosity displayed by a very mobile camera); the dreamlike, larger-than-life tone of such sequences suggests that to some degree Gale, Evelle and the Biker represent Hi's fears about himself as he tries to go straight and lead a normal family life. Smalls is lawlessness incarnate (he shoots at animals for the fun of it, tells Arizona he'll find the baby and punish his kidnappers whether he is paid to or not, and carries a battery of guns and hand-grenades – with which, when they finally meet, Hi manages to destroy him); sporting a tattoo announcing 'Mama Didn't Love Me', he also embodies a life devoid of love – and Hi, of course, sees love as his salvation.

< 173 >

It is only fitting, then, that when he and Ed, realising Junior must be missed by his family after all, return him to Nathan, the tycoon takes pity on their childless predicament and advises them not to separate as they intend. He suggests they sleep on the matter, and the film ends with another of Hi's dreams, in which Gale and Evelle (his 'bad side') return voluntarily to prison, Glen's vengeful efforts to inform on Hi and Ed go unheeded, Junior grows up to be a football star, and Ed and Hi, now old, are surrounded by their children and grandchildren. A happy ending, of course, but one recognised as a Utopian dream, as Hi inadvertently admits when he explains, in characteristically lofty clichés, 'It seemed like, well, our home: if not Arizona, then a land not too far away where all parents are strong and wise and capable, and all children are happy and beloved... I dunno, maybe it was Utah.'

That final injection of undermining satire into a coda that is otherwise an admirably po-faced parody of mainstream movie-style poignancy is fairly typical of the flip humour which here and there weakens the coherence of *Raising Arizona*'s inventive blend of credible human motivations and surreal, comic fantasy. Whereas in *Blood Simple* it was possible to root for Abby, caught up in a chain of events whose deadly outcome far outweighed any 'error' she might have made in simply sleeping with her abusive husband's best friend, it is very hard to care about Hi and Ed in *Raising Arizona* because the humour, much of which satirises their banal, inarticulate ideas of domestic bliss, is hammered home so relentlessly. That said, the film is very funny. Its fascination with dreams and nightmares, its sense of place as a state of mind (whereas *Blood Simple*'s Texas was all dark, overheated passions, Arizona is shown to be geographically and culturally as arid as Hi and Ed's vain attempts to conceive), and its intriguing use of couples (Hi and Ed, Glen and Dot, Gale and Evelle, the Arizonas) to evoke different kinds of morality and parental feeling, situate the film firmly within the linear development of the Coens' oeuvre.

Whereas emotional reticence, or lack of emotional depth, was perhaps the most conspicuous shortcoming of *Raising Arizona*, it became one of the central themes of their next film, *Miller's Crossing*. Even more than *Blood Simple*, the sheer wealth of detail in the Coens' storyline makes anything more than a very simplified synopsis out of the question in a study of this scope. Set in a north-eastern city during the early 30s, it centres on the rivalry between the gangs led by the Italian-American Johnny Caspar (Jon Polito) and the Irish-American Leo (Albert Finney), whose control of the city is challenged when Caspar demands he be allowed to kill the conniving bookie Bernie (John Turturro), the brother of Leo's young mistress Verna (Marcia Gay Harden). Leo's right-hand man Tom (Gabriel Byrne), who is secretly having an affair with Verna, advises his boss to sacrifice Bernie in order to avoid outright war with Caspar, but Leo, who believes Caspar murdered a detective he hired to tail Verna, sets about getting the police to clamp down on Caspar's various rackets. Convinced that Verna is only seeing Leo to safeguard her brother, Tom tells Leo about their affair; beaten up by his old friend, he

< **174** >

then goes to Caspar, offering to divulge Bernie's whereabouts. To prove his loyalty to Caspar, he then agrees to murder Bernie in the forest clearing of the film's title, but, unbeknownst to Caspar's men, lets Bernie go when he begs for his life, insisting that he leave town. After a few days, however, Bernie returns, demanding that Tom kill Caspar, or he'll start appearing in public. Meanwhile, Caspar's henchman Eddie Dane suspects Tom of deceiving Caspar, and takes him to search for the body in the forest; unexpectedly, they find a man with his face shot off (who later turns out to be Eddie's 'boy' Mink, shot by his former gambling partner Bernie). Tom now plays his trump cards: he tells Caspar it was Eddie, not Bernie who was cheating him, so that Caspar kills Eddie, and then after revealing that Bernie is still alive, sets up a meeting at which Bernie kills Caspar. When Bernie again begs for his life, Tom kills him, arranging things to look as if he and Caspar shot each other. At Bernie's funeral, Verna ignores Tom, but Leo, who chooses to believe his friend was acting on his behalf all along, asks him to come back and work for him. Tom turns down the offer, and watches Leo walk away through the forest.

< 175 >

While the film certainly impresses for its superbly complex 'whodunwhat' plotting (there are many more characters, subplots and twists which I've not had the space to mention), and for its evocative reworking both of the classic, uncluttered visual style of 30s gangster thrillers and of the literary style of Dashiel Hammett (whose *Red Harvest* and *The Glass Key* may have been an influence on the story), what is perhaps most extraordinary about *Miller's Crossing* is the way it uses an almost abstract series of variations on numerous motifs to explore 'Character, friendship and ethics' – words first spoken by Caspar in the film's opening moments, and often discussed both by him and by the other leading characters during the film. Even in the crime world, ethics are of crucial importance, as Caspar tells Tom: 'You're honest [he isn't, of course, though he is basically honorable] and that's something we can't get enough of in this business; I'll admit, since we last jawed, my stomach's been seizin' up on me. The Dane saying we should double-cross you: you double-cross once, where's it all end? An interesting ethical question.' And ethics, in a world less concerned with right and wrong than with allegiance and rivalry, comes down to a question of friendship, of loyalty, betrayal and trust. But when everyone is on the make, and apparent loyalty may really be betrayal, friends 'is a mental state' (to quote Caspar); trust can only be based on a perception of people's characters. And Leo, Caspar and Verna all, at some point, misread Tom's character, proving his argument that 'Nobody knows anybody – not that well.'

< 176 >

The reason for their not understanding him, however, derives not only from the lies he tells but from his emotional reticence: he will admit neither to his friendship for Leo nor to his love for Verna, who would readily give up her relationship with Leo if Tom would only say he wanted her, rather than asking her to give it up because he wants to help Leo. Tom repeatedly puts reason above appeals to love or friendship (that's why he manages to outwit everyone else); he's so closed off emotionally that, even at the film's end when his friend Leo walks away, he has to hide his saddened eyes under the brow of his hat. It's not that he has no feelings, merely that he can't, or won't, show them: the one time he does – when Bernie, in the forest, begs for his life, asking Tom to 'look into your heart' – he is betrayed, so that when Bernie uses exactly the same words towards the film's end, Tom – once bitten, twice shy – simply replies, 'What heart?', and kills him.

Tom manages to resolve the gang warfare to Leo's advantage by playing on the fact that no one (as in *Blood Simple*) has any idea what anyone else is doing, let alone why. (Once again, in the case of Bernie, Mink and Eddie, the living are believed dead and vice versa.) And the chess-like precision of his strategy is reflected in the film's structure, which not only consists of many scenes being repeated with only the slightest variation in content (the near-shootings in the forest, Tom's visits to Leo's bar and to Verna's apartment, Bernie's unannounced arrivals at Tom's place, the mayor and police chief being lectured first by Leo and then by Caspar, etc), but of 'doubled' characters and groups: Leo, Tom and Verna are mirror-images of Caspar, Eddie and Mink, with the double-crossing Bernie serving as a fragile link between the two groups. This element of formalism is perhaps most conspicuous in the many repeated phrases in the dialogue ('What's the rumpus?', 'I wouldn't want it any other way', 'You gotta lip on ya', etc) and in the opening credits sequence, in which we see a man's fedora being blown through the forest: the sequence is revealed to be Tom's dream (intriguingly, shots looking up at the trees are repeated during Tom's later visits to Miller's Crossing with Bernie and Eddie, as if the dream were a premonition). When Verna later asks what the dream meant – did he chase the hat? – Tom replies that there's 'nothing more foolish than a man chasing his hat', as if to admit that allowing others to see him follow his emotions is also out of the question; for Tom, as we see when he pulls the brim of his fedora down over his eyes after Bernie's funeral, a hat is a means of concealing emotions, rather than displaying something about his character, just as the forest is a place where, he hopes, his actions will remain invisible, and hence incomprehensible, to others.

< 177 >

If the Coens' use of these formal devices – not to mention the performances which, while utterly convincing in the context of the film, are just slightly off-kilter and non-naturalistic – ensured that *Miller's Crossing* stands at one or two removes from the traditional crime-thriller, it was even more difficult to categorise their next film, *Barton Fink* (1991), according to any one genre. Compared to its predecessor, its story is relatively simple, and yet its precise meaning is shrouded in ambiguity. Set in 1941, it centres on the young New York playwright Barton Fink (John Turturro), whose Broadway success with his new play about fishmongers leads to his being offered a Hollywood screenwriting contract by Capitol Pictures. After checking into the seedy Hotel Earle, Fink visits studio boss Jack Lipnik, who sets him to work on a Wallace Beery wrestling movie; plagued, however, by writer's block, Fink tries to enlist the help of Bill Mayhew, a famous but alcoholic novelist working without much success at Capitol, and his attractive amanuensis and mistress Audrey (Judie Davis). He soon, however, comes to despise Mayhew's drunken abuse of Audrey, and instead befriends Charlie Meadows (John Goodman), a cheerful insurance-salesman who lives in the next room at the Earle: for Barton, Charlie Meadows epitomises the 'Common Man', about whom and, indeed, for whom he intends to write. When the studio pressurises him to produce an outline of his script, Barton calls Audrey, who visits his room, reveals that she is the real author of much of Mayhew's work, and seduces the wary Barton; the next morning, however, he wakes to find her bloody corpse beside him. Disturbed by his screams, Charlie offers to help dispose of her body, before going away for a few days on business, leaving a small box containing all his belongings for Barton to look after. Shortly afterwards, Barton is visited by two detectives, who make enquiries about his neighbour, whom they know as the psychopathic murderer Karl 'Madman' Mundt, suspected of shooting and beheading an ear-doctor Charlie told Barton he was planning to visit.

< **178** >

Upset but strangely inspired by this shocking turn of events, Barton finally completes his script, but after celebrating at a dance (where he angers a sailor by insisting that, as a writer, he has a superior claim over a girl he is dancing with), he returns to his room where the detectives accuse him of helping Charlie to murder Audrey and Mayhew, both of whose headless bodies have now been found. As they are about to arrest him, Charlie returns, and while the hotel blazes in flames around him, kills the detectives and complains that Barton never once, during their conversations, really listened to him. After Charlie returns exhausted to his room, Barton leaves the hotel for the studio, where Lipnik tells him that his script – small fragments of which we have heard the detectives read, sounding almost identical to the ending of his Broadway play – is unacceptable: he will keep him on contract, but won't film any of his scripts until he grows up.

Despondent, and still carrying Charlie's box, he goes to the beach, where he watches a beautiful young woman looking out to sea: his view of her is identical to a picture which, hung above his typewriter on his hotel room wall, used to distract him from writing.

Even if one takes the story of *Barton Fink* literally (rather difficult, given Charlie/Karl's apocalyptic reappearance in the hotel corridors, surrounded by flames), the film is a magnificent *tour de force* in several respects. As a satire both of the left-wing/populist pretensions of playwrights of the 30s and 40s (Fink's play *Bare Ruined Choirs* is a witty pastiche based on Clifford Odets' *Awake and Sing*) and of the philistine tastes of the movie moguls during Hollywood's Golden Age, it is both funny and accurate. As played by John Mahoney, Mayhew bears an uncanny resemblance to William Faulkner (another southern novelist who had trouble functioning in the movie capital), while Lipnik's welcoming

< **179** >

Playwright Barton Fink (John Turturro) gets the Hollywood lowdown from eccentric movie mogul Jack Lipnik (Michael Lerner) in the Coens' surreal meditation on creative infertility in the Hollywood of the 40s.

speech to Barton – 'Bart, keep it simple; we don't gotta tackle the world our first time out. The important thing is we all want it to have that Barton Fink feeling. I guess we all have that Barton Fink feeling, but since you're Barton Fink I'm assuming you have it in spades' – perfectly captures the mix of artistic ambition and conveyor-belt business sense that ruled Hollywood.

As a Gothic horror film, too, the film succeeds in slowly but effectively building to the fiery, nightmarish climax of Charlie's murder of the detectives, with the hotel itself – all bizarre staff, shadowy rooms, dreary furniture, strange noises and peeling wallpaper – serving as an additional sinister character to threaten Fink's sanity. Perhaps unsurprisingly, the film's nightmarish evocation of the solitude and stress of Hollywood life has been compared both to Nathaniel West's *Day of the Locust* and to the writings of crime novelist Cornell Woolrich; at the same time, however, the measured pace and elegant compositions and camera-movements of its first half are in many ways reminiscent of the European art-movie, a form of film-making which frequently takes a very different approach from the narrative certainties favoured by Hollywood, and whose ambiguities are usually best understood on a metaphorical level.

For it is, finally, unwise to take the story of *Barton Fink* at face-value as the literal depiction of an encounter between two men, one of whom turns out to be a murderer. Disregarding, for the moment, the exact significance of the way the final shot of the film reproduces Barton's bathing-beauty picture, we should first consider the question of whether Charlie really is Audrey's killer, as the detectives imply and Barton comes to believe. When Barton wakes to find Audrey dead beside him, we may initially think that Mayhew, in a fit of drunken jealousy, somehow crept in to kill her; that, we later discover, is unlikely, since Mayhew's body has also been found and attributed to the homicidal Charlie. Our assumption, then, is that Charlie is the culprit – but could he really have killed her so very violently (her body is drenched in blood) while Barton slept on beside her? And how

< 180 >

and why would he have murdered Mayhew, whom he has never met? If anyone should be the prime suspect for these murders it's surely Barton himself. He was with Audrey at the time of her death, and had more than one possible motive for killing Mayhew: he felt contempt for his alcoholism, for his violent treatment of Audrey, and for the fact that he had not in fact been the author of his acclaimed novels; moreover, he may well have felt jealousy over Audrey.

While, however, it is just possible that Barton did commit the murders, it is certainly more likely that the killings, and even perhaps Charlie himself (at least in his later incarnation as Karl 'Madman' Mundt), are figments of his imagination. Barton, after all, is suffering from writer's block, and is so caught up with his ideal of writing for and about the 'Common Man' (even though he clearly knows nothing about such people, nor, for that matter, really cares about them) that he may well have fantasised Charlie/Karl into existence. Barton is preoccupied with 'the life of the mind': for all his rather patronising remarks about being interested in 'the average working stiff', he repeatedly ignores Charlie's offers to tell him 'a few stories', signally failing to heed Audrey's advice that 'empathy requires understanding'. He tolerates the insurance salesman only because he 'sells peace of mind' and listens to him in admiration; in truth, his ignorance of the Common Man results in his fearing him, so that he imagines Charlie as a psychopath (i.e. not a rational person as he likes to believe himself to be), and displaces his contempt for Mayhew and his sexual nervousness about women (he's embarrassed when Charlie refers to the 'saucy' picture on his wall) on to his neighbour. It is hardly surprising, then, that when Charlie charges down the blazing hotel corridor to kill the detectives who are about to arrest Barton, he bellows, over and over, 'I'll show you the life of the mind!'; it is as if Charlie, at least in his murderous incarnation as Karl 'Madman' Mundt, is Barton's id run rampant.

Whether Charlie actually exists or not, then, it's highly unlikely that he commits any murders: the killings are dreamed

< 181 >

up by Barton, partly out of frustration, resentment and a sense of inadequacy, partly as an attempt to overcome his writer's block. The creepy, stagnant hotel, which seems to have a life of its own and whose motto is 'A day or a lifetime', reflects Barton's own mental condition. Moreover, there are many hints that he lives in a dreamworld of his own making, and allusions to heads, minds and souls abound: Lipnik points out that 'the contents of your head are the property of Capitol Pictures', complains that he didn't want a script about a man 'wrestling with his soul' (Barton at one point has even wrestled with Charlie), and berates Barton for believing that 'the whole world revolves around whatever rattles inside that little kike head of yours'.

< 182 >

A more subtle but telling detail arises when Barton, still distracted in his room, opens a Gideon's Bible to read a passage about Nebuchadnezzar (the title, incidentally, of a novel Mayhew has handed him as a gift): 'And the king, Nebuchadnezzar, answered and said to the Chaldeans, I recall not my dream; if ye will not make known unto me my dream, and its interpretation, ye shall be cut in pieces, and of your tents shall be made a dunghill.' The dunghill apart (although the Earle is admittedly none too luxurious an abode), the quotation reflects both Barton's inability properly to recall his dream (i.e. his desire to kill Audrey and Mayhew) and his interest in severed heads. (It also reflects his delusions of grandeur: when later he calls his agent to tell him he has finally finished his 'really big' script, he compares the result to the Bible.)

The nightmarish scenario that constitutes the film's second half is therefore best read as the product of Barton's feverish imagination: of his feelings of frustration and fear at not being able to engage with the Common Man, of his jealousy about Audrey and Mayhew, of his inability to create a script even for a lowly wrestling picture. In the end, after Charlie/his id has told him he's 'just a tourist with a typewriter' and vanished once more into the darkness of his room (the interior of which neither we nor Barton have ever seen), and after Lipnik has cast him into a world of creative oblivion, Barton sits on the beach watching the girl look out to sea. Before she strikes up the pose that matches Barton's wall picture, she asks what's in the box (which Charlie eventually admitted was not his). Barton doesn't know; he doesn't even know if it belongs to him. Unsure, as it were, of his own identity and achievements, he gazes dreamily at a vision in which life imitates art; now more than ever, it seems, he is unable to distinguish between the two.

Disguised as a Hollywood-satire-cum-horror-thriller, *Barton Fink's* metaphorical study of madness, creative infertility and suppressed resentment may not have been properly understood (the Coens themselves were reluctant as always to discuss its precise meaning), but the sheer confidence of the writing and direction, the imaginative art direction and camerawork, and the excellence of the performances garnered it widespread critical acclaim. The same, sadly, could not be said of *The Hudsucker Proxy* (1994), which was widely and unwisely dismissed as a foolhardy, even arrogant attempt to revive the screwball/cornball comedy style of Frank Capra. True, the basic story, of an innocent hayseed who finally triumphs over the cynical big city business types who try to exploit him, is deliberately reminiscent of the comic fables of the 30s and 40s, but as ever the Coens' focus on more formal elements lends it a metaphorical sophistication lacking in those films. To be sure, if the film is finally less original than *Miller's Crossing* and *Barton Fink*, that is because it wears its pastiche status too conspicuously on its sleeve; nevertheless, few recent comparatively big-budget American films (one of its producers, rather surprisingly, was the action-movie mogul Joel Silver) have matched *Hudsucker's* inventive fecundity.

The film begins on New Year's Eve, with 1958 about to become 1959; while New York celebrates, Norville Baines (Tim Robbins) contemplates suicide on a ledge of the Hudsucker Building, home of the company of which he is president. The film flashes back to relate how this lowly business student from Muncie, Indiana, came to be there: after the suicide of Waring

< 183 >

< 184 >

Hudsucker, the company founder who leapt from the 48th floor, the board, led by scheming vice president Sidney Mussburger (Paul Newman), made mailroom boy Norville president, assuming his lack of acumen would make shares plummet, thus allowing board members to buy stock for themselves. Cynical journalist Amy Archer (Jennifer Jason Leigh) wheedles her way into a job as Norville's secretary to write an exposé of his appointment, but falls for his naive optimism. After Mussburger puts in motion one of the president's least promising projects – the development of the hula hoop – the company makes a killing, and while success goes to Norville's head, effectively alienating Amy, whose deception has now come to light, Mussburger puts out a story that Norville is an insane sham who stole the idea for the hoop.

Drunk and depressed on New Year's Eve, Norville climbs out on to the ledge and slips; as he plunges towards certain death, however, Moses, who tends the clock at the top of the building, jams its cogs and halts time itself. While Norville is suspended a few feet above the sidewalk, he is visited by the angelic ghost of Waring Hudsucker, who reminds Norville of a letter he failed to deliver in which he bequeathed his stock to whoever replaced him as company president. Surviving the fall, Norville makes up with Amy and returns to work where he introduces his latest idea – the frisbee.

Certainly, *The Hudsucker Proxy* succeeds for the most part as a cool, knowing but affectionate pastiche of Capra's sentimental comic parables like *Mr Deeds Goes to Town* (1936), *Mr Smith Goes to Washington* (1939) and *It's a Wonderful Life* (1946), from which the Coens borrow characters like the hick from the sticks, the hard-boiled newspaperwoman, and the angel who prevents the hero's suicide. Tim Robbins does a sterling job in the Gary Cooper/Jimmy Stewart role, Jennifer Jason Leigh's fast, staccato delivery is clearly a hommage to feisty but emotionally vulnerable actresses like Rosalind Russell, Katharine Hepburn and Jean Arthur, while the tradition of feelgood Hollywood fantasy is further alluded to in the use of deliberately artificial-looking sets (the opening shot, as the camera swoops through the snow and skyscrapers to zoom in on Norville perched high above the city, is particularly magical). At the same time, the Coens keep reminding us that this is just a movie: when music swells up to accompany a silhouetted kiss between Norville and Amy, there is a sudden cut to a woman saying 'Shhhhh' straight to camera, at which point the music is silenced; and when Moses stops time by jamming the cogs of the clock, he turns to camera to confess, 'I'm never supposed to do this, but have you got a better idea?' In true modernist fashion, both the fundamental artifice of the fiction and our own expectations and hopes as an audience are openly acknowledged.

< 185 >

That the film is a Faustian fairy-tale is reinforced by the angelic and demonic status accorded, respectively, to Moses and Waring Hudsucker and to Mussburger as they battle over Norville's destiny. Moses, who has control over time and an inside knowledge of everything that happens within the Hudsucker building, is not only a beneficent angel, however; he is also the narrator who, in delivering the monologues that open and close the film, points to its central motif: the circle. Not only is the circle a recurring spatial motif throughout the movie (when Norville tries, somewhat inarticulately, to explain his revolutionary new idea – 'Y'know, for kids!' – he merely holds up a slip of paper with a pencilled circle on it); it also relates to the passing of time. The film's narrative structure is circular, beginning and ending at roughly the same point in time; Moses introduces the imminent 1959 as 'the next ride round the sun' (as the camera zooms into focus on the circular clock – which is driven by circular cogs – ticking towards midnight); when Amy and Norville discuss the Hindu belief in reincarnation and an endless cycle of life, death and rebirth, she murmurs 'What goes around comes around'; Mussburger, who has a huge globe and a perpetual-motion toy in his office, decides to fight against Norville's success with the hula-hoop with the phrase: 'The music plays, the wheel turns, and our spin ain't over yet'; and, when time stands still,

Waring Hudsucker appears to Norville with a spinning halo hovering over his head (he calls it a celestial 'fad', its transient popularity resembling that of the hula-hoop and the frisbee).

The spatial and temporal dimensions of the circle are further linked to the concept of destiny: during the delightfully funny, beautifully choreographed and compiled montage that traces the rising fortunes of Norville's invention, a hoop, thrown out by a shopkeeper unable to shift his stock, rolls down the streets as if willed by its own sense of purpose, to land at the feet of the one small boy who has sufficient imagination to understand what to do with the new toy. Within seconds of screen-time, other kids catch on to the idea, the craze sweeps the nation, a boffin compares its dynamics to the spinning earth, and Norville's confidence in his future is amply rewarded: not for nothing did Mussburger sarcastically agree to develop his project with the words, 'Son, you've re-invented the wheel!' (Similarly, destiny

< 186 >

From mailroom boy to company president – Tim Robbins plays Norville Barnes in **The Hudsucker Proxy** (1994), the Coens' knowing pastiche of the cornball comic fables of the 40s.

had earlier led Norville to his Hudsucker job: after reading through the ads in a café, he leaves despondently, but his paper, blown by a mysterious breeze, follows him and wraps itself around his legs; when he picks it up, he finally sees the Hudsucker ad, with the company motto – 'The Future Is Now' – circled by the stain of his coffee cup.) Since destiny rules Norville's life, his present and future are inextricably intertwined: he first arrives at the Hudsucker building at the exact moment – 12 noon – when Waring is plunging to his death (or rebirth, as the film would suggest), and he himself is 'reborn' and sees his fortunes reversed when – at 12 midnight (the earth having turned around the sun) – he follows Waring's dive towards the sidewalk.

< 187 >

The Faustian aspect of *The Hudsucker Proxy* had, of course, been an element in all the Coens' earlier films, but it was in *Fargo* (1995) that the theme of a man selling his soul to evil with unforeseen disastrous results was treated most effectively. In order to get himself out of a financial crisis, Minnesota car sales-man Jerry Lundegaard (William H Macy) arranges for his wife Jean to be kidnapped by two strangers, Carl (Steve Buscemi) and Gaear (Peter Stormare); his plan is that Jean's father Wade (who owns the company where Jerry works, and who barely conceals his contempt for his son-in-law) will pay a million-dollar ransom, only $40,000 of which Jerry will hand over to the kid-nappers. The plan goes awry when Carl and Gaear kill a state trooper and a couple of passing drivers en route to their hideout; not only do the pair now demand $80,000 from Jerry, but a local police chief, the heavily pregnant Marge Gunderson (Frances McDormand), starts making enquiries about the murders. Though she knows nothing as yet about the kidnapping, her investigations lead her to the car salesroom, where she questions Jerry about a saloon (given to his partners in crime by way of part-payment for their scam). Wade, meanwhile, decides to deliver the ransom himself, but is killed by Carl who, shocked to find that the case contains $1,000,000, buries it in the snowy countryside, taking back to the hideout only $80,000, which he splits, as agreed, with Gaear. Gaear, however, who has murdered Jean for no reason other than sheer devilry, objects to Carl taking the saloon for himself, and kills him with a shovel. Marge, having again questioned Jerry, only to see him take flight in panic, hears about Jean's disappearance on her radio; putting two and two together, and seeing the missing saloon parked outside a cabin, she approaches Gaear, whom she finds forcing a body into a wood-chipper, and shoots him as he tries to escape. Before delivering him to her colleagues, she expresses amazement at how many people have died just because of money. Jerry is arrested in a motel, and Marge returns to her husband, congratulating him on the fact that one of his wildfowl paintings will grace a new three-cent postage stamp.

< **188** >

While *Fargo* reworked many themes and stylistic devices from the Coens' earlier work – the idea of deceit and distrust resulting in nobody knowing what anyone else is doing; the notion of a relatively minor misdemeanour leading to full-scale carnage; the repetition of dialogue and scenes to emphasise similarities and differences between characters; the juxtaposition of comedy and horrific violence – it displayed a new maturity in several respects. For one thing, the quieter, more classical visual style – the camera is largely static, and the compositions either long shots depicting the characters' relationship to their environment or close-ups accentuating their thoughts and emotions – allows for a more detailed, contemplative scrutiny of the characters than before, while the slower, less insistently snappy dialogue – resulting partly from the speech patterns of the Scandinavian population inhabiting Minnesota – seems genuinely human, rather than the product of deliberately colourful movie writing.

Most important, however, is the respectful depiction of the mutually supportive, if relentlessly banal, relationship between Marge and her husband Norm: not only was this the first time that the Coens had properly shown, without parody or cynicism, the existence and value of love, but the simplicity, warmth and tacit understanding of the couple's marriage highlights, by way of

Marge and Norm (Frances McMormand and John Carroll Lynch) represent a warmer core for the Coens at the heart of the cold moral wastes of **Fargo** (1995).

contrast, the sad, dysfunctional family life of Jerry, Jean, their son Scottie and Wade, and the endless bickering of Carl and Gaear. Moreover, Marge is that rare thing in American cinema: a genuinely 'good' person, who, nevertheless, is never sentimentalised. Whether inspecting corpses shot at the side of the road while suffering from morning sickness, or pragmatically waddling into the snow to fire a bullet into the fleeing Gaear's leg, she just gets on with her job, trusting to her professional expertise and common sense with hardly a thought for the danger she is putting herself in. She may be easy-going, but she's also firm and strong enough to deal with the likes of the uncooperative Jerry ('Sir, you have no call to get snippy with me; I'm just doing my job'), the demonic Gaear ('There's a lot more to life than a little money, y'know'), or an old schoolfriend who, after telling her a heart-rending – and as it transpires – wholly untrue story about his wife having died from leukaemia, makes an unsuccessful pass at her.

In stark contrast to Marge, Jerry, who is forever being used and abused by his wealthy, arrogant father-in-law, is so unhappy with his lot that he resorts to desperate deceit, placing Jean and his son at risk, lying to both his family and the kidnappers he hires, and unleashing, in the form of Gaear, a true force of uncontrollable, unrepentant evil. (Once again, it might be argued that Gaear is Jerry's id.) For Jerry and Wade, as for Carl and Gaear, human interaction has become an ongoing power struggle, a competitive arena where the contestants continually try to outwit each other in an ultimately futile effort to gain more money and have their own way; none of these characters knows a fraction of the happiness experienced by Marge and Norm in their boring but wholly trusting marriage, since, being dishonest themselves, they are constantly anxious about being cheated by others. It's as if they can't see the wood for the trees or – to borrow a visual metaphor from the film, which opens on a blinding white screen that only reveals itself to be a landscape shot after first a bounding woodpecker and then Jerry's car come into view through the blizzard – can't tell the earth from the sky, so murky is their view of the moral horizon.

Typically, the Coens scatter many delightfully witty moments through the film: the oft-repeated idiosyncrasies of the local dialect ('You're darned tootin', 'Okey-dokey, thanks a bunch', 'Oh geez!'); a fade from Carl and Gaear having wild sex with two hookers in a motel room to a shot of all four blearily staring at late-night TV; the complete inability of any witness to describe Carl except as 'kinda funny-lookin''; Marge and Norm's obsession with filling themselves with hot food at every opportunity; the consistently tacky décor of Middle America's diners, hotels and car showrooms; and Carl's attempts to appear sophisticated when he takes a hooker to a local nightspot and observes, 'Y'know, with Jose Feliciano, you got no complaints.' At the same time, the film achieves a gravitas unprecedented in the Coens' oeuvre, not only because of the horrific slaughter of innocent people, or

< **190** >

because of the warmth and devotion that makes Marge and Norm's marriage so rock-solid, but because finally we can't help but feel a sneaking sympathy for Jerry who, despite his blinkered moral vision, hardly bargains for the murderous nightmare that will befall his family simply because, oppressed by Wade and by his own panicky feelings of inadequacy, he makes a single, stupid error of judgement.

A kidnapping once again supplied the plot-motor for *The Big Lebowski* (1998), a quirky and relentlessly inventive variation on characters and situations from traditional hard-boiled crime stories such as were written by the likes of Raymond Chandler and Dashiel Hammett. After an opening prologue, spoken by an unseen narrator introducing the film's hero 'the Dude' to the strains of an antiquated cowboy ballad and shots of a tumbleweed being blown out of the desert into 90s Los Angeles (the movie is set around the time of the Gulf War) and down an empty freeway to a Pacific beach, the Dude (Jeff Bridges) – a laid-back, none-too-bright, dope-head slacker whose real name is Jeffrey Lebowski – returns home to his apartment to be beaten up by two thugs demanding the money his wife owes their pornographer boss Jackie Treehorn. After peeing on his carpet, they realise they've got the wrong Jeffrey Lebowski. The Dude – egged on by his bowling partners, the volatile Vietnam veteran Walter (John Goodman) and the slow-witted Donny (Steve Buscemi) – decides to visit the 'big' Jeffrey Lebowski (David Huddleston), a crippled philanthropist millionaire, and ask for recompense for the soiled rug. The man, openly contemptuous of the Dude's ex-hippy demeanour, refuses, but summons him back days later and asks him, in return for $20,000, to act as a courier in delivering the ransom for his now kidnapped wife Bunny, reckoning that the Dude might be able to confirm that the abductors are the same men who beat him up. The Dude agrees, but the handover goes wrong when Walter, convinced by a remark of Dude's that Bunny may have 'kidnapped' herself to pay off her debt to Treehorn, decides they should keep the money

< **191** >

for themselves and scares the waiting men off. After Dude's car, together with the briefcase containing the $1 million, is stolen from outside the bowling alley, he is consumed by guilt over Bunny's predicament, though the matter is further complicated when he is summoned by Lebowski's feminist-artist daughter Maude (Julianne Moore), who explains that the cash is not really her father's but in trust, and that in her opinion the kidnapping is a fiction dreamed up by her father in order to get his hands on the money, which she hires the Dude to recover for herself.

< **192** >

The plot thickens: Lebowski shows the Dude a toe allegedly cut from Bunny's foot by the kidnappers. A trio of German nihilists – one of whom the Dude recognises as a former porn-star associate of Bunny's – break into his flat and warn him off the case. The Dude and Walter trace the boy who stole the car but fail to regain the money. The two thugs return and take the Dude to Treehorn, who asks where Bunny is, wants the money as repayment for her debt, and spikes the Dude's drink before having him dumped and threatened with arrest at a local police precinct. The Dude is seduced by Maude, who then reveals she only wanted him to impregnate her, and learns that a man who has been following him for some time is a private eye hired by Bunny's parents. The truth finally dawns on the Dude and he visits Lebowski's mansion: Bunny is there, complete with toe – she was merely away visiting friends – and Lebowski confesses the kidnap story was a ruse by which he hoped to embezzle the $1 million from the philanthropic trust controlled by Maude. After discussing the affair with Donny at the bowling alley, the Dude and Walter are confronted by the three nihilists, who demand the money (still with the car thief or now with Treehorn – we never find out) by way of compensation for the hacked-off toe of one of their girlfriends; in the fight that ensues, Donny has a heart attack and dies. After haggling with the mortuary over the expense of an urn, his friends take his ashes in an empty coffee-tin and scatter them into the ocean. Consoling himself back at the bowling alley, the Dude once again bumps into a stranger in

'The Dude' (Jeff Bridges), seated here with his bowling partner Walter (John Goodman), becomes embroiled in a web of Chandleresque intrigue in early 90s LA in **The Big Lebowski** (1998)

cowboy garb, who after telling him to take it easy – 'I know you will' – turns to the camera to confide that he takes comfort from his friend's credo that 'The Dude abides', that it was a pretty good story (though he was sad to see Donny go), that there's another little Lebowski on the way, and that, as at the film's beginning, he's rambling again...

While the above synopsis may hint at the way the story in some ways resembles the novels of Chandler, with the Dude's involvement in the kidnapping case introducing him to a vivid gallery of variously wealthy, corrupt and dangerous characters and seeing him beaten up, drugged, duped, seduced, and threatened with arrest and murder, it hardly suggests just how much the film differs from the classic crime novels and movies about Southern California. For one thing, the tone is not only suspenseful but frequently comic (the Dude, Walter and Donny's banal, unfocused conversations are particularly delightful) and even, in places, surreally fantastic: when Dude is knocked out by Maude's henchmen, he dreams he is flying over LA, only to be brought tumbling towards death by the weight of the bowling ball on his arm, and when he is drugged by Treehorn, he fantasises he is in a bizarre Busby Berkeley-style musical called 'Gutterballs', complete with himself as a stud superstar, dancing girls in skittle headgear, Maude in Brunhilde costume, Saddam Hussein as a bowling-shoes attendant, and the nihilists coming at him with huge scissors, echoing the way they threatened his 'Johnson' when they warned him off the kidnapping case with a marmot thrown into his bath. Such scenes are not only amusing, virtuoso set-pieces, however; they also relate to the film's main theme, which is introduced by the cowboy narrator's opening ruminations about what it means to be a 'hero', and further extended by Lewbowski's musings, when he asks the Dude to act as his courier, about 'what makes a man?'

In this respect the prologue – with its intimations that we are about to watch a Western – and the two appearances in the bowling alley of the rambling, digressive cowboy stranger are not wacky red herrings but pertinent to the film as a whole: the Western, after all, is *the* genre about male heroism. Indeed, throughout the film, definitions of masculinity are suggested and tested. The 'big' Lebowski, a self-made man whose life is built on lies, seems to believe that power, riches and a young 'trophy wife' make a man; Walter, volatile, aggressively proud and prone to violence, equates virility with standing one's ground in the most macho way; Jesus (John Turturro in a memorably over-the-top caricature as an absurdly competitive bowler) resorts to peacock posturing, flamboyant fashion and taunting gestures and insults; Treehorn (Ben Gazzara, in another of the film's many judiciously cast cameos – others include Jon Polito and David Thewlis) puts his faith in business acumen and beach parties that extravagantly display nubile female flesh.

The Dude, however, seems to believe only in taking it easy –

< **194** >

bowling, listening to 'The Song of the Whale', smoking dope, driving around, having the occasional acid flashback... and, when the occasion demands, being prepared, as Lebowski puts it, to do the right thing. Though he initially takes the courier job as an opportunity to make some easy money, he does come to take his responsibility as the potential saviour of Bunny's life seriously, and so is motivated, finally, to seek out the truth behind her disappearance. The Dude may appear to be lazy and even slower-witted than Marge initially seemed in *Fargo*, but like her he has an honest integrity which makes him a good man – or if we accept the cowboy's cautious definition of heroism as being 'the man for his time and place', some kind of hero. It matters not that he appears to be plagued by anxieties about castration, female sexuality or whatever (besides the scissors and the marmot tossed into his bath, he also drops a lighted cigarette into his lap while driving, and is clearly perplexed by Maude's 'feminist' outspokenness about vaginas, nymphomania and so forth); the Dude is tolerant, loyal and finally confident and courageous enough to do the right thing, so that, like the cowboy, we are comforted by the fact that he 'abides'.

< **195** >

And just as the film echoes *Fargo* in its unsentimental study of a fundamentally decent person, so it echoes the earlier film's celebration of Marge and Norm's marriage with its portrait of the friendship between the Dude and Walter. With his violently angry outbursts (he's quite happy to turn a gun on a friend he suspects of cheating at the bowling alley), his endless allusions to Nam, and his inability to see the point of a conversation, Walter is evidently a headcase, and it is partly his fault that the Dude ends up in so much trouble. Nevertheless, as if aware that he at least means well, the Dude repeatedly forgives him, and when the two finally console each other with a hug on the cliffs above the Pacific, the scene is genuinely touching (even though the Coens, ever wary of maudlin sentimentality, have Walter miscalculate the wind and cover his friend in Donny's ashes). Compared to the way the other characters are only out for themselves, and are ready to cheat, steal and maim to get what they want, the relationship between the Dude and Walter, however flawed, seems humane indeed.

All of which may make *The Big Lebowski* sound overly serious; mercifully, the sheer wit and invention on view in the direction, the writing, the performances, the design, the sometimes inspired use of music on the soundtrack (which ranges from Dylan to Duke Ellington, Debbie Reynolds to Captain Beefheart, Mozart to Meredith Monk and from the Sons of the Pioneers to the theme from the *Branded* TV series), the smooth switches between 'naturalistic' suspense drama, comedy and fantasy all make the film enormously enjoyable. If it finally lacks the depth and assurance of *Barton Fink* and *Fargo* – which arguably remain, respectively, the Coens' most artistically audacious and most moving works – it is nevertheless a superbly amusing, offbeat and imaginative exercise in cinematic story-telling. (And should one suspect that the kidnapping plot was in the end something of a storm in a teacup, the Coens have covered themselves: as the cowboy confesses, in an admission not a little unlike the narration that closed *The Hudsucker Proxy*, the story was 'pretty good' but then again, he is prone to ramble...)

< **196** >

Despite returning repeatedly to semi-comic tales of violent crime, Joel and Ethan Coen have shown themselves to be remarkably versatile: each film, while sharing many stylistic and thematic elements with their other work, has not only differed from its predecessor in terms of mood and emphasis, but proved to be an ambitious step forward. While the Coens would probably argue that the repeated focus on double-cross and crossed purposes leading inevitably to carnage is a convenient dramatic strategy rather than a philosophical view of the human condition, there is an overall consistency to their films which distinguishes each as unmistakably a work by the Coen Brothers. They have brought a new formal sophistication to the crime genre, while their interest in metaphor has led them away from generic conventions to a more complex understanding of human psy-

chology than is usual in recent American cinema. Even before
Fargo they had established themselves as major, innovative talents,
but with the added warmth that characterised that film, they
seem to have reached a new maturity, their intellectual inventiveness being complemented by compassionate insights of emotional depth. It is surely significant that it is virtually impossible
fully to grasp or comprehend a Coen Brothers movie at first
viewing; the fact that the films all reveal more and more riches
with each repeated screening is testimony to their textual complexity and subtlety, and to the intriguingly skewed originality of
the fantastic but strangely familiar cinematic worlds they create.

< 197 >

8

spike Lee

< **199** >

Despite the sometimes controversial nature of the features Spike Lee made during the first decade of his professional career, there is no doubt whatsoever that he is one of the most important and influential directors in contemporary American cinema. Before Lee established himself with movies like *She's Gotta Have It* (1986), *School Daze* (1988) and *Do the Right Thing* (1989), African-Americans had found it extremely difficult to break into film-making; his success helped to pave the way for other black directors – including John Singleton, Carl Franklin, Robert Townsend, Charles Lane, the Hughes and Hudlin brothers, Mario Van Peebles, Matty Rich and Leslie Harris – to follow.

Lee's importance lay not only in the example he set for other would-be film-makers, but in his determination that his movies should depict, honestly and accurately, the everyday experiences of millions of African-Americans. Accordingly, few of his films have been overly concerned with a simple, classical, linear plot; more important to Lee has been the recreation of the texture of African-American life, and the exploration of both the external pressures and the internal divisions that affect that community. (In this respect, the occasional stylistic similarity of some of his films to those of Scorsese, which have done much the same for New York's Italian-American community, is perhaps unsurprising.)

If the latter aim has occasionally resulted in films marred by a rather schematic didacticism that sits uneasily with his talents as a faithful chronicler of the rich variety of African-American culture, there is no denying either his intelligence or his skill as a film-maker. His imaginative appropriation of stylistic tropes not only from, say, the French *nouvelle vague* or Scorsese (who taught him at NYU and co-produced Lee's *Clockers*, 1995) but from classical Hollywood film-making has resulted in movies that are at once accessible and distinctly at odds with the American mainstream.

< **200** >

Lee was born into an artistic, talented, middle-class family. His father Bill was a jazz bassist and composer, his mother a teacher, his brother David a photographer and his sister Joie and brother Cinque actors. He grew up in Brooklyn, the setting for many of his films, before attending first Morehouse College, Atlanta, then the film school at NYU. His graduation movie, *Joe's Bed-Stuy Barbershop: We Cut Heads* (1982), the first student film selected for the Lincoln Centre's prestigious New Directors/New Films series, also won an Academy Award. Despite this, to finance his first full-length feature, *She's Gotta Have It*, he was forced to forego studio investment and hustle the $175,000 budget from other sources. Whatever the film lacked in terms of production values – though elegantly shot in black and white, it looks a little rough and ready compared to his later work – it certainly made up for in inventiveness and originality. For one thing, the film's heroine, Nola Darling (Tracy Camila Johns), was a sexually liberated black woman, whose refusal to settle down with any of her lovers – the sincere, poetically inclined Jamie Overstreet, the rich, vain male model Greer Childs, and the wisecracking, immature Mars Blackmon (Lee himself) – Lee accepts rather than condemns. For another, the film eschews a classical, 'realist' storyline for a fragmented, impressionistic collage consisting of brief dramatic vignettes, documentary-style, straight-to-camera 'interviews' with the main characters, montages of stills and talking heads, and even – in colour – a dance sequence reminiscent of the classic MGM musicals of the 40s and 50s. The film opens with Nola waking up in her bed (which is surrounded by candles, as if it is a shrine to her sexuality and independence – she won't have sex anywhere else) and telling us that she has agreed to be interviewed only on condition that she can contest the notion that she's 'a freak' because she has three lovers. A doctor she later visits confirms that her interest in sex is healthy and normal, but her lovers are too self-centred and possessive to agree. Even after the caring but obsessive Jamie 'punishes' her promiscuity (though she says she loves him, he has come to the conclusion that she feels only physical desire, not love) by effectively raping her, violently forcing her to agree that her 'pussy' is his, not hers, Nola insists, at the end of the film, that she is 'not a one-man woman'; indeed, she has by then finished with all three of her lovers, and returns to her bed alone.

< **201** >

Although Nola's decision to maintain her independence entails a degree of solitude, the film – which, like much of Lee's later work, reveals him to be something of a sensualist – celebrates the fact that she remains confidently in control of her body. Conversely, her lovers give the impression that they will be 'complete' only if they are allowed to feel that they, and nobody else, take priority in her affections. Men, in fact, are seen as somewhat pathetic: an extremely funny montage shows a variety of men using pitifully clichéd chat-up lines (ranging from absurd professions of love to crude, arrogant promises about sexual prowess and penis size); Greer is ludicrously preoccupied with his stylish appearance (he takes an age neatly folding all his clothes before climbing into bed with Nola); Mars is like an eternal, boastful adolescent unable to take seriously anything other than his own fantasies; and Jamie's love for her is based not on true understanding but on a desire for her to be something she is not. Not that the movie's female characters are much more sympathetic to Nola's needs: her lesbian friend Opal finds it hard to accept that she's merely curious about the way women make love together and doesn't actually want to be seduced, while her three lovers' jilted girlfriends (whom Nola dreams about) accuse her of being an irresponsible home-breaker while simultaneously complaining that too many black men are either homosexual or in prison.

Though the film primarily focuses on Nola's needs as an individual, it's fair to say it also addresses wider aspects of society in general: Jamie, Mars and Greer are 'types' representing different facets of black manhood (solid bourgeois respectability, devil-may-care irresponsibility, upwardly mobile ambition). Here already, and rather schematically, Lee is tracing the diverse threads that make up the social tapestry of African-American life.

< 202 >

That tendency was still more evident in his first film for a Hollywood studio, *School Daze*, an energetic but not particularly amusing campus comedy in which the students and staff of Mission College (a Southern black university rather like Morehouse) serve as a microcosm of contemporary African-American society. As usual in the genre, much of the movie revolves around romantic intrigue and the rituals and rivalries of various cliques, fraternities and sororities, although Lee puts an original spin on the formula not only by interspersing the narrative with big song-and-dance numbers but by making the disparate groups representative of socio-political attitudes. The Gamma-Phi-Gamma fraternity, led by Big Brother Almighty (Giancarlo Esposito), is a reactionary group devoted to tradition and organised along robotic military lines; the Gamma Ray sorority (or 'Wannabees': wannabe white, that is) is distinguished by its members' light skin tones, tinted contact lenses and straightened hair, and by the fact that they readily serve, sexually and domestically, their fraternity counterparts; the 'Jigaboos' are a group of dark-skinned, afro-haired girls who seem to view most male students as 'dogs'; and finally, there is a small group of men led by radical black nationalist Dap (Larry Fishburne), who despises the fraternity his cousin Half-Pint (Lee) wants to get into and tries to persuade the other students to join him in pressurising the staff to divest the college of its investments in South Africa.

Little happens in the way of plot: Dap falls out and makes up with his dark-skinned girlfriend (who, when he objects to her pledging to a sorority, accuses him of going out with her only for political reasons); Half-Pint is accepted into the Gamma-Phi-Gammas after losing his virginity to Big Brother's Wannabee girlfriend Jane (whom the frat leader then dumps for obeying his order that she have sex with Half-Pint); and Dap, disgusted by this last incident, rouses the students and staff from their beds to tell them to 'Wake up!' – presumably to their responsibilities to one another and other blacks around the world, by putting aside the prejudices, traditions and attitudes that divide them as a community.

< **203** >

Though the film's message is both heartfelt and sensible, the execution leaves much to be desired. The characters are one-dimensional ciphers; the comedy is broad, obvious and – with the sole exception of the film's sharpest scene, which pits Dap and his friends against some townsfolk who voice their under-standable resentment against the privileged students – devoid of satirical bite. Many of the jibes the characters direct against each other are homophobic; the attitude to Jane in particular and the Wannabees in general is misogynist; and the musical scenes, while certainly lively, are clumsily staged and – with the exception of a number titled 'Straight and Nappy', in which the Wannabees and Jigaboos 'fight' with each other in a beauty salon – superfluous to the thematic and dramatic development of the narrative. Moreover, elements of the story don't make sense: why does Dap do his best to ensure that Big Brother accepts Half-Pint into the fraternity when he despises it so much? And why does Big Brother, a sworn enemy of Dap and his 'African mumbo-jumbo' throughout the film, suddenly join the black nationalist at the end of the film and, like him, stare meaningfully at the audience as Dap begs us, with an alarm clock ringing in the background, to 'Wake up'?

Happily, *Do the Right Thing*, which begins with the sound of an alarm clock as the radio DJ Mister Señor Love Daddy (Samuel

African-American Mookie (Spike Lee) and his Italian-American pizzeria-owning boss Sal (Danny Aiello) get heated as racial tension reaches boiling point in **Do The Right Thing** (1989)

L Jackson) exhorts his listeners to wake up, was an altogether more coherent, persuasive and dramatically satisfying call to action. The film charts 24 sweltering hours in the life of a few streets in the predominantly black and Puerto Rican Brooklyn neighborhood of Bedford-Stuyvesant, at the centre of which is a pizzeria owned and run by the Italian-American Sal (Danny Aiello), assisted none too enthusiastically by his sons Pino (John Turturro) and Vito (Richard Edson) and his delivery boy Mookie (Lee). Though Pino, who hates blacks, repeatedly tries to persuade his father to sell up and open a diner in their own neighborhood, Sal, like Vito, feels perfectly at home with the locals, who have been buying his food for 20 years. The heat, however, takes its toll on everyone. Pino berates Vito for befriending Mookie, who is in turn berated by his Puerto Rican girlfriend Tina (Rosie Perez) for spending so little time with her and their baby, and by his sister Jade (Joie Lee), whose apartment he lives in, for not getting a better job. Mookie's friend Buggin' Out (Esposito) complains that Sal's Wall of Fame photo display includes Italian-Americans but no blacks; Radio Raheem (Bill Nunn), who repeatedly plays Public Enemy's 'Fight the Power' at full volume on his ghetto-blaster wherever he goes, annoys Sal by refusing to turn it down in the pizzeria; Pino vents his anger at Smiley (Roger Smith), a speech-impaired derelict who sells photos of Malcolm X and Martin Luther King; and various long-term residents express their resentment about a Korean couple who have recently opened a corner foodstore.

< 205 >

By the evening, tempers are well and truly frayed, and when Buggin' Out, Smiley and Radio Raheem (armed with pounding stereo) storm into the pizzeria demanding that the Wall of Fame be replaced with pictures of African-Americans, Sal smashes the cassette player and a fight breaks out; when the cops intervene, one, losing his head, chokes the barely controllable Radio Raheem to death. After Mookie, already angry with Sal for having paid what he thinks is too much attention to his sister, throws a garbage can through Sal's window, a riot ensues, and the pizzeria is vandalised and burned to the ground. The next morning, after Mister Señor Love Daddy awakens the neighbourhood with the question 'Are we going to live together?', Mookie asks the despondent Sal for his wages, and encouraged by the DJ, goes to visit his son. As children play in the sun once more, Love Daddy exhorts listeners to register to vote, and the film closes on two quotes: the first, by Martin Luther King, argues that violence is immoral and self-defeating, while the second, by Malcolm X, argues that violence is excusable if resorted to in self-defence, and that the power held by bad people should be taken away from them by any means necessary; the final image is a photo of the two activists smiling together.

< **206** >

This final note of ambiguity – it's unclear whether Lee is condoning or condemning the riot as a reaction to Radio Raheem's death at the hands of the (perhaps predictably white) policeman – is symptomatic of his approach throughout the film, in which the only definitively 'bad' person is the openly racist Pino. (It may well be that this unsettling, provocative ambiguity – whether intentional or otherwise – is perhaps the only realistic response to a social and historical problem so complex and ingrained that it sometimes seems unresolvable.) For all their good intentions, many other characters, at one point or another, contrive to do the wrong thing: Sal, while generally beneficent to the locals and quite within his rights to decorate his pizzeria as he chooses, is a little insensitive to their feelings in his refusal to include a few African-Americans in his Wall of Fame; Buggin' Out is presented as a somewhat hysterical trouble-maker in his attempts to force Sal to change his mind; Raheem displays scant consideration for others in drowning out all other sounds with his ghettoblaster; and Mookie, unwilling to take responsibility for his actions towards his family, gives way to his anger over Raheem's death and to his suspicions about Sal's kindness towards his sister by indulging in a destructive act with no thought for its probable consequences. The point is not that Sal's pizzeria, which he has so proudly built up over 20 years, has been destroyed (more tragic, of course, is Raheem's death); what is crucial is that the riot's only achievement is to fan the flames of interracial hatred even higher. Lee understands the reasons for racial tension, but offers no easy solution to what is clearly a frighteningly urgent social problem (except perhaps for the suggestion that oppressed ethnic groups begin to take power for themselves by registering to vote and by putting aside the many differences that divide each group to achieve some semblance of political unity).

'Message' aside, *Do the Right Thing* is a remarkably powerful and sophisticated piece of work. Although the narrative observes the Aristotelian unities of place and time and the characters are sufficiently deftly drawn (and superbly played by the cast) never to become mere mouthpieces for a particular ideology or attitude, Lee's aesthetic is anything but 'realist'. As in *She's Gotta Have It*, the characters often speak directly to camera, most memorably when Radio Raheem uses his knuckleduster-like rings marked LOVE and HATE to deliver a parable about life's eternal conflict that is borrowed from *Night of the Hunter*, and in a montage of shots showing, in sequence, Mookie, Vito, a Puerto Rican, a white cop and the Korean store-owner each stringing together a series of insulting (albeit amusingly colourful) racial slurs aimed at, respectively, Italian-Americans, blacks, Koreans, Puerto Ricans and whites.

Certain characters function almost like a Greek chorus, notably three ageing, happily idle blacks who trade jokes, insults, anecdotes and comments on the events around them as they sit like spectators in front of a red brick wall. Action, too, is often stylised: as the fluidly mobile camera traces the criss-crossing paths of the various characters, their movements seem almost choreographed, an impression echoed in the evocative use of music. Much of this emanates from Mister Señor Love Daddy, whose comments on the world outside his studio remind us not only that it's crucial to stay cool, physically and emotionally, on such a hot day, but also, as he intones a long litany of musical names (from Louis Armstrong and John Coltrane to Otis

< **207** >

Redding and Prince), that the black community has a great artistic tradition to take pride in. (This celebrity roll-call, incidentally, plays in serious counterpoint to one of the film's most tellingly witty scenes, in which Pino, forced by Mookie to admit that he admires Magic Johnson, Prince and Eddie Murphy, is put into the absurd position of insisting that his heroes are not 'niggers' or even black, but 'more than black'.)

Most impressive of all, perhaps, is Lee's assured sense of pace and mood: as the film progresses, the scenes get more languid during the midday heat, then steadily become less comic and more tautly edited as evening approaches until, with Raheem, Smiley and Buggin' Out's sudden, unwelcome dash into the pizzeria to confront Sal, the violence erupts in a matter of seconds, so that no one involved even has time to think about doing the right thing. However easily the terrifying, fatal riot that ensues might have been avoided, the forceful narrative thrust suggests there is also, sadly, a dreadful inevitability to the way the petty tensions that plague the community finally turn into outright, undiscriminating physical violence.

The escalating tension between conflicting needs and desires that both defines the Bed-Stuy community and drives the narrative in *Do the Right Thing* recurred in a more intimate context in *Mo' Better Blues* (1990), Lee's response to what he believed were the negative stereotypes about black jazz musicians conveyed in films by white directors such as *Round Midnight* (Bertrand Tavernier, 1986) and *Bird* (Clint Eastwood, 1988). The film is not only about the divisions within a rising New York jazz quintet, but within its leader Bleek Gilliam (Denzel Washington), whose single-minded devotion to improving his trumpet expertise had been fostered by his mother in the late 60s when, as a child in Brooklyn, he had been forced to persevere with his practice at home rather than go out and play with his friends. As a result, Bleek has grown up to view relationships and responsibilities to others as secondary to the demands placed upon him by his artistic ambitions; not only is he unable to commit fully to

< **208** >

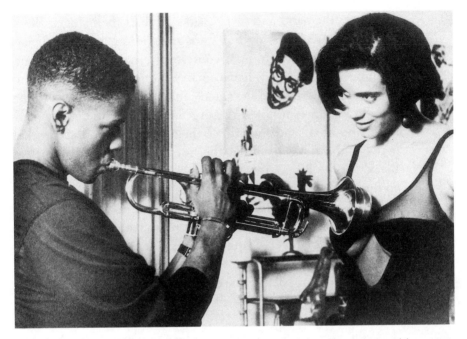

Jazzman Bleek Gilliam (Denzel Washington) puts artistic ambition before relationships and responsibilities in Lee's **Mo' Better Blues** (1990) – pictured with Cynda Williams as singer Clarke Betancourt.

either of his two lovers – the teacher Indigo (Joie Lee) and the aspiring singer Clarke (Cynda Williams), whom he refuses to help professionally – but his not entirely democratic leadership of the band means that he is often at loggerheads with Shadow (Wesley Snipes), a saxophonist whose spontaneous solos are frowned on by both Bleek and his friend Giant (Lee), the band's manager who is addicted to gambling. The film sketches in these and other tensions – such as the band's attribution of the unpunctual tendencies of pianist Left Hand (Giancarlo Esposito) to his excessive affection for his white, French girlfriend – before focusing more squarely on Bleek, who faces a crisis when both Indigo and Clarke decide that they no longer wish to share him, and when, protecting Giant from thugs hired by his creditors, he is so violently beaten that his mouth is badly injured. After a year's absence from the music scene, during which time Shadow takes over the band and gives Clarke a job as their singer, Bleek returns to guest at a gig but finds that he can no longer play. Depressed, he visits Indigo, confesses he has been selfish and inconsiderate, and begs her to marry him: it is the only way to save his life. Hesitantly, she agrees, and in a final montage, to the sound of John Coltrane's 'A Love Supreme', we see their marriage, the birth and growth of their son and, in a scene that matches the film's opening, the boy practising the trumpet at Bleek's family home: this time, however, the child is allowed to go out and play in the street with his friends.

< **210** >

While *Mo' Better Blues* certainly succeeds in avoiding the traditional depiction of the black jazz musician's life as ruined by drugs and alcohol, it simply replaces one cliché with another: that of the driven artist who can't relate properly to his lovers and friends, who can't balance the conflicting demands of life and art. Only when Bleek finds himself physically unable to play does he finally admit his need for and responsibilities to others. The turning point comes when he is beaten by Giant's creditors, immediately prior to which he sees them telling his unconscious friend to 'Wake up!' Moreover, the film's 'happy ending' is predicated on the fact that Indigo, hitherto treated selfishly by Bleek, is finally prepared to sacrifice her own independence to his needs. Indeed, the film's depiction of women leaves something to be desired. Indigo and Clarke are presented merely as ciphers, so bereft of individual characteristics that they are viewed as virtually interchangeable (both by the bewildered Bleek, and by the film which, in a cleverly edited scene which brings the two women together through montage, has him first making love with and then being berated by them at the same time), while in the opening sequence the musician's mother is depicted as needlessly harsh and disciplinarian. Lee also lay himself open to charges of anti-Semitic stereotyping in his one-dimensional portrayal of the Flatbush brothers (John and Nicholas Turturro), the owners of the club at which Bleek's band plays: not only are they exploitative and penny-pinching, refusing to renegotiate the band's contract as they pull in ever larger audiences, but the pair's identical gestures and speech patterns rob them of individuality, turning them into grotesque comic-strip caricatures.

That said, *Mo' Better Blues* does have its virtues. Ernest Dickerson's warm, fluid camerawork complements the mostly smooth, lyrical jazz (played and composed, in fact, by stalwarts of the modern scene like Branford Marsalis, Terence Blanchard and Donald Harrison) which accurately reflects the somewhat conservative approach to jazz adopted by the smartly suited groups of the 80s. (It might have been more interesting to focus the film more closely on Shadow, whose feeling for the liberating, spontaneous, wilder aspects of the music is rather more appealing than Bleek's tight-assed, almost academic attitude towards improvisation.)

< 211 >

The ensemble scenes between the members of the band also ring true, displaying a vitality and exuberance sadly lacking in much of the movie, which often seems undecided as to whether it is a love story, a buddy movie, or a film which uses the jazz world as a microcosm of black cultural life, in which the achievements and talents of African-Americans are exploited by whites while being neglected or underrated by blacks themselves. (At one point Bleek complains that he's tired of playing to everybody but his own people, to which Shadow replies, with some justification, that he should play what people want to hear, echoing his opinion, stated earlier to Clarke, that 'All Bleek cares about is Bleek.') In the end, in fact, it is Bleek's egocentricity that robs the film of its emotional punch: there is little reason for us to care deeply about him, so that his final 'redemption' through love seems to be merely a neat, contrived way of bringing the movie to a close.

Rather better, if at times similarly unfocused, was Lee's next film, *Jungle Fever* (1991), a profoundly ambiguous study of the myths and prejudices surrounding the subject of inter-racial sex. The aptly named Flipper Purify (Wesley Snipes) – he turns away from his destiny for a while, but soon recognises the error of his ways – is a well-to-do architect living happily in Harlem with his wife Drew (Lonette McKee) and daughter Ming. Embarking impulsively on an affair with his secretary Angie (Annabella Sciorra), a working-class Italian-American who also keeps house for her father and two brothers in Bensonhurst, Flipper is found out when the wife of his friend Cyrus (Lee) tells Drew about the romance. Thrown out, he goes to stay with his parents, but his conservative, religious father (Ossie Davis), who has already banned Flipper's crack-addict brother Gator (Samuel L Jackson) from his home, strongly disapproves of adultery, and when Angie is beaten by her irate, racist father, the couple move into an apartment together. Their happiness is soon eroded, however, by the racism around them, and even though Flipper's attempts to make up with Drew are unsuccessful, he breaks with Angie, who returns to her family. Gator, meanwhile, has stolen his parents' television; Flipper tracks him down to a crack den but, finding it has been sold for drug-money, disowns him. When their father returns home to find Gator threatening his wife for more money, he shoots him dead. Flipper, meanwhile, is now allowed occasional visits to Drew and Ming. As he walks the girl to school, a crack addict offers to fellate him for two dollars; hugging Ming close to him, Flipper screams 'No'.

Like *Do the Right Thing*, *Jungle Fever* – which was inspired partly by the real-life murder of Yusuf Hawkins, a young African-American who visited the Bensonhurst neighbourhood to buy a car and was killed by Italian-Americans for (in Lee's words) 'alleged reckless eyeballing' – impresses through its use of a wide range of characters to explore attitudes to racial interaction. Angie's intensely macho family and the Italian-Americans who frequent the diner run by her friend Paulie (John Turturro) simply hate blacks and abhor the idea of white women being sullied by sexual contact with black men; Drew and her friends, on the other hand, who moan that too many black males are gay, drug-addicts and bad fathers, believe that white women throw themselves at black men out of a fascination with the 'Zulu dick' myth

< **212** >

of sexual prowess, and that black men have been conditioned to prefer light-skinned women, the ultimate trophy being a white woman. Flipper's father, meanwhile, who has a picture of a white Christ on his wall, simply insists (apparently due to some private guilt about his own past) that the sins of the flesh are the work of the Devil. Even Flipper is adamant that he'd never want to father mixed-race children and, when he breaks with Angie, claims they were each attracted to the other mainly out of curiosity about what it would be like to have sex with a person of a different colour.

< 213 >

If there's no evidence that Lee himself agreed with any of these myths, which are rooted in notions of racial purity, he does at least appear to have been sympathetic, while making the film, to the deeply conservative, even reactionary idea that miscegenation derives from curiosity rather than from real sexual attraction, let alone love (reserved in the movie for Flipper and Drew's initially blissful marriage). It is as if he feels, like Flipper at the film's end, that since mixed-race relationships are about curiosity rather than love, it isn't worth enduring the racist hostility they provoke; besides, people will probably be happier with their own kind. A degree of ambivalence nevertheless remains, expressed in Angie's silence when Flipper dismisses their feelings as misguided curiosity, in the genuinely sensual way in which Lee stages and photographs their couplings, and in Paulie's decision, despite being insulted and beaten up by his resolutely separatist customers, to go ahead with his plans to date an African-American woman.

Though the film's exploration of various racist myths takes place within a overall structure that is deeply problematic (the simplistic contrast between Flipper's idealised middle-class home life and Angie's primitively patriarchal family does not help in this respect), the characterisation is dramatically rich enough to counterbalance any schematic/didactic flaws in the narrative. The interplay between the Italian-Americans at Paulie's diner and between the women who console Drew in her solitude reveals an ear for dialogue that makes the groups' respective racist remarks all too plausibly symptomatic of the oppressive attitudes Flipper and Angie face; likewise, a black waitress who pointedly ignores them as they try to order, and two white cops who assume Flipper is about to rape Angie while they are fooling around in the street, exemplify the hostile attitudes even total strangers take towards mixed-race lovers prepared to flaunt their relationship publicly. (That said, whether the world still frowns on mixed-race romance quite as much as Lee seems to believe it does is a moot point.) Moreover, Lee often avoids cliché by means of unexpected twists and reversals. It is Flipper's family, rather than the Italian-Americans, who are financially well-off; at the same time, while his middle-class career and home life are at first presented in a fairly idealised light, we soon see that, for all his affluence, he suffers indignities at the hands of white bosses who refuse to make him a business partner; what is more, his parents' equally middle-class home has produced not just an architect but a crack addict. (Sadly, while the scenes with Gator 'fill out' this facet of Flipper's background, and point to a serious problem faced by the black community, they also interrupt the film's narrative flow and distract our attention away from its concern with inter-racial relationships.)

< 214 >

Impressive, amidst all the racist and sexist contempt and hostility, are the film's occasional moments of tenderness: not just Flipper and Angie's early courtship, but Angie's confessional, mutually supportive friendship with Paulie, and Flipper's relationship with his daughter. Indeed, such scenes indicate, perhaps, the most crucial shortcoming of the treatment of Flipper and Angie's affair. Had Lee actually allowed love, as opposed to physical sexuality, to develop as an openly admissible factor in their brief encounter, the film would have benefitted from greater depth and complexity. As it stands, there is no real sense of Flipper's emotional investment in their affair (nor do we even find out what happens to Angie when she returns home), so that when he makes up with Drew, his view of life apparently as unchanged as that of the other characters in the film, our final impression may be that (with the exception of Gator's death) we have witnessed a storm in a teacup.

Almost as if to make amends for this shortcoming, Lee's next film, *Malcolm X* (1992), was precisely about man's capacity – and need – to change, to wake up to socio-political, spiritual and moral horizons that stretch beyond personal experience. When Lee first announced his intentions of making a biographical film of the late black leader, there was a common assumption – following what some had seen as the separatist ideology underlying *Jungle Fever* – that the film would quite probably feature a hard-line endorsement of the segregationist tenets of the Nation of Islam as advocated by Malcolm while under the spell of the movement's leader, Elijah Mohammad. To many, then, it came as something of a surprise when the film's final scenes voiced a more concil-iatory, optimistic view than that which simply pointed out the evils of the white man (the 'greatest murderer, kidnapper, robber and enslaver on earth') as listed during its opening credits.

< 215 >

In tracing Malcolm's life and achievements, the film falls into three distinct parts. The first, covering the period from the mid-40s to 1952, follows his progress from a smalltime Boston hus-tler (known as 'Red' due to his dyed hair) who survives partly by dating rich white women, to a spell in Charleston State Prison after turning to crime under the far from benign influence of a Harlem numbers-racketeer. At first, Malcolm's proud contempt for his white warders conspires only to land him in solitary; but after meeting Baines, a prisoner whose resistance takes the more purposeful form of self-education and enlightenment through the Islamic teachings of Elijah Muhammad, Malcolm begins to read and hence to understand the history, methods and implica-tions of the white man's oppression of the black race.

The second part of the film traces his development as a thinker and spiritual/political leader in the outside world where, under Elijah Muhammad's aegis, he helps to raise African-Americans' awareness of their plight so successfully that he is viewed with suspicion not only by the authorities, who fear a violent outcome to his denunciations of the white man as the devil, but by the leaders of the Nation of Islam itself, who see him as overly ambitious and powerful, and who are embarrassed when Malcolm implies that the assassination of John F Kennedy was justifiable.

In the third part, Malcolm, banned by Elijah Muhammad from making further public speeches, and fearing for the lives of his family after hearing rumours that the NOI plans to take its revenge on him for setting up a rival organisation called Muslim Mosque Incorporated, makes a pilgrimage to Mecca and the Middle East, where his encounters with white Muslims lead him to renounce his earlier separatist views. Returning home, he finds he is still reviled by whites and followers of NOI alike. In 1965, soon after his house has been firebombed, he is killed by gunmen (presumably working for the NOI, though Malcolm had his suspicions that the NOI was colluding with other bodies) as he takes the stage at a public meeting.

Despite a number of artistic misjudgements which allow the film to slide into the realm of sentimental hagiography – most notably the introduction of Elijah Muhammad (Al Freeman Jr) when he appears as a vision of glowing, smiling, beneficent wisdom in Malcolm's prison cell, and the final coda, in which none other than Nelson Mandela stands up before a schoolroom of small, cute kids to pay tribute to Malcolm's enduring influence – *Malcolm X* remains impressive both for its epic sweep and for its plausible account of its protagonist's transformation from devil-may-care, politically unaware hustler to profoundly influential demagogue.

The early part of the film, with its brilliantly choreographed dance sequence and noir-ish scenes of Malcolm's involvement with the Harlem underworld, hardly prepare one for the comparative austerity of the central section, which concentrates more on subdued conversational encounters – with Elijah Muhammad, with Malcolm's wife-to-be Sister Betty (Angela

< **216** >

Bassett), and with his former partners in crime Shorty (Lee) and Archie (Delroy Lindo) – than on action, or for the horizon-expanding trip to Mecca and Egypt which, in the final part, mirrors Malcolm's deeper grasp of experiences besides his own. Holding these disparate parts together is Denzel Washington's sensitive, understated, dignified performance, which never downplays the stubborn pride or even the vengeful hatred that were part and parcel of his rise to power (flashbacks recall how his minister father was killed in Nebraska by the Ku Klux Klan – the murder was covered up as a suicide – in the 30s).

Also crucial to the film's coherence, however, is the way Lee constantly emphasises the fact that Malcolm's life is itself an education of sorts. Whether he is the 'country nigger' taught to dress less flamboyantly when he arrives in Harlem; the troublesome prisoner encouraged by Baines to think about history, language and God, and to take pride in his race rather than try vainly to

< **217** >

Denzel Washington plays the lead in **Malcolm X** (1992). The film impresses through the diversity of visual styles used to convey the education, spiritual and moral progress of a remarkable individual.

imitate the white man's ways; the disciple of Elijah Muhammad forced reluctantly to recognise the existence of devious politicking within the NOI (typically for Lee, when Betty asks him to consider if Baines is really his friend, she tells him to 'Wake up'); or the segregationist who comes to see that morality is not simply a question of black and white – throughout the film, Malcolm's life is seen as a learning curve which brings him closer to the truth. (Hence that schoolroom coda may be justified thematically, even if it is dramatically embarrassing.) In many respects, then, since *Malcolm X* allows its characters to develop, it is subtler than Lee's earlier work in which characters reflect different attitudes and experiences but never change very much.

< 218 >

Technically, too, the film impresses through diversity. Not only because its three parts adopt appropriately different visual styles (the central section, which is most concerned with the ideas behind Malcolm's oratory, is the most spatially static and confined of the three). But because, as Malcolm becomes more of a public figure whose every word is noted by the NOI, the FBI and all those interested in the cultural advancement (or, indeed, the oppression) of African-Americans, Lee intersperses the narrative with 'fake' black and white documentary-style footage reminiscent of television and newsreels to emphasise how Malcolm's teachings were disseminated across the nation.

Malcolm's enduring relevance to the present and future of African-American life is also made plain, both by the opening credits sequence (which intercuts the American flag burning into the shape of an 'X' with footage of Rodney King being beaten by the LA police) and by the insistence that racial oppression has been a constant historical force against which progress can yet be made, from the flashbacks to the Klan's murder of Malcolm's father to the appearance of a free Mandela in the final sequence.

The only major flaw in the film is its negative attitude towards women, who are shown almost exclusively as poor black girls doomed for prostitution, white women who lust after the forbidden thrill of black flesh, or in the case of the followers of the

NOI, saintly types who happily submit to Elijah Muhammad's belief that women 'have too much of the devil in them' and should simply sew, cook, raise children and be supportive of their men. (Indeed, even the notion that a man should marry only if he finds a woman who is half his age and the right height seems to be accepted by the film; it appears that Lee, in trying to present as positive an image of the NOI as possible, decided to sidestep any opportunity for criticising such archaically misogynist ideas, just as in the end he leaves it rather unclear as to whether Elijah Muhammad and the NOI were really behind Malcolm's assassination.) That said, *Malcolm X* must surely be seen as one of Lee's most impressive efforts, a lucid and intelligent attempt to explore political, spiritual and moral ideas through the life of a remarkable individual.

< **219** >

Since *Malcolm X*, which with its large cast, its recreation of the 40s and 50s, its scenes shot in the Middle East, and its 201-minutes running time, was Lee's biggest, most complex film by far, he has tended to work on a smaller, more intimate scale, as if going back to his roots. That, certainly, seems to have been the thinking behind *Crooklyn* (1994), a semi-autobiographical tale of a young girl from a middle-class Brooklyn family growing up in the early 70s, co-written with the director's brother and sister Cinque and Joie. In terms of plotting, little happens: teacher and mother Carolyn (Alfre Woodard) manages to hold the Carmichael family together, instilling a sense of discipline and order into her one daughter, Troy, and her four sons, while husband Woody (Delroy Lindo), a none too successful jazz musician, prefers to win their affections with a soft touch. When Woody sides with the rowdy children against her, Carolyn asks him to leave; when he is allowed to return after a few days, the fact that he has failed to pay the electricity bill only makes matters worse, and Carolyn sends Troy to spend the summer with relatives in Virginia. While the girl gets on well with her cousin Viola, she soon tires of her deeply religious, disciplinarian aunt. Returning home, she is met by another aunt and uncle who inform her that her mother is in hospital. After Carolyn dies, Troy reluctantly attends her funeral, and for a while is haunted by dreams that her mother is still alive; eventually, however, she eventually comes to terms with the death, and begins to take special care of Jimmy, the youngest of her idle and less responsible brothers.

Although, as ever with Lee, the film is partly constructed around social conflict – most notably between Woody, reluctant to compromise his art by acting responsibly as the family bread-winner, and Carolyn, whose pragmatic desire to give her family a decent upbringing frequently alienates both husband and children – much of it is simply concerned with the texture of life as seen through the eyes of nine-year-old Troy. Accordingly, many of the scenes are brief impressionistic vignettes of the children arguing together over the dinner table, playing in the street, or singing along together to *The Partridge Family* on television. The tone, for the most part, is nostalgic and gently comic: the Brooklyn on view seems to be a far safer, happier place than the explosive melting-pot shown in *Do the Right Thing*, and much innocent fun is had at the expense of the fads – sartorial, tonsorial and cultural – of the early 70s, making it Lee's warmest and least didactic film to date. As if to underline the fact that the movie is partly a hymn to happier times – at least for Troy, before her mother's sudden death thrusts her closer to the adult world of responsibility, loss and grief – Lee fills the soundtrack with an evocative roster of soul and pop classics.

Dramatically, however, the film is deeply flawed, not merely because the rather routine melodrama of the later scenes follows uneasily upon the predominantly laid-back humour that offsets the occasional domestic crises of the film's first hour, but because, to accentuate the strangeness and claustrophobia felt by Troy when she stays with her aunt in Virginia, Lee squeezes the image with an anamorphic lens: the effect may make metaphorical sense but, deployed throughout a sequence lasting approximately 20 minutes, it is clumsy, tiresome and heavy-handed. Finally,

< 220 >

too, the rag-bag, anecdotal form of the piece as a whole is too weak and loose a structure on which to hang the narrative peg of Troy's eventual shift from childhood innocence towards adolescent experience, and the implication – with Troy taking up the mantle of her mother's responsibility to her comparatively lazy, live-for-the-moment brothers – that history is about to repeat itself.

An altogether darker picture of the lives of young African-Americans was to be found in *Clockers*, an adaptation of Richard Price's novel about drug-related violence in a Brooklyn housing project. Sixteen-year-old Strike (Mekhi Pfifer) makes his money selling drugs on the street, and is promised 'promotion' by local crack dealer Rodney (Delroy Lindo) if he kills Darryl, whom Rodney claims has been cheating him. Trying to work up courage, Strike tells his strait-laced brother Victor (Isaiah Washington) that Darryl deserves to die for beating up a teenage girl, and is surprised when Victor says he may know someone who could do the job. After Darryl is found dead, Victor turns himself over to the police, saying he killed him in self-defence, but detective Rocco Klein (Harvey Keitel), believing he's covering for Strike, begins to pressurise the younger brother, who is already being harangued by local cop Andre and by the mother of Tyrone, a child who hero-worships Strike and wants to get into dealing himself. When Rocco arrests Rodney, implying that Strike betrayed him, Strike decides to leave the neighbourhood and goes to say farewell to his mother and sister-in-law: Errol, an ailing junkie who works for Rodney, waits for him to leave his mother's apartment, but before he can shoot Strike, Tyrone, who has 'borrowed' his idol's gun, kills Errol. Andre begs clemency of Rocco, who shows mercy to Tyrone when the child tells him where he got the gun. Beaten up by Andre for getting Tyrone into trouble, and pursued by Rodney, Strike takes refuge in the police station, where Rocco tries to make him confess to Darryl's murder, until his mother arrives and admits that it was indeed Victor who committed the crime in a moment of crazed depres-

< 221 >

Rocco Klein (Harvey Keitel) at the 'office' bench of drug-dealer Strike Dunham (Mekhi Pfifer) in **Clockers** (1995). Lee tackles the problems of crime and violence in a culturally and economically impoverished environment.

sion. Strike's car having been smashed up by Rodney, Rocco drives the boy to Penn Station, where he takes a train west to start a new life.

In adapting Price's novel with the author, Lee jettisoned much of the book's material on Rocco Klein's off-duty life and his relationship with his less idealistic partner Mazilli (John Turturro) in favour of focusing on the dilemmas faced by Strike. Raised in the impoverished projects, where drug-dealing and crime have become a short-term means of survival for the young, Strike is a 'clocker' (the lowest form of dealer) not because he takes drugs – he doesn't – but because it provides the money which he believes will eventually take him out of the projects; he doesn't care that he is 'dealing death' (as Tyrone's mother puts it) until it begins to affect him directly, with Victor in prison and Tyrone involved in a manslaughter case. Only then does he fully realise the consequences of his actions, and – with a firm but helping hand from the likes of Rocco and Andre – decide to start out afresh, away from the violent Rodney, the AIDS-ridden Errol, and the other clockers in the neighbourhood.

As a crime mystery or thriller, *Clockers* lacks surprise and suspense: right from the start it's pretty clear that Strike did not kill Darryl, while a couple of scenes depicting his innocent, childlike obsession with model trains suggest that he'll finally make it safely out of town. (The closing shots of the film evoke his feeling of freedom as he looks out on the wide-open vistas of the western landscape at sunset, even though a shot of one of his fellow clockers lying dead on the sidewalk reminds us that the problems facing poor young blacks still persist.) Rather, Lee is concerned to show the difficulty of avoiding crime and violence in a culturally and economically impoverished environment: even the law-abiding Victor, who has to hold down two jobs in order to support his family, is driven to kill in a fit of despair. With comparatively wealthy kingpins like Rodney preaching a religion of self-improvement through dirty money, the kids face temptation on every street corner, while even younger children like Tyrone, inured to violence not only by seeing how older kids behave but by playing video games and reading comic strips, are in danger of following suit. Be it with drugs or guns, young African-Americans are killing each other; as the film shows, unless those in power start caring enough about the black underclass to do something to stop them killing each other, the circle of violence will remain unbroken.

< 223 >

Accordingly, *Clockers* is without doubt Lee's darkest movie to date. Images of violence abound, from the opening credits' montage of police-style photos of black men's bodies torn apart by bullets, through the shots of crowds staring impassively at Darryl's corpse, to the comic strips and video games enjoyed by Tyrone. The location camerawork has a raw, grainy, vérité feel, highlighting the grim reality of life in the projects, while the scenes of interrogation in the police precinct, shot in high-contrast tones verging on black and white, have the quality of a claustrophobic nightmare. And if, finally, the film has little to say that is genuinely original about the limited options faced by young blacks living in impoverished inner-city environments, it performs a skilful balancing act, refraining from sentimentality, didacticism and sensationalism. Moreover, its absolute refusal to romanticise, glamorise or condone any kind of violence whatsoever places it at an admirable distance from many other ''hood' movies of the period, which tended to view the macho behaviour of the young with a degree of complacency or even approval.

< 224 >

While *Clockers* offered a despairing account of the prospects facing many poor young black men in contemporary America, *Girl 6* (1996) took a light-hearted look at the options available to young black women, or at least one young woman (Theresa Randle) who fantasises about following in the footsteps of her idol, Dorothy Dandridge, to make it as a famous actress. The reality, of course, is rather different: after walking out of an audition because the hotshot film director (played by Quentin Tarantino) insists she take her top off, Judy, tired of poorly paid jobs, finds work with a phone-sex company. Though her neighbour Jimmy (Lee) is appalled, 'Girl 6', as she is known at the office, gets on well with her colleagues, and soon finds she enjoys the work: she manages to satisfy her callers, retains control of her body, and gets well paid into the bargain. The job has its drawbacks, however, when she becomes too involved in it: after she becomes attracted to one regular caller, she arranges to meet him but is stood up, while another client, who has disturbingly sadistic tastes, reveals that he knows where she lives. Distraught, she decides to give up her job and head for California, planning to resume her career as an actress. After bidding farewell to her ex-husband, and giving some of her earnings to a young girl who is recovering from having fallen down a lift shaft, Judy attends a Hollywood audition...where the director asks her to take her top off. She refuses, but completes the monologue she has started before calmly walking out, integrity intact.

Spike Lee and Theresa Randle in **Girl 6** (1996) – an amusing, off-beat exploration of the way women may be constrained by being defined as types, and a return to the themes of **She's Gotta Have It**.

It is far from insignificant that the monologue Judy quotes at each of her auditions is actually Nola Darling's speech from the opening of *She's Gotta Have It*. Not only was Lee responding, perhaps, to those critics who had complained about his lack of interest in creating fully rounded female characters by reminding them that his very first feature centred on a proudly independent woman; the allusion to the earlier film also serves to introduce the theme of a woman whose multi-faceted, arguably 'disreputable' character is actually a means of self-determination (whereas Nola was regarded as a 'freak' because of her decision to have three lovers, the celibate Judy is viewed with suspicion by the men in her life because she works as a phone-sex operator).

But *Girl 6* also bears a resemblance to Lee's feature début in that it adopts a more free-wheeling, experimental narrative style than most of his work: while there is little 'story' as such, the narrative is fleshed out with numerous fantasy sequences in which Judy, in an array of wigs and costumes, impersonates both female stars (most notably Dandridge and blaxploitation star Pam Grier) and female stereotypes (the sharp-suited career-woman, the blonde bimbo, etc). As a result, the film both serves up some amusingly offbeat genre parodies and explores the way we try to restrict women by defining them as types; Judy resists such categorisation since, as a would-be actress and a phone-sex operator who plays, unseen, upon her callers' fantasies, she can become anyone (and, indeed, any colour) she wants.

< 226 >

Except, of course, that she can't; in her work at least, the client ultimately calls the tune. Indeed, the film's attitude to her job is, typically for Lee, ambivalent: on the one hand, the office where she works is seen as an efficient, warmly supportive matriarchal environment, and Judy initially finds her work oddly therapeutic; on the other, she gets so involved in it that she virtually has a breakdown, especially when the sadistic caller gets too close. (The threat of punitive violence is reminiscent of Jamie's rape of Nola in *She's Gotta Have It*.) Not that Lee is making any particularly serious points in the film, whether about the illusory appeal of stardom, the way men think about women, the career options available to black women, or the pros and cons of the sex industry: rather, the film is a scatter-shot comedy-fantasy, full of bright colours and elegant camera movements, and centred on a genuinely playful approach to the question of human identity. Indeed, for all its energy, visual invention, and the engaging versatility of Randle's performance, the film finally gives the impression of being rather too slight, unfocused and incoherent for its own good. (Quite what Judy's fascination with the girl who fell down the lift shaft is all about is anyone's guess.) Despite the several insights it offers en route – for example, the idea that whiteness has become a *sine qua non* for female movie stardom – by the time it reaches its conclusion, the film never quite seems to add up to the sum of its parts.

The same might be said of the very different *Get on the Bus* (1996), a determinedly small-scale film (it cost only $2.5 million) which paradoxically sets out to convey some idea of the wide diversity of African-American manhood. The film is basically a road-movie: the bus in question is filled with a cross-section of black men whose only common aim, initially, is to attend the Million Man March organised by the Muslim leader Louis Farrakhan in Washington DC in October 1995. As the group make their three-day journey from South Central LA, the tensions and attitudes that divide African-American men come to the fore. An apolitical delinquent teenager reluctantly goes along simply because he is shackled, by dint of a court order, to his estranged father; a boastful actor argues constantly with the other passengers, most notably a gay couple in the process of breaking up; an old man is travelling to the march to make amends for the fact that he was too afraid of losing his job to attend a demonstration in the 60s; a light-skinned cop (his mother was white) discovers that a now devout Muslim used to be a gangbanger and threatens to turn him in for murder upon their return; a young film student shoots his fellow travellers' conversations with a video camera; a white Jewish driver, though an avowed liberal, hands the wheel over to the group's organiser because he disapproves of Farrakhan's anti-Semitic statements; and a black self-made businessmen given a lift in Tennessee is ejected from the bus after admitting that he simply sees the march as an opportunity to network and offending the entire group with his disparaging remarks about blacks being too idle and irresponsible to build a proper life for themselves.

< **227** >

This is the only time before the bus reaches Washington that all the men temporarily put aside their differences. Ironically, however, a genuine sense of unity only arises when the old man has a heart attack as the bus enters the city: the men never get to the march – most are reduced to watching it on television as they await news of his progress in hospital. When he dies, they finally realise that their shared hopes and experiences outweigh their differences. Chastened but with a new sense of purpose, they begin the journey home, leaving the shackles that bound the teenage boy and his father on the steps of the Lincoln Memorial.

Get on the Bus finds Lee at his most schematic. As the men discuss skin-colour, homophobia, sexism, history, class, music, religion, crime and so forth, many of the characters in Reggie Rock Bythewood's screenplay seem little more than ciphers whose sole function is to represent certain attitudes and experiences and thereby to clash with their opposite numbers. The arrogant, ferociously ambitious, dark-skinned actor Flip (Andre Braugher), for instance, immediately seems destined to come into conflict with the half-white cop Gary (Roger Smith) and with the openly gay Kyle (Isaiah Washington), who equally predictably manages to beat Flip when the braggart challenges him – an ex-marine, as it conveniently transpires – to a fight. Likewise unsurprising are the various revelations that Evan Sr (Thomas Jefferson Bird) has not hitherto been the most responsible father to his wayward son, that wise old Jeremiah (Ossie Davis) is homeless, and that the Muslim Jamal (Gabriel Casseus) used to be a gangbanger. Nor are the kindly patriarch Jeremiah's death and its unifying effect on the others unexpected; indeed, the observation by group organiser George (Charles S Dutton) that 'We have come 3,000 miles just to bury another black man' is symptomatic of both the contrivances of the script and the film's final shift towards sentimentality.

Besides the film's schematic use of stereotypes, however, a more subtle flaw undermines its status as an accurate political text. Although it was ostensibly inspired by the Farrakhan march, next to nothing is made of Farrakhan's politics. At the start of the film, Gary's girlfriend notes that, in being exclusively for men, the march is 'sexist', while the Jewish driver points to the demagogue's reputation for being anti-Semitic; these, however, are relegated to being small, 'negative' points made by minor characters who are not part of the film's overall thrust towards a sense of black male unity. Intriguingly, too, the one and only passenger on the bus

< **228** >

who, judging by his clothes, is evidently a member of the Nation of Islam doesn't utter a single word or do anything of note in the entire film; one can only assume that Lee is reluctant to confront the problematic political realities of Farrakhan's ideology. Such an interpretation may help to explain why the bus fails to reach the march – we the audience are thus prevented from hearing what the Muslim leader actually said.

There are, then, serious shortcomings to the film's claims to be a serious analysis of the current state of African-American masculinity. Despite its political and dramatic flaws, however, the film is notable for the way Lee keeps what is essentially a conversation piece engrossing throughout. For all the stereotypes and predictability, Lee's fluent direction makes us forget that the action is restricted for most of the film to the confines of the bus, while the excellent cast invest their cardboard cut-out roles with a vitality and colour lacking in the script. The film is not entirely without interest (it does reflect the diversity of black masculine experience); the problem is that, in arguing that unity might arise from that diversity, it resorts to maudlin contrivance, clichéd characterisation and – in signally failing to address the actual political implications of Farrakhan's rally – ideological manipulation.

< 229 >

Similarly low-key, Lee's first documentary feature, *4 Little Girls* (1997) was also notable for its conciliatory attitude towards the age-old problem of racist hatred and violence. Not that the film ever conceals the obscene injustice and bigotry that brought about the terrorist bombing of Birmingham, Alabama's Sixteenth Street Baptist Church in 1963, which not only left four young members of the black congregation dead, but also constituted a turning-point for the civil rights movement. But while the film charts the history of racial inequality and oppression which fuelled the tragedy, it also focuses on the recollections of the four girls' family and friends, all of whom are understandably sad and angry about their loss, but none of whom express hatred or a desire for revenge; indeed, in the final sequence one of the girl's mothers explains that, with the passing of time, she was able to overcome her feelings of hatred, since her life has been filled not only with the grief of losing her loved ones but also with the joy of seeing other family members grow up, a joy that has enabled her to carry on in the face of adversity.

While the film is admirably lucid in its use of personal testimony, newsreel footage and photos (including, shockingly but justifiably, brief shots of post-mortem pictures of the girls, showing their shattered bodies) both to convey the small, telling details of black family life in the early 60s, and to chart the wider social and political events of the time, it is also, for the most part, a rather conventional, linear assembly of talking heads alternated with archive documentary material. The virtue of talking to the victims' families is less one of emotional force (though the enduring trauma of losing a child is all too evident from the interviews) than of illustrating, on an intimate, more familiar scale, the sheer iniquity of being forced to live each and every day in a segregated society: even though racism is still rampant in many parts of the world (and Lee includes news reports of more recent attacks on Southern black churches), it is salutary to be reminded just how bad things were when parents had to try and explain why exactly they, unlike white folks, were not allowed to buy their child a cake in a store, or why they had to use different water fountains. Lee's decision to focus so much on personal reminiscence gives the film a genuinely human slant on history as it is experienced not just by important, influential political celebrities but by ordinary people simply trying to get by in life.

At the same time, however, the newsreel footage and the interviews with various ministers, lawyers, politicians, civil rights activists and media commentators locate the girls' deaths within a clearly defined historical context. Birmingham, a blue-collar steel town, had a history of labour violence; expansion brought with it rural racism, so that even by the end of the 40s bombings were a regular occurrence in the black neighbourhood known as 'Dynamite Hill'. Many police were members of or sympathetic

< **230** >

to the Ku Klux Klan, and police brutality towards blacks was common; the commissioner 'Bull' Connor saw nothing wrong with turning dogs and hoses on civil rights demonstrators, or indeed locking up children who supported the movement for several days, while Governor George Wallace took it upon himself to resist Kennedy's integrationist policies. (One of the most remarkable moments in the film is a present-day interview with Wallace, who argues that he was only doing what Alabama had always understood, and insists repeatedly that his best friend is black – a rather embarrassed-looking aide who understandably says nothing by way of agreement or otherwise.) Even though Martin Luther King's SCLC was making headway among blacks and liberals, it was, the film argues, the girls' murder that finally broke the camel's back, and brought home to people just how hateful the white racists were. Even so, such was the cloak of silence among those in positions of power and authority that not until 1977 was the unrepetentant Bob Chambliss indicted and found guilty of organising the bombing.

< 231 >

Lee proves an expert interviewer, and assembles his footage with intelligence and sensitivity, smoothly shifting between more personal recollection and historical commentary, and making fine use of John Coltrane's 'Alabama' as the girls' relatives recall the events of the fateful day. If the use of interviews with such famous faces as Ossie Davis, Jesse Jackson and Bill Cosby seems a little superfluous, there is no denying the sincerity of the film as a whole; indeed, for all its formal conservatism, it is one of Lee's most eloquent, subtle and poignant tributes to the courage and dignity of African-Americans in recent years.

It must be said, sadly, that since *Malcolm X* Lee's work has gone into decline, even though he remains a fine visual stylist, an expert director of actors (like many of America's finest film-makers, he has repeatedly used the same performers, most notably Ossie Davis, Bill Nunn, Giancarlo Esposito, Delroy Lindo, Roger Smith, John Turturro, his sister Joie and himself), and an able, fluent storyteller who seldom feels the need to adhere to the strict conventions of genre (most of his films are remarkably difficult to categorise in that respect). If we may applaud his determination to deal with the socio-political issues of African-American life, we must also note his tendency towards schematic simplification and stereotypes, and his films' occasional lapses into misogyny and homophobia (the result perhaps of an inability, rather than a reluctance, to distance himself clearly from some of his characters' more reactionary statements). Moreover, as his films have come to exhibit an increasingly tolerant attitude towards the diversity of human behaviour, they also seem to have lost the energy that distinguished his early work (this may be due to his increasing involvement in other business interests, such as fashion, music, video promos, ads, etc). Nevertheless, his status in the modern cinema is assured: as a chronicler of twentieth-century African-American life, he is unrivalled.

< **232** >

todd Haynes

< **233** >

As the director of the Sundance prize-winner *Poison* (1990) and the long-term business partner of Christine Vachon (who produced such films as Tom Kalin's *Swoon*, 1991, Steve McLean's *Postcards from America*, 1994, and Mary Harron's *I Shot Andy Warhol*, 1996), Todd Haynes is widely acknowledged as a leading light of what came to be known, in the early 90s, as the 'New Queer Cinema'. The accolade is both just and accurate: Haynes' influence has been considerable on other gay film-makers, his work is certainly marked by what may tentatively be termed a 'gay sensibility', while he himself has noted that his films have been made partly in response to AIDS and to the way western society has reacted to the virus and its devastating effects, particularly on the gay population. Nevertheless, it's fair to say that Haynes is far more than 'a great gay film-maker', since he is, without qualification, one of the most intelligent, ambitious and truly distinctive film-makers of the last decade.

His work is formally adventurous and imaginative, intellectually rigorous, and deeply political in its analysis and interrogation of contemporary myths and social practices; at the same time, however challenging or subversive his films may be in generic terms – the narrative style tends to be oblique but densely informative, the tone serious yet ironic – wit, imagination and a keen understanding of his characters' emotional lives ensure that they are never less than compelling. Moreover, in his exploration of popular culture, Haynes goes far beyond the flip name-check syndrome beloved by, say, Tarantino and his acolytes, and delves deeply into how music, television, fashion, fame and other such modern phenomena both reflect and affect contemporary life on a psychological, social, political and ethical level. Indeed, it's arguable that no other American film-maker working today is as fascinated by, or as alert to, the complex, fraught, symbiotic relationship between image and 'reality', between life as it is presented in the public domain and life as it is experienced in the deepest, darkest realms of the individual psyche.

< 234 >

Haynes grew up in the suburbs of Los Angeles before moving East at the age of 18. At Brown University, he studied art, semiology and psychology, and began making short films on Super-8mm; one, *Assassins*, was about Rimbaud and Verlaine, another, *The Suicide*, concerned contemporary teenage life. After graduating, he moved to New York where, with Vachon and Barry Ellsworth, he set up Apparatus, a company devoted to developing and producing low-budget independent films, and in 1987 he wrote and directed *Superstar: The Karen Carpenter Story*, a 43-minute biopic of the late 70s pop star who in 1983 died from anorexia. Remarkably, the singer, her brother Richard, her parents, and all the other dramatic characters were 'played' by Barbie dolls, photographed on miniature cardboard sets or against projected backdrops. The only humans seen are a handful of vox-pop interviewees (including Haynes himself in shades as DJ Todd Donovan, pontificating on how the Carpenters' 'sound' was a cleaner, purified version of the Burt Bacharach/Herb Alpert sound of the 60s).

The film plays as a pastiche docu-melodrama: after an opening 'dramatisation' in which 'subjective', hand-held monochrome footage allows us to see through Karen's mother's eyes as she finds the singer dead on her bedroom floor, a man's voice asks, somewhat rhetorically: 'What happened? Why at the age of 32 was

this smooth-voiced girl from Downey, California, who led a rau-
cous nation smoothly into the 70s, found dead in her parents'
home? Let's go back, back to Southern California, where Karen
and Richard grew up, back to the home in Downey where their
parents still live today…' At which point, over grainy colour shots
of squeaky-clean suburban homes, we hear Karen begin to sing,
plaintively, 'Long ago and oh so far away, I fell in love with you…'

Already, even before the 'simulation' that is the main body of
the film has commenced, Haynes' tone, methods and concerns are
clear. The mock-documentary introduction suggests that this will
be an investigation into the causes of Karen's death; that the answer
may be found within the family; that Karen had a 'smooth', calm-
ing effect on America's troubled/troubling youth; and that the
lyrics of her songs may reflect on the emotional realities of her life.
To some extent, what follows is a standard soap opera about a girl-
next-door-type whose rags-to-riches career conceals a tragic
secret: the onset of anorexia which leads eventually to her early
death. But as the story proceeds, Haynes not only emphasises the
clichéd artifice of such a story, by means both of the dolls and the
hilariously hackneyed dialogue (the A&M record producer who
'discovers' Karen and Richard promises that, with their help, he'll
'make young and fresh a happening thing'), but repeatedly interrupts it with asides on pop culture, politics, medical theory, and
the psychology and sexual politics of eating disorders. The
Carpenters' rise to popularity is examined in the context of the
social dynamics of 70s America: their pristine, wholesome,
almost asexual image and restful but heartfelt music are an anti-
dote to the unrest of a country beset by the Vietnam War, student
riots, free love, drugs, and hard rock, and heading towards the
Watergate scandal, which broke, we're told, when the duo hit the
peak of their popularity. And yet that 'pure', happy, sanitised image
is a lie, both for America in general and for the increasingly sickly
Karen, whose obsession with food and body size and bouts of
vomiting and depression are seen by her family as problems that
can be solved simply by 'fattening up'.

< **235** >

Haynes, however, knows otherwise. Through captions, voice-overs, interviews and documentary inserts, various statistics and theories about food and eating disorders are offered. After the rationing of World War Two, we're told, the popularity of fridges and supermarkets eliminated the need for daily shopping and led to people buying more than intended. Another voice-over explains that anorexia plagues many women, usually arises from a distorted perception of body size and often involves a sufferer's menstrual cycle ceasing, as if she wished to return to pre-pubescence. Such a diagnosis might certainly be applied to the film's Karen, who begins to worry about her figure after a columnist describes her as 'chubby'. Even if she wanted to grow up, not only does the group's fresh, clean image suggest arrested development, but her family, in particular her mother, are so keen to maintain the appearance of a happily united family that they are reluctant to let her move into an apartment of her own; indeed, when a doctor insists her anorexia will take three years to cure, during which time she must stay in New York, they object, rejecting the notion that family life might play a part in her illness.

There is, however, perhaps another reason why Karen may be emotionally tied to those childhood years 'long ago and oh so far away'. Many of the songs in the film provide a commentary on her life ('We've Only Just Begun' as the band start to take off; 'Rainy Days and Mondays' as she considers leaving the band), and the recurrent use of 'Close to You' suggests she herself may not be altogether happy with the idea of leading an independent life away from her family. Intriguingly, when she embarks on a short-lived romance and marriage with Tom, she says that he reminds her of Richard, who now has his own 'private life'. (Might this be a hint that he is gay? Certainly, when she threatens to tell their parents about it, he becomes angry and calls her a bitch.) While the film never explicitly suggests that the relationship between the siblings was incestuous, the implication remains thematically resonant, playing on the duo's image of a girl singing love songs with, and perhaps to, her equally adoring

< **236** >

brother. At any rate, as time passes, the pair are shown to grow ever further apart as Karen becomes more obsessed with her body and Richard becomes ever more tyrannical and insensitive to her condition, dismissing it – as patriarchal society has always tended to do with women's illnesses – either as hysteria, or as a deliberate, self-centred attempt to ruin his career.

That Haynes could deal with so many cultural, sociological, political, historical and medical issues in such a short, cheaply made film and do so in a way that was provocative, witty, moving, original and entirely relevant to the way society views illness (including, of course, AIDS) was a superb achievement, which far outweighed the mere 'infamy' of having dared to depict real-life stars by using Barbie dolls. (Richard Carpenter himself added to the film's notoriety and cult status when he issued an injunction preventing it from receiving any further screenings – ostensibly because of its use of Carpenters songs, although the fact that he was not portrayed in the most favourable light in terms of his treatment of his late sister may also have been a motive for his suppressing the movie.) Indeed, even without its 'subversive' and inspired use of Barbie dolls, *Superstar* would have been one of the most impressive débuts in recent years; fortunately, Haynes' subsequent work has more than lived up to that initial promise.

< 237 >

With *Poison*, he again employed a variety of narrative styles to explore how society reacts to and demonises illness, deviancy and transgression, although this time his method centred on the interweaving of three apparently unrelated stories each defined by a different generic style. In 'Hero', the story of a seven-year-old boy who murdered his father and then vanished, according to his adoring mother, by flying out of the window, is related as a case-history investigated by a TV documentary; 'Horror', about a scientist who accidentally drinks the human sex-drive serum he has isolated and turns into a hideous mutant who is persecuted for starting an epidemic, is a marvellous parody of the creakily moralistic, sensationalist sci-fi paranoia thrillers of the 50s; while

< 238 >

'Homo' (based on Jean Genet's *The Thief's Journal*) offers a weird, potent mix of grim prison drama and lyrical art-movie as it charts the faltering progress of an intense affair between two inmates who spent their youth in the same reformatory. Though the three stories are interwoven to proceed in parallel, rather than related one after the other, at first they seem to be linked in a wholly arbitrary manner: the chronological settings (the present, the 50s and a timeless era evocative of both the 20s and 40s), the generic styles and even the 'deviancies' and 'transgressions' (parricide; diseased mutation due to an excessive interest in the libido; openly gay love in a milieu where homosexual activity is practised as sado-masochism rooted in violent machismo and power hierarchies) are transparently different in each story. Yet it is this very refusal to establish clear narrative connections that forces us, as it were, to fill in the thematic 'void' between the stories by considering their structural similarities.

It is not only 'Homo' and 'Horror' (clearly, for all its gleeful parodic gibes at 50s sci-fi conventions, a dark parable about the way the world – especially the media – has elected to dismiss the majority of people with AIDS as outcasts who deserve to die for their reckless sexual 'indulgences') which deal with sexuality; in 'Hero' young Richie shoots his father when he finds him beating his mother for having had sex with their Hispanic gardener (indeed, the boy witnessed her adultery). Also common to each story is a strong strain of scatology: a neighbour confesses that she saw Richie defecating in her garden; Graves, the mutant boffin, drips pus and blood constantly and is known as the Leper, since he infects anyone he kisses; and when the prisoner Broom rapes his lover Jack Bolton, he not only uses his saliva as a lubricant, but is reminded of the time in reformatory when he saw Bolton being humiliated by the other boys who made him stand with his mouth open while they spat at him. Moreover, like Bolton, Richie was an outcast often bullied at school, just as Graves' experiments with the sex serum alienate him from the scientific establishment. And in each story, violence itself is

Larry Maxwell as Dr Graves in the 50s sci-fi paranoia pastiche 'Horror'– one of the trilogy of stories that make up Haynes' **Poison** (1990). All three tales are concerned with the way society reacts to transgressive behaviour.

infectious. Richie, who played 'spanking games' with a schoolchum (probably in imitation of his father's methods of chastisement), punishes his father's violence towards his mother by shooting him; Graves, who dementedly beats and kills a woman who screams when she finds his kiss has infected her, is hunted down by a mob; and Broom and Bolton's tender love turns violent partly out of jealousy, partly because sado-masochism is the sexual currency of prison life.

Each story, then, features certain motifs: persecution and alienation, sex, scatology and violence. Furthermore, in 'Hero' and 'Horror', Richie and Graves are in their own different ways viewed by the world around them as 'monsters'. It might be said, then, that Broom and Bolton are regarded as monsters too, since their love for each other doesn't conform with the cruel denial of affection and homosexuality practised by the other inmates; in raping his lover, Broom finally yields to that ethos, whereas Bolton tries to escape from the prison, and is shot. Graves, too, is sacrificed to society's sense of 'normality', jumping to his death before the taunting mob and cops can get him. Richie, on the other hand, if we are to trust his mother's testimony, finds salvation when he makes his own leap into the void: instead of plunging to his death, she says, he flew up and away, like an angel. Then again, even though the film's final shot adopts his point of view, with the camera panning upwards and the image fading to white as he leaves the window ledge, are we really to believe this doting, guilty parent, who has already claimed that her son was 'a gift from God'? Even at the film's end, the note of ambiguity, even mystery, that has characterised Richie's case history, remains intact.

< **240** >

That mystery, also reflected in the seemingly arbitrary way the three stories relate to one another, is crucial to the film's meaning. It is precisely because the actions and motives of the various protagonists are unfathomable to the 'normal', conformist world that surrounds them that they are viewed and/or persecuted as outcasts, deviants, monsters. (That 'normality' is relative and not absolute is clear from the fact that the prisoners who look down on Broom and Bolton's openly homosexual love for each other are themselves outcasts from conventional society.) Haynes, then, is not concerned with 'moral' transgressions as such, but with the way society defines as transgressive anything which is sufficiently different or non-conformist as to defy explanation in terms of conventional behaviour: in a repressive world which refuses to accept the diverse mysteries of human experience, that which is merely 'unusual' or inexplicable comes to be viewed, out of fear or suspicion, as unclean, deviant, monstrous and 'wrong', and therefore undesirable, deserving of eradication. As the film shows, however, such 'transgressions' may be the product of love; indeed, the lyrical eroticism of 'Homo' and final shot of 'Hero', suggestive as it is of Richie's redemption, imply that Haynes, at least, finds much to celebrate in transgressive behaviour – a genuinely radical attitude fully in the spirit of Genet, whose writings inspired the entire movie.

That unusually positive attitude towards behaviour widely deemed as 'abnormal' or 'unhealthy' was also present in his next film, a short entitled *Dottie Gets Spanked* (1993), in which a small boy, growing up in the 60s, is obsessed with watching a TV comedy series starring a Lucille Ball-like character named Dottie Frank. As a result he is not only ostracised by his schoolmates, but chastised by his father for watching a programme primarily directed at women; his mother, more indulgent, gets tickets to take her son on set, but the combination of the other children's teasing, his father's criticisms and threats to spank him, and the experience of watching the sitcom's larger-than-life power-games between Dottie and her screen partner (who 'spanks' her in the episode the boy goes to see being recorded) causes him to have strange dreams and fantasies, imagining himself as a fairy-tale king exerting his power over his minions (including Dottie herself in drag as a knight), and being spanked by the 'strongest man in the kingdom' (Dottie, again, alternating with his father and other threatening adults). Finally, one night, waking from a dream, he folds up a drawing he has done of Dottie being spanked (with exposed buttocks), creeps downstairs, wraps it in kitchen foil, and buries it – his secret – in the garden.

< **241** >

Typically for Haynes, the film is packed with a wide variety of stylish imaginative touches (the dream sequences, especially, are often reminiscent of German expressionist movies and classic film noir, and yet sit quite happily within a narrative that is for the most part 'naturalistic'), and finds space for moments of finely judged comedy (here, some deft parody of 60s TV) amidst the more serious insights. As in Haynes' two previous films, the family is seen as a source of confusion and repression, as the boy's father not only chastises him for his viewing habits, but repeatedly accuses his wife of allowing their son too much leeway with the television, his magazines and his scrapbooks filled with pictures of Dottie.

A scene from Haynes' short **Dottie Gets Spanked** (1993). As with most of his other films the light-hearted, parodic approach to genre and style are always underpinned by serious political intent in terms of content.

Even more unusually, the sexual aspect of the six-year-old's obsession is explicit: his fears of being spanked by his father find an echo in his fantasies about spanking and being spanked by Dottie. At the same time, it's characteristic of Haynes that he presents the boy's obsession and fantasies as natural, rather than problematic. When he buries his drawings in the garden, the impression is not that he is acting out of shame, but that he is beginning to find his voice, standing his ground, storing up his true needs and desires until he is old enough to reveal them to a world that doesn't understand them. Again, as in *Poison*, society, not the individual, is the problem; the boy may be different from his friends and may not live up to his father's ideals, but only by remaining true to himself, even if he must do so in secret for a while, has he a chance of finding happiness and a sense of his own identity.

Notwithstanding his often light-hearted, free-wheeling, even parodic approach to genre and style, Haynes' films are always distinguished by a fundamental seriousness of purpose in terms of content. Nowhere was that more evident than in *Safe* (1995), which, despite having a far more straightforward linear narrative than his earlier films, was if anything more radically subversive than its predecessors. The story is simple: Carol White (Julianne Moore), a comfortably-off 'home-maker' (a term she prefers to the more demeaningly passive 'housewife') who lives with her husband Greg and her stepson Rory in the San Fernando Valley, begins to suffer from inexplicable coughing and choking fits and rashes which she suspects are allergic reactions to the chemicals in her food, in her clothes and furniture, and in the atmosphere. Though doctors can find nothing physically wrong with her, her condition deteriorates and she decides to take up residence at the Wrenwood Centre, a remote community in the New Mexico desert whose proprietor and guru, Peter Dunning – himself apparently a chemically sensitive person with AIDS – oversees a holistic 'new age' regime which requires inmates not only to isolate themselves from the outside world and give up their usual material comforts, but to become aware of their own culpability in developing the 'environmental illness' and overcome it by learning properly to love themselves. Though Carol, after some initial doubts, devotes herself whole-heartedly to the Wrenwood philosophy and tells Greg and Roy, on one of the rare visits they are allowed, that she is convinced her stay there will cure her, she makes no discernible progress; indeed, her breathing, now aided by an oxygen cylinder, becomes worse, she develops lesions on her forehead, and she asks to be moved from her cabin to an even more isolated and sterile igloo-like 'safe-house' empty since its last inhabitant died. The film ends with her standing before the mirror, telling herself, as recommended by the Wrenwood team, that she loves herself.

A sickness-movie which foregoes both the facile options of lachrymose melodrama and the sensationalist diversions of

< 243 >

'body-horror' (the film couldn't be further from respected genre landmarks like Jonathan Demme's *Philadelphia*, 1993, or David Cronenberg's *The Fly*, 1986), *Safe* is remarkable not only for refusing to provide the happy or 'tragic' endings customary in such movies, but for avoiding any clear, satisfactory (and therefore comforting) 'explanation' of Carol's condition; indeed, we are never quite sure whether it is purely physical or at least partly psychologically-induced. Haynes' keeps the film so low-key – not only in terms of its emotional tone (Moore's performance is intentionally blank, and neither she nor those around her show or voice very much sadness, anxiety or anger), but in terms of its refusal to forge strong, easily defineable links of cause and effect – that it is impossible to gauge what, exactly, is behind her illness.

< 244 >

On the one hand, we see her reduced to a coughing fit after she follows a truck spewing out fumes in her car, and collapsing after a visit to the dry cleaners; on the other hand, there are times – such as when she becomes agitated at the fact that the sofa she has ordered is delivered in the wrong colour, or when she has a respiratory attack at an afternoon gathering of her equally affluent, directionless 'home-maker' friends, or when she shuts herself off at a dinner party by not listening to one of Greg's friends tell a crude joke about a woman with a vibrator stuck inside her – when her condition seems to be the result of psychological panic, born of fears that her ordered, immaculately 'tasteful' existence may be vulnerable to dirt, infection, chaos. It seems that her illness could be caused both by everything and anything around her, and by her anxieties, which are themselves probably related to the fact that she and her husband have set out to make such a 'safe' (i.e. artificially sanitised) life for themselves: their home is distinguished by its cool, off-white tones, their neatly landscaped garden consists of electric lights and carefully cultivated, entirely un-wild lawns and flower beds, and Carol is visibly upset when Rory discusses a school essay he is writing about LA's violent street-gangs. Carol's life, then, is 'unreal' in the sense that she is effectively alienated from the chaotic realities of the world (a nice satirical touch which points to the complacent purposelessness of her existence comes when she expresses awe and surprise that one of her 'home-maker' friends has actually wrapped a present herself); the irony is that in retreating into a neat, hygienic, 'safe' world, she seems to have reduced her natural immunity against the 'dirtier', less controllable physical and psychological aspects of life.

Not that Haynes downplays the very real damages done to the environment by our efforts to create an affluent western society: his images of LA repeatedly show traffic fumes, smog, humming pylons and so on, while the script, through the meetings Carol attends and various documentaries she watches, points out that there are some 60,000 chemicals in everyday use, only 10 per cent of which have been tested for toxicity. In exploring possible reasons for 'twentieth century disease', the film remains admirably ambivalent, just as it refuses either to condone or condemn outright the medical establishment which, having failed to diagnose a physical cause for Carol's illness, tends to suggest that it simply isn't 'real' and must therefore be psychological.

< **245** >

Similarly, Haynes never implies that the ascetic, 'holistic' Wrenwood community is any better or worse than the materialistic San Fernando Valley Carol leaves in her attempt to find a cure. Like Carol herself, Wrenwood strives to shut out the surrounding world, but in vain: while its inmates live in isolation not only from their families and material comforts but, for the most part, from each other, coyotes prowl the edge of the enclave, a nearby highway wafts traffic fumes downwind, and inmates die. Worse, Dunning's smug, woolly philosophy – according to which sufferers are encouraged to blame their illness on the fact that they have not learned to love themselves properly – is as blinkered, self-centred and ultimately unhelpful as that of the world Carol has left behind. (It's notable both that Dunning is shown, in a very brief shot, to live in a huge mansion on a hill high above his 'disciples' and that, though he's rumoured to be ill himself, he shows no symptoms of any disease whatsoever.) Indeed, for all his insistence on the importance of love and caring, his message is profoundly reactionary: not only his attacks on drug-abuse and promiscuity, but his theories that we alone are responsible for our illnesses and that recovery can be achieved only by adhering to some notion of the transcendent self, are reminiscent of the ideas of the right-wing fundamentalists whose radio programmes can be heard on Carol's radio as she drives around LA. (Moreover, the conceit that we are ourselves to blame for our illnesses may remind us of some responses to people with AIDS, especially gays and drug-addicts; nevertheless, while Carol's wasting, apparently incurable immunity deficiency is in many ways suggestive of AIDS, Haynes has rightly pointed out that *Safe* is no simple allegory, since at least we know that AIDS is a physical phenomenon and how it is caused, whereas the environmental illness featured in the movie is, at least at the time of writing, a problem about which we know considerably less.)

< 246 >

Safe, then, proposes neither an explanation nor a possible cure for Carol's illness; indeed, like *Superstar* and *Poison*, it is less concerned with the disease itself than in responses to it. The establishment doctors dismiss it as psychological since they can find no physical reason for it; Greg, initially, reacts as if it is merely a form of female hysteria, a ploy adopted by his wife to avoid having sex; Dunning regards it as a failure of self-knowledge and self-respect; Carol herself at first realises that it cannot simply be explained away, though she is habitually so passive that she eventually resorts to the Wrenwood philosophy of recovery through self-love and isolation from the world. In so doing, she merely replaces one artificial, cosseted existence with another.

What is crucial, at the film's end, is not that she is still ill and even, probably, deteriorating, but that she has abandoned all semblance of a normal, socially interactive life. As she stares at herself in the mirror in her empty, grey bubble of a room, she has cut herself off from the world around her and hence from her reasons for living; at the same time, ironically, she has perhaps begun at last to be in touch with herself, or at least to communicate with herself on a deeper level. It is as if, in becoming ill and therefore more constantly aware of her body, she has finally been given and, perhaps, accepted an opportunity to discover a sense of her own identity, to think about what she wants from life as opposed to what she feels is 'right', 'normal' or 'tasteful', or to what her family and friends expect of her. Of course, whether she will achieve this self-esteem is left as uncertain as whether she will ever recover from her illness, but at least (as is demonstrated by the film's visual style, which has shifted from long, wide-angle shots of her dwarfed by or alienated from her immaculately tidy house and the cold, ultra-modern LA cityscape, to less conspicu-ously formal compositions making more frequent use of close-ups) there is a small glimmer of hope that she is now perhaps 'closer' to some kind of self-awareness, however depressing that may be, than she was at the film's beginning.

< 247 >

Julianne Moore (centre) plays Carol White, a closeted middle-class housewife in **Safe** (1995) – a sickness movie which eschews melodrama, sensationalist diversions and the traditional comfort of an unequivocal conclusion.

Indeed, the look of the movie is crucial to its tone and meaning. In maintaining a discreet distance from Carol, Haynes' camera not only avoids the melodramatic emotional manipulations traditional in films about illness but makes us aware of the many diverse factors – socio-political, cultural, psychological and environmental – that intrude upon and affect her life. Carol's isolation from the world around her is expressed spatially (she is frequently shown sitting or standing alone, apart from other people and detached, as it were, from the architecture around her). Furthermore, Haynes uses colour – the black sofa brought into the cool, off-white pastels of her sitting-room, the bright red of a nose-bleed running down her pale face after she has had a perm at the hairdresser's (one of her few impulsive actions in the movie) – to suggest violation, pollution, the invasion of 'dirt': not merely the onset of her illness but the arrival of chaos into her obsessively ordered existence (not for nothing is her surname White).

< 248 >

The result is not unlike a Sirk or Minnelli melodrama drained of lurid colour and overheated passions; the effect is lucid, dispassionate and analytical, yet never cold or heartless, since Haynes never allows us to forget the genuine psychological and physical distress Carol is going through. He simply denies us the traditional comforts offered by such movies: either a 'feelgood' ending in which she would be cured, or the consolation that, even if she herself is doomed, her suffering would be somehow worthwhile in improving the prospects of other victims. Neither a cure nor a ground-breaking discovery about her illness is forthcoming, so that the future – both Carol's and the world's, beset as it is by pollution and disease – remains uncertain. Small wonder, then, that *Safe* – complex, low-key, ambivalent and ironic – was widely regarded as so chilling that, despite considerable critical acclaim, it never achieved the commercial success it deserved; indeed, even many of its admirers tended to downplay its overall bleakness by preferring to view it as a satire either against San Fernando materialism, or against 'new age' hypocrisies, or against

Californian lifestyles in general, whereas whatever satirical thrust
it had was not only admirably even-handed but more than outweighed by its quiet seriousness and its heartfelt sympathies for
Carol's predicament.

That bleakness, at least, was nowhere to be found in *Velvet
Goldmine* (1998), which was otherwise so rich – in terms of tone,
texture, style and content – that in some respects it seemed to be
something of a summation of all Haynes' work to date, and more
besides. In the most superficial terms, it might be described as a
somewhat unlikely (since British-set) exercise in nostalgia, a rags-
to-riches cautionary tale charting the rise and demise of a rock
star from the headily hedonist glam-rock era of the early and
mid-70s to the comparatively joyless, more middle-of-the-road
days of the mid-80s. Such a thumbnail synopsis, however, does
no justice whatsoever either to the narrative sophistication or to
the thematic and stylistic invention of the film; indeed, a study
of this length allows insufficient space to give anything more
than an introductory reading of a film whose richness really
deserves a chapter of its own.

< **249** >

The film is structured as an investigation into the brief but
glittering career of Brian Slade (Jonathan Rhys Meyers), a Bowie-
like glam-rock star who slid into obscurity soon after his assassination on stage by fellow musician Jack Fairy was revealed
simply to be a publicity stunt devised with his image-obsessed
manager Jerry Divine (Eddie Izzard). Ten years later, Arthur
(Christian Bale), an English journalist working in New York, is
reluctantly sent to Britain to find out what became of Slade,
whose whereabouts are now unknown, because, as a teenage fan
of the glam-rockers, Arthur had witnessed the 'shooting'. As
Arthur tracks down and interviews Slade's first manager and his
ex-wife Mandy (Toni Colette), and remembers his own experiences during the years of Slade's phenomenal stardom, he
finally realises the truth, partly due to a meeting with Curt
Wild (Ewan McGregor), an American proto-punk rocker of the
early 70s whose drug-blighted career had been briefly revived

by a musical collaboration with the admiring Slade: the missing star transformed his identity and became Tommy Stone, now a very successful middle-of-the-road pop singer whose current endorsement of the President would appear to be a complete betrayal of the (pan-)sexual revolution of which he was once both demonised and revered as an outspoken leader. Arthur's disillusion-ment at his former hero's change of heart, however, is counter-pointed by his own poignant memories of how he himself, as a provincial schoolboy hanging out on the fringes of the glam-rock scene, had long ago found liberation in a sexual encounter with Wild following an end-of-glitter-rock concert.

< **250** >

If the basic plotline of *Velvet Goldmine*, shorn of both its sex-ual politics and its teasing parallels to various real-life figures from the 70s (not merely David and Angie Bowie, but the likes of Iggy Pop and Lou Reed), sounds vaguely familiar, that is because Haynes here and there pays homage to *Citizen Kane*: not only does a journalist investigate the enigma of a celebrity who fell from grace, but certain sequences – Arthur's editor sending Arthur on his mission; Slade's first manager Cecil introduced, like Jedediah Leland, in infirm old age; Mandy discovered, like Susan Kane, in an empty nightclub – explicitly borrow mood and milieu from Welles' classic. But Haynes' film echoes its famous ancestor not only in terms of discreet cinephile allusions; it is also an exploration of the concept of shifting, unfathomable identity, and it finds Haynes deploying an astonishing array of narrative and visual tropes to construct a complex, flashback-led narrative that examines a man's private life and public image, his effect on those around him, and the times in which he lived. In this second respect, Haynes proves himself even more eclectic and imaginative than he did with *Superstar* or *Poison*.

While much of the film is given over to a gloriously evocative and extraordinarily accurate (given that Haynes was in America at the time) recreation of the glam-rock era, with its feather boas, stacked shoes, lamé suits, glittery make-up and all the attendant extravagant attitudes and behaviour, *Velvet Goldmine* is never an

Rock star Brian Slade (Jonathan Rhys Meyers) and his ex-wife Mandy (Toni Colette) in **Velvet Goldmine** (1998) – Haynes' thematically rich and stylistically ecclectic take on the rise and fall of a 70s glam-rock icon.

exercise in mere nostalgia. Instead, Haynes uses a remarkably coherent collage of various visual and narrative styles to convey the heady excitement of the era for those caught up in the glam-rock scene, to provide a diversity of perspectives on the events under investigation, and to place the 'sexual revolution' on view within a (partly fantasised) historical context. The mood of the 70s is conveyed by 'realist' dramatic scenes; stylised concert performances and rock promos; grainy vox-pop interviews; a press gathering for Slade's artistic and sexual manifesto shot like a circus act; party and orgy scenes shot in druggy slo-mo; several musical/dramatic montages, one of which – with Roxy Music's 'European Song' overlaying a range of scenes as different bands and singers take up the lyrics – recalls Mamoulian's similarly inventive staging of 'Isn't It Romantic?' in *Love Me Tonight* (1932); and even a brief scene (as a witty nod to *Superstar*) in which Slade and Wild are represented by dolls.

As if this weren't enough, in contrast to the saturated, luridly glossy hues of the 70s, Haynes shoots the 80s scenes in drab, muted grey-green tones, often with extras acting like automata, to stress the comparative joylessness of that era (at least as perceived by the nostalgic Arthur). He stages flashbacks to Slade's childhood with a bright, almost cartoon-like simplicity; and prefaces the film with an extraordinary fantasy prologue blending sci-fi and history, in which a flying saucer descends through the night sky to 1854 Dublin, to leave on a doorstep the infant Oscar Wilde, who in the next scene announces to his schoolteacher that his ambition is to become a pop star!

< 252 >

Such an intentionally fanciful opening might seem irrelevant and indulgent were it not in keeping with the inventive, eclectic methods of the rest of the film and were it not for the fact that the film (dedicated to Wilde 'for posing as a sodomite') alludes several times to the once notorious, now hallowed Irish wit and writer: once through a reference to *The Picture of Dorian Gray* (a book taught to Slade at school), which introduces the themes of secret double lives and the unwelcome effects of ageing, but more frequently through a luminous green bauble – a badge, as it were, of transgressive sexuality and, perhaps, love – which arrives on Earth with the baby Wilde, and is later passed from Fairy to Slade, and then to Wild, who finally gives it to Arthur.

The thematic meat of the movie concerns the relationship of individual transgressive sexual behaviour (here bi- or pan-sexual as opposed to merely homosexual) to the wider context of history. For Haynes, as for Arthur and many glam-rock fans, not only the era's androgynous costumes and make-up but its relatively open-minded attitude towards sexual proclivities of whatever hue represent a period of individuality and liberation. The various relationships between Slade, Wild and Fairy are not only professional and artistic but physical, while young Arthur's fascination with his heroes is both cultural and erotic: in one montage, superbly cut to Eno's blistering 'Baby's On Fire', Haynes intercuts Jerry Divine taking a new female employee to an orgy, Slade 'fellating' a band member's guitar in concert (as notoriously mimed by Bowie and Mick Ronson in real life), and Arthur masturbating over music-mag photos of the act in his bedroom. Just as glam-rock encouraged many to 'come out', so in other eras, Haynes suggests, transgressive sexuality manifested itself in other, less open ways: not only Wilde, forced to 'pose' as a sodomite, but drag artists in English variety shows (visited by Slade as a child), and rock 'n' roll singers like Little Richard (whom Slade, made-up and appropriately singing 'Tutti Frutti', imitates as a young boy). In other words, such frowned-upon, allegedly 'abnormal' sexuality has always been with us; the glam-rock phenomenon was merely a blossoming forth which, though the fashions may have given way to the greyer, more conformist lifestyle of the 80s, left a fruitful legacy for all those who dared to live out their innermost fantasies and desires.

< 253 >

Not that *Velvet Goldmine*, for all its gleeful recreation of 70s styles, glamorises the era and its emphasis on conspicuous consumption, outrageously extrovert behaviour, sex 'n' drugs 'n' rock 'n' roll. Slade's world may be liberating and fun, but it has its casualties: his first mentor and manager Cecil is shafted by the ruthless, egomaniacal Divine; Slade abandons Mandy almost as soon as he discovers his erotic attraction to Wild and yields to the sexual temptations faced by anyone rich and famous; drugs take their toll; stardom is based on an illusion, an image constructed for the public, in which it is all too easy to begin believing oneself. In the end, Slade is so caught up in his own Maxwell Demon *alter ego* image that he feels quite justified in deceiving both his fans and Mandy with the staged 'assassination' – in so doing he loses their love, respect and adulation and destroys his own career, so that he is eventually obliged, in order to regain fame, to remake/remodel himself as the strait-laced, mainstream (and presumably American Republican) pop singer Tommy Stone. Like Dorian Gray, to achieve eternal youth (the aim, surely, of any rock star), he sells his soul; as with Kane, his identity, as perceived both by himself and by those once close to him, is finally so shiftless (over the years he has been too many things to too many people) that he no longer knows who he is or what he wants, and he betrays the 'revolution' he once led.

Far from being merely a *film-à-clef* or an indulgent exercise in nostalgia, then, *Velvet Goldmine* is characteristic of Haynes' work in that it offers an ambivalent, ironic, complex account of the way transgressive or 'deviant' behaviour was both lived out and regarded by society at a particular period of time. Like *Superstar* it examines the pitfalls of fame and maintaining a public image, and makes expert use of the lyrics and music of popular classics of the era (either original versions by the likes of Eno or Roxy Music, or cover versions by modern bands like Radiohead and Elastica, alongside a number of songs composed specially for the film) to comment on the drama as it unfolds. Like *Poison* and *Dottie Gets Spanked* it combines a variety of cinematic styles to provide different perspectives on a theme, and celebrates transgression. And like *Safe* it adopts a subtly subversive attitude to an existing genre to conduct a probing analysis of a lifestyle symptomatic of a particular time and place which is viewed both ambivalently and sympathetically. If it differs from Haynes' other work, it is in the sheer scope of its concerns and the rich diversity of its stylistic strategies; all his previous films had been distinguished by their wit, inventiveness, complexity, and acute analytical insights, but *Velvet Goldmine* has a narrative sweep, a formal sophistication and a sense of the importance of mythology (rock stars are for many the legendary heroes of the modern age) that at times raise the film into the realm of the epic.

Though he has yet to achieve the commercial and critical recognition he deserves (probably because he is still rather simplistically regarded in some quarters as a gay, and therefore marginal, film-maker), Haynes' work is among the most innovative and rewarding being made today. His political commitment and engagement never decline into facile sloganeering or simplistic solutions (the implication that Dunning, in *Safe*, might perhaps be duplicitous and exploitative was intended as a provocation to

< **254** >

any viewers who might assume that Haynes, as a leading figure in the 'New Queer Cinema' would automatically show a gay, reputedly HIV+ character in a favourable light). His interest in illness and 'abnormality' as indexes of society's values and as potential sources of self-definition is both topical and subversive. His awareness of how individual lives are shaped by psychological, sexual, economic, historical, political and cultural factors is sophisticated and lucid. His fascination with the gulf between reality and 'image' – a product, probably, of his interest in semiology – and with the concomitant discrepancy between private life and public profile is illuminating in an era obsessed with success, fame, fashion and the media. And his recognition of the damage done by our inability and reluctance to accept that certain aspects of life, including illness, desire and human identity, may finally be unfathomable is philosophically astute.

< 255 >

Cinematically too, however, he is impressively ambitious and talented, deploying all the stylistic and narrative tools at his command to explore fresh ways of approaching his material, and playing with and undermining traditional genres to illuminate and question the assumptions popular culture makes about the world. In terms of subject, style and analytical methodology, his work is determinedly modern – no other American director seems so alert to the lessons to be learned from semiology – and as long as critics and audiences are prepared to accept – or even to try and understand – the ambivalence that is regularly a defining element in his work, his future as a film-maker should be bright indeed.

steven soderbergh

< **257** >

When 26-year-old Steven Soderbergh, reacting to the fact that
his début feature *sex, lies and videotape* (1989) had just won the
Palme d'Or and the Best Actor prize at the Cannes Film Festival,
half-joked that 'It's all downhill from here', he could not have
known just how accurately his prediction would turn out. Not
that Soderbergh's subsequent output has been especially disappointing in artistic terms – indeed, he has proved to be a consistently interesting, albeit rather erratic, film-maker – but none of
his films has managed to match either the unexpected commercial success or the critical plaudits which greeted his début, which
he made, as some have pointed out, at the same age as Welles was
when he made *Citizen Kane*. The lack of attention his later work
has attracted may simply be due to the fact that *Kafka* (1991),
the eagerly awaited follow-up to his first film, was so different
from its predecessor in every respect that it was widely (and, in
this writer's view, unfairly) dismissed as a pretentious failure, thus
establishing its maker's reputation as something of a one-hit
wonder. At the same time, however, Soderbergh's current low
profile may also be attributed to the fact that his talent is difficult to categorise. With no discernibly consistent style or thematic preoccupations, it is hard to make convincing claims that
he is an *auteur*, while his recent decision to withdraw from

commercial film-making into more experimental, low-budget work has ensured, somewhat ironically, that he is no longer regarded as a significant player on the American independent scene.

< **258** >

Nevertheless, Soderbergh has continued to produce ambitious, intriguing, sometimes startlingly original movies; and while it's true that the sheer diversity of subject matter and styles in his work to date prevents our categorising him along the lines of any *auteur*-based theory, the fact that he deploys whatever cinematic style he deems appropriate for the material in hand has resulted in films that exhibit an unusually coherent approach to questions of form and content. Indeed, it may be argued that there is after all a preoccupation that inflects much of his output: the search for new nuances of film language unexplored by the conventional syntax of the Hollywood mainstream.

A movie fan since childhood, Soderbergh began making shorts on Super-8mm with equipment borrowed from students at Louisiana State University. Foregoing college, he went straight from school to Hollywood, where he found work as an editor while trying his hand at writing film scripts. Frustrated, he returned to Baton Rouge (still, at the time of writing, his home and work-base) where he met, through a friend, the rock group Yes, who invited him to shoot the band on tour: the assembled footage became a Grammy-winning video entitled *9012 Live* (1986). Soderbergh's next move was to use personal experience – a failed relationship – as the fictional basis for *sex, lies and videotape*, made in Louisiana on a budget of $1.2 million. Notwithstanding the alluring title, the resulting film was a subtle, thought-provoking comedy-drama about contemporary sexual mores, its mature insights and assured tone belying its maker's tender years.

The story centres on the intimate interactions between four characters: thrusting young lawyer John (Peter Gallagher) and his demure, elegant wife Ann (Andie MacDowell); Ann's sister Cynthia (Laura San Giacomo) with whom, unbeknowst to Ann,

John is having an affair; and John's old college friend Graham (James Spader), whose return to the neighbourhood after a long absence provokes a series of revelations that will expose the lies the other three tell to themselves and each other. Not only do John and Cynthia conceal their clandestine meetings from Ann, but John is blind to the fact that he has never managed to satisfy his wife sexually, while Cynthia is seeing her brother-in-law not out of any genuine desire for him, but out of a contemptuous dislike for her sister which masks her guilt and insecurities about her own emotional shortcomings. Ann, meanwhile, deludes herself about her marital happiness by focusing her attention on her immaculate home, by retreating into anxieties about garbage and the starving millions (as she confesses to her shrink at the start of the film), and by refusing to talk or think about sex (she has never knowingly had an orgasm, and constantly reproaches her sister for her predatory behaviour). Only when the gently spoken, apparently unthreatening Graham responds to her admission that she considers sex overrated by confessing that he is impotent does an opportunity arise for the other three characters to do away, once and for all, with the deceits that define their lives.

< **259** >

Not that the film follows the course we might expect. The intimacy that has grown up between Ann and Graham – both shy and sexually innocent (or so it seems) compared with John and Cynthia – is suddenly broken when Ann discovers he has his own secret: a collection of videotapes he has recorded of women talking frankly about their sexual experiences and fantasies, an ongoing project which has nothing to do with sociological research and everything to do with Graham's inability to maintain a physically satisfying relationship with, as it were, a woman in the flesh (we later see him masturbating as he watches them). Shocked and disgusted, Ann leaves his apartment, but when Cynthia sees he has somehow upset her sister, she decides to visit Graham, whom she has never met, and, intrigued by his tape collection, agrees to an interview. The experience arouses her: she

not only dashes off to have sex with John, but gleefully confesses to Ann that she masturbated on camera. Distraught, Ann finds
the courage to ask her husband if he's sleeping with Cynthia; he
lies, accusing her of paranoia. It is John, however, who becomes
paranoid after Cynthia breaks with him and admits she spoke of
their affair on tape (which Graham insisted would remain confi-
dential); to make matters worse, after Ann finds Cynthia's earring
in her bedroom, she visits Graham to ask why he didn't inform
her about the affair, and returns home to tell her husband that
she wants out of their marriage and that she too has made a tape
with Graham. John visits Graham, assaults him and, watching
the offending cassette, learns not only that he has never satisfied
his wife but that Graham is impotent – an affliction he suspects
was cured by Ann after the camera was turned off. After John
leaves, Graham destroys his tapes and camera. Some time later,
we see him tentatively enjoying his new relationship with Ann,
with whom Cynthia has made up; meanwhile, John, whose
career is beginning to suffer, half-heartedly boasts to a colleague
that he's perfectly happy no longer being married.

< 260 >

The prime virtues of Soderbergh's film are the subtlety of its
moral and psychological insights and the generosity extended
towards the characters. At first sight, it might appear that Ann
and Graham are the innocents and John and Cynthia the duplicitous baddies, but while Soderbergh's sympathies for the gentler,
more vulnerable pair are obvious, he never makes facile judge-
ments. If John is the 'villain' of the piece, who not only lies outright to his wife but, in so doing, is even more irresponsible
towards her than Cynthia (who rightly points out that she never
took a vow of fidelity to her sister), he is also the most pitiable
character: whereas Graham's impotence is a result of his not
being properly in touch with his physicality, John's inability to
admit the truth even to himself after Ann has left him shows that
he is out of touch with his own emotions. Similarly, Cynthia's
competitive rivalry with and dishonesty towards Ann derive from
her concern, expressed to Graham's camera, that she is not as

Intimate encounter: Graham (James Spader) and Ann (Andie MacDowell) in **sex, lies and videotape** (1989). Soderbergh deploys video to foreground the act of voyeurism involved in cinematic storytelling.

attractive as her sister, and from an inability to admit to feelings for others (she enlists Ann to buy a present for their mother's fiftieth birthday). It is Graham's honesty and video camera that force the characters' various deceits and delusions into the open; at the same time, Soderbergh never glosses over the fact that Graham's video obsession is symptomatic of his hang-ups (he admits to having once been a pathological liar, and worries about getting too close physically to women, due to a disastrous affair some years previously). While the tapes serve to reveal the truth to the other characters, for Graham they are a defensive means of keeping the world at a distance, of refusing to accept the fact that he has an effect on, and therefore a responsibility towards, other people. Only when Ann turns the camera towards him, asking him about his own emotions, and points out that she is about to leave her husband partly because of the effect he, Graham, has had on her life, does he find the strength to destroy the camera and tapes and face up to the truth of his own responsibilities, needs and desires.

Soderbergh's use of video, however, not only reveals how, in the modern world, people often use technology and the media as a substitute for the potentially more troublesome but ultimately more fulfilling realities of proper human contact; it also allows him to play with the viewer's expectations of filmic storytelling and to force us to acknowledge our own status as voyeurs. Just as the film's provocative, faintly lurid title is belied by the fact that we see no graphic depictions of nudity or sexual activity, so Soderbergh deploys the video recordings both to arouse and to disappoint our curiosity about the progress of the narrative and any sexual activity therein. When Graham interviews Cynthia, her confessions are interrupted by a cut to a shot of her leaving his apartment; later, when we get to see the tape itself, we see only her face as she removes her skirt and then, as the TV screen is replaced by a shot of Graham's face, we *hear* him comment on the fact that she's wearing no underwear, at which point the film cuts to another scene – Soderbergh is deliberately withholding information and images we may prefer or expect to see. Likewise, Ann's interview is dealt with in two scenes. In the first we see her waiting for Graham to turn on the camera, followed by a jump cut to the pair staring at each other in a composition suggestive of post-coital bliss; in the second, John – reflecting our own curiosity – watches the tape to find out if Ann has had sex with Graham. As the tape plays, the image changes from black and white to colour, signifying that we have flashed back 'into the room' with the pair, and so are likely to see everything that 'really' happened. All we see, however, is a very long conversation, until Ann and Graham finally kiss; then, just as they seem about to engage in something more physically intimate, we see Graham lean over to turn off the camera and, like John, are left looking at a screen blank except for electronic interference, wondering what exactly Ann and Graham did once the camera

< **262** >

stopped recording. The effect is both frustrating (the experience of watching movies is primarily about the pleasure of wondering, anticipating and being shown what happens next) and entirely appropriate to the film's concern with honesty and deceit (i.e. information revealed and withheld), with the psychology that explains and defines physical behaviour, and with the way technology situates us at a remove from reality.

If this analysis of Soderbergh's ideas and methods make *sex, lies and videotape* sound drily academic, nothing could be further from the truth. The film is often very funny, the characters – beautifully played by the four leads – are rounded and utterly convincing, and there is a genuine erotic frisson – heightened rather than diminished by the lack of explicit sex scenes – to the sequences involving Ann and Graham. Moreover, while the film is in no way moralistic, it is refreshing to see a contemporary film which suggests, without a hint of cynicism or manipulative sentimentality, that honesty – to oneself and to others – is the best way forward in attempting to find a mutually fulfilling relationship. As such, the movie cannily reflected the zeitgeist of a world in which AIDS had made 'liberated', phallocentric sex problematic, while never resorting to reactionary dogma or solemn didacticism. *Sex, lies and videotape* proved once and for all that it was quite possible to make a critically and commercially successful film on a low-budget, using a small cast of comparatively unknown actors, a handful of locations and a low-key, sensitive, literate script; as such, it was influential in encouraging other young American film-makers to follow suit in making character-driven chamber-pieces.

< **263** >

It was perhaps ironic, then, that the commercial success of the film enabled Soderbergh himself to make the considerably more expensive and technically ambitious *Kafka*. Emphatically not a biopic, the film situated the Czech writer within a nightmarish fiction which he might have written, or which at least might well have served as the inspiration for one of his novels. In Prague shortly after the First World War, Kafka (Jeremy Irons), a mild-mannered clerk for an insurance company, whose stories, written in his spare time, are just beginning to establish his reputation in artistic circles, tries to discover the whereabouts of Raban, a colleague who has mysteriously disappeared. Through the missing man's lover Gabriela (Theresa Russell), Kafka becomes acquainted with an anarchist group with whom Raban was involved, but refuses to write propaganda for them, partly because he doesn't agree with their aims, partly because he feels he is being watched both by the police and by an officious messenger at his office. After Gabriela also disappears and he narrowly escapes being killed by a diseased lunatic, Kafka visits the anarchists only to find them murdered by the very same maniac, whom he follows to a patch of wasteland where the man is stabbed to death by an accomplice. When the eccentric, childlike twins who have been appointed as his assistants 'arrest' him and start taking him to the Castle, the city's mysterious, apparently impenetrable seat of power where all files are kept, he is rescued by a stonecutter he has recently befriended, who shows him a secret passage into the Castle. Carrying Raban's briefcase (which Gabriela told him was really a bomb), Kafka enters the Castle where he meets Dr Murnau (Ian Holm), a scientist conducting terrible experiments on the exposed brains of men abducted from a rural mining community, in the hope of finding a way to abolish individuality and thereby to increase human efficiency. (The insurance firm pays compensation to the supposedly dead guinea-pigs' families.) Though Murnau says he and Kafka are alike in their vision of a new modern world, the writer refuses to condone his plans; when the bomb explodes, the twins, the maniac's accomplice and Murnau himself are killed, and the laboratory destroyed. Having successfully escaped, Kafka is asked by the police to identify Gabriela's body: though he knows that she too was tortured in the Castle, he admits he'd 'have to agree' to a verdict of suicide. After returning to work to find that an order summoning him (like Raban before him) to the Castle has been cancelled, Kafka writes to his father that now, knowing the truth rather

< 264 >

than living in ignorance, he feels he is a part of the world around him.

Though Lem Dobbs' script offers a rather pat distillation of Kafka's preoccupation with individuality, alienation, bureaucracy and oppression, and is occasionally stilted in its references to the author's own works (the clumsy allusions in the dialogue to 'The Penal Colony' and 'Metamorphosis' are little better than the 'Hello Brahms, hello Liszt'-style embarrassments of Hollywood's artistic biopics), the film does make a fair stab at evoking the kind of half-real, half-fantasy world which might have inspired Kafka to write novels like *The Trial* and *The Castle*. Crucial to the creation of a sinister, nightmarish atmosphere of paranoia and isolation is Soderbergh's adoption of a shadowy, black and white visual style reminiscent of the German Expressionist films of the 1910s and 20s (the period in which the film is set): not for nothing is the scientist named Murnau and another character Orlac.

< **265** >

Jeremy Irons plays Kafka in Soderbergh's second feature (1991). Soderbergh used a shadowy black and white expressionism to create a sinister, nightmarish atmosphere of paranoia and isolation.

(When the film bursts into colour for Kafka's visit to the Castle, the change, albeit justifiable in suggesting that Kafka is at last able to see the full story, makes the film's 'climax' seem altogether more conventionally mainstream.) At the same time, the use of occasionally 'lop-sided' camera angles, of Prague's dark streets and towering monumental architecture, and of the enormous office in which Kafka and his colleagues toil, echoes more recent films about missing persons and oppressively bureaucratic Middle European states: *The Third Man* (Carol Reed, 1949) – Harry Lime is as contemptuous of the faceless masses as Dr Murnau – Orson Welles' adaptation of Kafka's *The Trial* (1962) and *Brazil* (Terry Gilliam, 1985). These resonances, also present in Woody Allen's even more pretentious *Shadows and Fog* (1992), offer a visual shorthand suggestive of the unspeakable horrors and injustices perpetrated by authorities so dedicated to order and efficiency that individual freedom and non-conformism are regarded as serious threats to the *status quo*. Similarly, the presence of Kafkaesque characters like the infantile but malicious twins (who look nothing like each other), the enigmatic police chief and the office messenger who informs his superiors of every misdemeanour perpetrated by the clerks, evoke a world where no unauthorised act, however petty, passes unnoticed.

Though the film is too self-consciously 'arty' to build up sufficient mystery and suspense to impress as a proper thriller, it nevertheless succeeds in its efforts to 'explain' how Kafka might have arrived at some of his ideas: the film's Prague is situated, as it were, midway between historical reality and the fictional universe of his novels. In this respect, Jeremy Irons' restrained performance, devoid of the hallmarks of 'genius' that are usually drawn on to suggest a tormented, visionary artistic temperament, is appropriately passive and watchful: as his final monologue confirms, his chastening experiences bring him to a clearer, more empathetic understanding of the predicament of his fellow men, and will be put to good use in his future writings. Indeed, almost all the performances, pitched carefully between naturalism and

< 266 >

unsettling eccentricity, do justice to the uneasy, nightmare-like tone of the film; only Theresa Russell, with her flat, American-accented delivery, fails to convince.

Notwithstanding its flaws, *Kafka* was far more intelligent than its reputation suggested; one can't help wondering whether some of its detractors resented an American (and a 'boy wonder' at that!) taking on a story that was in many ways distinctly and inherently European (albeit written by another young American). Whatever, his next film, the altogether more conventional and American *King of the Hill* (1993), met with a far warmer critical reception, even though it failed to ignite in box-office terms. Based on a memoir by AE Hochner, the film tells of the hardships suffered by a 12-year-old boy during the Depression.

< **267** >

Though his family is poor and lives in a dilapidated St Louis hotel, Aaron (Jesse Bradford) is blessed with a vivid imagination that allows him not only to shine at school but to conceal his impoverished circumstances from his better-off schoolmates with made-up tales of his air-pilot father. The truth, however, eventually asserts itself after his younger brother is sent away to live with an aunt and uncle, his ailing mother (Lisa Eichhorn) is sent to a sanatorium, and his father (Jeroen Krabbe) finally finds a job selling watches out of state. Left to fend for himself, Aaron sees his life gradually fall apart: an epileptic girl he has befriended in the hotel leaves town for reasons of health, his romantic fantasies about his family life are exposed as fiction at a party following graduation, his friend Lester – who helps him survive by outwitting the hotel's malicious bellboy Ben – is arrested for taking part in a battle between the police and the city's homeless, and a seedy hotel guest (Spalding Gray) who has promised to deal with the hotel manager's demands for outstanding rent commits suicide. Reduced to near-starvation, Aaron begins to suffer stomach upsets and hallucinations, but with the return of his brother (the result of a letter Aaron sends to his relatives in his father's name) and his father, who has been offered a job in St Louis with the

WPA, he avoids death and rejoins his mother in their new home – but only after tricking Ben by leaving the hotel with all his belongings and without paying the bill.

Though easily the most conventional of Soderbergh's movies to date, *King of the Hill* is far from being without interest. For one thing, its sensitive portrait of an intelligent, resourceful, vulnerable child who manages to overcome adversity through a mix of imaginativeness, courage and sheer determination makes it a distinctive addition to a very honourable tradition of movies, fine Hollywood examples of which include *The Night of the Hunter* (Charles Laughton, 1955), *Driftwood* (Allan Dwan, 1947) and *The Curse of the Cat People* (Robert Wise/ Gunter von Fritsch, 1944). For another, while the slightly sepia-tinted photography suggests that the film might be just another exercise in nostalgia, the generally unsentimental tone and the subtle insistence on the harsh realities of the Depression as experienced by

< **268** >

Aaron (Jesse Bradford) and his father (Jeroen Krabbe) in **King of the Hill** (1993). An intelligent and unsentimental tale of a 12-year-old boy's experiences during the Depression, it is Soderbergh's most conventional film.

Aaron, his family, the other hotel guests and the dispossessed of St Louis ensure that romanticism is for the most part held effectively at bay.

Best of all, however, is the way in which Soderbergh, helped no end by Bradford's extraordinarily fine performance, manages to show how Aaron's life is a complex, precariously balanced mix of playful childish fantasy, adolescent bravado and an almost adult pragmatism born of the necessity for survival in difficult circumstances. Ever inventive, Aaron concocts a bold if doomed scheme to supplement his family's income by breeding canaries to sell to a pet shop (sadly, the first brood is entirely female, and so produces no songbirds); facing starvation, he cuts photos of food from magazines, places them on his plate, and eats them; visiting his mother at the sanatorium, he tells her everything is fine, knowing that the truth would only upset her and possibly put her improving health at risk.

< 269 >

With such small, relatively undramatic details, Soderbergh paints a vivid, insightful portrait of a boy whose fundamental innocence is threatened by rude experience. For the most part the narrative avoids big dramatic moments (though a sequence in which Aaron steers his father's car away from repossession agents, his feet unable to reach the brake-pedal, is genuinely thrilling); the texture of Aaron's life, and our sense of his character, derives instead from an accumulation of details supplied in brief vignettes. For all his storytelling and sense of mischief, for example, Aaron's decency is quietly but quickly established in a handful of short, seemingly unimportant scenes, as when he keeps his word and visits the neighbour whose epileptic fits scare him, or when he manages to elicit a beautiful smile from a bored, black elevator girl by thanking her for the gum she's given him as a graduation present. The unassertive tone of these and other such scenes, moreover, is mirrored by Soderbergh's unflashy but telling direction. The imagery and editing are unobtrusively 'realistic' throughout, save for a rapid montage evoking Aaron's exhilaration at winning a game of marbles and a very convincing oneiric sequence depicting his hunger-fuelled hallucinations, but they are never lazily arbitrary. A typically evocative sequence occurs when Aaron and his brother, elated at living in a proper house at last, run from room to room, simultaneously hiding from and shouting to each other; the sense of space, freedom and wonder at no longer having to share the cramped hotel room with their parents is palpable. In such moments, the warm humanity and cinematic intelligence of Soderbergh's film are admirably clear.

< **270** >

Soderbergh's next movie, *The Underneath* (1995), was another very American subject, albeit filtered through a narrative style more akin to that of the European art-movie. For one thing, in adapting Don Tracy's crime novel (filmed by Robert Siodmak in 1948 under the book's title, *Criss Cross*), Soderbergh went beyond the relatively straightforward flashbacks common in film noir to create a complex three-part time structure; for another, in place of the 1948 film's typically noir conception of its protagonist as a man fatally obsessed with a *femme fatale*, in Soderbergh's movie Michael Chambers' motives and personality are altogether more ambiguous.

The plot itself is a fairly standard labyrinth of desire and treachery. Reformed gambler Michael (Peter Gallagher) returns to Austin, Texas, ostensibly to attend his widowed mother's wedding to security guard Ed (Paul Dooley) but also, perhaps, to get back together with his ex-girlfriend Rachel (Alison Elliott), whom he deserted without warning some time previously, leaving her to pay his gambling debts. Though she is living with crooked club-owner Tommy Dundee (William Fichtner), Michael stays in town after Ed gets him a job driving armoured cars; occasionally dating a local bank-teller, Susan (Elizabeth Shue), he nevertheless persists in trying to persuade Rachel to leave the insanely possessive Tommy. After she agrees to go away with him for a few days but stands him up, Michael finds that she has married Tommy; when she comes to his house claiming that Tommy abuses her, her husband follows her, and Michael makes the excuse that he was asking her if Tommy would be interested in participating in a robbery he has planned. Tommy agrees, insisting they work with an anonymous crew, while Michael makes plans with Rachel to double-cross her husband. On the day of the robbery Michael is alarmed to find his partner in the armoured car is Ed, who is killed by the crew while Michael protects Susan from their bullets. Wounded, he wakes in hospital to find he is considered a hero, though his brother David (Adam Trese), a cop who is himself obsessed with Rachel, suspects the truth. Fearing Tommy will take revenge, Michael asks a hospital visitor to sit with him; the man abducts him and takes him to Rachel and Tommy, who immediately kills the kidnapper. While he is disposing of the body, Michael persuades Rachel to give him the gun, but after he has killed Tommy and been wounded himself, Rachel drives off alone with the money, only to be followed by the anonymous crew – led by Michael's boss at the security firm.

< **271** >

As may be seen from the above synopsis, the tortuous plot of *The Underneath* serves up a heady brew of deceit and betrayal, both premeditated and unplanned, with the various machinations of Michael, Rachel, Tommy and David (who, jealously infatuated with Rachel, threatens to frame her if she leaves Tommy for Michael) capped by those of Hinkle (Joe Don Baker), the security firm boss who gave Michael his job and hypocritically thanks him for his 'heroism' in trying to fend off the robbers (i.e. his own men) at the bank. But while Soderbergh creates sequences of considerable unease – most notably the scene in the hospital (shot almost entirely from the vulnerable, bed-ridden Michael's point of view) when neither he nor we have any idea whether the hospital visitor he asks to sit with him will protect or kill him – he seems less interested in suspense, action and the thematic traditions of the crime movie than in exploring the motivations that lead the self-destructive, strangely noncommital Michael into a maelstrom of lies and distrust. By dividing the narrative into three carefully interwoven time frames (the robbery and its aftermath, the events leading to the crime after Michael returns home, and the events leading to his earlier departure from Austin), Soderbergh points to the self-negating contradictions that constitute Michael's personality.

During his gambling period he is barely attentive to Rachel, who rightly tells him that he seems to be 'somewhere else' and is 'not very present tense'; though he insists that he loves her, he repeatedly ignores her requests to put aside his winnings for their future, and is able to walk out on her without explanation when his debts threaten to catch up with him. When he returns to Austin, he is no better: he vacillates between Rachel and Susan (whom he tells 'There's what you want and what's good for you – they never meet,' hinting at his indecision); neglects to buy a wedding present for his mother; and is insufficiently concerned by the possibility of Ed getting injured or killed to stop the armoured car robbery going ahead. Michael gambles with lives – including his own – but doesn't seem particularly bothered about winning, or even to know what he wants: while he appears to dream up the bank job as a way of persuading Tommy that he has not been trying to seduce Rachel, the fact that he comes up with the plan as soon as Tommy confronts him suggests that he may have had it in mind for some time, and that winning back Rachel, for all his declarations of love, is no more important to him than the money. (No wonder that at the end of the film, she explains her decision to leave him by saying he made her feel 'interchangeable'.)

Unlike the other characters in the film, who seem to know exactly who they are and what they want (Rachel wants money, Susan wants Michael, Tommy and David want Rachel, and Michael's mother and Ed want each other), Michael is defined by his lack of genuine desire, passion and commitment: he exists at a distance from the world around him, as is suggested by the way Soderbergh repeatedly frames him behind glass, usually tinted blue, green or yellow – cold colours, all. Moreover, Michael seems aware of his condition; he reads books like *Self-Esteem: A*

< **272** >

User's Guide and *Saying Hello to Yourself.* But he has no real sense of self, let alone of anyone else, as is shown by his embarrassed expression when Ed, happily admitting to the fortuitous circumstances that have brought him and Michael's mother together, pointedly remarks that for some people 'the planets just don't line up, and there's nothing you can do about it'.

For all its tortuous, maze-like plotting, *The Underneath* is essentially a portrait of a man without qualities, whose purpose in life is unknown both to others and to himself. In this regard, it may be useful to quote Jorge Luis Borges' review of *Citizen Kane*, another film noir with a fragmented time-structure, which, incidentally, Borges likened to the work of Kafka: 'The subject, at the same time metaphysical and detective story-like... is the discovery of the secret soul of a man... We understand at the end that the fragments do not have a hidden unity: the unhappy Foster Kane is a shadow, a mere chaos of appearances... Nothing is more frightening than a centreless labyrinth. This film is just that labyrinth.' While it would be foolhardly indeed to claim that *The Underneath* is anything like as impressive as Welles' début, it is certainly true that Michael may be described as the metaphorical void at the heart of Soderbergh's existential thriller.

< 273 >

The writer-director, however, professed himself unhappy both with the movie and with commercial film-making in general; by way of proof, his next film, *Schizopolis* (1996) – which was made on a micro-budget with a group of friends – was his most bizarre and experimental to date. At first it seems to be a chaotic, hit-and-miss assembly of very tenuously connected comic sketches, put together virtually at random, but as it proceeds and a semblance of a story begins to emerge, it begins to make a kind of 'sense'. As far as it can be said to have a plot, it runs as follows: when an office colleague dies suddenly, Munson (Soderbergh), who works at a company where paranoia about industrial espionage is rife, is told by his boss to take over the writing of a speech for the company's owner, the new age 'Eventualist' philosopher T Azimuth Schwitters.

Already obsessed by masturbation, and too preoccupied with speech-writing and the intrigues at work to respond to his wife's advances, he fails to notice that she is having an affair with a dentist, Dr Korcek, who is Munson's double. Meanwhile, his colleague Mr Nameless Numberheadman is so worried that he might be thought to be an industrial spy that he starts acting oddly and is sacked for espionage; as revenge, he passes on company secrets to a rival organisation. When Munson's wife decides to move in with the dentist, it is too late, for Korcek has already fallen for a new patient, who bears a strange resemblance to his mistress; unfortunately for him, Attractive Woman # 2 responds to his love letter by accusing him of sexual harassment. Meanwhile, a woman who is Munson's wife's double cheats on her Japanese-speaking husband (Soderbergh again) by having an affair with his Italian-speaking lookalike; when she moves in with the latter, he tells her he is about to take a job elsewhere. Shocked, she goes to a café where she notices Munson's wife, before meeting and beginning an affair with a Frenchman who looks exactly like her husband and lover. Munson, meanwhile, has completed the speech, and with his wife, now returned home, attends a lecture given by Schwitters, who is shot and wounded by Elmo, a womanising pest-controller-turned-macho action star. Munson then tells us that in the next few years his wife will leave him and he will almost die in a snow-storm.

It should be said that some of the details in this synopsis may be incorrect; it is never made entirely clear, for instance (nor, probably, is it of any great importance in such a playful piece of nonsense), whether the Japanese- and Italian-speaking lookalikes are really distinct characters from Munson and Korcek, or whether they are Munson and Korcek as perceived by Munson's wife, who takes over as the focus of attention in the third part of the film, the 'narrative' of which consists largely of scenes repeated from the first two parts, albeit with dialogue spoken in different languages. (The first part centres on Munson, the next on Korcek, and the third on Munson's wife or her double, while

< **274** >

Elmo and the many other characters recur throughout the movie.)

In terms of plot, then, it is hard to say that the film is about very much at all; while it satirises, with variable success, male paranoia, corporate business politics, new age philosophies, the American obsession with dental hygeine, and soap-style melo-drama, its often bewildering use of physically identical characters is too haphazard to be interpreted, for example, as an exploration of repetitive patterns of human behaviour or of the philosophical concept of parallel universes. As Soderbergh implies in speeches (to an empty cinema) that open and close the film, the film is not meant to be taken seriously: though he claims it is 'the most important motion picture' we'll ever see, he warns that we are unlikely to understand it unless we watch it over and over again (which will make him lots of money), and when he invites queries about what we have just seen, he simply answers 'yes' repeatedly to unheard questions.

< 275 >

That said, Schizopolis is not entirely meaningless, since it is really 'about' language. In the first part the pest-controller Elmo converses with his female conquests in gobbledegook: only after a few scenes do we figure that repeated phrases like 'Nose army', 'Jigsaw' and 'Sneeze' are probably equivalent to 'Later!', 'Hello' and 'Cheers'. Munson and his wife, meanwhile, communicate in a different kind of language which *describes* rather than uses the words and phrases that express meaning, welcoming each other with 'Generic greeting' and 'Generic greeting returned', and dis-cussing dinner as follows: 'Imminent sustenance!'; 'Overly dra-matic statement regarding upcoming meal'; 'False reaction indi-cating hunger and excitement' – it is as if someone has had an idea for a scene but hasn't yet written the precise dialogue.

Though this may all sound quite pretentious on paper, on screen, accompanied by vocal inflexions, facial expressions and gestures, it is often very funny. Equally amusing are a funeral where the preacher, instead of delivering the expected eulogy, says exactly what he's thinking (the widow's a babe, many wives would probably like to kill their husbands for the insurance, let's go have a drink), and the absurd attempts at love poetry in the ludicrously boring Korcek's letter to Attractive Woman # 2, which includes such marvellously prosaic flights of fancy as 'The wind sings your name endlessly, although with a slight lisp that makes it difficult to understand if I'm standing near an air-conditioner'.

If the film's playfulness with language has any relevance, it is partly in the way it reflects on the pretentious nonsense spoken by the evangelical Schwitters, who is nevertheless viewed as a kind of new Messiah by his gullible admirers, and partly in the way Soderbergh experiments with film syntax to construct the jigsaw puzzle of his film. The narrative consists of a seemingly disconnected jumble of scenes ranging from straight drama and comic sketches to bogus documentary interviews, speeded-up action sequences (in the wacky style of Soderbergh's idol Dick Lester), disruptive news flashes, and moments when the characters address the camera directly (as when Elmo the pest-controller, offered a better role in another movie by a couple who have been watching his antics, turns to insult the makers of *Schizopolis* before storming off, only to reappear later as an action hero who does nothing apart from beat people up). If the film's story finally means very little, at least Soderbergh makes us 'work' to piece it together; however erratic and wayward its individual scenes, its self-reflexive, witty and imaginative approach to film syntax and structure ensures that *Schizopolis* deserves to be regarded as innovative and ambitious 'guerrilla' film-making.

Soderbergh's next film, also determinedly small-scale, was more accessible. Like *Swimming to Cambodia* (Jonathan Demme, 1978) and *Monster in a Box* (Nick Broomfield, 1991), *Gray's Anatomy* (1996) was essentially a filmed record of one of Spalding Gray's bizarre, digressive, confessional comic mono-logues, with the writer-raconteur for the most part sitting at a table as he tells the surreal, shaggy-dog story of his lengthy search for a cure for an eye complaint. Nevertheless, Soderbergh makes the most of the limited cinematic tools at his command to lend atmosphere and dramatic tension to Gray's already engrossing

< **276** >

story. Besides interrupting the monologue at regular intervals with black and white interview footage of people describing their own grotesque experiences with damaged sight (one woman relates how she poured superglue instead of drops into her eye, while a man tells of how he used pliers to remove a piece of wire that had punctured his iris), he also shoots Gray against diverse photographic backdrops (forests, wigwams, an enormous staring eye); makes use of a wide array of different-coloured lighting effects; and alternates static shots with a variety of camera movements (as Gray tells of the sensation of detachment he felt with a taciturn doctor, the camera slowly pulls backwards, while the agitation he felt during a visit to a weird Filipino 'psychic surgeon' is reflected by the camera tracking at speed). While *Gray's Anatomy*, then, is first and foremost a Spalding Gray film, Soderbergh's contribution in enhancing and enriching the storytelling should not be dismissed as mere window-dressing, but seen as yet another exploration of the nuts and bolts of film language.

< 277 >

Though Soderbergh has never quite lived up to the promise of his début, he remains one of the more adventurous and intelligent young film-makers currently at work in America. Apart from his evident fascination with film syntax, he is also of interest for the almost European sense of cool, ironic detachment evident in films like *sex, lies and videotape*, *Kafka* and *The Underneath* and for the psychological subtlety of his characters. In this last respect, his assurance with actors is enormously fruitful: the performances of all four leads in his début, of Jeremy Irons in *Kafka*, of Jesse Bradford in *King of the Hill*, and of Peter Gallacher, William Fichtner and Paul Dooley in *The Underneath* are especially memorable. It is only to be hoped that the fact that he hasn't made a hit for some time, and his desire to withdraw from mainstream production (*Schizopolis* only gained an extremely limited release) do not mean that he disappears from film-making altogether.

Hal Hartley

< **279** >

While all the film-makers discussed at length in this volume are distinguished by a robust creative idiosyncrasy which makes it unlikely that they will ever fit comfortably into the mainstream, it's probably true that, with the possible exception of Jarmusch, none of them so embodies the spirit of contemporary indie film-making in America as Hal Hartley, whose work is so far removed from the conventional genres that it is perhaps best understood as a genre unto itself. Even the films of Jarmusch and Haynes, finally, may be regarded as distant relations of, say, the road movie or Western, sickness movie or rags-to-riches melodrama, whereas Hartley's work – even the 'thriller' *Amateur* (1994) – bears only the faintest passing resemblance to established genres. Accordingly, of all the film-makers whose work is analysed in some depth in these pages, he is perhaps the hardest to pin down or neatly categorise, since his output raises sundry paradoxes and contradictions. Each of his films, on a narrative level, is packed with incident, yet the 'plot' seldom seems to be of prime importance; indeed, some of his more experimental shorts are to all intents and purposes 'plotless'. While his characters – played mostly by a repertory group of actors (Martin Donovan, Robert Burke, Bill Sage, Adrienne Shelly, Karen Sillas, Elina Lowensohn and Parker Posey) – are colourful, eccentric and vividly drawn, he encourages his actors to underplay, as if they were figures in a landscape, objects to be set alongside furniture, architecture, cars, trees, earth, sky and other structural features in the overall scheme of his visual design; moreover, it would be hard to argue that his films were essentially character-studies. Structurally, his films share certain elements with the mystery or suspense film (crime or violence often feature at some point) or melodrama (many concern dysfunctional families and/or the search for love, and include more than their fair share of coincidence), yet these elements are often stressed so little in terms of drama that we may barely register them as a major part of the narrative.

< **280** >

Moreover, while they are clearly very personal works, they never appear to add up to some forceful personal statement, nor do they stress autobiographical input or aim for a big emotional punch; they are discreet, reserved, unassertive and modest in the extreme. And though aspects of his style – the playful way with narrative, the stylised dialogue, offbeat characters and deadpan humour – have encouraged some critics to discern the influence of *auteurs* as diverse as Godard, Truffaut, Hawks, Sturges, Lynch and Jarmusch, his movies are not really like those of anyone else. Even characterising them as primarily concerned either with 'ideas' or with the formal properties of narrative cinema reaps limited rewards, since they seem to be more about questions than fully formed hypotheses, and are considerably more entertaining, interesting and involving on a human level than most studies in formalism. In the end, then, a Hal Hartley movie is exactly that, and unless he decides to change direction drastically, it is hard to imagine either that he would be able to make films acceptable to Hollywood or, indeed, that he would ever want to.

There is, however, another aspect to his films that makes them rather more difficult to write about than those of the other *auteurs* featured in this book. Not only are his stories, however full of incident, not of prime importance (which is not to say, of course, that they are without interest or meaning), but they frequently bear a strong resemblance to one another; it is as if

Hartley regards each movie as part of a larger work in progress, made in a quizzical spirit of enquiry. More so even than Sayles, Jarmusch or Haynes, all of whom repeatedly return to certain preferred themes and stylistic devices, it is as if Hartley is constantly reworking his material, refining his art, trying to find fresh ways of looking at the same handful of subjects that obsess him. Not that an overview of his career to date reveals no discernible progress. To the contrary: because he proceeds, as it were, one or two steps at a time, but always in the same general direction, it is easy to see how he is growing more assured and ambitious with every film. Thus, an overview of his work reveals at once that *Amateur* or *Flirt* (1995), say, are more audacious, confidently executed and mature than *The Unbelievable Truth* (1989) or the shorts he made before that first feature; by the same token, since he moves so methodically (by which I certainly don't mean cautiously) from one film to the next, and since the style and content of his films are so idiosyncratic and personal, it is immediately evident that the maker of, for example, *Kid* (1984) or *The Cartographer's Girlfriend* (1987) is also the creator of *Simple Men (1992)* or *Henry Fool* (1997).

< **281** >

Before moving on to a consideration of the individual films, it may be useful to point to some of the most immediate defining stylistic characteristics of his work as a whole. We have already noted that he prefers actors to give understated performances – not flat, exactly, but low-key, a little morose, and generally deadpan, especially in the delivery of the funnier lines – and to position themselves carefully within the frame, avoiding grand gestures except at specific moments involving spontaneous, often violent activity. (Sudden slaps, punches, scuffles and kisses regularly punctuate his work, which otherwise consists largely of conversation.) Moreover, the dialogue is generally written and delivered as if in quotation marks. In naturalistic terms, it's usually slightly off-kilter: philosophical and literary in tone (characters read from books, slide into aphorisms, or converse in strangely forthright fashion as if thinking or feeling aloud), bluntly confrontational (they constantly question, contradict and argue with each other), and sometimes intentionally repetitive, either to stress the habits and limits of human communication, to underline the obsessions of a particular character, or to stress a formal or thematic point.

Likewise, the visuals are not quite naturalistic; though the films are shot on location in mundane, unremarkable settings, there is a frequently a preponderance of primary colours in the decor, accentuated by Michael Spiller's crisp, sharp camerawork which tends to make use of claustrophobic medium shots or close-ups, slightly skewed angles or flattened, tableaux-like compositions to render the familiar fresh and even faintly unfamiliar; camera movement, meanwhile, is usually brief, measured, discreet and kept to a minimum, deployed mainly to track characters in motion. The overall effect is not entirely unlike, say, a Hopper or Hockney painting come to life: never picturesque, but simple, precise, informative, detached: a cool, clear-eyed interpretation of the real world. This slightly austere, pared-down visual aesthetic is reflected in his rigorous editing style: his narrative methods tend towards the elliptical, with scenes often starting, as it were, in mid-sentence, with an action or discussion already underway, and establishing shots avoided. It is as if Hartley is concerned only with the bare essentials: the tone of his films, at once serious, ironic, and regularly punctuated by injections of deadpan satire and dark absurdist humour, is fundamentally intimate and miniaturist. The focus is squarely on the reactions of individuals to each other and to their own psychological, emotional, moral and existential dilemmas and obsessions; if we are to draw any conclusions about the wider concerns of society in general, they derive less from individual films than from the repetitive nature of Hartley's body of work as a whole.

Hartley grew up in the working-class commuter belt of Long Island (the setting for most of his early films) before studying painting at the Massachusetts College of Art in Boston, where he began making movies in Super 8mm. It was only, however, when he moved on to film school at the State University of New York

< 282 >

that he really began watching and reading about movies seriously.
He then did a series of jobs, working in a lowly freelance capacity on a number of commercials and 'answering the telephone'
for a TV company producing public service announcements; at
the same time, he also made a number of shorts which reveal
Hartley's style and thematic obsessions in embryonic form. His
graduation film, *Kid*, for example, deals with the frustrations of
smalltown life; with its moody young hero attempting to leave
Lindenhurst to seek out a girlfriend in the city, only to be
detained by friends in need of help or trying to seduce him, the
territory is recognisably part of the Hartley landscape (and not
just because some of the cast will regularly reappear in his features). Ricky doesn't get on with his dad, is easy prey for any
female who shows interest in him, and needs to 'loosen up'; his
peers, meanwhile, include indecisive women, and men who are
either aggressively possessive of the women they know or
unhinged by the conformism of parochial life. Moreover, the
narrative style is economic and elliptical and the dialogue
tersely literary or aphoristic in places: one character, for example,
'knows the beauty of cold, tyrannical indifference'. Even more
non-naturalistic and enigmatic is *The Cartographer's Girlfriend*
(1987), in which a surveyor obsessed, somewhat metaphorically,
by the problems of mapping the world, enters into a sudden,
troubled affair with a mysterious young woman; not only do the
couple differ in their opinions about the nature and value of love,
but Bob barely communicates with his family, is confused by
advice given about women and sex by a friend, and again needs
to 'loosen up'. Once more the protagonist is torn between love
and work, head and heart, fear and desire; this time, however, the
narrative and dialogue are more heavily stylised than in *Kid*,
sometimes a little pretentiously, at others with a nice line in ironic, absurdist humour, especially in Bob's dealings with his would-
be womanising friend. Finally, even *Dogs* (1988), an updating of
scenes from Eugene O'Neill's *The Iceman Cometh* which concerns the emotional dilemmas of a group of young friends on the

< 283 >

eve of one of their number's marriage, is fairly typical; while their morose bewilderment over sexual matters and smalltown ennui prefigure both *The Unbelievable Truth* and *Trust* (1990), the cut-aways to slo-mo shots of snarling dogs, analogous to the boys' barely suppressed aggression towards each other, are a clumsy device he would avoid in his later work.

Though all these shorts showed considerable promise, it was only when Hartley, encouraged and financed by his TV company boss Jerome Brownstein, made his feature début with *The Unbelievable Truth* that he achieved the right balance between stylisation and narrative clarity. Described in very superficial terms, the plot sounds a little like a slightly bizarre updating of themes from a Western (mysterious, possibly violent stranger arrives in small town) and a Romeo and Juliet-style romance (young lovers are kept apart by parents and friends): when Josh (Robert Burke) returns to Lindenhurst after years in prison, Audry (Adrienne Shelly), a 17-year-old reluctant to go to college because she believes the world will soon be destroyed by nuclear war, and who has just broken with her boyfriend Emmet because he doesn't understand her fears and needs, is attracted to him as a soul-mate. Though her father Vic gives Josh a job as a mechanic at his garage, he warns him not to see Audry, since the town is rife with rumours about Josh's imprisonment for killing his former girlfriend (sister of Audry's friend Pearl) and her father. Audry, only two at the time of the killings, is intent on seeing him anyway, even after he admits he was responsible for Pearl's sister's death in a drunk-driving accident, and that he killed her father in self-defence; but when he resists her advances, she leaves for New York with Todd, a photographer who promised Vic he could make her rich as a model. Shortly afterwards, Vic and his wife are shocked to see a nude Audry in a magazine jewellery ad, and give the impoverished Josh $500 to visit her in the hope that the reunion will result in her coming home. In New York, however, Josh realises that she is now living with Todd and, in despair, gives the money to a derelict, throws a book Audry gave

< 284 >

him about George Washington through her window, and returns to Lindenhurst. Happily, she had been breaking up with Todd and, seeing the book, returns home; on arrival, she finds her family and friends at Josh's house, all in turmoil over his relationship with Pearl, who is asleep in his bed after telling him he didn't kill her father (who knocked the drunken Josh unconscious before falling downstairs, startled by the sight of Pearl). After it transpires that Josh and Pearl have not slept with each other and the truth about the killings comes out, Audry tells Vic she alone will decide whether she goes to college, and embraces Josh as they listen for the sounds of war.

< 285 >

While the mystery over the killings and the romance between Josh and Audry are clearly the motors that drive the narrative (which in terms of detail is far more convoluted and complex than in the above synopsis), the resolution of neither plot strand is particularly important or satisfying on a dramatic or emotional level. Rather, they serve merely as threads in a larger tapestry which, at its most basic level, satirically depicts the economic mindset that informs smalltown life and which, on a deeper level, explores the relationship between truth and falsehood, knowledge, opinion and rumour; in each respect, trust is signally lacking. In the first, human interaction is largely a matter of give and take carefully calculated: people only give when they know they will get something in return. Most notably and hilariously, this defines the relationship between Audry and Vic, which has nothing to do with familial love and everything to do with transaction: Vic wants her to go to college, but nowhere too expensive, while she will only take the courses he wants if he makes a donation to her chosen charity; later, it is the lure of money that makes Vic encourage her to take up modelling, and money (given to Josh as a way of tempting her home) with which he tries to buy back his self-respect, dashed by the nude photo session he inadvertently pushed her towards. Crucially, Josh is concerned with money only insofar as it meets his basic, everyday requirements; and Audry 'finds' herself when, at the film's end, she hands Vic a cheque for the money she's saved as a model, telling him that henceforth all such deals are off; she'll determine her future according to her own needs and feelings.

Such deals imply a lack of trust in relationships, and it is the lack of trust regarding the newly returned Josh that creates all the complications and misunderstandings in the film; everyone – whether out of fear, desire, or laziness – is too willing to listen to rumour and rely on dim, distant memories ever to try and discover the truth, which would necessitate them bringing up an awkward topic with Pearl, who alone really knows what befell her father, and who has kept silent out of hatred for Josh's role in her sister's death. Again, it is crucial that Josh, like his and Audry's hero George Washington, cannot or will not lie; just as his presence throws the community into chaos, so his honesty acts as a catalyst whereby things are eventually brought out into the open and relationships set on a more even keel. At the same time, he and Audry have to learn to trust one another: he over her dealings with Todd, she over his with Pearl. It's significant that when, at the film's close, they decide to go off together (with Josh still claiming he trusts no one, even though he loves her), she tells him to 'Listen!' – ostensibly to the sound of war-planes which she hears but he doesn't, but also, by implication, to the truth. To gain knowledge, we should trust to our own experience rather than to the hearsay of others; and to give and receive trust, we should listen to our own instincts, just as Audry did about Josh when all around her were telling her he was a dangerous murderer.

All this might be dismally pretentious, were it not for the wit and originality of Hartley's writing and *mise-en-scène*. The notion of human interaction as barter is hilariously embodied in the ludicrously complex deals and sub-deals Vic and Audry hammer out in their endless bargaining with each other. The prevailing air of distrust and suspicion is marvellously evoked at the end of the film when all the main characters gather at Josh's beach-house, spying on each other through windows and passing from room to room as if in some demented, farcical game of hide and seek.

< **286** >

The banal limitations of daily human discourse are suggested in a scene with Josh being vainly chatted up by a waitress, where an identical sequence of phrases is repeated, like a litany, three times in succession, and in the numerous times Josh is asked by different characters whether he's a priest (noting only his black garb and the fact that he doesn't drink, they are loath to accept the truth that he's an ex-con and a mechanic). Such playful anti-naturalistic devices extend to the narrative as a whole, with Hartley filling in the ellipses between scenes with intertitles announcing 'MEANWHILE', 'BUT', 'THEN' and 'A MONTH, MAYBE TWO MONTHS LATER', as if editing conventions were unable to provide all the information we need, or as if the film-maker were unable quite to make up his mind about the order and time-scale of the narrative. Not all the humour is in this formalist vein, however; much of it derives from ludicrously excessive behaviour or choice dialogue. Emmet's jealousy over Audry's feelings for Josh is expressed in pathetic flirtations with any passing female and equally risible fights with any nearby male; Vic's assistant Mike explains at length to the virgin Josh how having a girlfriend entails improving personal hygiene, such as washing one's back; and Vic, keen to get Josh to entice Audry away from Todd, tells him she's crazy about him, adding: 'I ain't kidding – the girl sleeps with your crescent wrench!' (Indeed, she does – a token of desire that is characteristically absurd and mundane in this community where almost everyone, except Josh, seems to be caught up in his or her own obsessions; small wonder they find it so difficult to hear and see the truth.)

< 287 >

In terms of basic plot and characters, *Trust* is in many ways surprisingly similar to its predecessor, concerning as it does a girl, Maria (Shelly again), at a crossroads in her life and involved with an honest man, Matthew (Martin Donovan), who has a history of violence and who, like her, is trapped in a troubled relationship with a parent. Maria's home problems arise when she announces she is pregnant and leaving school; her father keels over and dies when she slaps him for calling her a slut, and her mother first throws her out of the house, then accepts her back only on condition that she work like a slave. Matthew, meanwhile, is even more violently abused by his father, and frequently loses his temper when confronted by inefficiency and crookedness at the computer factory where his technical expertise is appreciated but his idealism frowned on; he also prefers books and Beethoven to television (which he detests), and carries a grenade... When these two outcasts meet, with Maria in despair after having been abandoned by the jock father of her unborn child, a healing process begins for both, when Matthew moves in with Maria, her single-parent sister Peg, and their mother Jean. But their path to happiness is strewn with obstacles: Maria is undecided over whether to have an abortion or to marry Matthew as he proposes; they become involved in a search for a woman whom she suspects has kidnapped a child to replace her own dead daughter; Matthew's father continues to bait him; and Jean tries to pair him off with Peg, even going so far as to get him drunk and putting him in the elder sister's bed. Maria, who has by now taken a job and begun reading in earnest under Matthew's tutelage, finds him asleep in bed with Peg and has an abortion the following day, after which she tells Matthew, who has by now left his job in disgust again, that she no longer wants to get married. Leaving her a thesaurus as a gift, Matthew takes his grenade to the computer factory; Maria follows him and, amidst the panic, takes the unexploded grenade from him and throws it away. When it does explode, she tells him she'll tell the police the explosion is her fault, and as she watches him staring back at her as he is driven away, she puts on the reading glasses which she always felt made her look stupid, but which he advised her to wear...

Again, this synopsis gives little idea of the immense detail with which Hartley invests the film, but it does suggest the way Maria and Matthew's stunted, frustrated, oppressed lives are redeemed through mutual support: Martin gives Maria the

< **288** >

Jean Coughlin (Merrit Nelson) and Matthew Slaughter (Martin Donovan), in **Trust** (1990) – a heavy brew of dysfunctional family life leavened by Hartley's absurd comic antics and witty dialogue.

respect, education and wider ambitions that enable her to move on from her hitherto unprepossessing prospects of dull, reluctant motherhood; she gives him the trust in his future that his father, his bosses and his own capacity for violent rages have hitherto denied him. (In one particularly engaging scene, the couple attempt to define love as an equation involving respect, admiration and trust, after which Maria proves her trust in him by falling backwards from a concrete edifice, convinced he'll catch her.) But *Trust* is certainly no mere remake of *The Unbelievable Truth*; not only is it considerably darker than its predecessor, dealing as it does with parental abuse, unwanted pregnancy, child kidnapping, sexual harrassment (at one point a liquor owner tries to assault Maria), guilt, and thoughts of suicide, but it is more complex in probing the psychology of the various characters. Even Matthew's father, it transpires, has a reason, albeit no excuse, for his abuse of his son (to whom he proudly refers in public as a genius): his wife died giving birth to Matthew. Jean's cruel domination of Maria, meanwhile, at first seems simply vengeful, but during her drunken session with Matthew, she confesses that the reason she doesn't want Maria to marry him is because she doesn't want her to make the same mistake she and Peg did: she was relieved at the death of her husband, who had poisoned her life for 20 years (a credible claim, given his insults to Maria in the opening scene).

< **290** >

This bleakly unappealing prospect of family life haunts the film. As Maria agonises over whether to have an abortion, she is confronted by visions of how her life might evolve: the woman who abducts a child because her life seems empty since her daughter died; Peg, divorced and living with her mother while trying to raise two children; Jean, bitter as hell; and men, selfish as her jock boyfriend, meekly conformist as the kidnapper's husband (who in a very funny scene is seen to dress identically to all the town's other commuters), lecherous as the liquor-store owner, or volatile as Martin and his dad. Guilty over the death of her own father, Maria must move forwards, look to her own needs, desires and talents instead of listening to her family. Likewise Martin, guilty over the death of his mother (whose more modest, 'grown-up' dress, in a rather Freudian twist, Maria presently takes to wearing), must stop bending to the will of his father out of fear and unspoken pity. It is fitting, then, that at the film's end, his grenade (brought back by his father from Korea) explodes, as if ridding him of guilt and suicidal impulses, just as a traffic light above Maria's head, in the final shot, indicates that she can now proceed forwards.

True to form, Hartley leavens what might otherwise have been a heavy brew (there are implications that the initially brattish Maria achieves an almost saintly selflessness in her dealings with her mother and Matthew) with humour: not merely the sight gags involved in the couple's naive, Hardy Boys-style search for the abductor's overcoated, pipe-smoking, trilby-sporting commuter husband, but Matthew's absurdly sudden, extreme outbursts of rage (punching out men who get in his way in a bar, placing a detested employee's head in a vice). Nevertheless, the movie, for all that it succeeds as a comedy of manners, is symptomatic of Hartley's readiness to tackle serious social issues; indeed, its indictment of corporate dishonesty at the computer factory (which knowingly and happily sells flawed goods to an unsuspecting public), its sympathetic depiction of an abortion clinic nurse harrassed by pro-life campaigners, and its tacit endorsement of a woman's right to choose arguably make it his most overtly political film about contemporary America to date.

< 291 >

Even though Hartley's first two features are hardly plot-led or even particularly 'resolved' in comparison with most American films, Hollywood or independent, in 1991 he made two shorts and a featurette for television which allowed him to move still further away from conventional narrative arcs. Indeed, both *Theory of Achievement* and *Ambition* are virtually without 'plot' as such. The former concerns a group of Brooklynites – 'young, middle-class, college-educated, broke, unskilled, white... and drunk' for some of its duration – endlessly arguing whether Brooklyn, seen by one of their number as future capital of the art world, is an affordable place to live, and discussing the value of work, creativity, happiness and self-knowledge; they quote from books, list their heroes, sing eccentric songs (including a roisterous prayer to win the lottery), fall out and make up. In the latter (Hartley's most Godardian film to date), a young New Yorker who keeps insisting 'I'm good at what I do' learns from a woman that 'the world is a dangerous and uncertain place'; he repeatedly and successfully fends off muggers in the street, discusses work and his philosophy of life with strangers, and in an office defends himself against an unheard interrogator before being repeatedly chased and beaten up, in slow-motion, in a corridor, while still proclaiming his worth and his love of England 'for rock and roll and Virginia Woolf'. Both are wry, satirical portraits of the predicament of the young, contemporary would-be artist, playful experiments made with his friends (many of whom have appeared in other Hartley films) in how to assemble small cinematic vignettes without recourse to or the need for a neat, coherent story. If they finally don't add up to anything very substantial in terms of theme, they do display Hartley's growing interest in staging scenes involving action, be it inspired by slapstick comedy or by music and dance.

Though the hour-long featurette *Surviving Desire* was rather more closely aligned to traditional narrative – it concerns a young college professor, Jude (Martin Donovan), who embarks on a brief, doomed love affair with one of his students, Sophie (Mary Ward), who's anxious that others might think she's sleeping with him to get better grades – Hartley still took the opportunity to avoid the kind of tidy, naturalistic storytelling favoured in most television films (or, indeed, in most theatrical features): the much mulled-over affair fizzles out almost before it's begun. Again, the dialogue is unusually literary in tone (not only is Jude obsessed by a paragraph about love from Dostoevsky's *The Brothers Karamazov* which, much to his pupils' dissatisfaction, he's been going over for a month and a half, but Sophie speaks and writes about their relationship in poetic terms, and a barman waxes philosophical to him about Americans liking their tragedies to have a happy ending). Again, characters speak their innermost thoughts undiluted by social niceties (Sophie asks Jude, 'Will you carry your disappointment around with you forever?' if he never sees her again – to which, in a nice wry touch, he raises his eyes in exasperation, replying, 'I'll risk it'). Again, too, the film explores the need for trust, the conflict between the head and heart (Jude discovers through the disastrous affair that 'Knowing is not enough'), and different attitudes to finding a suitable partner: Jude's theology student friend Bob believes, like Luke, that we should love and cherish whoever is before us and so ends up engaged to a mad woman who asks any passing man to wed her – whereas Jude is caught up in delusions of romantic destiny. Most memorable, however, is a scene in which Jude,

< 292 >

elated at Sophie kissing him in a bar, runs out into a backyard and, together with two men who happen to be passing, performs a bizarre little dance, unaccompanied by music. The movements and gestures – which evoke, among other things, Gene Kelly, Madonna and the crucifixion – suggest romantic ecstacy, sexual desire and suffering; but the real pleasure to be had from this brief, funny interlude is in seeing Hartley completely turn his back on naturalism to work his own modest but affecting variation on a stylistic convention familiar from classic Hollywood escapism.

< 293 >

Over the next few years, Hartley would regularly make shorts as a way of exploring more experimental techniques. *NYC 3/94*, for example, which intercuts scenes of three characters caught up in violence on the streets of New York with a man at a microphone commenting on urban life, is an exercise in narrative coincidence and the juxtaposition of image and sound (the violence is heard rather than seen); *Iris*, which features two young women lifting weights, discussing money problems and repeating an incantation about the hours that must pass until Iris sleeps over, is a fragmented (and, it must be said, fairly impenetrable) study in representation, again with sound (rock music, dripping water, bird noises) used to unusual effect; while *Opera No 1* is a minimusical, set in what appears to be a derelict warehouse and with music by Hartley himself (as Ned Rifle he has been composing his own scores since 1991), in which two scruffily garbed, cigarette-smoking fairies on rollerblades engineer the romantic union of a bookworm and a girl tired of sleeping alone. Ornate yet funky to look at, with memorably mundane lyrics (when the man croons to one of the immortals, 'I feel my hands were simply invented to caress your thighs', she sings sweetly, 'Take your mind out of the gutter and your hand off my leg') offsetting the fairy-tale romanticism, the film is gleefully, whimsically modern, a witty variation on opera conventions that includes transvestism, magic spells, mistaken identity and an intermission title accompanied by overdubbed applause. Indeed, the relationship between sound and image is a constant motif in Hartley's later shorts, and inflects even some of his pop-video promos: as the song plays in 'From Motel 6', we simply see the band Yo La Tengo setting up its equipment, the guitarist playing a furious but very brief solo, and then the band packing up and leaving again, while for 'The Only Living Boy in New York', the band Everything But The Girl mime to the song without actually opening their mouths – as if Hartley is taking his renowned preference for understated acting to its logical conclusion to offer a sardonic commentary on how gestures and facial expressions in rock performances tend towards histrionic excess.

< **294** >

His features, meanwhile, would steadily become more assured without any compromise in terms of style or content. *Simple Men*, the last of his 'Long Island films' (though it was actually shot in Texas), returned to the themes of suspicion and trust, truth and rumour, troubled families, and the search for love, while complicating the issue further by doubling the number of central characters. The men in question are two brothers: Bill (Robert Burke), a petty criminal who at the film's start is betrayed by his girlfriend when she deserts him with their partner in crime and the takings of an armed robbery, and Dennis (Bill Sage), a rather serious student obsessed with tracking down their father, a former baseball hero who 20 years ago was imprisoned for the murder of seven people with a bomb planted at the Pentagon. Only reluctantly does Bill accompany his brother to Long Island to find their father (who escaped during a hospital visit), since he is more concerned with fleeing the police and taking his revenge on women than in reuniting with a man he considers crazy and a poor father to boot. En route, however, the impoverished brothers help a woman, Kate (Karen Sillas), tend to her epileptic friend Elina (Elina Löwnsohn), and Bill abandons his plans to seduce and ruin women when he falls for Kate, who partly from gratitude, partly from fear of her psychotic ex-husband Jack (just released from prison), invites the brothers to stay awhile at her place. Meanwhile, Dennis finds himself attracted to the enigmatic Elina, whom he suspects is his father's mistress, and whom he eventually follows to a boat in which his dad, still an anarchist and still protesting his innocence, plans to escape. By now the police, alerted to the presence of strangers in the area, are looking for Bill; at a garage (run by Vic and Mike from *The Unbelievable Truth*) they hold Dennis by mistake, while Bill – who has already seen off Jack (harmless, as it turns out) – asks Kate to lie to the cops so that he may escape with his father. Constitutionally unable to lie, and angry that all the men in her life seem to be criminals, she refuses, but is later reconciled to him when he returns to give himself up, having decided at a brief, wordless encounter with his father to stay put and face the consequences.

< **295** >

Though *Simple Men* shares many themes with *The Unbelievable Truth* and *Trust*, it explores them in rather more complex fashion. The brothers' mixed feelings about their father may recall the abusive parents and erroneous rumours in the earlier films, but because of the political nature of his crime (as a baseball star he's an establishment hero, as an alleged terrorist he's a 60s radical scorned in the 90s), his presence in the narrative also serves to allow his sons – one law-abiding, the other a thief who eventually reforms – to discuss the relationship of crime, justice, government and the law. Moreover, the fact that Elina is his lover reinforces the Oedipal aspect to his sons' feelings – partly hostile, partly solicitous, partly curious – about him: when Dennis, in response to Elina's accusation that he doesn't respect his father, says he at least respects his taste in women, she replies, 'So then go make love to your mother!'

Indeed, the film is primarily about how the brothers think about women, and how their simplistic moral systems collapse when they meet Kate and Elina. Betrayed by his lover and estranged from the mother of his child (he's not so good a father himself), Bill plans to make the first good-looking woman he meets fall in love with him by pretending to be 'mysterious, thoughtful, deep but modest', and then to fuck her, use her up

< 296 >

'like a little toy' and throw her away. But the first such woman he meets is Kate, strong, intelligent and honest, and he immediately falls for her and abandons his scheme, only for her to tell him (in a memorably droll scene) that he strikes her as mysterious, thoughtful and deep; when he tries to deflect the compliment, she tells him he's being modest. Nothing, in other words, is as he expects it to be; past experience has led him to view women with suspicion and make absurd generalisations about life, but meeting Kate and letting down his defences enables him to face the truth, admit to his own vulnerability and needs, and give up a life of crime in which, evidently, he wasn't especially successful. Dennis too entertains a simplistic view of women, apparently inspired by his protective love of his mother (his distaste for his father stems less from his infamy as a terrorist than from his womanising); he is not only distinctly uncomfortable about Elina being the lover of an older, still married man, but so innocent that at one point he can't understand how he might be doing anything untoward when he gropes between the legs of a strangely mature young schoolgirl for a note containing his father's phone number. Bill starts off hating women for their treachery; Dennis puts them on some sort of pedestal, only vaguely aware of their sexuality; the truth, somewhere in between, only dawns on them during their encounter with Kate and Elina.

Hartley derives much comic mileage from confounding the expectations of both his simplistic men and his audience. When Bill, heartened by Kate's compliments, kisses her, she slaps him… only to tell him at their next meeting that he may kiss her again (it was his presumption that angered her). His theory, based on the slap, that Kate and Elina are lesbians could not be more mistaken. The schoolgirl Dennis meets is watched over by a nun, who chain-smokes and is not averse to fighting cops in the street should the occasion demand. The psychotic Jack turns out to be a docile sort who only wants to collect his jacket from Kate's. The cop hunting down Bill is so lovelorn that instead of doing his job efficiently, he mopes around bemoaning how put upon and lone-

The enigmatic Elina (Elina Löwensohn) leads brothers Bill (Robert Burke) and Dennis (Bill Sage) in a dance to the sounds of Sonic Youth in **Simple Men** (1992).

ly he is and wondering why women exist. And Mike, Vic's assistant, spends all his time playing loud electric guitar and learning French (very badly) in order to date a local check-out girl – who, Vic later informs him, is Italian. Nobody conforms to stereotype, so that the men are confused, and lack control of their emotional lives, whereas the women know what they want and are not prepared to accept anything less. (It's no accident that during one drunken after-dinner discussion about the exploitation and representation of women, Elina voices admiration for Madonna for her image of strength, self-determination and for maintaining control over her career.)

< 298 >

Simple Men is no less interesting on a stylistic and formal level. The narrative is, if anything, more audaciously elliptical and pared down than before. It begins with Bill in mid-robbery, telling a blindfolded security guard 'Don't move!'; we are thrown abruptly into the story without preamble or explanation, just as later on we suddenly 'lose' the brothers for a while – the film fades to black and begins again, as it were, on an image of Kate and Elina (whom we haven't seen before) in mid-conversation in a field. The effect is disorientating, encouraging close attention lest we miss anything, such as Vic and Mike's having walked in from an earlier movie, or another repeated, circular conversation like the one in *The Unbelievable Truth*, or a hide-and-seek scene again evocative of a weird farce, or the sundry narrative details and coincidences scattered through the movie. Moreover, Hartley develops on the dance sequence in *Surviving Desire* to marvellous effect: after Kate's friend Martin (Martin Donovan), jealous at her attraction to Bill, drives into the country, kicks his cap around (in typically volatile Donovan style) and angrily screams 'I can't stand the quiet!', the film cuts suddenly to Elina, Kate, Martin and the brothers in Kate's bar, with Elina gradually leading the others into a weird, eccentrically stylised formation dance to a song by Sonic Youth, the various groupings, glances and gestures serving to illuminate the shifting allegiances and suspicions of the five dancers. The scene both serves as an unexpected musical interlude and furthers the narrative; such flashes of inspiration display Hartley's increasing maturity and confidence. (Another is the way the film's final words, spoken off-screen by the cop come to arrest Bill as he lays his head on Kate's protective shoulder, are identical to those which opened the film: 'Don't move!'. This time, however, the roles are reversed, with Bill now vulnerable – he's being held at gunpoint and he's in love – and not even wanting to move.)

If *Simple Men* sometimes looked (somewhat deceptively) as if it were about to turn into a road-movie, *Amateur* made similarly beguiling moves towards the crime thriller. It begins with a shot of a man, Thomas (Martin Donovan), lying unconscious with a head wound in a New York street; a woman, whom we later learn is Sofia (Elina Löwensohn), timidly inspects his body and runs off. Thomas revives and staggers into a coffee-shop, where he is found to be suffering from amnesia and taken home and tended to by Isabelle (Isabelle Huppert), a former nun trying, with little success, to make a living as a writer of pornography; a virgin who considers herself a nymphomaniac, she asks if he will make love to her, but he is too tired. Meanwhile, Sofia contacts her accountant friend Edward (Damian Young), telling him that she's killed her husband Thomas, a violent crook who forced her into prostitution and made her act in porn films made by the crime organisation for which Edward used to work. Learning that Thomas was trying to blackmail the organisation's Dutch boss Jacques with records of arms deals stored on computer disks, Sofia, who wants to start a new life, phones Jacques and asks for the money herself; he responds by sending two thugs, Jan and Kurt, who torture Edward in an attempt to discover Sofia's whereabouts. Isabelle, meanwhile, recognises Sofia in a porn video, and since Thomas has mentioned her name in his sleep, they visit her apartment in the hope she'll tell them about his identity and past. Finding the place empty, she puts on Sofia's sexy clothes, but as the couple begin to make love, they are disturbed first by the thugs then by Sofia. When Jan goes out for a

< **299** >

while, they emerge from hiding to save Sofia from torture, forcing Kurt out of the window to his death, and escape in Jan's car to an upstate hideout recommended to Sofia by Edward. He, in the meantime, has been wandering the city deranged by his ordeal at the hands of Jan and Kurt; after being arrested and shooting a cop who tries to prevent his escape, he too heads upstate in a stolen police car. After Isabelle relieves Sofia (who will still only reveal that Thomas is dangerous) of the incriminating disks and posts them to her publisher, Jan catches her and takes her to the house where he is shot dead by the recently arrived Edward; sadly, Sofia is also wounded. Isabelle, accompanied by Thomas and Edward, takes her for treatment at her former convent, where she learns the truth about Thomas; when he apologises to her without knowing what he's done, she asks him if he will still make love to her. Assenting, he goes to fetch the car, but as he emerges from the convent, he is shot dead by the police who have been trailing Edward. When they see their mistake, they ask Isabelle if she knows the dead man; she replies that she does.

< **300** >

Befitting Hartley's description of the film as 'an action thriller, with one flat tyre', *Amateur* is packed with his usual delightfully eccentric characters and absurdly po-faced jokes. Isabelle – a character written specifically for Huppert after she wrote saying she'd enjoyed *Trust* and suggesting they work together – is a particularly engaging creation, explaining the fact that she believes she's a nymphomaniac despite never having had sex with a morose 'I'm choosy', and patiently pointing out to Thomas that the men looking for him 'work for a highly respectable yet ultimately sinister international corporation with political connections'. But many of the other characters are equally vivid, offbeat variations on traditional movie types: Sofia, the porn star who determines to become 'a mover and shaker' without having a clue how to do so; Jan and Kurt, forever arguing about the best kind of mobile phones or, in the latter case, asking Sofia, even as he prepares to torture her, if she resents being a commodity in the motion picture industry; Isabelle's publisher, complaining that he

Isabelle Huppert and Martin Donovan in **Amateur** (1994) – described by Hartley as 'an action thriller with one flat tyre'.

always really wanted to work in 'defamatory journalism'; the female cop Patsy whose sympathies for the unfortunates she deals with cause her regularly to burst into tears. All this is deliciously amusing, but also wholly to the point, since the film is about people who are all 'amateurs' at what they do, and would like to start out anew. Only Thomas, who has lost his memory and former identity, is given a real chance to do that – but, the film asks, how possible is it for a person to change completely, and how far can Thomas be held culpable for his criminal past now that he is reborn as a fundamentally decent man? Sofia, a victim of his violent iniquities, can't forgive him and doesn't want to forget; but for Isabelle, who comes to love him, his past matters only insofar as she feels a need to rectify his 'mistakes' by taking Sofia under her wing (just as she eventually rectified her own by leaving the convent after 15 years).

For Isabelle, despite her attempts at writing pornography, is convinced she has a mission, ever since she had visions of the Virgin Mary as a child; when she sees Sofia in the porn video, she recognises her from a previous visit to the cinema, links her with the name Thomas mentioned in his sleep, and believes it is a heaven-sent 'sign' that her encounter with him is fated and will allow her to fulfil her destiny by helping Sofia. (Incidentally, Hartley based the frozen video image of Sofia's face as she has sex on a photo of Bernini's statue of St Teresa.) For Thomas, and perhaps for the writer-director, of course, it may be coincidence rather than destiny that is at work; nevertheless, Isabelle does 'save' Sofia, albeit at the cost of the life of the man she has come to know and love. In this sense *Amateur* is a tragedy (its ending is certainly more emotionally affecting than those of his earlier films): though Thomas, ironically, is killed for a crime he didn't commit, it is his own past actions that set in motion the chain of events leading to his death, at the very moment when he had learned to accept love and trust another person, and when Isabelle was on the brink of belatedly achieving another mission – losing her virginity and finding the love hitherto denied her.

Amateur, then, is a very tender film, for all its humour and its interest in crime, pornography and violence. Indeed, Hartley uses these elements in a fresh, intriguing way, far removed from the mainstream's titillating clichés. The context of organised crime, as suggested by talk of 'highly respectable but ultimately sinister corporations', is evoked in cursory, ironic fashion, as if guying conspiracy-thriller conventions, while the pornography never results in prurient imagery but is implied through dialogue (not only Isabelle's stilted, overly 'poetic' writings, but also Thomas' unlikely discussion with a teenage boy – played, as it happens, by a young woman – about the attractiveness of models in a porn mag lent him by Isabelle), through the strangely chaste video sequence of Sofia, and through the 'sexy' clothes Isabelle borrows from Sofia's wardrobe. Violence, meanwhile, is depicted in a way that is never gratuitous but which also never

< **302** >

shies away from its horror: when Kurt tortures Edward by applying electric flex to his temples, though we briefly see his agonised face, his pain is conveyed at greater length by a shot of twitching ankles; when Isabelle forces Kurt out of the window, her advance upon him in the sexy clothes and armed with a power drill comes over as an absurdly excessive pastiche of a kinky *femme fatale* (she is an ex-nun, after all); and when the deranged Edward fires again and again at Jan, the repetition, the jerky cartoon-like choreography of the men's movements, and the fact that the scene is tracked in long shot all make the sequence seem oddly unreal, even as its crazy brutality remains evident throughout. Hartley's stylisation has always had a purpose, but here it serves him well as a means of representation without exploitation.

< 303 >

The poignancy of Isabelle's quiet assertion, 'I know this man', at the end of *Amateur* was unprecedented in Hartley's work, as if he'd finally decided (or learned) to invest his films with heartfelt emotion as well as intellectual substance. A similar tenderness concluded *Flirt*, which in every other respect is the most formally rigorous and experimental of his features. It comprises three identically plotted parts (shot intermittently over three years), set in New York, Berlin and Tokyo. In each, a 'flirt' – whether real or perceived as such – is about to see their partner depart to spend several months working abroad, where an old flame lives, and doubts exist as to whether the relationship should continue. Intentionally or otherwise, and unbeknownst to the partner, the flirt has already become involved, through a kiss, with another prospective (married) lover, and after a series of encounters with various individuals (acquaintances of those involved in the romantic triangle, or simply passers-by), he/she is wounded in the face by a gun-shot. Subsequent hospital surgery, so painful that the patient is encouraged to think of something specific (which in each case turns out to concern sex), wrecks the flirt's plans to drive their partner to the airport and to confirm once and for all whether or not he/she is ready to commit more fully.

Where Jarmusch's *Mystery Train* explored aspects of cinematic storytelling by means of three roughly contemporaneous episodes, set in and around the same hotel, which are gradually revealed to intersect in various ways with one another, Hartley goes one step further by basing each of his stories on almost identical dialogue and events. Repetition has always been a feature of his work, but here it lies at the very heart of the film. At the same time, each episode differs subtly from the others, and not only because the different settings shape the narratives, the milieux, the characters and overall atmosphere. In the first, the 'flirt' is a white heterosexual male (Bill Sage) who, despite his claims to sensitivity, appears chronically unable to commit to anyone, let alone his partner (Parker Posey). In the second, it is a gay, black American (Dwight Ewell), whose cool air of indifference belies the fact that he doesn't respond especially flirtatiously to the various people he encounters – perhaps he is considering committing to his German lover (Dominik Bender) after all. And in the third, the protagonist is a Japanese girl (Miho Nikaidoh) who is far too serious to be a flirt – she is merely regarded as one by a dance-troupe colleague and by the suicidally possessive wife of her choreographer, Mr Ozu, who is seen kissing Miho after she comforts him in a moment of depression. Indeed, Miho is actually very concerned about Ozu's wife, and it is her attempts to help her – coupled with misunderstandings over a gun which result in her being briefly held by the police – that delay her efforts to join her departing film-maker boyfriend, Hal (Hartley himself).

Not only the cities' special imprints – New York with its street and café culture, Berlin with its art, prostitution and vibrant gay life, Tokyo with its traditional and experimental theatre, youthful fashions and sense of propriety – but the flirts' gender, race and sexual proclivities shape the dynamics of each episode. Though, as we have noted, the dialogue and basic elements of the storyline are almost identical in each episode, Hartley reorders and rearranges them, adds and subtracts details, and

< 304 >

makes telling changes in terms of who says or does what to whom, not to mention how, where, when and why. Hence, Bill is accidentally shot by the despondent husband of the woman he's been seeing; Dwight is (presumably – it occurs off-screen) shot by the wife of his potential lover when his reluctant sexual attempts to comfort her are interrupted by the arrival of the drunken husband; and Miho accidentally shoots herself when, taking the gun from Ozu's wife, she is surprised by two policemen.

Hartley makes other radical changes from episode to episode. In the first, Bill enters a bathroom in a café, asks for and is (hilariously) given remarkably forthright, philosophical advice on his emotional predicament by three men, one urinating, another slumped on the floor and the other sitting on a toilet stall. In the equivalent Berlin scene, Dwight pitches these questions at a friend, before the film cuts to three builders who discuss among

< **305** >

Miho (right), the main character from the Tokyo segment of **Flirt** (1995) – the most formally rigorous and experimental of Hartley's films, in which the same script is delivered three times by three different casts in different locations resulting in a variety of tones, nuances and outcomes.

themselves not only Dwight's problems but the definition of flirtation and the meaning, purpose and artistic shortcomings of the film they're in. (In so doing, they not only shatter the already fragile 'realist' illusion of the movie, but clarify its methods and concerns for the viewer.) In the third story, Miho is confronted in a police cell by three schematically different Japanese women (or movie stereotypes: a traditionally demure wife, a tense, chic career woman, and a tough biker) who all speak at the same time, offering their various opinions on men and how to treat them.

< **306** >

A still more dramatic shift occurs in the Tokyo story, which begins with a lengthy, almost silent rehearsal of an experimental dance which to some extent plays out, through its gestures, the events that will follow. In the first two episodes, many actions (notably the fateful kiss) were merely described or discussed, whereas the third depicts them: not only are they seen by the audience, but they are witnessed by other characters – fittingly, in that the 'flirt' in this instance is defined less by what she actually does than by how she is perceived by a watchful society concerned with correct behaviour. (Miho is reported to and arrested by the police simply because she's been seen in the street with a gun.)

When Bill and Dwight are told while under surgery to think of something specific, they respectively describe in detail hetero- and homosexual love-making (though both, to the doctors' bemusement, use the antiquated word 'spooning'), whereas Miho, who passes out from the pain, simply dreams about sex: we see her in bed with various lovers, the last of them Hal. Moreover, there is notably less dialogue in the Tokyo story, so that the overall mood is sometimes rather reminiscent of the mime in *butoh*, a form of dance related to experimental theatre. While this paucity of words almost certainly results in part from Hartley's unease with the Japanese language, it also suggests that while he is already acclaimed as a writer of dialogue, he is eager to explore other modes of film language.

Formally, then, *Flirt* is his most audacious and inventive feature to date. At the same time, however, it transcends mere formalism by offering a conclusion that pays emotional dividends. Bill emerges from hospital too late to take his girlfriend to the airport, but orders a cab announcing he's going to Paris anyway – we have no idea whether she'll be glad to see him, given that he failed to meet her ultimatum and commit before her departure. Dwight tries to reach Johan, realises he has missed him, and visits a roadside snack-bar where he is charmed by a man who, solicitous about his wounded face, offers him his jacket. Dwight's future seems even more uncertain than Bill's. When Miho emerges from surgery, she finds Hal asleep in the waiting room. Evidently, he has decided to delay his journey in order to await the outcome of her operation, and Miho, without even waking him, simply places his arm around her and closes her eyes. This particular 'flirt', who was no such thing, is willing and able both to give and accept commitment. Furthermore, this tentative, gently hopeful image of easy togetherness – perhaps the most genuinely romantic and affecting in the film-maker's career – achieves an additional power in light of the fact that Hartley – here appearing in one of his films for the first and, so far, only time – went on to marry Miho Nikaidoh in real life. *Flirt* may be seen as something of a personal love-letter.

As if in reaction to the structural rigours and subtle miniaturist nuances of *Flirt*, *Henry Fool* is, by Hartley standards, a sprawling, shaggy dog of a movie, dealing with diverse themes and satirical targets as it ranges through a variety of moods. Simon Grim (James Urbaniak) is a shy, taciturn, sexually naive garbage man, oppressed by his foul-mouthed, work-shy, promiscuous sister Fay (Parker Posey) and his depressive, couch-potato mother Mary (Maria Porter), and bullied and ostracised as a retard by other inhabitants of his working-class New Jersey hometown. Until, that is, (as if in answer to his prayers) the arrival of Henry Fool (Thomas Jay Ryan), an egocentric, self-appointed philosopher, rebel and bum whose articulacy, confidence and non-conformism make him strangely charismatic to all who meet him.

< **307** >

Prone to borrowing money at every opportunity, Henry moves into the Grims' seedy basement where, between claims about the world-shaking import of the 'Confession' he has been writing for years, he encourages Simon to put his own thoughts to paper. Though barely literate, the results – written, inadvertently, in iambic pentameters – convince Henry that his friend and disciple is a great American poet. While a handful of friends agree, Simon's family and others in the town (where a right-wing back-to-basics political campaign is being waged) consider his work at best insignificant, at worst pornographic. Undeterred, Henry (who, it emerges, has just been released from a seven-year prison sentence for having sex with a 13-year-old girl) agrees to give the increasingly self-confident Simon the address of Angus, a publishing friend in the city; he, however, denies all knowledge of Henry (though his secretary Laura tells Simon he worked there as a janitor), and deems his writing irrelevant and unprintable. Citing this as proof that the world is afraid of his revolutionary insights, Henry, who has by now not only had sex with Mary (who subsequently killed herself) but impregnated and somewhat reluctantly married Fay, arranges for Simon's work to be put on the Internet, whereby he achieves sudden fame and notoriety.

Bored by domestic life, Henry asks his now much-courted writer friend to use his influence with Angus to get his own book published; though unimpressed by what he reads, Simon attempts to do so, fails, and signs a contract with Angus himself, with the result that Henry accuses him of betraying their friendship and mutual contempt for a shitty world. Five years on, Henry is working as a garbage man; Fay is so appalled by his bad influence on their son that their marriage is on the rocks. Nevertheless, he is sufficiently reformed that when a 13-year-old offers sex in return for murdering her abusive father, he rejects the offer and visits her parents in an effort to sort things out, though he ends up stabbing the father in self-defence and being wanted for murder and sex with a minor. His son tracks down

< 308 >

Simon (now living with Laura in New York) who arranges for Henry, armed with his own passport, to leave the country and collect his own Nobel Prize. On the airport runway, however, Henry, undecided whether to turn back or go and accept the coveted award, simply starts running…

In certain respects, *Henry Fool* constitutes something of a summation of Hartley's preoccupations to date. The emphasis on the importance and limitations of trust; the discrepancy between reality, rumour and reputation (though Henry is for the most part scandalously outspoken and honest, he is both deluded about his own importance and prone to being economical with the truth); the oppressively dysfunctional families; the relationship between an educating mentor and a younger, unformed disciple; the wariness of committing to a steady job and marriage; the narrow conformism of smalltown America – all are familiar from earlier films.

< **309** >

Where the movie differs from its predecessors is in the way it tosses all these themes into the pot together, and in its ambivalent stance on certain issues. It's true, for example, that Simon, once famous, agrees to have his work published even though he promised to reject any such offers if Henry's magnum opus were not also accepted for publication. On the one hand, Henry's right to feel betrayed, but on the other, how realistic or fair is it to expect Simon to sacrifice his own ambitions for a friend who, as he points out, merely sat around talking while he toiled away at his writing? Simon does repay his friend in the end, not only by offering him the opportunity to collect his own Nobel Prize, but by believing in his innocence even though his criminal record might suggest otherwise: Henry's initial faith in Simon is eventually returned with interest.

Similarly, the characterisations are more ambiguous than in previous work. Henry, especially, is a morass of contradictions: he is intelligent, erudite and articulate, yet his 'Confession' is deemed worthless by both Simon and Angus (though, as with Simon's poetry, we never actually hear it for ourselves); he gives

Simon great encouragement, help and inspiration, yet he is not beyond taking sexual advantage of his emotionally unstable sister and mother when the opportunity presents itself; he has strength and integrity, but is not averse to drunken carousing, theft or, at least in the past, indulging a 'weakness' for a 13-year-old girl. Nor are the other characters static or one-dimensional. Besides Simon's dramatic transformation, Fay changes from a promiscuous, lazy haridan, first into a daughter wracked with guilt over her mother's suicide (she was too busy seducing Henry at the time to notice anything wrong), then into a responsible mother concerned about the way Henry is allowing their five-year-old son to smoke, drink and attend topless bars with him. Even relatively minor characters are deftly drawn: Warren (Kevin Corrigan), the abusive father killed by Henry, started out as a bullying punk, became so infatuated with a woman that he turned ultra-straight and began canvassing for a right-wing politician ('He takes complicated issues and simplifies them... I appreciate that'), and then, disenchanted by the candidate's failure, became an embittered practitioner of patriarchal violence.

< **310** >

As much of the above may suggest, *Henry Fool* is Hartley's darkest film in several respects. Besides being largely shot in sombre browns, greys and blacks (rather than the previously favoured primary colours), in an assortment of none too glamorous locations (seedy bars, the garbage plant, a tyre dump, the gloomy basement), the ubiquitous violence, the reactionary smalltown comformism, Maria's suicide, Fay's unwanted pregnancy, Henry's sexual offence with an underage girl, a priest suffering a crisis of faith, Henry's inability to get work as a librarian because of his record, the hypocrisy of the publishing world – all would appear to endorse Henry's view that 'the world is full of shit'. Even the humour (the film is very funny) is darker than usual and often surprisingly but suitably scatological. Besides an early scene in which Simon is forced publicly to kiss Warren's girlfriend's bared arse (he immediately vomits over it), there's also a hilarious, outrageously excessive sequence in which Henry, having OD'd on coffee, sits on the toilet, his bowels exploding loudly over and over again. Suddenly, Fay emerges in horror from the shower, but then, noticing a gasket ring beside him (he found it in the garbage), she assumes he is going to propose marriage, and hugs and kisses him, now apparently oblivious to the odour, while he sits too embarrassed to apprise her of her mistake.

Not all the comedy is in this bawdy vein (besides the usual witty wordplay and deadpan eccentricities, there are lovely gags concerning the way the likes of Camille Paglia – shown in a news broadcast – and the Pope respond to Simon's writings), but such scenes are in keeping with one of the film's central themes: how any creative output, especially if it is so idiosyncratic as to confound middlebrow expectations, may either be lionised as great art or demonised as pornographic filth. (It's crucial that we the audience never hear Simon's poetry and so cannot make up our own minds about it according to personal taste.) The film shows how controversy may on the one hand threaten to undermine an artist's faith in himself, and on the other endow both the work and the artist with a celebrity far more commercial than that achieved by less notorious works. Celebrity and controversy, however, give no real indication of artistic worth: value, in a world hungry for heroes and villains, dominated by the media, and suspicious of originality but obsessed with novelty, is calculated primarily in terms of reputation, profitability and impact on society, rather than in terms of what the art actually means and whether it accords with its creator's intentions. Furthermore, all too often society judges art simply by assessing the appeal of its subject matter: though Henry tells Simon that the poet should contemplate anything, regardless of whether the subject matter is sordid, works about sex, violence or similar topics are frequently deemed inherently bad by association. Henry, then, for all his egomania, is no fool when it comes to the ethical standing of art, even though no one may appreciate his own particular 'Confession'.

There is, then, perhaps an element of autobiography to the film, since Hartley himself has been ploughing his own special

< 311 >

furrow for almost a decade, and has presumably found that while some have lionised his work, others have deemed it insignificant, irrelevant or even, figuratively speaking, 'pornographic' – as a film-maker who is too experimental and eccentric for those with conventional tastes, he has surely suffered animosity towards his work. Typically, however, there is no special pleading in the film, simply a witty, ironic, clear-eyed assessment of the place of the unconventional artist in contemporary western society. On a more positive level, however, it also celebrates art as a means of self-expression and discovery: Simon is utterly transformed by his writing. This too, presumably, has personal import: Hartley appears to have found his vocation, and it is to his credit that in continuing to make non-mainstream films which pay scant regard to passing fashions and are true to his own peculiar vision of the world, he has managed also to create a body of work which is illuminating, relevant and highly entertaining for many others. In this respect, he is the embodiment of all that is valuable and rewarding about the contemporary American independent scene.

< 312 >

Quentin Tarantino

< 3¹3 >

Whatever his standing as an artist, Quentin Tarantino is most certainly a remarkable cultural phenomenon. In the mid-90s, though still in his early thirties and having directed only two complete movies, he was, alongside Steven Spielberg, probably the best known film-maker in the western world. Even though, by the standards of Hollywood blockbusters, *Reservoir Dogs* (1991) and *Pulp Fiction* (1994) had performed only moderately at the box office, they had come to be seen by many cinema-goers and video-buffs – particularly young males – as landmarks in contemporary American film-making. Scenes such as the ear-lopping torture in *Reservoir Dogs* and lines of dialogue like 'I'm gonna git medieval on your ass' (*Pulp Fiction*) were endlessly repeated, discussed and analysed in conversation, the press and on the Internet (I shall try, therefore, not to spend too much space in this chapter going over well-trodden ground), while Tarantino and his films were constantly being given coverage, alluded to and imitated by the media (including other movies). Indeed, the writer, director and occasional actor had achieved a cult celebrity normally accorded only to major rock stars. The Palme d'Or awarded to *Pulp Fiction* in Cannes had not only shown that he was not a one-hit wonder but served to lend him a certain respectability; Cannes, after all, was the world's most prestigious and high-profile film festival where, notwithstanding a string of recent American winners like *sex, lies and videotape*, *Wild at Heart* and *Barton Fink*, the main prize was regularly given to such worthy, serious art-movies as Kurosawa's *Kagemusha* (1980), Pialat's *Under Satan's Sun* (1987), Bille August's *The Best Intentions* (1992) or, the year before Tarantino's triumph, Jane Campion's *The Piano* and Chen Kaige's *Farewell My Concubine*. *Pulp Fiction* was different: like *Wild at Heart*, it was energetic, foul-mouthed, violent and amoral, but unlike Lynch's film, its more amoral aspects could not be explained away in terms of a surrealist's desire to shock the bourgeoisie; Tarantino seemed to delight unselfconsciously in his film's disreputable subject matter simply for what it was, rather than as an arty aesthetic. Emphatically, he just 'got off', as it were, on serving up violence, profane dialogue and allusions to kitschy pop culture because that was what he loved and remembered from all the movies, television shows and records he had immersed himself in since childhood.

And it's almost certainly that unbridled enthusiasm for all aspects of modern popular culture, however obscure, tacky, banal or 'politically incorrect', that was the prime reason for his popularity. There are some who would attribute his success to his unrepentant fascination with low-life violence, but while that has undeniably been an important factor in helping to build his rather controversial reputation, it is far from the whole story. Certainly, Tarantino's work – including his scripts for *True Romance* (Tony Scott, 1993), *Natural Born Killers* (Oliver Stone, 1994) and *From Dusk Till Dawn* (Robert Rodriguez, 1995), each of which he originally hoped to direct himself – is notable for its unusually visceral depiction of violence, even though the body count is generally lower than that in the more routine action fare starring such cartoon-style superheavies as Schwarzenegger, Stallone or Steven Seagal. But for all the fuss made about the dismemberments, the blood and gore and the deadly 'Mexican stand-offs' that recur in his films, Tarantino is in no way a typical action-movie director. For one thing, much of his work is finally more concerned with the events that lead up to or follow on from violence than with the violent acts themselves; he appears to be more interested in the emotions, character traits and situations that give rise to violence, or in the anxiety and recrimination that result from it, than in moving on as quickly as possible from one bloody encounter to another.

Accordingly, conversation plays an usually large role in his films, which allows him both to sketch in his characters' personalities with a degree of vividly coloured detail seldom found in modern action fare, and to indulge his obsession with popular culture. And in focusing closely on what criminal types do when they are not committing crimes – his almost certainly justifiable contention is that they are as likely to discuss movies, television programmes, the lyrics to a Madonna song or fast-food joints as the rest of us – he not only parades his own interests and erudition, but touches directly on many of the subjects that fascinate his audience. His films are as much 'about' the popular culture of which they are a part as they are 'about' crime and violence; the way they reflect the spirit of the times in this regard is surely a crucial aspect of their appeal.

The endless allusions and hommages to cult heroes and celebrities, favourite movies, TV shows, comic-strips and songs, urban myths and brand names, not only establishes a direct line of contact and complicity with the audience which exists over and above his storylines (we don't necessarily need to care much about the plot details or the fates of the various characters to be caught up in his movies, though the fact that the characters share our interests may make it more likely that we will), but encourages viewers to think about Tarantino and his films in the same obsessive way. The trivial but knowing dialogue enables him, as it were, to hit the right buttons, so that we experience a welcome feeling of recognition – we may not have personal experience of the violence his characters are involved in, but we know what they are talking about. Despite, therefore, the violence and the

< 315 >

sometimes slightly challenging structures of his narratives, Tarantino, as obsessed by and nostalgic about the ephemera of modern culture as most of his audience (in interview he has done nothing to hide the fan-boy side of his personality), comes across as a film-maker of and for the people. (Ironically, this, of course, has only served to establish him as a cult hero of almost Godlike status for those more impressionable fans who, only vaguely aware of the tradition he's very consciously working in, see him as a complete original.)

< 316 >

There is another sense, however, in which Tarantino appears to embody the spirit of the times, in that he himself displays scant regard for 'originality'. Aware that in storytelling there is nothing new under the sun, he has not only alluded to movies by way of hommage but actively 'borrowed' from them. Disregarding the question of the exact nature of the authorial contributions made to some of his films by his former friend and collaborator Roger Avary, it has been pointed out, for example, that *Reservoir Dogs* bears a strong resemblance not only to Kubrick's 1956 heist movie *The Killing* (a debt acknowledged from the start) but to Hong Kong director Ringo Lam's *City on Fire* (1987). Moreover, elements from *Du Rififi Chez les Hommes* (Jules Dassin, 1955), *The Wild Bunch* (Peckinpah, 1969), *The Taking of Pelham One Two Three* (Joseph Sargent, 1974), *Q – The Winged Serpent* (Cohen, 1982) and *Casualties of War* (De Palma, 1989) are integrated into the movie, just as some of his other films rework scenes and situations from earlier movies: notable among the 'references' in *Pulp Fiction* are those to *Kiss Me Deadly* (Robert Aldrich, 1955), *Bande à Part* (Godard, 1964), *Deliverance* (John Boorman, 1972) and *La Femme Nikita* (Luc Besson, 1990), while his script for *True Romance* was clearly influenced by *Badlands* and his 'The Man From Hollywood' episode for *Four Rooms* (1995) openly inspired by an instalment in the *Alfred Hitchcock Presents* TV series. Such 'steals' recall the playfully referential methods adopted in the early work of Tarantino's hero Godard, which constituted a (self)conscious interrogation of genre born of the French *auteur*'s love-hate attitude to Hollywood; more importantly, however, in terms of Tarantino's appeal among younger audiences, they relate to the aesthetic of 'sampling', whereby it is seen as perfectly valid to appropriate, magpie-fashion, elements of other people's work and, by means of collage and quotation, to revamp them into something fresh. For older viewers such a strategy may smack of plagiarism, but for those accustomed to the practice of 'sampling' in music who surely account for many of Tarantino's greatest admirers there is no problem; indeed, the very act of trying to spot and identify 'steals' may provide pleasure in itself. (Tarantino even offers a bonus for fans who enjoy such pursuits by extending this intertextuality to his own work; in *Reservoir Dogs*, verbal allusions are made to *Pulp Fiction*'s Marsellus and *True Romance*'s Alabama, a character named Bonnie gets a name-check in all three films, while it's distinctly possible that *Reservoir Dogs*' Vic Vega, played by Michael Madsen, is meant to be the brother of *Pulp Fiction*'s Vincent Vega, played by John Travolta.)

< 317 >

Nevertheless, despite having made a significant contribution to Tarantino's popularity among the more trainspotter-like of his fans, if these references and 'steals' and his focus on violence were the only reason for enjoying his work, he would hardly merit consideration as a film-maker of importance. Happily, he displays genuine talent both as writer and director, a product, surely, of a childhood and adolescence devoted to the consumption of cinema; though he never shone at school, he read and watched films and TV voraciously. In his teens he acted at the Torrance Community Theater Workshop, which he followed in the early 80s with a spell at the James Best Theater Center; a later stint under the tutelage of Allen Garfield led to his first notable role as an Elvis impersonator in an episode of television's *The Golden Girls*. At the same time, he entertained ambitions to become a fully fledged film-maker: while working at LA's Video Archives store (which allowed him to indulge his cinephilia to the full), he embarked with colleagues on two no-budget, never-completed movies – *Lovebirds in Bondage* (1983) and *My Best Friend's Birthday* (1984-87); the latter, abandoned after the two final reels were destroyed in a lab accident, included a number of elements which he recycled in *True Romance*.

Neither that script, nor *Natural Born Killers* or *From Dusk till Dawn* (which was based on a story by a friend who worked in special effects), was initially well received in Hollywood, where they were regarded as too violent; only when rumours began to circulate about his promising début with *Reservoir Dogs* – which had got off the ground when his producer Lawrence Bender attracted the interest of director Monte Hellman and actor Harvey Keitel, who both ended up with producer credits – did the industry really take notice. (Since Tarantino didn't direct these three scripts himself – indeed, he disagreed with the changes made to *True Romance* by Tony Scott and, even more so, with Oliver Stone's extensive rewrites for *Natural Born Killers* – I shall not devote further space to them; whatever is interesting about the movies in terms of what they tell us about Tarantino is present in far less diluted form in his own work.) *Dogs*, however, fulfilled the young writer-director's wildest dreams; it made a splash at Sundance, Cannes and every other festival it played at, and immediately established him as a promising new talent to be reckoned with.

In terms of its story, the film is not particularly original (we have already mentioned its similarity to various other heist-gone-wrong movies). A gang of criminals, hitherto unknown to one another, is assembled by an ageing gangster to carry out a daring jewel robbery. After one loses his cool and starts shooting, the cops arrive; two of the gang are killed and one seriously wounded in the carnage that ensues. One by one the survivors arrive at a warehouse as planned. Besides wondering about the whereabouts of the diamonds, they begin to suspect, given the amazingly prompt arrival of the cops at the jeweller's, that they had been tipped off; accusations are made, frequently at gunpoint, about who the traitor might be, a cop who has been taken hostage is

< 318 >

tortured in the hope that he'll betray the culprit, and when the boss finally arrives, all but one of the gang end up shooting one another. Out of gratitude to the gangster who defended him against accusations of treachery, the traitor – an undercover cop wounded in the robbery – reveals his identity; his colleague shoots him in the head, knowing that the action will mean he himself is killed by the cops, who have just entered the warehouse after apprehending the sole survivor of the bloodbath as he was trying to escape.

What chiefly distinguishes the film from other heist-gone-wrong movies is less any particular insights into the age-old theme of honour among thieves than the vibrancy of Tarantino's dialogue and the film's structural eccentricity. Perhaps the most immediately notable aspect of the narrative is that we are not shown the robbery itself. The film begins with the various gang members discussing, over coffee, the meaning of Madonna's 'Like a Virgin' and the ethics of tipping in restaurants (neither crime in general nor the heist in particular are mentioned, though the profane language and jokes about shooting each other alert us to the possibility that these men, most of them in sharp dark suits and ties, may not be ordinary business types); then, as the credits roll to the sound of a song announced on the radio programme 'K-Billy's Supersounds of the Seventies' (already name-checked in their conversation), it observes them in slow-motion-relaxed, cool, some still chatting – as they walk out of the pancake house to go to work. An abrupt cut, slightly anticipated by the sound of a man screaming in agony, takes us directly into the aftermath of the heist: Mr Orange (Tim Roth), blood pouring from the gun-shot wound in his stomach, is in the back of a car being driven at breakneck speed by Mr White (Keitel), who tries to reassure him that he won't die because Joe (Lawrence Tierney), the boss, will fix him up with a doctor. (Joe has given the gang aliases and insisted they don't talk about themselves so that they can't inform on each other after the robbery.) Cut to the two men arriving at the warehouse, where they are presently

< 319 >

Harvey Keitel (Mr White) faces off with Mr Pink (Steve Buscemi) in **Reservoir Dogs** (1991) – a heist-gone-wrong movie celebrated largely for its vibrant dialogue, but just as impressive for its imaginative structural sophistication.

joined by Mr Pink (Steve Buscemi), who argues that a traitor must have set them up with the cops; by Mr Blonde (Michael Madsen), who started shooting people at the jeweller's and who has brought along the injured cop Marvin with the alleged intention of discovering the traitor's identity through torture; and finally by Nice Guy Eddie (Christopher Penn) and his father Joe who, finding their friend Mr Blonde and the cop dead, are convinced one of the others must be the traitor, so that a shoot-out erupts of which, as mentioned above, the sole survivor is Mr Pink, who is arrested as he leaves the warehouse with the jewels.

Into this tense, suspenseful but straightforward narrative, which focuses exclusively on the questions of who is the traitor and who will survive what is evidently a very volatile situation, Tarantino inserts several flashbacks, showing how Mr Pink escaped from the robbery; how Mr Blonde (who had served time in prison without betraying Joe and Nice Guy Eddie) and Mr White were brought into the gang; how plans were made for the robbery; and, most crucially, how Mr Orange, the undercover cop, managed to worm his way into the gang by gaining their confidence (Joe knew everyone else from previous collaborations) with a made-up tale of past misdemeanours.

It is this last, lengthy flashback which best displays the writer-director's talents. Coming immediately after Orange's true identity is revealed to the audience (but not to the other gang members, who have left the warehouse for a while) by his having shot Mr Blonde to prevent him setting alight the petrol-soaked Marvin (and to stop Marvin, already in agony after having his ear sliced off, giving the game away), it begins with Orange/Freddy in a diner telling his colleague Holdaway about how he has won the trust of Joe and the gang.

< 321 >

The narrative then flashes still further back to the time when, high on a roof, Holdaway taught Freddy how to act, advising him that it is the little details he inserts into a drug-deal yarn Holdaway gives him to tell the gang which will finally convince them of his reliability. The film then begins to flash forwards, step by step, as it cuts to Freddy in his apartment, reading and memorising the drug story from a piece of paper; to Freddy back outdoors, continuing the story in a visibly more confident performance to Holdaway; to Freddy 'in character', continuing the story in a bar for the benefit of Joe, Nice Guy Eddie and Mr White who, though they ask questions (to which he can give ready, persuasive answers), are clearly lapping up every word; and then, most remarkably, to Freddy actually 'in' his own fiction, which we hear him continuing to relate in voice-over, complete with further offscreen interruptions from Eddie. (Though Freddy himself doesn't speak 'within' the story, we do hear a sheriff in it talk – and he too is relating an anecdote to his colleagues!) At the end of Freddy's story, we return first to a shot of Joe expressing satisfaction with the anecdote (and with Freddy's cool behaviour in it), then to Holdaway in the diner, asking for more information about Joe, then to Freddy – now accepted into the gang – in his apartment, being phoned by Eddie and joining him, White and Orange as (followed by an unmarked cop car) they travel to a briefing with Joe, then to the post-robbery escape scene in which Freddy/Orange is shot by and kills a woman whose car he and White try to hijack, and finally back to the warehouse, with the gang returning to find that he has shot Mr Blonde, who, he claims in one last lie, was planning to make off with the jewels after killing the rest of the gang.

< **322** >

This Chinese-boxes sequence, with its tales within tales and complex time structure, sees Tarantino's writing and direction at their most sophisticated and imaginative. Though the contents of Freddy's anecdote are only mildly diverting, it is the manner of its telling that is extraordinary, not only due to the typically racy dialogue, but because the narrative does precisely what Holdaway tells Freddy to do: in gradually becoming more and more detailed, it brings the story literally to life, so that we no longer simply hear it being told but see it enacted. Moreover, both Freddy in the story and Freddy telling the story embody one of the film's themes: the need to keep cool in a risky situation, to act rationally and professionally at all times, regardless of fear, a desire for revenge, or considerations of friendship. Even under torture, Marvin resists giving Freddy's game away lest he jeopardise the police's chances of capturing the whole gang; Mr White, however, allows the pity and friendship he feels for the wounded Freddy/Orange to blind him to the fact that he is the most likely betrayer of the gang. And had Freddy not given way to emotion and admitted his true identity to White, he would most likely have lived, given that he made his confession only seconds before the arrival of the police. Only Mr Pink, who throughout acts logically and in his own interests, and warily avoids close attachments, lives to see another day, albeit in prison.

Not that Tarantino invests his film with any strong ethical considerations. Though some of his characters act out of loyalty

(Joe and Nice Guy Eddie trust Blonde because he proved a stand-up guy during his stint in prison; White helps Freddy/Orange out of a sense of honour and friendship), most die, partly because, as Pink alone realises, distrust is endemic in an operation where no one, Joe included, really knows the other players, partly, one suspects, because Tarantino just preferred it that way: outright carnage, with no survivors, makes for a neater, more dramatic and more unexpected outcome. For all that some have likened *Reservoir Dogs* to, say, Jacobean tragedy, Tarantino does not appear to be concerned with the moral implications of the film: rather, it is primarily a stylish variation on traditional genre conventions, designed to thrill, shock, amuse and surprise the viewer with its sudden shifts in tone, its charismatic characters, its outbursts of violence, its profanely demotic yet ornately stylised dialogue and the sheer joy taken by its maker in the art of storytelling. The much-discussed violence, frankly, is amoral (as opposed to immoral); while it occurs with some regularity, and while it may sometimes be executed in a way that makes some viewers question its tastefulness (though can violence ever be 'tasteful'?) – as when Mr Blonde does an amusing little dance to the strains of Stealer's Wheel's innocent, innocuous ditty 'Stuck in the Middle With You' before stopping, with evident sadistic pleasure, to cut off Marvin's ear with a razor – Tarantino never lingers over the actual act of violence. (Indeed, as has often been pointed out, he has the camera discreetly avert its gaze towards a wall during the ear-slicing sequence.)

< **323** >

Violence for Tarantino is simply part and parcel of the crime movie; it is dramatic spectacle, not to be leered over (though there's plenty of blood splattered around in his films, he tends to avoid gory close-ups), but simply to be enjoyed as part of the action, just as his dialogue is meant to be savoured for its colourful cadences, its unexpected turns of phrase, its unlikely subject matter (while the gang are driving to their briefing, they discuss not the robbery but the theory that black women are less submissive than white women, which includes, naturally, a name check for Pam Grier, future lead in *Jackie Brown*), and its wealth of anecdote. The violence, finally, is no more disturbing or morally offensive than his profligate use of such problematic words as 'nigger', 'bitch', 'faggot' or 'motherfucker'; it may be flip, even insensitive or immature, and it certainly doesn't make for any kind of artistically serious statement, but it does catch the flavour of how criminals (or at least low-life movie criminals) think, act and speak. Moreoever, his skill at choreographing scenes of sudden violence and writing witty, engrossing, memorable dialogue makes him as adept in the realm of pulp poetry as writers like Jim Thompson, James Ellroy, and Elmore Leonard.

< 324 >

Since Tarantino is arguably a genre stylist, a *metteur-en-scène* whose films are largely inspired by other films (as opposed to a fully-fledged *auteur* with a persuasive, coherent world-view or with an interest in radically transforming film syntax), it is the details of his films, rather than any overall 'meaning', that are of most interest. In *Reservoir Dogs*, surprisingly (given his popularity among younger fans), the style is mostly subtle and classical. For all the complexity of the narrative structure, the editing is sharp, simple and to the point, and avoids the kind of bombastic MTV-style gimmickry seen at its most flashy in *Natural Born Killers*. The colour is mostly naturalistic and muted: red, black, white and flesh tones. The camera moves when appropriate: circling the restaurant table in the opening scene to introduce the gang (including Tarantino's Mr Brown and Eddie Bunker's Mr Blue, barely seen thereafter since they are killed in the robbery); tracking rapidly along a street to show the panic of the thieves' escape from the robbery; and gradually becoming more animated as Freddy's flashback 'comes to life'. The compositions in the warehouse are generally more static, partly to reflect the tense, claustrophobic mood of waiting and entrapment, partly to focus attention squarely on the actors. (One of Tarantino's great strengths is his ability to elicit strong performances from well-chosen casts, which is enhanced by the way he never allows his cutting or compositions to distract attention from the actors.)

Just occasionally, he does something a little unusual – as when Blonde fetches his gasoline can from his car and, as the camera follows him out from the warehouse and back again, the volume of the music playing inside gradually drops then rises once more – but such moments are rare and, when they do occur, quite logical in terms of their execution.

If Tarantino is a stylist, then, his most conspicuous digressions from the norm lie in his accent on characterisation. In most crime films, the characters exist almost solely as pawns in the power-game that is the plot; there is seldom any emphasis on those areas of their lives which are not directly affected by the crimes that make up the storyline. *Reservoir Dogs*, however, allows ample space for the characters simply to joke, argue over their obsessions (mostly related to sex, music, TV and movies), tell stories about people they've known, and generally rabbit on about anything that comes into their heads. This shtick was even more conspicuously on display in *Pulp Fiction*, a film noticeably more ambitious (and extenuated) than *Reservoir Dogs* but rather more uneven in its execution.

Again, the most intriguing aspect of the film is Tarantino's skilful deployment of an unusual narrative structure, which here consists of two prologues and three separate but linked stories, one of which begins with a brief dream sequence/flashback (though since it precedes the story it cannot strictly be described as a flashback) which serves as another little story in itself. Before the credits, a young couple are sitting in a coffee shop: Pumpkin (Tim Roth) explains to Honey Bunny (Amanda Plummer) his plans to rob the clientele, and the sequence ends abruptly as they rise from their chairs, guns drawn, to commence the hold-up. After the credits, two suited hitmen, Jules (Samuel L Jackson) and Vincent (John Travolta) discuss their boss Marsellus' possessive attitude towards his wife Mia (whom Vincent has been asked to chaperone for an evening in Marsellus' absence) on their way to killing a group of young men who have failed to deliver the contents of a mysterious briefcase to Marsellus (Ving Rhames);

< 325 >

the sequence again ends abruptly after Jules has killed two of the men, at which point the first story proper, 'Vincent Vega and Marsellus Wallace's Wife' begins. After a scene at Marsellus' club, where Jules and Vincent, now in shorts and T-shirts, deliver the briefcase and Vincent, in a brief, hostile exchange, meets Butch (Bruce Willis), a boxer whom Marsellus has just paid to throw an upcoming fight, Vincent, suited once more, visits his drug-dealer Lance (Eric Stoltz).

< **326** >

After fixing heroin, he goes to collect Mia (Uma Thurman) for their night out together; at a kitschy theme restaurant devoted to the 50s, they get to know each other and win a dance trophy, but having taken her home, Vincent, mindful of how Marsellus treats those who have overstepped the mark with his wife, decides to make his excuses and leave. Too late: while he's in the bathroom, Mia, who unbeknownst to him has been doing coke all night, finds his stash of heroin and OD's; in panic, he takes her to Lance's, where he is shown how to plunge a syringe filled with adrenaline directly into her heart. Mia revives, and after he takes her home, they shake hands, agreeing that it's mutually advantageous to keep the night's events a secret from Marsellus.

After a brief fade, the film recommences with a vignette in which an Air Force officer (Christopher Walken) tells the young Butch how he managed to bring back his dead father's watch from a Vietnam POW camp (the sentimental souvenir had been concealed up the arse of each man). We then cut to the adult Butch, waking up just before going into the fight; after the title 'The Gold Watch', we see him furtively escaping the auditorium in a taxi – having bet on himself to win, he has killed his opponent, so that Marsellus is out for blood. Returning to his girlfriend Fabienne (Maria de Medeiros) at a motel, he discusses their plans to flee the country and live somewhere exotic, but their idyll is broken when he finds she's left his watch at his apartment. Cautiously, he returns, picks up the watch and, hearing the toilet flush, kills Vincent with a gun found in the kitchen as

Marsellus' wife Mia (Uma Thurman) at the 50s restaurant with Vincent in **Pulp Fiction** (1994) – more ambitious than **Reservoir Dogs**, though more uneven in its execution and overly concerned with pop-culture references.

he emerges from the bathroom. While making his escape, he collides with Marsellus and the pair end up fighting in a pawnshop run by a survivalist, who ties them up at gunpoint, takes them to his basement, and invites a cop friend over. While the pair are buggering Marsellus in another room, Butch starts to escape but, finding a samurai sword, returns to rescue Marsellus. He kills the survivalist, while the cop is shot in the crotch and theatened with torture by Marsellus, who – still unaware that Butch has killed Vincent – agrees to let him go as long as his ordeal remains a secret. Butch promises to say nothing, returns to collect Fabienne, and they set off for a new life.

The third story, 'The Bonnie Situation', takes off where the second prologue ended, with Jules and Vincent in the apartment; another man emerges from the bathroom, but none of his six shots even scratches the hitmen. After killing him, Jules decides their survival is a miracle, and together with Marvin, a fourth man who was working as an insider, they head off to meet Marsellus. In the car, however, Vincent's gun accidentally goes off and kills Marvin, and the pair visit Jules' friend Jimmie (Tarantino) in order to hide out, clean up and dispose of the body. Worried lest his wife Bonnie return from her nursing job, Jimmie insists Jules phone Marsellus, who sends The Wolf (Harvey Keitel) to organise the operation as quickly as possible. Due to his efficiency, they manage to clean up the car and themselves and to dump the body in record time; exhausted, and dressed in unappealing shorts and T-shirts, Jules and Vincent breakfast in a diner, where the former explains that their miraculous survival is a sign from God that he should give up working for Marsellus and 'walk the earth'. Accordingly, when Pumpkin and Honey Bunny hold up the diner and ask for his wallet and briefcase, with the help of Vincent who has emerged from the toilet with his gun, he overpowers the young thieves and, on condition that they put down their guns and leave Marsellus' briefcase, allows them to depart with his money. After paying the bill, Jules and the bewildered Vincent, still sporting their 'dorkish' garb and packing automatics, leave the coffee-shop to go see Marsellus.

As with Jarmusch's *Mystery Train*, it has been necessary to describe the plot of *Pulp Fiction* in some detail, not only to give some flavour of the story but, more importantly, to suggest how the film's various parts intersect; on first viewing, it only becomes clear that the stories are related to one another during 'The Gold Watch', and it is not until Vincent reappears in 'The Bonnie Situation', after we've seen Butch kill him, that we can be sure that the stories are not ordered chronologically. Indeed, had Tarantino structured the film chronologically, the sequences would have run as follows: the second prologue, with Vincent and Jules killing the young men at the apartment; then 'The Bonnie Situation', with the first prologue, featuring Pumpkin and Honey Bunny, inserted after Vincent and Jules leave

< 328 >

Jimmie's for the diner; then 'Vincent Vega and Marsellus Wallace's Wife'; and finally 'The Gold Watch' (although whether the Walken vignette would start this section or come at the very beginning of the film depends on whether one regards it as a dream sequence or a flashback to Butch's childhood). By ordering the narrative the way he has, as opposed to relating it in straightforward linear fashion, Tarantino turns what would otherwise have been a loose, rambling, unfocused yarn into a series of self-contained short stories, each of which serves as an off-kilter, de-centred pastiche of a familiar Hollywood sequence. The coffee-shop hold-up ends before it has even begun, while the scene of the hitmen's contract killing stops before reaching its logical conclusion; we are diverted instead to Vincent's drugs-score and disastrous date with Mia. The story of the boxing fix omits to show us both the build-up to the fight and the bout itself, directing attention instead to Butch's lengthy tryst with Fabienne, his unexpected encounter with Vincent, and the still more surprising nightmare to which he and Marsellus – tough guys both – are subjected by sadistic hillbilly perverts. And 'The Bonnie Situation' finale ties up a number of threads from the movie's early moments before closing on a scene which, chronologically speaking, is not an ending at all, since one of the figures we see calmly walking off down the road is, as far as we're concerned, already dead.

< **329** >

Not only does the film's structure allow Tarantino to mount a number of generic pastiches and to create a kind of narrative jigsaw puzzle which the audience may gain pleasure from solving, but it also means that all the main stories follow roughly the same format. Each begins with a number of somewhat directionless scenes involving a great deal of conversation which is (or at least appears to be) irrelevant to the progress of the plot: Mia and Vincent's extended discussion and dance in the 50s diner; Butch and Fabienne's endless and, it must be said, embarrassingly childish endearments; Jules and Vincent's discussion of miracles, the shtick about coffee and home-decorating at Jimmies, and so on.

Each also includes or works towards a set-piece centred on surprising, disturbingly grotesque violence (Mia's adrenaline shot plunged through her breastbone, Butch and Marsellus' grim ordeal in the basement, and in the last episode, both Marvin's sudden, needless death and the potentially deadly diner stand-off). Finally, each concludes on a somewhat unexpected note of calm reconciliation: Mia and Vincent quietly agreeing to keep their secret from Marsellus, Butch and Marsellus agreeing to keep theirs from everyone, and Jules giving up his life of violence and letting the couple who, in robbing him, would normally have fallen foul of his 'great vengeance and furious wrath' (to quote the passage from Ezekiel with which he customarily prefaces his killings), walk away unscathed.

< **330** >

To recognise the formal ingenuity of this structure does not, however, entail accepting Tarantino's claim that the film ends with Jules' redemption: for all that he changes his ways and decides henceforth to interpret the Ezekiel passage differently, so that he will try to become 'a righteous man' who 'shepherds the weak through the valley of darkness', rather than part of 'the tyranny of evil men', the film is too flip and comic-strip-like ever to convince as any kind of moral fable. For the most part, Tarantino's dramatic strategy is one of shock and surprise rather than of serious contemplation, encouraging the audience not to ponder the moral, spiritual or philosophical implications of his characters' actions and experiences, but to embark on a roller-coaster ride that will have them laughing, screaming and wondering about what will happen next, all in quick succession.

Mostly, it must be said, he succeeds in this aim, although there are a few too many moments when one can't but feel that Tarantino the director should be less indulgent to Tarantino the writer: partly, perhaps, because he was as yet not very adept at creating convincingly rounded female characters, the sequences between Vincent and Mia and between Butch and Fabienne seem hollow, coy and over-extended. Moreover, while the endless prattle about pop culture is amusing as long as it lasts, be it

Vincent explaining to Jules the little differences between American and European junk food as they make their way to their hit, or Mia recalling a 'Charlie's Angels'-style TV series she used to act in, it seldom serves any real purpose in terms of story or characterisation, so that it tends to slow down the narrative and weaken the overall dramatic structure; too often, the verbiage relegates scenes to the level of mildly diverting but redundant anecdote. Indeed, one can't help feeling at times that Tarantino is overplaying his hand in this particular regard: while certain eccentricities, like the disorienting Biblical quotations and polite questions about burgers Jules uses to terrify his victims, are dramatically effective, other details, such as the kitschy 50s diner where they serve Amos and Andy shakes and Douglas Sirk steaks ('burnt to a crisp, or bloody as hell'), or the lecture on body piercing given by Lance's girlfriend (Rosanne Arquette), are so knowing and determinedly 'hip' that they look rather like crowd-pleasers for those who congratulate themselves for spotting a reference, for getting a gag, or for not being shocked by some deliberately provocative action or dialogue.

< **331** >

Certainly, in this last respect, the film differs noticeably from most mainstream fare. Jules and Vincent's discussion about the distinction between giving a foot massage and 'eatin' pussy', the violent adrenalin injection, the jokily unrepentant attitude to the accidental killing of the innocent Marvin, and the scene in the survivalist's cellar all suggest that Tarantino was trying to push back the boundaries of what is deemed acceptable in the commercial American cinema. To some degree, it must be said that he succeeds, although the nightmarish nature of the buggery scene does smack of homophobia in a way that his characters' frequent use of the term 'faggot' does not. And while it would be foolish to argue that the scene is any more offensive than most of the anodyne stereotypes of homosexual behaviour which can be found in mainstream films, it does suggest, along with his rather immature conception of women, that its creator was taking inspiration from the lurid clichés of pulp movies and comic-strips rather than from the realities of the world around him.

That said, for all that his direction indulged his writing, the former was again largely in keeping with the pulp aesthetic of the situations he was dealing with. The luridly colourful characters, complete with costumes that tell us at once where they are coming from (Jules' 70s-style sideburns and haircut are a particularly fine touch, especially given his plans to walk the earth 'like Caine in *Kung Fu*'), are well served by the often kitschy décor and by the simple, mostly static camerawork: the preference for medium-shots and close-ups, and the frequent use of tilted shots looking up at the characters are both reminiscent of comic-strip art. Again, however, the accent is on the actors, and while Maria de Medeiros and, to a lesser extent, Uma Thurman are rather ham-strung by being given so little of interest to do, the cast in general does full justice to the felicities of the writing, with Jackson especially forceful and credible as Jules.

Any reservations raised by *Pulp Fiction* about Tarantino's self-indulgent tendency towards meandering, irrelevant dialogue and an over-dependence on knowing references to pop-culture were exacerbated by the episode he wrote, directed and acted in for the hugely disappointing compendium-movie *Four Rooms*, a dismal folly about the experiences of a hapless, innocent bellhop (Tim Roth in unusually hammy form) at the Monsignor Hotel. Certainly, Tarantino's episode was marginally more tolerable than those by his friends Alison Anders and Alexandre Rockwell, but only Robert Rodriguez showed any real understanding of the short-story format or any flair in the editing department. Tarantino's 'The Man from Hollywood' exhibits his worst excesses. The story is hand-me-down: the bellhop is called to a suite by a flashy, temperamental movie star (played as a sledge-hammer caricature by Tarantino himself) who, inspired by his memories of an episode of the old *Alfred Hitchcock Presents* TV series, has entered into a drunken wager with one of his entourage: if the man succeeds in igniting his Zippo lighter ten times in succession, he'll win the star's car; if he fails, he will have his little finger

< **332** >

chopped off with a hatchet (wielded by the impartial bellhop in return for $1000).

Crucially, the story lacks the suspense of Hitchcock's 'The Man from Rio', partly because the dialogue (which includes a riff on Jerry Lewis' 1960 comedy *The Bellboy*) and performances are far too concerned with crudely outlining, in very broad strokes, the bellhop's gormless gullibility and the star's voluble arrogance and patronising pretensions, partly because Tarantino's direction is so clumsy. He uses very long takes which, in following the five characters' movements around the apartment, frequently defy logic in their evocation of the suite's geography and the spatial relationships between the characters; he often has them address the camera directly at such length that tedium sets in and the shortcomings of the performances are highlighted; worst, he opts unsuccessfully for comedy (none of the episode is remotely funny) instead of building up the tension of the situation, so that

< **333** >

The bellhop, played by Tim Roth, with Quentin Tarantino as Chester Rush in 'The Man from Hollywood' segment he directed for **Four Rooms** (1995) – inspired by an episode of the old **Alfred Hitchcock Presents** TV series.

the whole redundancy of the episode is made evident when the lighter fails to ignite first time, the bellhop chops off the finger and runs with his money from the room, and the other characters are left screaming in panic as they search for the finger with the intention of rushing the victim to hospital to have it sewn back on. The whole thing, in short, looks like nothing more than a misbegotten vanity project intended to cash in on Tarantino's cult popularity; as such, it raised serious doubts about his future as a film-maker of importance.

< **334** >

Happily, with *Jackie Brown* (1997), made after a lengthy period during which Tarantino appeared content to perform the odd acting turn – most substantially in *From Dusk Till Dawn* – and to work, with noticeably lively results, as a script-doctor on *Crimson Tide* (Tony Scott, 1995), any such doubts were allayed. Indeed, the film's comparative maturity suggested that Tarantino had spent much of the time since *Pulp Fiction* and *Four Rooms* not only considering the various criticisms made by some against those films, but actually taking them to heart and acting upon them. Though this respectful adaptation of Elmore Leonard's novel *Rum Punch* is again a crime film which, like *Reservoir Dogs*, is partly concerned with the themes of loyalty and betrayal and the need to keep one's head in potentially deadly situations, it differs conspicuously from its predecessors in several respects. There is far less violence than before, and what there is is barely visible on screen; there is far less babble about pop-culture; there are two strong, well-drawn female characters; the narrative structure is for the most part straightforwardly linear; and, a few very minor moments excepted, one rarely feels that Tarantino is 'grandstanding' or resorting to gimmicks in any way, either as a writer or as a director.

Jackie (Pam Grier), an air stewardess in her mid-forties who supplements her meagre income by acting as a courier for Ordell (Samuel L Jackson), a Los Angeles gun-trader whose fortune is kept largely in Mexico, is intercepted at LAX airport by a couple of cops and found to be carrying $50,000 and a bag of cocaine.

Released from jail after Ordell hires bondsman Max (Robert Forster) to arrange bail, Jackie realises the cops had acted on a tip-off from Beaumont (Chris Tucker), a small-time associate of Ordell's, whom she suspects (and as we have seen in the film's preceding scenes) was bailed out of jail then killed by the gun-runner lest he give evidence against him in court. Unable to face a spell in prison but wary of Ordell's murderous ways, Jackie persuades the cops to let her continue in her job so that she can set up Ordell for them, and then tells Ordell that she has made the deal so that she can get his money out of Mexico for him; meanwhile, she informs Max, who is clearly attracted to her, that her real plan is to trick both Ordell and the cops and make $500,000 dollars for herself. The scheme, which involves two exchanges of bags at a shopping mall – the first involving a small amount of cash to convince all concerned of her integrity, the second the rest of Ordell's illicit fortune – goes ahead as planned, but after the second hand-over, things go awry when Ordell's former cell-mate Louis (Robert De Niro) angrily shoots Ordell's girlfriend Melanie (Bridget Fonda), who has vainly attempted to persuade him to trick their mutual friend by making off with the money for themselves. Irate and suspicious, Ordell kills Louis, and swears revenge on Jackie, who has gone into hiding with the money. The police, meanwhile, having found a number of marked bills on Melanie, and not realising that Jackie has the rest of the money, believe she has kept her word and agree to be present when she arranges, through Max, a meeting with Ordell; he, persuaded that fear has driven her to give up the cash, doesn't realise he is being set up. At the meeting in Max's office, the cops, thinking Ordell is about to take revenge on Jackie, shoot him dead. A few days later, she arrives there with the money and invites Max to go with her to Spain; torn, he declines, but then changes his mind – too late, since she has already driven away.

The first thing one notices about *Jackie Brown* is just how conventional it is compared to his previous features. There are only a few of the playful, 'clever' stylistic flourishes beloved by

< **335** >

many of Tarantino's fans: a brief resort to split-screen, a map showing an animated plane's progress from Mexico to LA, a handful of intertitles announcing location, including one which jokily informs us that the Del Amo Mall in Torrance (where the director grew up) is the 'largest indoor mall in the world'. Nor do the characters rap repeatedly about pop-culture; besides the odd reference to the Delfonics (whose soul records are used as an index of the growing affection between the similarly middle-aged Jackie and Max), and an opening sequence in which Ordell bemoans the fact that Hong Kong films like *The Killer* (John Woo, 1989) have encouraged Americans involved in street crime to favour the wrong kind of guns, there is little of the shtick that frequently held up the action in *Pulp Fiction*. Indeed, the dialogue overall is less insistently flamboyant, more naturalistic and concerned with the issues at hand: characters discuss themselves and their own feelings rather than TV shows, music, movies and so on, and the result is a sharper focus both on the characters' emotional and psychological lives and on the movie's main themes.

Similarly, the fact that the narrative structure is linear (with the notable, justifiable exception of the second exchange of money being shown three times in succession, from the point of view of Jackie, Louis and Max, which not only allows us to see the exact mechanism of Jackie's complex plan but reflects on how everyone involved in the story is caught up in their own private schemes, largely ignorant of other people's motives and actions) ensures that we have an opportunity to get to know the characters more fully than in the earlier films. While the first hour, with its long conversational scenes and leisurely pace, may seem a little slow, the details served up about the various characters enable us clearly to grasp their needs and desires, suspicions and fears, relationships and preoccupations, with the result that, when things finally speed up in the film's second half, the emotional consequences count for rather more than they would have had Tarantino simply plunged straight into the action. Crucially, we

< **336** >

Queen of blaxploitation, Pam Grier, in Tarantino's **Jackie Brown** (1997) – his most conventional film to date, and thematically and stylistically his most mature.

understand why Jackie takes the risky course of playing off all sides against each other; as a middle-aged black woman in a none-too-rewarding job, faced with the alternatives of a stretch in jail or the deadly self-protective ploys of Ordell, she has no option but to take a gamble and go for broke.

It is this aspect of the film that makes it Tarantino's most mature and emotionally satisfying work to date. Treachery, trust, deceit and loyalty are a stock element of such movies, and *Jackie Brown* handles the various shifts in allegiance with assurance and subtlety (Louis' reluctance to betray Ordell, despite his intial attraction to Melanie, is handled with fine understatement). But it is the accent on ageing, and its effects on how we reconsider our lives, that most distinguishes the movie from *Reservoir Dogs*. Jackie, besides being aware that her looks are beginning to fade, is anxious that a prison sentence would wreck any possibility of a decent job and a comfortable life; Max, having met a woman he genuinely respects and even perhaps loves, is tired of his seedy job, and would like to do something more emotionally rewarding – such as take off with Jackie – before it's too late; Ordell is terrified that he may have lost his entire life's savings; and Louis, a quiet man who we gradually see has been broken by the years he has spent in prison, is not only unable to perform well sexually in his hasty liaison with Melanie, but is sufficiently nervous and 'past it' to lose his cool at the mall when the money is exchanged. (As Ordell says to him in anger and sadness just before killing him, 'What the fuck happened to you, man? Your ass used to be beautiful.') This sense of lives being overtaken by time, of diminished opportunities and failing faculties – rather reminiscent of the mood that permeates Hawks' *El Dorado* (1966), a kind of sequel to *Rio Bravo* (1959), often cited by Tarantino as his favourite film – lends the film depth and poignancy, so that when Max realises he's left it too late to go abroad with Jackie and start life anew, the sense of loss for both is palpable.

There is, then, a faintly elegiac tone to *Jackie Brown*, a tone well served by the almost classical understatement of the film's visual style. Even more than in *Reservoir Dogs*, camera movement and emphatic angles are used sparely; the camera tracks at length with and circles around Jackie, for instance, conveying her panic after the exchange of bags as she searches for the cops in the mall. Remarkably, given Tarantino's previous two features, the depiction of violence is extremely restrained. When Ordell kills Beaumont in the trunk of his car, the scene is played out in long-shot; when Louis shoots Melanie, she dies offscreen; when Ordell shoots Louis in the stomach, the camera, positioned in the rear of their truck, simply observes the blood splattering across the front windscreen; and when the cops shoot Ordell in Max's office, the action takes place in near-darkness. In none of these instances are there explicit shots of wounds, gore or bullets entering flesh; it is as if Tarantino is not only mindful of some of the

< **338** >

criticisms made against his earlier films, but aware that scenes of graphic violence would somehow disrupt the quieter, even contemplative mood that marks much of the movie.

Likewise, the performances are less 'upfront' than in his other work: Grier and Forster, hitherto best known for their work in the relatively lowly areas of, respectively, blaxploitation and TV series, bring a genuine tenderness, dignity and thoughtfulness to their roles, while Fonda and Michael Keaton (as one of the cops) are more impressive than in most of their films. Samuel Jackson, while given perhaps the most colourful role in the film, still makes the character considerably more credible than was Jules in the larger-than-life comic-strip world of *Pulp Fiction*, while Robert De Niro's taciturn, self-effacing performance is notably more engaged and less self-consciously understated than his other quiet men of recent years.

< **339** >

Though one may entertain minor reservations about *Jackie Brown* – the intertitles announcing location are redundant tics, the first hour of the film is a little too talky in places – it does constitute a major step forward for Tarantino on an artistic level. While it remains a genre film in every respect, it is more disciplined and purposeful than *Pulp Fiction*, more affecting and subtly shaded in terms of its characterisations than *Reservoir Dogs*, and notably less dependent on movie pastiche and more perceptive about the emotional realities of contemporary life than any of his work to date. It may be a little less immediate in its appeal than its predecessors, but in terms of its thematic content and wealth of psychological detail, there is considerably more substance. Whereas the first two films looked like promising calling-cards, the product of a feverishly inventive cinephile but ultimately adolescent imagination, *Jackie Brown* suggests that if Tarantino can rein in the more flamboyant side of his artistic personality, he may have the makings of a film-maker in the mould of genre specialists like Hawks, Peckinpah, Michael Mann or even Jean-Pierre Melville. He has the cinematic talent; what remains to be seen is whether he has the depth of insight to become a great film-maker. But, after the disastrous self-indulgence that was *Four Rooms*, it seems he is not only willing but able to learn from his mistakes. In this respect, *Jackie Brown*, which stands head and shoulders above the work of Tarantino's many imitators, bodes very well indeed.

< **340** >

13

New Kids on the Block

< 341 >

Over the last decade or so, the number of indie film-makers working in the American cinema has grown from a small trickle into a raging torrent. Inspired by the examples of Jarmusch, Soderbergh and Hartley, countless young writers and directors have managed to find finance for their low-budget films from sources that have little or no connection with the major studios. At the same time, Hollywood, ever on the look-out for new, potentially profitable talent, has not only seen fit to finance idiosyncratic figures like Tim Burton and Robert Rodriguez, but has forged links with independent production and distribution outfits like Miramax and October Films while setting up its own comparatively small, specialist divisions like Fox Searchlight and Sony Classics. The result has been a veritable explosion of product, some of it exciting, adventurous and original, much of it sadly and even brazenly imitative of the work of directors like Scorsese, Lee, the Coens and Tarantino.

Because of this high degree of imitation, it is easy to note certain trends within the morass of comparatively low-budget films made in recent years. The influence of Scorsese (notably with *Mean Streets* and *GoodFellas*) and Tarantino, for instance, has spawned endless crime films, often set on or around the blue-collar streets of New York or LA, and featuring a close-knit group of colourful characters prone to express themselves in fast, pro-fanely demotic dialogue and macho, Method-derived gestures. Rob Weiss (*Amongst Friends*, 1992), former Hartley editor Nick Gomez (*Laws of Gravity*, 1992), James Gray (*Little Odessa*, 1994), former Tarantino associate Roger Avary (*Killing Zoe*, 1994), Matthew Harrison (*Rhythm Thief*, 1995, *Kicked in the Head*, 1997), Sal Stabile (*Gravesend*, 1996), Alan Taylor (*Palookaville*, 1997) and many others have mined this particular territory with varying success, although none has done it with as much intelligence, insight and originality as either Bryan Singer, whose *The Usual Suspects* (1995) echoed vintage Hollywood examples of the genre with a wonderfully labyrinthine plot and a genuinely epic sense of evil, or Boaz Yakin, whose *Fresh* (1994) used the metaphor of a chess game to explore the strategies used by a young black kid to haul himself and his family out of a mael-strom of inner city troubles related to drugs and gang crime.

< 342 >

Closely aligned to this vein of storytelling were the various films about life in the 'hood made by black film-makers inspired by the example of Lee's *Do the Right Thing*. Most notable was John Singleton's *Boyz N the Hood* (1991), which tempered its depiction of South Central gang violence with a polemic about irresponsible absent fathers, though he failed to live up to his début's promise with *Poetic Justice* (1993) and *Higher Learning* (1995); most raw in its emotionalism was 19-year-old Matty Rich's *Straight Out of Brooklyn* (1991), which bemoaned the lim-ited options available to kids living in impoverished city projects; most insistently, even over-emphatically stylish Albert and Allen Hughes' *Menace II Society* (1993), which charted much the same territory as Singleton and Rich's films; and most hackneyed the sensationalist, gloatingly macho gangsta thrillers typified by Melvin Van Peebles' *New Jack City* (1991). After Lee, in fact, per-haps the most interesting African-American film-maker – and one who avoided the inner-city clichés of the 'hood genre – was Corman graduate Carl Franklin who, with *One False Move* (1991) and *Devil in a Blue Dress* (1995), used classical thriller conventions to mount intelligent, sophisticated analyses of the relationship between race, gender, money and class; crucially, in each film Franklin allowed socio-political issues to emerge subtly and naturally from the story, characters and milieu, rather than foregrounding them through preachy or attitudinising dialogue.

Women directors, meanwhile, continued to have a pretty hard time of it. With the notable exception of Kathryn Bigelow, who in working (very) faintly feminist variations on the action movie in films like *Blue Steel* (1990), *Point Break* (1991) and *Strange Days* (1995) aligned herself ever more closely with the mainstream, it evidently remained difficult for women directors to work as regularly as their male counterparts and hence to assemble a major body of work. Alison Anders followed the promising domestic drama *Gas Food Lodging* (1991) with the disappointing gang movie *Mi Vida Loca* (1993), an episode in *Four Rooms*, and the likeable but minor pop saga *Grace of My Heart* (1996); Maggie Greenwald's ingenious thriller *The Kill-Off* (1989) was followed by the ambitious but flawed feminist western *The Ballad of Little Jo* (1993); while Nancy Savoca displayed a flair for witty, offbeat naturalistic romance with *True Love* (1989) and *Dogfight* (1991). Otherwise, all too often either women directors have managed to make just one feature, or their follow-ups have been promoted so poorly that they remain best known for one film only: Julie Dash (*Daughters of the Dust*, 1991), Stacy Cochran (*My New Gun*, 1992), Leslie Harris (*Just Another Girl on the IRT*, 1992), Tamra Davis (*Guncrazy*, 1992), Darnell Martin (*I Like it Like That*, 1994) and Stacey Title (*The Last Supper*, 1995). Perhaps the most promising débuts by women, however, were Nicole Holofcener's *Walking and Talking* (1996), a touching, perceptive, often genuinely painful comedy about a close friendship menaced by marital entanglements and romantic rivalry, and Rose Troche's *Go Fish* (1994), a lively, engagingly matter-of-fact comedy about lesbian life which avoided the usual stereotypes and special pleading.

Troche's film was welcomed as part of the 'New Queer Cinema'

< **343** >

pioneered by Haynes and his producer Christine Vachon, who also oversaw Tom Kalin's *Swoon* (1991), a determinedly modernist, bold reworking of the story of real-life murderers Leopold and Loeb, which was far more successful in attempting to create a new 'gay' aesthetic than such well-meaning but stylistically conservative portraits of the gay community (and its devastation by AIDS) as *Parting Glances* (Bill Sherwood, 1985) and *Longtime Companion* (Norman René, 1990). Also regarded as part of the (international) new movement were Marlon Riggs' documentary *Tongues Untied* (1989), about gay experience within the black community; Christopher Munch's *The Hours and Times* (1991), an impressive speculative drama about the relationship between John Lennon and Brian Epstein; and the films of Gregg Araki – *The Living End* (1992), *Totally F***ed Up* (1993), *The Doom Generation* (1995) and *Nowhere* (1997) – whose stylistic diversity and shock-tactic strategies were often undermined by a posturing emphasis on terminal ennui.

< **344** >

Indeed, apart from a few practitioners of the New Queer Cinema and some of the *auteurs* covered in the main chapters of this book, very few indie film-makers came up with anything very innovative on a formal level. Michael Almereyda experimented with the other-worldly, grainy, soft-focused images of Pixelvision in the determinedly arty *Another Girl, Another Planet* (1992) and *Nadja* (1994); Lodge Kerrigan used a fragmented, impressionistic narrative and an expressionistic barrage of aural and visual devices to explore the consciousness of a schizophrenic in *Clean, Shaven* (1993); Scott McGehee and David Siegel's *Suture* (1993) analysed questions of identity, memory and the duality of mind and body through non-naturalistic dialogue and performances (including the unremarked-on fact that two 'identical' brothers were played by physically dissimilar black and white actors) and austerely formalised black and white compositions; while Errol Morris, in his more recent films like *The Thin Blue Line* (1988), *A Brief History of Time* (1992) and *Fast, Cheap and Out of Control* (1997), effectively blurred and interrogated the distinctions made between fiction and documentary by using a variety of highly stylised visual tropes for interviews, reconstructions and actual events alike. (Though Morris is one of the most accomplished and fascinating American film-makers to have emerged in the last two decades – his début, *Gates of Heaven*, was made back in 1978 – as a documentarist he stands outside the range of this study.)

Mostly, then, indie film-makers were content to fall back on more traditional forms of storytelling, particularly in the realm of comedy and drama (areas in which the influence of Woody Allen could often be discerned: studies of fraught romantic affairs and dysfunctional families proliferated). Troubled relationships and domestic tensions were a constant in the films of the Taiwanese-American Ang Lee (*The Wedding Banquet*, 1993; *Sense and Sensibility*, 1995; *The Ice Storm*, 1997), and central features in Ed Burns' *The Brothers McMullen* (1995) and *She's The One* (1996); in Alexandre Rockwell's *Sons* (1989) and Joe Roth's *Coupe de Ville* (1990); in David O Russell's *Spanking the Monkey* (1994) and *Flirting with Disaster* (1996), Doug Liman's *Swingers* (1996) and Bart Freundlich's *The Myth of Fingerprints* (1997); and in Nick Cassavetes' *Unhook the Stars* (1996) and *She's So Lovely* (1997) (the latter based on a script by the director's late father, but directed with little of his insightful mastery). However diverse in style and quality these films were – and it must be said that *Spanking the Monkey* (a sensitive but often darkly comic study of a mother-son relationship that results in incest) is far wittier, more provocative and less hackneyed than, say, Burns' derivative romances – it did sometimes seem as if the constant dependence on the same kind of material and milieux sometimes reflected not only budgetary constraints but a failure of the imagination.

The same might be said of some of those actors who tried their hands at writing and directing, even though the finished results were mostly more polished and rewarding, if only because, like most movies directed by actors, they usually offered a range of superior performances. John Turturro examined fra-

< **345** >

ternal relationships in *Mac* (1992), Stanley Tucci and Campbell Scott treated the same subject (albeit more warmly and comically) in *Big Night* (1996), while Kevin Spacey and John Cusack turned to the milieu of petty crime in, respectively, *Albino Alligator* (1997) and *Grosse Point Blank* (1997 – directed by George Armitage, but written and produced by Cusack). Meanwhile, just as Robert Duvall revealed his admiration for Ken Loach with *Angelo My Love* (1982) and *The Apostle* (1997), so Sean Penn, as a follow-up to his 60s-style début *The Indian Runner* (1991), opted, often rather clumsily, for Cassavetes-style realism in *The Crossing Guard* (1995). Best, arguably, were the directorial débuts of Billy Bob Thornton and Steve Buscemi: the former, *Sling Blade* (1996), was a moving, subtly-observed drama about a retarded murderer's attempts at rehabilitation after years in an institution for the criminally insane, while the latter, *Trees Lounge* (1996) was a beautifully low-key comedy-drama about a feckless boozer's inability to take responsibility for his unwittingly self-centred attitude towards all around him.

< **346** >

There were, of course, a handful of movies that didn't fit readily into conventional categories. With his rambling, grainy, controversial look at young teenagers in *Kids* (1995), Larry Clark somewhat dubiously took the pseudo-documentary realist style as far as it would go to paint a sensationalist, contrived portrait of young lives devoted to sex, drugs, booze and macho misogyny and overshadowed (in a strained moralistic subplot) by the threat of AIDS. More honest, effective and disturbing as a meditation on the anguish, cruelty and loneliness of puberty was Todd Solondz's carefully stylised black comedy *Welcome to the Dollhouse* (1995), while Neil LaBute's *In the Company of Men* (1997), which likewise owned up to its artifice through elaborately wrought dialogue and tableau-like compositions, could have taught Clark a thing or two in the way it cleverly and wittily distanced itself from the misogynistic schemes of the petty, vengeful businessmen who were its central characters. Best of all, perhaps, and certainly most original and unusual, was Al Pacino's

Looking for Richard (1996), a self-financed, supremely inventive essay-movie about the appeal and problems of staging Shakespeare, which intercut interviews, snippets of historical information, discussions and rehearsals with a very abridged but finally thrillingly directed version of *Richard III*. Such departures from the norm, however, were few; all too often, the indie scene's dependence on a limited variety of hand-me-down stories, characters and styles ensured that many films soon became virtually indistinguishable in the memory.

That said, besides the directors covered in the preceding chapters, a number of more distinctive stylists have emerged. The most successful in mainstream terms has been former animator Tim Burton who, whether working in offbeat fantasies like *Pee Wee's Big Adventure* (1985), *Beetlejuice* (1988) and *Edward Scissorhands* (1990), or in the big-budget comic-strip adaptations *Batman* (1989), *Batman Returns* (1990) and *Mars Attacks!* (1996), has shown a preference for dark, troubled fairy-tales populated by lonely, frustrated, even tormented social outcasts; though Burton clearly has an eye for the authentically Gothic, his visual flair is all too often let down by lackadaisical storytelling. Indeed, it's perhaps no accident that by far his finest film, *Ed Wood* (1994), which charts the absurd exploits of an ever-optimistic but wholly incompetent Z-grade Hollywood film-maker of the 50s in a way that is both funny and poignant, was inspired by the life and career of a real person; not only was Burton able to draw on his evident empathy for the 'visionary' Wood, but the film-maker's progress through Hollywood, as distilled in a fine script by Scott Alexander and Larry Karaszewski, supplied a firm narrative structure which Burton could embellish with his own special brand of wry, whimsical fantasy.

Likewise closely aligned to the mainstream were two genre specialists. With the overly allusive and schematic private-eye movie *Kill Me Again* (1989), John Dahl at once announced himself as a film noir buff, before moving on to confirm his credentials with the rural neo-noir *Red Rock West* (1992), which

< **347** >

playfully took the genre into Western Gothic territory with an impressively tortuous, tongue-in-cheek plot. Neither film, however, prepared audiences for *The Last Seduction* (1993), a ferociously fast and enjoyably amoral tale of cross and double-cross featuring, in Linda Fiorentino's Wendy, one of the most duplicitous, sexually predatory and brilliantly cunning *femmes fatales* ever portrayed in the movies. Sadly, the Byzantine plotting and taut, stylish direction that made the film so intriguing and gripping were conspicuously absent from Dahl's bigger-budgeted follow-up, the far-fetched, lacklustre *Unforgettable* (1996).

< **348** >

Another specialist in crime films, though of the action-movie variety, was Robert Rodriguez, whose Mexico-set début *El Mariachi* (1992) – famously proclaimed to have been shot and edited for just $7,000, although when Columbia decided to release it, post-production and print blow-ups took the final budget way higher – enlivened a fairly routine plot about an innocent loner hunted by murderous gangsters with frantic, superbly edited set-piece shoot-outs, engagingly witty dialogue and characterisation, and a plethora of playful cinematic tricks. To all intents and purposes a bigger-budget remake of his début, *Desperado* (1995) may have lacked the light touch of its predecessor, but the sheer skill and bravado Rodriguez displayed in mounting scene after scene of thrillingly dynamic (if gleefully gratuitous) violence and mayhem compensated for the comparative disappointment of his episode for *Four Rooms*. The same could be said for the Tarantino-scripted *From Dusk Till Dawn*, although the film's puerile sexism and its reliance on comic-strip horror once its group of robbers and hostages are beseiged in a truck-stop cantina populated by vampires inevitably led to a coarsening in tone. Nevertheless, if Rodriguez ever gets to work on a more adult, substantial action-thriller, his technical expertise should stand him in good stead.

At the other end of the spectrum from Dahl and Rodriguez are the comparatively arty, even whimsical talents of Gus Van Sant and Tom DiCillo. After making waves with his $25,000 début

Matt Dillon and Max Perlich in Gus Van Sant's **Drugstore Cowboy** (1989) – noteworthy for its refusal to take a moralising stance toward the antics of its characters.

Mala Noche, a bittersweet account of a gay romantic triangle set on and around the rainy streets of Portland, Oregon, Van Sant remained in the Pacific Northwest for two similarly offbeat, down-beat tales of feckless youth with *Drugstore Cowboy* (1989) and *My Own Private Idaho* (1991). Though each film was impressive both for the excellence of its performances and for refusing to adopt a moralising stance towards the antics of its characters (drug-addicts and gay hustlers, respectively), each also suffered from Van Sant's rather clumsy use of occasional 'surreal' imagery, while the over-emphatic allusions to Shakespeare's Falstaff in *Idaho* made for gobbets of indigestible dialogue that likewise sat uneasily amid the prevailing mood of laid-back naturalism.

Van Sant's next film, an adaptation of Tom Robbins' cult novel *Even Cowgirls Get the Blues* (1993), was widely dismissed as an unamusing, misbegotten foray into feminist allegory, with the result that he changed tack dramatically with *To Die For* (1995), a splendidly splenetic black satire about a ruthless, go-getting young woman who will literally do anything to become a television celebrity; far sharper, faster and funnier than Van Sant's other work, the film may perhaps be better understood as the work of screenwriter Buck Henry (though Van Sant's direction is superb).

Whatever, a certain anonymity seems to have settled upon his work of late: while the admittedly affecting *Good Will Hunting* (1997), about a young man whose intellectual brilliance (particularly in the field of mathematics) is countered by anti-social behaviour and an inability to enter into close human relationships, bears witness to the director's abiding interest in troubled youth, it is his most conventional film by far and, for all its sensitivity and superior acting, not so very different from a sentimental Hollywood tract like, say, *Dead Poets Society* (Peter Weir, 1989).

Tom DiCillo is an altogether more erratic talent, and might not deserve special consideration were it not for his second film. A former cameraman for Jarmusch, he made his début with the lightly likeable *Johnny Suede* (1991), a fable about a young rock 'n' roll poseur forced to choose between his fantasies and the love of a good, comparatively mature woman. Though the film had a nice line in gently absurdist humour and featured what would later prove to be a typically excellent performance by Catherine Keener (one of the most interesting actresses to emerge from the indie scene), it often looked like DiCillo was trying a little too hard to emulate Jarmusch's expert balancing act between cool characterisation and incisive irony. Certainly, it hardly gave notice that his next film, *Living in Oblivion* (1995), would be one of the funniest, most inventive and insightful comedies made by the indie sector. A satire about the various egos involved in the shooting of an arty, low-budget independent movie – complete with ambitious *auteur*, a lead actress he's secretly enamoured by, a long-suffering cameraman, lowly technicians keen to direct, and a vain, temperamental Hollywood star slumming

< **350** >

Brad Pitt plays Johnny Suede, in Tom DiCillo's gently absurd first feature (1991). DiCillo was formerly Jim Jarmusch's cameraman.

because he's heard the director knows Tarantino – the film also makes play with the very process of cinematic storytelling, repeatedly confounding audience expectations about whether any given sequence is real, dreamt, imagined or part of the film-within-the-film. At the same time, the movie is something of a *tour de force* in making comic mileage out of all the technical things that can go wrong during shooting under straitened circumstances and, in an extraordinary sequence in which Keener is made to act out a scene over and over again, in revealing the artifice, serendipity and sheer hard work that are combined in the construction of a filmed performance. In short, *Living in Oblivion* stands as the ultimate indie feature about indie movie-making (it is far more authentic and amusing than, say, Alexandre Rockwell's *In the Soup*, 1992); sadly, its affectionate wit and sharp insights were nowhere to be found in *Box of*

Moonlight (1996), a rather woolly and predictable comic fable about a workaholic who is rejuvenated by his encounter with an anarchic young back-to-nature type living outside the confines of conventional society.

Comedy was also the dramatic form chosen by two very different film-makers, each of whom was acclaimed especially for the facility of his writing. Kevin Smith first drew attention with his ultra-low-budget *Clerks* (1993), a scabrous, incredibly profane conversation-piece in which a group of young friends, hanging out at a convenience store and a neighbouring video shop in suburban New Jersey, endlessly discuss anything that enters their feverishly adolescent minds: sex, the subtext of *Star Wars* and its sequels, job prospects, sex, customers, videos, toilet tissue, more sex. With only scant regard for dramatic structure, camera placement, editing or whatever, the film came across not unlike a dangerously extenuated riff from *Pulp Fiction*, only even more

< **352** >

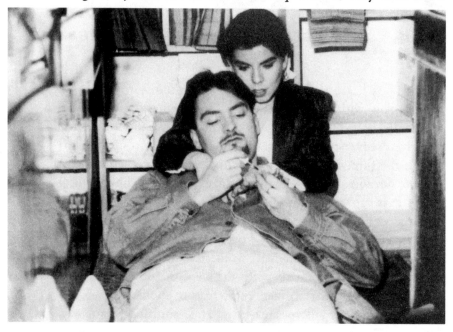

Kevin Smith's hilariously scripted **Clerks** (1993) was shot in and around a New Jersey convenience store for $27,575.

trivial, sexist, scatological, foul-mouthed and immature; so funny was the writing, however, and so natural the performances of the unfamiliar young cast, that somehow, against all odds, the film succeeded as a comedy firmly locked into the mood of a particular place, time and generation. When Smith tried to repeat his success with the larger-budget *Mallrats* (1995), the result was dismally lame, so that the hitherto good-humoured sexism and profanity felt not just wearisome but even vaguely offensive. Mercifully, however, with *Chasing Amy* (1997) he not only grounded the persistent babble within a dramatic structure (a young comic-strip artist falls for a girl only to find she's lesbian; when she reciprocates his feelings, his friend becomes jealous), but actually began exploring the emotional and social implications of the affair with some intelligence and insight. True, the funny moments (fewer than in *Clerks*) still mostly centred on topics such as injuries sustained during oral sex, but in acknowledging that there is more at stake for the heroine if she changes her lifestyle than there is for the hero if they get together, and in showing how difficult it is for people to come to terms with a lover's past, Smith at least showed that as a writer (rather than as director) he had matured, even if his male characters had not.

< **353** >

Like Smith, Whit Stillman is also fascinated by the tribal rites of the young and immature, but where Smith's characters are likely to discuss 'sucking dick', *Return of the Jedi* or bitches and sluts, Stillman's are more prone to wax pensive about the advantages of going out with a homely rather than a beautiful girl, the novels of Jane Austen, and the downward mobility of UHBS (the 'urban haute bourgeoisie'). Not that the latter are any less preoccupied with sex, matters of the heart or the ethics of social interaction; it's just that Stillman is dealing with young men and women who are wealthier, more conventionally educated and, in their own sniping, snobbish, superior way, more concerned with the niceties of human intercourse than are Smith's blue-collar kids. Indeed, besides the wit and erudition of his finely turned dialogue, Stillman is remarkable in American indie cinema in dealing with the unfashionably well-to-do and conservative. In *Metropolitan* (1989) – incidentally one of the finest Austenesque movies ever made, even though it was not based on an Austen novel (there are, however, allusions made to *Mansfield Park*, which it resembles in certain key repects) – a group of New York preppies 'adopt' a relatively lowly young man with a distaste for wealthy privilege who, during the course of the debs' coming-out season, falls for one of their number. And in *Barcelona* (1994) – not a little reminiscent of Henry James in its tale of an encounter of American innocence and Old World experience – an awkward young businessman and his tactless cousin (a NATO fleet representative, and therefore frowned on as an imperialist by Spaniards at the start of the 80s) find themselves bewilderingly involved in a series of romantic encounters with girls working at the Barcelona trade fair. In each film, the personal intersects with the social and political: sexual insecurity makes for aggression, desire and love for unexpected alliances across the cultural divide, so that Stillman's romantic comedies turn out to be far more complex than they first appear. Crucial in this respect are his talents as an ironist: he never lets us forget that his characters – who for all their self-assured announcements about the world remain, like most young people, profoundly confused – may not mean what they say or say what they mean; they are simply trying to make a mark on those around them. Accordingly, Stillman effortlessly succeeds in the difficult task of making us understand and even sympathise with his spoiled, arrogant, even priggish creations who, after all, are just as likely and entitled to worry over their lives as the rest of us.

Where Stillman most differs from Smith, however – besides the fact that his dialogue bears more resemblance to such elegant wordsmiths as Wilder, Sturges and Mankiewicz (not to mention the aforementioned Austen and James) – is in his abilities as a director. Not only does his ironic tone extend to the somewhat detached (albeit unpatronising) way his camera stands back from his characters to view them in a clearly defined social, cultural

< **354** >

and political context, but he is adept at evoking milieu and mood in economic but expressive ways. The glamorous, lit-up, Christmas New York conveys both the seductive appeal and the rather frosty social codes of the rich, would-be sophisticated set; Barcelona, on the other hand, is not depicted as the usual picture-postcard tourist Mecca, but as a working, living city where the endless parties, picnics and political discussions of the young locals only highlight the expatriate cousins' sense of alienation and confusion over the comparatively liberated sexual habits of the Spanish. In his directing skills, then, just as in his writing, Stillman reveals himself as a classicist in the Hollywood mould, even if his acute sense of irony aligns him more closely with a European tradition of writing than with its American counterpart.

< **355** >

The same, perhaps, might be said of Richard Linklater, whose serio-comic studies of disaffected American youth to some extent reflect his interest in European *auteurs* better known for observing human behaviour than in telling tight, tidy stories. (Eric Rohmer is a particular favourite.) Linklater, whose début feature, *It's Impossible to Learn to Plow by Reading Books* (1988), received only limited screenings, first scored a success with *Slacker* (1991), a plotless series of vignettes featuring a large, sometimes bewildering array of obsessives and eccentrics – con-artists, conspiracy theorists, Catholic psychos, whores, astrologers, film-makers – doing not very much in the director's hometown of Austin, Texas. As one brief episode leads into the next, with the camera often turning from one character to follow another who is passing by, the film gradually turns into a filmic portrait gallery consisting of people far too caught up in their own peculiar preoccupations and self-images ever actually to do anything of note. Although patchily amusing, both dramatically and as a thesis the film is of limited interest (even though it helped popularise the word 'slacker' as a term for a particular kind of idle, nihilistic young person); however, the freewheeling narrative – vaguely reminiscent of Otar Iosseliani's *Favourites of the Moon*, 1984, or

Ethan Hawke and Julie Delpy in Richard Linklater's **Before Sunrise** (1995) – a dazzling, perceptive variation on the traditional romantic motif of 'meeting cute'.

certain films by Jacques Tati or Miklos Jancso – is unusually loose and experimental for the American cinema, its closest antecedent probably being Altman's *Nashville*.

A marginally more conventionally structured portrait of teen life in the mid-70s, which darts to and fro between some two dozen kids as they go through the customary rituals of school, dating, cruising around and generally hanging loose, *Dazed and Confused* (1993) came over as a naturalistically written and acted update of a film like *American Graffiti*, albeit without the plot contrivances or glowing, portentous nostalgia. Polished but just a little pointless, it was easily overshadowed by Linklater's next film, the genuinely insightful and remarkably affecting *Before Sunrise* (1995), a dazzling variation on the 'meeting-cute' romance in which a young American at the end of a European trip persuades a Parisian student he meets on a train to spend 24 hours wandering around Vienna with him until he catches his flight back to the States. If the basic situation was familiar, the execution was not: boldly using long uninterrupted takes to show how the couple's conversations gradually shift from the general to the particular, from the trivial to the relevant, from the impersonal to the pointed, the film echoes Rohmer in the way it explores the gulf between what is said and what is meant; the American, especially, is so keen to impress the girl as a man of the world that he only hesitantly admits to his true feelings. Not only is the film a *tour de force* of naturalistic, seemingly semi-improvised acting (it was actually scripted from start to finish), but in showing how well the couple get on with one another, only to leave us uncertain whether they will meet up again in six months as promised (it's admittedly improbable), it achieves an extremely poignant sense of lives afflicted by force of circumstance, by problems of time and distance, and by one-off opportunities grasped then wasted. Ending with a montage of shots showing places the pair visited, now empty and bereft of the magic invested in them by the presence of the young lovers, the film is that rare thing: a truly romantic modern American movie.

< 357 >

With *subUrbia* (1997), an adaptation of a play about a group of directionless, frustrated young kids hanging out one night at a corner convenience store, Linklater returned to the themes of *Slacker* and *Dazed and Confused*, albeit – given the theatrical contrivances of his material – with rather less originality and scattershot insight. Nevertheless, Linklater's assured control of mood and his skill with actors remained firmly in evidence, and he looks set to become, alongside Stillman, one of the mainstays of the indie scene. More than Burton, Rodriguez, Dahl or Van Sant, each of these two writer-directors exhibits a sensibility which may be too uncompromising and idiosyncratic to be contained within the mainstream sector of the movie-making world; more than DiCillo, they have both a distinctive style and a preoccupation with particular themes and milieux; and more than Smith, they are very able directors, and have displayed a maturity of vision which, financiers willing, should allow them to continue making entertaining, thought-provoking and personal films.

< **358** >

conclusion

< **359** >

While I hope I have shown that the directors whose work is examined at greater length in this book all have distinctive artistic personalities, it may be useful to consider what they have in common. Most obviously, of course, they are American and work largely outside the confines of the Hollywood mainstream. But these two shared characteristics have further repercussions.

The very fact that they have grown up and mostly worked in a country that has dominated world film-making since the start of the century, but have chosen not to align themselves closely, in either industrial or cultural terms, with Hollywood is indicative both of the circumstances which fostered their maverick learnings and of their various methodologies regarding form and content. All, for instance, grew up in the 60s or 70s when it was possible to see not only the mainstream Hollywood studio product that had always dominated American cinema screens but also – in arthouses, on college campuses, and, in later years, on video – films from Europe, Asia, Latin America and, just as importantly, the American 'underground'. Encouraged, no doubt, by the examples set by Cassavetes and those Hollywood mavericks (Altman, Penn, Peckinpah, Malick, Scorsese *et al.*) who in the late 60s and early 70s stretched the aesthetic boundaries of popular film-making in various ways, they were also able to see and learn from those foreign directors who had, since the late 50s, attained an unprecedently high international profile. Indeed, it was probably the example set by Europeans like Godard, Rohmer, Truffaut, Antonioni, Fellini, Bertolucci and, later, Fassbinder, Herzog and Wenders that not only showed the young American film-makers of the future that they too could become *auteurs*, but also suggested some of the ways they could do so. Hence, most of the directors examined in this volume would have seen nothing extraordinary about wanting to write their own material (rare in Hollywood, but common in Europe); moreover, like, say, the film-makers of the French *nouvelle vague*, Bertolucci, Fassbinder or Scorsese, they would have found it quite natural to quote and borrow from other films, either by way of homage or criticism, in their own work.

This last tendency was not only facilitated and encouraged, however inadvertently, by the fact that many film-makers of this generation attended film school or university film courses – an option which began to become widely available only in the 60s and 70s – but was part of a general movement towards intextextuality and democratisation in the cultural arena.

Barriers between diverse art forms began to shift or break down; pop art, especially in forging closer links between painting and sculpture, comic strips, music, movies, television, photography and advertising, challenged the values that distinguished between 'high' and 'low' art. Andy Warhol involved himself in all manner of creative activity (including, of course, film-making), questioning notions of authorship, appropriate subject matter and the very essence of artistic values and methodology. The Beatles and Bob Dylan were mentioned in the same breath as established classical composers and poets; modern jazz, with John Coltrane, Ornette Coleman and Cecil Taylor in its vanguard, experimented with free-form improvisation and structural complexity in a way reminiscent of avant-garde music; in the 70s punk made the ethos of low-budget 'amateurism' not only acceptable but an attractive option. In cinema, meanwhile, the French *politique des auteurs* (which was championed and to some

< **360** >

extent developed upon by, among others, the influential American critic Andrew Sarris) had argued that relatively lowly or populist Hollywood directors like Ray, Fuller, Sirk and Minnelli were as worthy of study and acclaim as acknowledged cinematic masters like Renoir, Eisenstein, Bergman and Fellini, on the assumption that the line dividing mere 'entertainment' from art was arbitrary and artificial.

In short, a more open-minded, catholic attitude towards creative endeavour became the order of the day. Almost anything could be 'art' on its own terms if one chose to present it as such; everything was up for grabs in terms of subject and style. And in independent, non-mainstream cinema, genres could be mixed and deconstructed, stars and sumptuous production values dispensed with, discreet 'realism' exposed as artifice, movie allusions made, and other art forms plundered willy-nilly, in a way that Hollywood itself had rarely dared. Fertile creative territory was just waiting to be explored and cultivated by anyone keen to express some kind of personal vision and less than happy with the artistically and politically conservative style of film-making favoured by the studios. At the same time, however, since narrative film-making, other than at the most basic or 'underground' level, tends to be a rather more expensive pursuit than, say, writing, painting, sculpture or most musical composition and performance, and while many independent-minded *auteurs* wanted to offer an alternative to Hollywood conventions, it still made sense, where appropriate, to make use of existing narrative forms that audiences could feel familiar with, enjoy and understand.

Hence, genre, virtually a *sine qua non* of mainstream movie-making, remains an important aspect of most American independent production; even if one is to interrogate, deconstruct or mount a critique of traditional forms of cinematic storytelling, it is still necessary to take account of the audience's awareness of certain iconographic, stylistic, ideological and narrative conventions. The film-makers in this book have reacted to genre in various ways. Only Jarmusch, Hartley and, just occasionally, Soderbergh

< 361 >

have chosen to dispense with American genre virtually entirely, opting instead for a modernist exploration of cinematic language to treat subjects which may be seen as unusually intimate and personal in comparison to those of most American films. Jarmusch, whose films bear only a passing resemblance to road-movies and the Western, is clearly influenced in part by comparatively minimalist directors such as Warhol, Ozu, Antonioni, Bresson, Wenders and Fassbinder; Hartley, whose work sounds the faintest echoes of the romantic melodrama and crime thriller, has been compared, somewhat justifiably, with Godard; while Soderbergh's *sex, lies and videotape*, *Kafka* and *The Underneath* are more reminiscent of the European art-movie, and *Schizopolis* of a demented, highly experimental hommage to the 60s comedies of Dick Lester. In these three's films, familiarity with the conventions of mainstream American genre is of secondary importance to an understanding of their intentions; more useful by far is an awareness of how they are experimenting with film's formal aspects – most notably narrative structure – and of the film-makers' respective thematic preoccupations and stylistic strategies.

< 362 >

Sayles, Wang, Lee and Haynes, on the other hand, display a tendency to use (and abuse) genre to a political end, employing and subverting traditional stereotypes and narrative structures to interrogate notions of class, race, gender, sexuality, power and cultural identity. Each questions dominant mythologies in a different way. Sayles is perhaps the most concerned with the broader tapestry of American history and culture, using generic narratives to dissect and analyse the various socio-political elements that constitute the fabric of American society. Wang, a more eclectic and erratic talent, combines American genres with narrative and stylistic tropes borrowed from European and Oriental cinema (most notably Godard, Ozu and contemporary Chinese directors like Chen Kaige and Zhang Yimou) to investigate questions of cultural identity, with specific regard to the experience of Chinese-Americans. Lee, while often making use of the playful narrative devices familiar from the work of the French *nouvelle vague*, also draws heavily upon traditional Hollywood genres like the domestic melodrama, the musical and the biopic, and foregrounds key aspects of African-American culture in his use of music, dance, design and quotations from black political figures: the result is an on-going exploration of the tensions both between African-Americans and other ethnic groups and between different groups within the black community itself.

Finally, the most subversive use of genre for political ends is that of Haynes who, in examining questions of sexuality, deviance and 'normality', conformism and transgression, health and sickness, has also engaged with the semiology and syntax of film in his profoundly ironic, ambivalent approach to representation and concepts of closure and meaning. While he situates his films within traditional American genres like the melodrama and the biopic, his refusal to abide by the narrative 'rules' or remain within the stylistic parameters of those genres makes for fresh, challenging and frequently provocative viewing.

< 363 >

Lynch, the Coens and Tarantino use genre differently again. Without any obvious political or clear moral import, their films may at first seem simply like idiosyncratic, playful exercises in style for style's sake; indeed, since they tend to work in the crime and horror genres, with a concomitant amount of violence on display, detractors have occasionally complained of a fundamental amorality (or even immorality) in some of their films. While the film-makers' reluctance properly to discuss the moral substance of their work, and the fact that the films' exact 'meaning' is often buried beneath their stylistic and narrative surface, lend some weight to such criticisms, I hope I have shown that there is meaning and a degree of moral content in their work. True, until *Jackie Brown*, Tarantino appeared to be primarily a stylist, more concerned with surprising and entertaining his audience and with playing around with narrative chronology than with investigating the moral issues inherent in his tales of crime and punishment, loyalty and betrayal; in his third feature, however, his more evident interest in emotional attachment, the difference between greed, expediency and necessity, and the confusions, anxieties and pressure that come with age lent the film considerably more substance. Lynch, on the other hand, uses a surreal/expressionist approach to genre to explore his personal fantasies, fears and sense of life's mysteries; though the moral content in films like *Blue Velvet, Wild at Heart* and *Fire Walk With Me* is complicated and even perhaps compromised not only by his use of kitsch and naive, if ironic, cliché and by a sometimes seemingly prurient fascination with grotesque, lascivious or violent spectacle, there can be little doubt as to the humanistic sympathies of *The Elephant Man* or to the deeply felt anxieties that permeate most of his work. The Coens, meanwhile, operate in a rather different way: while a superficial examination of their films suggests a primary interest in innovation and complexity in the areas of narrative structure and overall style, as with Jarmusch and Hartley analysis of their formal qualities reveals a deeper moral concern with questions of trust and loyalty, commitment and integrity, heroism and goodness.

However genre is used by these film-makers, they all, to some extent, follow in the footsteps of predecessors like Godard and Altman in drawing attention to cinematic artifice. Any sense of a seamless, 'realist' narrative is avoided in various ways. Surrealism, expressionism and fantasy are common denominators in the work of Lynch and the Coens. A vigorous, visible, non-realist visual style inflects their work, just as it does, in different ways, many of the films of Lee, Haynes, Hartley and Tarantino. Genres are combined or turned upon their heads. Lynch, Wang, the Coens and Tarantino often juxtapose violence, horror and comedy, the banal and the extraordinary, in disconcerting, unexpected ways. Dialogue and performance, especially in the work of Lynch, the Coens and Hartley, may be emphatically non-naturalistic or ironic, as if delivered in quotation marks. Lynch, Lee, Wang, the Coens, Hartley and Tarantino have all, in different ways, made use of sequences reminiscent of the song-and-

< 364 >

dance musical. The narrative may be interrupted, as in *She's Gotta Have It, Blue in the Face, Schizopolis* or some of Haynes' work, by straight-to-camera 'interviews' and other techniques (hand-held camera, video footage) familiar from documentary. Furthermore, it may be broken up, scrambled, fragmented or even repeated, as in the films of Jarmusch, Wang, Soderbergh, Hartley or Tarantino, so that it is simultaneously laid bare as a fictional construct, opened up to a multiplicity of perspectives, and transformed into a kind of puzzle which the audience must work on in order to reassemble it and make sense of it.

< **365** >

Moreover, allusions to other movies abound, either through plot resemblance, dialogue, characters, or stylistic pastiche. In part inherited from older film-makers like Godard, Scorsese and Wenders, this tendency is also part and parcel of the post-modern fascination with intertexuality, which in quoting, reworking, and sampling other texts assumes an erudite, sophisticated and cineliterate awareness on the part of the audience. Whether used by way of hommage or critique, it ensures that individual films are commentaries not only on the world they depict but on themselves and the cinematic medium: they encourage us to view them both in the context of cinema history and as self-reflexive, artificial constructs.

In this respect, cinematic intertextuality is closely related to the allusions to other aspects of pop culture, which may be found throughout these film-makers' work, not only in the many references to television shows, junk food, cultural heroes, sport, advertising slogans, brand names, etc, but in the almost ubiquitous use of pop music. Whether it is Lynch using the songs of Roy Orbison to sinister effect; Sayles establishing time and milieu and celebrating community with a particular standard; Jarmusch embellishing atmosphere with Screaming Jay Hawkins, Tom Waits or Neil Young; Wang using Chinese rock 'n' roll to suggest the complexity of cultural identity; Lee paying tribute to black musical tradition in all its variety; Haynes using lyrics to comment on the action; or Tarantino using favourite tracks from the 70s to help delineate character – these and other examples of the use of popular music in independent films reflect not only the close, even symbiotic relationship between the two art forms, but the various ways in which music has been used to contribute meaning and mood to a narrative. While Hollywood now tends simply to compile a soundtrack of golden oldies in the hope of creating a merchandising spin-off in the form of a hit album, the *auteurs* in this book, like Scorsese before them, use music not as a symptom of their hipness but as a precise, resonant way of adding to the overall thematic and textural richness of their work.

< **366** >

What these *auteurs* really share, however – besides their readiness to work on comparatively low budgets without the resources and constrictions of a big Hollywood budget (in which respect their preference for working repeatedly with the same technicians and actors serves as a financial as well as an artistic advantage) – is their restless adventurousness, their desire to explore fresh ways of using the cinematic medium to tell new, interesting and relevant stories and to investigate intriguing ideas. Each displays a willingness to experiment and to break with convention; each, however, also has a desire to entertain rather than simply indulge in solipsistic navel-gazing. Most importantly, each is possessed of a robust, idiosyncratic creative personality and a reluctance to compromise. And it is finally that spirit of independence, combined with an assured sense of purpose and personal vision – qualities which both unite them as a disparate group and distinguish them as creative individuals – which ensures their place in the artistic forefront of contemporary American cinema.

index

< **367** >

< **368** >

< **369** >

< **370** >

< **371** >

< **372** >

< **374** >